Gravity and Grace
Essays for Roger Pearson

LEGENDA

LEGENDA is the Modern Humanities Research Association's book imprint for new research in the Humanities. Founded in 1995 by Malcolm Bowie and others within the University of Oxford, Legenda has always been a collaborative publishing enterprise, directly governed by scholars. The Modern Humanities Research Association (MHRA) joined this collaboration in 1998, became half-owner in 2004, in partnership with Maney Publishing and then Routledge, and has since 2016 been sole owner. Titles range from medieval texts to contemporary cinema and form a widely comparative view of the modern humanities, including works on Arabic, Catalan, English, French, German, Greek, Italian, Portuguese, Russian, Spanish, and Yiddish literature. Editorial boards and committees of more than 60 leading academic specialists work in collaboration with bodies such as the Society for French Studies, the British Comparative Literature Association and the Association of Hispanists of Great Britain & Ireland.

The MHRA encourages and promotes advanced study and research in the field of the modern humanities, especially modern European languages and literature, including English, and also cinema. It aims to break down the barriers between scholars working in different disciplines and to maintain the unity of humanistic scholarship. The Association fulfils this purpose through the publication of journals, bibliographies, monographs, critical editions, and the MHRA Style Guide, and by making grants in support of research. Membership is open to all who work in the Humanities, whether independent or in a University post, and the participation of younger colleagues entering the field is especially welcomed.

ALSO PUBLISHED BY THE ASSOCIATION

Critical Texts
Tudor and Stuart Translations • *New Translations* • *European Translations*
MHRA Library of Medieval Welsh Literature

MHRA Bibliographies
Publications of the Modern Humanities Research Association

The Annual Bibliography of English Language & Literature
Austrian Studies
Modern Language Review
Portuguese Studies
The Slavonic and East European Review
Working Papers in the Humanities
The Yearbook of English Studies

www.mhra.org.uk
www.legendabooks.com

EDITORIAL BOARD

Chair: Professor Jonathan Long (University of Durham)
For *Germanic Literatures*: Ritchie Robertson (University of Oxford)
For *Italian Perspectives*: Simon Gilson (University of Warwick)
For *Moving Image*: Emma Wilson (University of Cambridge)
For *Research Monographs in French Studies*:
Diana Knight (University of Nottingham)
For *Selected Essays*: Susan Harrow (University of Bristol)
For *Studies in Comparative Literature*:
Dr Emily Finer, University of St Andrews, and
Professor Wen-chin Ouyang, SOAS, London
For *Studies in Hispanic and Lusophone Cultures*:
Trevor Dadson (Queen Mary, University of London)
For *Studies in Yiddish*: Gennady Estraikh (New York University)
For *Transcript*: Matthew Reynolds (University of Oxford)

Managing Editor
Dr Graham Nelson
41 Wellington Square, Oxford OX1 2JF, UK

www.legendabooks.com

Gravity and Grace

Essays for Roger Pearson

Edited by
Charlie Louth and Patrick McGuinness

LEGENDA
Modern Humanities Research Association
2019

Published by Legenda
an imprint of the Modern Humanities Research Association
Salisbury House, Station Road, Cambridge CB1 2LA

ISBN 978-1-78188-787-5 (HB)
ISBN 978-1-78188-788-2 (PB)

First published 2019
Paperback edition 2021

All rights reserved. No part of this publication may be reproduced or disseminated or transmitted in any form or by any means, electronic, mechanical, photocopying, recording or otherwise, or stored in any retrieval system, or otherwise used in any manner whatsoever without written permission of the copyright owner, except in accordance with the provisions of the Copyright, Designs and Patents Act 1988, or under the terms of a licence permitting restricted copying issued in the UK by the Copyright Licensing Agency Ltd, Saffron House, 6–10 Kirby Street, London EC1N 8TS, England, or in the USA by the Copyright Clearance Center, 222 Rosewood Drive, Danvers MA 01923. Application for the written permission of the copyright owner to reproduce any part of this publication must be made by email to legenda@mhra.org.uk.

Disclaimer: Statements of fact and opinion contained in this book are those of the author and not of the editors or the Modern Humanities Research Association. The publisher makes no representation, express or implied, in respect of the accuracy of the material in this book and cannot accept any legal responsibility or liability for any errors or omissions that may be made.

Trademark notice: Product or corporate names may be trademarks or registered trademarks, and are used only for identification and explanation without intent to infringe.

© Modern Humanities Research Association 2019

Copy-Editor: Charlotte Brown

CONTENTS

	Introduction	1
	Poem: 'A Cricket for Pirandello' ANGELA LEIGHTON	5
1	Traces of Grace in Contemporary Fiction: Ali Smith's *There but for the* CLARE CONNORS	6
2	Weight and Wit: The Grace of Voltaire's Enlightenment T. J. REED	24
3	Gravity, Grace, and Gore: French Gloves in the Nineteenth Century ANNE GREEN	28
4	'Marcher droit sur un cheveu': Tightrope Walking and Prose Poetry in Flaubert KATE REES	40
5	*Le Juste Milieu*: Political Pornography in Numa's 'pièce à porte' NATASHA RYAN	55
6	'Grâces sataniques': Laughter, Redemption, and Poetic Self-Awareness in *Les Fleurs du mal* KATE ETHERIDGE	70
7	Quant au Livre de Mallarmé BERTRAND MARCHAL	85
8	Gautier, Leconte, Mallarmé: Gravity Redeeming Grace? TIM FARRANT	93
9	Rediscovering Beckford's 'Satiric Gravity': Mallarmé's Rehabilitation of the 'French' *Vathek* DAMIAN CATANI	112
10	Literary Translation, Responsibility, and the Linguistic Lightness of Being CLIVE SCOTT	130
11	Fighting Against the Fall: Gravity and Grace in Beckett's *Nouvelles* ADAM WATT	146
12	Gravity and Grace: Bonnefoy's and Bergson's 'Monde-images' EMILY MCLAUGHLIN	161

13	Grace and Gravity in Philippe Jaccottet CHARLIE LOUTH	178
14	Feathers, Scales, and Hollow Eggs: Lightness and Weight in Mercè Rodoreda's *La plaça del Diamant* LAURA LONSDALE	195
15	The Permissions of Translation PATRICK MCGUINNESS	207
	Poem: 'Dancer' DAVID CONSTANTINE	227
	Index	228

INTRODUCTION

Charlie Louth and Patrick McGuinness

Gravity and Grace is of course somebody else's title, though not exactly Simone Weil's, since *La Pesanteur et la grâce*, which founded her reputation when published as her first book in 1947, was a posthumous gathering of extracts from her notebooks, edited and entitled by Gustave Thibon. When translated as *Gravity and Grace* in 1952, 'pesanteur' shed some, perhaps most, of its negative weight (unignorable in Weil), not just because the connotations of heaviness, of being burdened, are displaced by ones of solemnity and *gravitas*, but because the words of the title seem to complement as much as work against one another, to consort rather than to oppose. *Gravity and Grace* suggests a complicity, one word and what it stands for helping out the other; and even if we narrow the focus to the shared element in the idea of gravity as 'the attractive force by which all bodies tend to move towards the centre of the earth' (*OED*), the English title implies an interdependence between its terms — perhaps without gravity there is no grace? — which *La Pesanteur et la grâce* tends to simplify into light-footed grace's bid to escape the encumbering, inevitable pull of circumstance.

For Weil, *pesanteur* is what drags us down; it produces 'bassesse'. Yet there is also a 'pesanteur morale' which 'fait tomber vers le haut'.[1] And grace, too, while being an 'ascending movement', can also be a way of 'descending without gravity'. Though Weil's preoccupations are primarily ethical, they have aesthetic implications: 'La création est faite du mouvement descendant de la pesanteur, du mouvement ascendant de la grâce et du mouvement descendant de la grâce à la deuxième puissance'.[2] 'Le double mouvement descendant n'est-il pas la clef de tout art?', she asks.[3] Grace might be said to occur when natural laws and the laws of art coincide, but as something mobile — 'grace, indeed, is beauty in action' (Disraeli)[4] — it cannot be grasped as such. 'Grace is grace', Lucio says in *Measure for Measure*, it cannot be compared to anything else, and 'grâce' seems to translate readily as 'grace'; and yet it is a precarious word, valuable because it intertwines various strands of meaning, aesthetic, social, theological, and ethical, but always in danger of becoming gratuitous, losing its weight in 'airs and graces'.

The double sense of 'gratuitous' — 'freely bestowed or obtained; granted without claim or merit' and 'done without any good ground or reason; unwarranted; uncalled-for'[5] — inhabits grace itself, which seems to come from nowhere and whose value is thus uncertain. We cannot get at grace, and if we try to it seems to disappear or not to amount to very much. It is not just, as Geoffrey Hill says with regard to Hopkins, that 'the determining of grace necessitates at times a graceless articulation', but that any determining of grace is going to be graceless, come away without grace.[6] Felicity is a question of being lucky, or seems to be, and the Latin root *gratia*, which at first just means 'favour', a 'pleasing quality', lucked out in leading to all the implications of 'grace', which is certainly what William Empson called a 'complex word'.

The element of this complexity which has to do with 'ease or refinement of movement' (*OED*), grace as a form of beauty, is commonly thought of in contradistinction to the labour or effort that accompanies other modes. Grace is, precisely, effortless, unstrained, showing no signs of striving after the effect it achieves. This is again to do with the gratuitousness of grace, it just happens. But the relation between grace and work may be more complicated, as can be seen from Marianne Moore's poem about 'The Frigate Pelican' who:

> appears to prefer
> to take, on the wing, from industrious crude-winged
>   species
> the fish they have caught, and is seldom successless.
> A marvel of grace, no matter how fast his
>   victim may fly or how often may
> turn.[7]

Grace here is set against industry, but the frigate bird must have learnt to steal other birds' catch, just as they have learnt to fish out of the sea. This 'marvel of grace' looks like a marvel because it is so accomplished, so unerring: what looks like grace (in its rightness and unanswerability) is in fact (just, also) precision, efficiency, an 'art' that is 'full | of feints'. It is like what Catholic theology calls 'efficacious grace' because it 'effects the end for which it is given' (*OED*), except that it is only partly given, and partly acquired through trial and error.

If, as against divine grace, the grace that inhabits a poem or other form is the product of work, is something achieved, a matter of poise and articulation like the lines of Moore's verse, it can still feel like something given, something efficacious because perfectly right. Finding the right words has an effect which exceeds the words themselves. In art, grace means the combination of a graceful movement and the sense of something bestowed, so that it is the movement itself, the gracefulness, that does the bestowing, a moment of beauty which seems a pure increase or blessing of the world, an inexplicable addition to it, even though it may in fact be a reiteration of what is there already. We receive a sense of something given, or about to be given, by a work as we encounter it, something incalculable, perhaps accidental, but vital and regenerative. Stendhal thought beauty a kind of promise, and like a promise this phenomenon needs gravity as well as grace: it must not be the thing itself, which is yet to come, but neither must it be purely formal. It thus functions like a glimpse, only half-seen but the more poignant and powerful for it, more of a *gift* for it: 'le rien de mystère, indispensable, qui demeure, exprimé, quelque peu' (Mallarmé).[8]

All the pieces here, whether implicitly or explicitly, gravitate round Roger Pearson himself, the person and the pen, their composure and grace.

Being Roger's colleague was to be aware of how much there was to live up to, but also of how unassumingly the example was set. To be his student was to benefit from a stringent intellect and a generous sense of humour, and from the kind of pedagogical attention that universities like Oxford boast about in prospectuses. On his reading lists, his own books, milestones in their subjects, always 'out' from libraries because they were always recommended by other tutors, were noted with self-deprecating asides such as: 'if you can face it' or 'by a local author'.

Roger's range as a scholar has been as remarkable as his productivity: three books on Mallarmé, two books on Voltaire, a book on Stendhal, and most recently a 630-page volume, entitled *Unacknowledged Legislators: The Poet as Lawgiver in Post-Revolutionary France*. The latter is by no means the last, either: as Roger tantalizingly and Mallarméanly writes in his acknowledgments, the book and its 'potential sequel(s)' are part of an ongoing project. There is, there are, 'Livre(s) à venir', but knowing Roger there will be no endless deferral. To these substantial scholarly achievements, enough in themselves for two or three parallel careers, Roger has added expertly-translated and enablingly-introduced classic translations of Zola, Voltaire, and Maupassant, as well as many articles and book chapters.

To list Roger's books is not enough, however — even if, judging by the temper of today's university sector, future research assessment exercises will count words rather than read them. A few comments about Roger's writing are in order. It isn't just the intellectual scope and ambition of his books that make Roger stand out as a scholar, or indeed the sureness of his sense of audience (general reader, specialist, student, reader of blockbusting biographies), but the delicacy and the scrupulousness of his writing, and the way he manages to put detailed close-readings to the service of large but never over-generalized theses. This limpidity in the midst of often highly imbricated material is as much a service to the reader as it is to the authors he so obviously admires. The reader responds, too, to the evident pleasure Pearson takes in sharing his scholarship, and which fills his pages in the guise of graceful formulations, tidy phrasings, amusing jokes, and quotable distillations.

Criticism, even the most rigorous, as Roger's is, is a way of sharing pleasure as well as recording it. So, for all the weight, the gravity, the *pesanteur* of his scholarship, Pearson's students, critics, and reviewers have also noted the lightness of touch and the wit of his writing. Even his jokes and bon mots are offered in the knowledge that we, as readers, teachers, students, and (always) lovers of literature, are part of a community. Roger's achievement as a Mallarmé scholar, for instance, was to demonstrate the fiendish complexity of Mallarmé's mind without ever losing sight of its capacity for sympathy, for seeking out affinities, and for making sense of the world. We come away from *Unfolding Mallarmé* or *Mallarmé and Circumstance* realizing that there is as much mystery in understanding something as there was mystification in not understanding it. The Mallarmé whose poetry can seem like a hall of ice-mirrors is also the Mallarmé who signed off his letters with the warmly affectionate 'ta main', who invoked the touch of the hand that holds the pen, and who underpinned and underscored his ideal words with the celebration of real people and real friendships in the here and now. As Roger glosses it: 'give me your hand and take what mine has written'. There is something of this in Roger too, in Roger the writer not just of books and articles, but of letters and emails to colleagues in the administrative *quotidien* of university life: punctilious, warm and *solidaire*.

In the prologue to *Unacknowledged Legislators*, Roger writes that 'poetry continues to matter profoundly'. He is one to whom it does, and it has been exhilarating to see how *Unacknowledged Legislators*, for all its range and brilliance, functions also as an article of faith in great literature's gravity and grace. Our book celebrates Roger the writer, the colleague, and the friend, and celebrates, too, the knowledge that there is more to come.

Notes to the Introduction

1. Simone Weil, *La Pesanteur et la grâce* (Paris: 10/18, 1962), pp. 11 & 13.
2. Ibid., p. 13.
3. Ibid., p. 151.
4. Quoted in *OED*, 'grace'.
5. Leaning on *OED*.
6. Geoffrey Hill, 'Our Word Is Our Bond', in *The Lords of Limit: Essays on Literature and Ideas* (London: Deutsch, 1984), pp. 138–59 (p. 157).
7. Marianne Moore, *Collected Poems* (London: Faber, 1951), p. 31.
8. Stéphane Mallarmé, 'L'Action restreinte', in *Igitur, Divagations, Un coup de dés*, ed. by Bertrand Marchal (Paris: Gallimard, 2003), pp. 261–66 (p. 262). Cf. Roger Pearson, *Unfolding Mallarmé: The Development of a Poetic Art* (Oxford: Clarendon Press, 1996), p. 8.

A Cricket for Pirandello

Angela Leighton

> Nascere grilli è pure qualche cosa.
> PIRANDELLO

Our trade's translation, whether poems or prose —
    and here in Rome
struggling to render Pirandello's 'crickets'
I must lose the creature or else the dream,
meaning's gravity or else the grace.
Nascere grilli, he writes, to signify
fancies, daydreams, born on the hop ...
but no insect makes a leap that's fit
for Englishing that device of wit.

So here's a leap-poem, Roger. It goes
    channel-hopping
from me to you, scrambling the frontiers —
since we who traffic from tongue to tongue,
mother to other, native to strange,
must make thought's impulse dance to the tune
that words call, by whims of their own:
idiom or pun, some self-stranging homonym,
the distant phones that ring in a phoneme.

Now skip: think ragwort, that hardy immigrant,
    taking root
in Oxford's first botanical garden,
later, on Isambard's cinder-tracks
riding westwards, seeding the dry ways —
but remembering still in the rails' sapped clinker
how once it rode the charcoal flows
of Etna's pyroclastic scree —
one hop ahead, gold-gracing earth's gravity.

So *Nascere grilli* ... On a Sicilian plain
    small jumping jacks,
blue and orange in the hot afternoons,
would gleam beside his rockfast tomb —
flashes of insight, lost as seen.
We'll dream — so words go jumping free
from page to eye, from mouth to ear,
to hatch wild fancies in translation —
cricket-strangers on the ground's foundation.

— 1 —

Traces of Grace in Contemporary Fiction: Ali Smith's *There but for the*

Clare Connors

Welcome, welcome! Roger, let me introduce you to Ali Smith. Ali: Roger Pearson. Have you met before? Perhaps not. I'm not even sure you have immediate friends in common. You've never mentioned Voltaire, Stendhal, or Mallarmé, have you Ali? Or maybe I've just missed them amongst your crowd, which includes everyone from Ovid via the metaphysical poets to Jackie Kay, everyone from Giorgione to Cézanne to Hockney to Tracey Emin, everyone from Beethoven to Boy George and Beyoncé. That litany suggests why I think you two might get on, though. Each of you has an interest in literature and art that refuses to be corralled into the usual stand-offs between the (neo-)classical and the modern, the realist and the romantic, the traditional and the experimental. So, it's not so much the proper names or references you share as some disposition or relation — a stance of (nonetheless discriminating) generosity or hospitality towards a variety of cultural forms; and along with that an ongoing interest in the question of how they work in the world.[1] *Hospitality and art are both arenas in which grace is at issue, and so let me introduce that, too, as my theme. It is a word or concept with a variety of valences — aesthetic, ethical, social and theological — and furnishes helpful ways to explore that abiding concern of yours: the question of what art makes happen. And it is having something of a renaissance in contemporary Anglophone fiction, for reasons I think you, Ali, might help me to explore.*

Other guests will arrive soon. In the meanwhile, I hope you won't think it rude if I point out our surroundings. We find ourselves here in a Festschrift, *a sort of writing-feast. As you've said yourself, Roger, and more elegantly than I could hope to, this is a genre that carries certain risks. For a start, while 'the honorand may take passing pleasure in seeing his name once more upon a title page [...] it now stands there associated with all manner of opinion over which he has no control' so that 'the most judicious of minds [are] honoured by the least discriminating of assertions'.*[2] *Not unlike being guest of honour at someone's 'annual alternative dinner party', and then finding you loathe your fellow diners, here you cannot choose your company.*[3] *Meanwhile it is anxious times too for the other guests who — and this I can certify — write in 'keen awareness' that 'the recipient of the putative honour may read what is written in his name'.*[4] *But it seems churlish or, worse, seems to accuse you of churlishness, to quote back to you your own words of modest and hospitable disclaimer, Roger, now that the feasting tables are turned. The positions of guest and host are necessarily dissymmetrical, and what is gracious to say as the former would disgrace the latter. And so, let us affirm that the risks of the* Festschrift *are also its possibilities. In an 'era where [...] studying the humanities has to be rhetorically and economically justified', an academic publication envisaged not primarily as an 'output', to use the graceless jargon, but as a gift or tribute must — whatever favour it finds — be considered in principle to offer a cherishable chance.*[5] *And more particularly, this seems a felicitous genre for the particular writing-celebration and celebration of writing I propose here, insofar as thinking about gifts already brings us into the province of grace: grace can mean at once a gift or favour, and thanks-giving for the receipt thereof. (The word derives from the Latin* gratia, *a pleasing quality, goodwill, or gratitude, and is cognate with the Sanskrit* gūrtá-s, *meaning welcome, from* gír, girás, *'praise' or 'song'.) We find ourselves in a place, then, where we are already muddled up (and the French equivalent for* Festschrift, *as I don't need to tell Roger, is* mélanges*) with the thing we are talking about — and must negotiate that situation as best we can. A* Festschrift *essay on grace, that is to say, might turn out to be as crass or clodhopping as they come, but it cannot simply dodge, as other forms of writing might, the question of its own grace. It already operates in an arena in which grace is at issue. That being the case... But excuse me for a moment. I can hear other people arriving.*

Grace

> I draw a small smiley face in a patch of condensation and I think *Joy* and then I think *Grace* and then I change the smiley mouth to one pointing downwards, and then I rub it out altogether.[6]

This seems no bad place to begin an exploration of 'grace' in contemporary fiction. It's from Sophie Mackintosh's 'Grace', which won the *White Review*'s 2016 short story prize. In it, the narrator describes a coach journey towards a destination that only at the end reveals itself to be a cliff-top whence the travellers will leap to their deaths. The referent of Mackintosh's title is never entirely clear. Is 'grace' the possibility for human intervention that the duration of the journey holds out? We learn that any passenger whose family or friends can overtake them is obliged to give up their death-wish and return home: the journey is a sort of grace period. Or is grace the intervention itself, the act which (as with Christian grace of whatever theological colour) offers the possibility of salvation from otherwise pre-determined perdition? Or, conversely, is grace the death which awaits, a final salve or solution, or a *coup de grâce*? More locally, in the lines just quoted, things are no more decidable. Like the coach window on which the narrator draws, Mackintosh's sentence is rather opaque — a 'patch of condensation' indeed. It's not obvious whether 'grace' is a synonym or an antonym or modification of 'joy', nor in which of its overlapping discursive senses it is being used. Is it noun or verb, or are both '*Grace*' and '*Joy*' proper names? It's even hard to keep our signifiers apart from our signifieds here: when the narrator 'think[s] Grace' is she mentally rehearsing the sound-pattern or grapheme 'grace', or entertaining in some manner the concept which attaches to these? And what corresponds with this thinking: the smiley face, the sad face, the overwriting of one by the other, or the act of erasure itself ('and then I rub it out altogether')? Traced over the condensation, in other words, is a series of displacements. The syntax doesn't help — parataxis renders causation enigmatic too — 'and', 'and then', 'and then', all sequence, no motivation or animating oomph to get us from happening to happening, just an inexorable onwardness. We might think it rather graceless prose.

The appearance and then disappearance of grace here mimics *in nuce* an emerging trend in contemporary Anglophone fiction. There are quite a number of novels from the last few decades whose title invokes 'grace' but at the same time 'rub[s] it out', disfigures it, or renders it approximate or embattled: to wit Margaret Atwood's *Alias Grace* (1996), J. M. Coetzee's *Disgrace* (1999), Anthony Doerr's *About Grace* (2004), Ali Smith's *There but for the* (2011), Kirsty Logan's *The Gracekeepers* (2015), and Tahmima Anam's *The Bones of Grace* (2016). And then there are also novels in which grace crops up quasi-symbolically but similarly expunged or exhausted, such as the second part of Zadie Smith's novel *NW*, a quite overtly allegorical story in which Felix ('"Listen: know what 'Felix' means? Happy. I bring happiness, innit?"') is murdered for the gifts his girlfriend Grace has given him;[7] Chris Kraus's *Aliens and Anorexia* (2000), which narrates the travails and failures of her film *Gravity and Grace*; Ben Johncock's *The Last Pilot* (2015) which tells the story of how test pilot and would-be astronaut Jim Harrison's quest for the stars comes at the expense of his marriage to Grace;[8] and Sarah Perry's *The Essex Serpent* (2016) in which, at a crucially disclosive moment, the eponymous serpent turns out in fact to be the wreck of a ship, named 'Gracie'.[9]

Each of these novels deserves close analysis for its singular thinking of grace, but from our armchairs we could diagnose the more general phenomenon of an erased or dissed grace in a number of ways. We might read it, for example, as a symptom of our mournful post-secular condition, a condition characterized by what Habermas calls 'an awareness of what is missing' from secular discourse.[10] G̶r̶a̶c̶e̶ here would advert to the loss of any belief in a salvific dispensation. Or else we could take grace's erasure as signalling and lamenting the decline and ruin of an inherited classical aesthetic category — the kind of achieved ease Vasari sees in Michelangelo say, '*una grazia più interamenta graziosa* [a grace more completely graceful], a superlative grace'.[11] Or bringing these two together, we could understand it as combining these theological and aesthetic melancholies, and marking 'the collapse of the idea of art as a channel of grace'.[12] Or, last, we could see it as tutting at a decline in contemporary mores or behaviour, in grace as a form of understatedly elegant comportment or self-effacing interpersonal thoughtfulness and care. That partial list of possible diagnoses certainly indicates the cultural, historical, social, and intellectual territory in which these novels are situated, and even gets at something of the pathos that attends them. But it's only part of the story. What it overlooks are the ways in which grace, across a variety of discourses, has *always* been conceived in relation to erasure and negation. In many cases, this erasure may be conceived as that of the *self* or of properties of the self, to permit grace's advent — a vatic emptying to allow God, or genius, to work; or in aesthetic terms an effacement or supercession of the appearance of artisanal labour or artfulness in the achievement of the work of art itself; or socially as the repression of any appearance of effortfulness in one's interactions. But grace itself must similarly be understood in relation to a withdrawal of its phenomenality. As, precisely, gratuitous, it is perforce chancy and adventitious. Thus we find Schiller, for example, arguing that, insofar as grace is accidental and mobile, disappearance is part of its essential possibility: 'Grace is a *movable* beauty, a beauty that can appear in a subject by chance and disappear in the same way' ('Anmuth ist eine *bewegliche* Schönheit; eine Schönheit nehmlich, die an ihrem Subjekte zufällig entstehen und eben so aufhören kann').[13] So, grace is one of those concepts which will always be ruined by the attempt to account for its attributes in terms of their presence: it cannot be discussed or written about, ever, as though it is too unequivocally there. In its gratuity, we might connect it with the gift, and with the an-economic 'logic' of the gift as best articulated by Derrida — the thinker and writer above all others devoted to tracing those aspects of our thinking and living which cannot be said to be uncomplicatedly present.[14] In *Given Time*, Derrida argues that a 'true' gift must always efface itself. For a gift to appear as such, however discreetly, would still be to vaunt itself *as a gift* and so already to assure some economic return; in psychological terms, for example, through complacency or simply pleasure in giving, or socially, through the gratitude or recognition the gift elicits. Any such pay-off would ruin the very nature of the gift. (That our concept of the gift as gratuitous and an-economic is itself but the fruit of the already-givenness of our language and inherited thought also forms part of Derrida's thinking.) Discussing alms-giving, Derrida explicitly connects the gift and grace: 'alms fulfils a regulated and regulating function; it is no longer a gratuitous or gracious gift, so to speak, which is what a pure gift must be'.[15] Grace and gift turn out to be inter-implicated: as grace is a species of gift, so the 'pure gift' must always be gracious. And so, just as with the gift, any marking of grace's gracefulness, any ostentation, and so, finally, any appearance of grace *as such*, would already be graceless.

To sum up, then, the repeated figure of an erased grace legible across a number of works of contemporary Anglophone fiction, on the one hand seems to register a loss, which can be described in historical and cultural terms. 'Grace' is felt to be missing, socially and aesthetically, in a late twentieth- and early twenty-first-century, 'post-secular' context. But on the other hand, and picking up on the concept of grace as it is given to us by a long tradition of Western philosophical and aesthetic thought, grace 'itself' is never something which can be said to have been ungainsayably there. The gesture of placing grace 'sous rature' in that case no longer simply marks a loss, but is in fact truest, in its very gawkiness, to grace's own-most evanescent essence. And so, we might begin to suggest that what we glimpse in this fiction is precisely, if paradoxically, a coming-into-its-own of grace.

Here is where we might pause to wonder. Why here and why now? And what work is ~~grace~~ doing in these novels? Beyond the local interest of these questions, I think they are worth pursuing for two related reasons. First, thinking about grace offers a contribution to the emerging conversation as to what might mark the particular aesthetic properties, as well as the ethical and political substance and commitments, of contemporary fiction. Contemporary fiction has sometimes been described in terms of an attenuation of the playfulness of postmodernism, and a qualified return to the realist project;[16] or else in relation to a 'meta-modernism' oscillating 'between a typically modern commitment and a markedly postmodern detachment'.[17] Something of the oscillation or ambivalence these descriptions point to is certainly there in the concept of grace, but grace summons longer traditions of aesthetic and ethical thinking too. Its art-historical lineage connects it with the traits of classicism — formality, placing, a replete restraint — while its affiliations with the marvellous and the supra-rational, on the other hand, are redolent of romance. So, the renaissance of 'grace' opens up larger scales and longer histories within which to conceive of the writing of our moment, and enriches the ways we might describe its particular feel and tone. And, importantly, it does so in terms which this writing *itself* quietly proffers and theorizes. This in turn points us to the second reason the phenomenon of erased grace commands our attention. 'Grace' as an aesthetic category has received relatively scant attention in the writings which constitute what, in the giddying merry-go-round terminology of intellectual history, is referred to as the 'aesthetic turn'. Much of this work evinces a renewed interest in Kant, and in the language of the beautiful and the sublime, and the fruitfully fuzzy terrain of aesthetic experience which takes place in the vicinity of these, which we inherit from the thinking of the Third Critique.[18] Meanwhile, the inventive work of Sianne Ngai, in her *Our Aesthetic Categories: Zany, Cute, Interesting*, extends the range of aesthetic categories beyond the classical sublime/ beautiful dyad in order to attend to a set of low-key contemporary ways in which we frame our aesthetic experience (what she calls '"minor" aesthetic judgements') in an era in which art has become irremediably intertwined with commodity culture and our encounter with it 'is no longer automatically equated with awe, or with rare or conceptually unmediated experience'.[19] In neither of these (very swiftly sketched) ways of reconceiving the aesthetic does grace, whose intellectual history stretches back to Greek accounts of *charis* and continues through the Renaissance, to the eighteenth-century, to its present usage, get much consideration.[20] In a local and small-scale way, this essay offers some preliminary attempts to repair that omission.

There but for the

Of the novels I've mentioned, Ali Smith's *There but for the* offers the most sustained meditation on grace. As a novel which itself reflects on contemporary art, its account also opens out onto the larger cultural field in which it participates. For these reasons, it's with Smith that I'll tarry in what follows. I'm going to begin by exploring how Smith's ~~grace~~ summons up a particular and agonizing *ethical* situation — and one which has implications for questions of fictional character, narrative style, and writing — before, in the final section of the essay, exploring what this has to do with 'grace' conceived under its more explicitly 'aesthetic' aspect.

Markedly excised from its aposiopetic title, grace returns motivically throughout the text of Smith's novel. It is there as a proper name in anecdotes about Grace Meyer (p. 182) and Gracie Fields (p. 230); as an acronym for an automatic telephone exchange, the Group Routing and Changing Equipment (p. 130); as an adjective in the commodified jargon of the estate agent ('our gracious old historic Greenwich townhouse' (p. 103)); and in a variety of idiomatic locutions, such as 'days of grace' (p. 205) or 'fall from grace' (p. 230), as well as in one of the novel's five epigraphs (from *The Winter's Tale*) 'every wink of an eye some new grace will be born'. Moreover, while this is never spelled out, the names of three of the novel's characters also derive from words to do with grace: Miles from the Slavic *milu*, meaning gracious, and Hannah and Anna both from the Hebrew *channa*, meaning grace or favour.

The word 'grace' and its cognates are manifestly played upon throughout the text, then. But Smith's attention to grace extends beyond this collection of grace-notes, and forms part of the ethical and formal thinking of the work as a 'whole'. Her novel is built around a central and rather fantastical or romantic conceit — that of 'a man who, one night between the main course and the sweet at a dinner party, went upstairs and locked himself in one of the bedrooms of the house of the people who were giving the dinner party' (p. 3). The man, Miles Garth, remains immured for many months. While the dinner party is represented as being fairly ghastly to any liberal or left-wing sensibility, the larger motivations for this gesture remain mysterious. Miles is as withdrawn from the narrative as he is from the world he so dramatically abjures. At times he appears to be an anchoretic figure (p. 67) and at others to conjure Bartleby ('No really, Miles keeps saying, I'd prefer not to', p. 114), but the novel explicitly rebuffs any attempt interpretatively to co-opt him. His own story is never told outright, though aspects of it can be inferred from those of others — Anna, Mark, May, and Brooke — through each of whom one of the four main sections of the book (entitled 'There', 'But', 'For', and 'The') is idiomatically focalized. These four characters' lives touch on, and are changed for the better by, that of the cloistered Garth. To this extent their 'long short stor[ies]' (p. 10) might be read as secular gospels: tales that tell of something good happening. Certainly their names syllabically echo those of the evangelists, and there are other parallels too. Anna gives up a job at least as odious as that of the erstwhile tax-collector Matthew, resigning her role working for the immigration authorities (a job designed 'to make people not matter so much', p. 54), and later organizing the group of people who gather outside the window of Miles's 'cell' to send him provisions. Meanwhile we are given enough information to figure out that May Young dies at the age of eighty-four, as the evangelist Luke is said to have done, and nine-year-old Brooke, who records all the events in her Moleskine, is, like John, the youngest gospeller. But *There but for the* is not concerned to spread *to euangelion tes charitos tou Theou*, the gospel of the grace of God (Acts 20:24). It is true that Miles's final act at the dinner party (his last supper, as it were) is surreptitiously to swap a glass of white wine for red, so that his friend Mark is left with something he is able to drink. But, while tradition puts the evangelist Mark at the marriage at Cana, *this* act is neither the turning of water to wine, nor a symbolic or actual transubstantiation. It is, rather, an overtly a-theist or secular transposition, which works through a different disposal of the available materials, rather than by divine intervention.

So, we can begin to see that Smith's novel reframes 'grace' in relation to a set of economic and ethical questions, in a broadly atheist, affluent, Western, twenty-first-century context. Indeed, most of *There but for the*'s main characters explicitly underline the absence or abstention of a deity: Berenice Bayoude is 'writing a paper about how nature says that God is dead' (p. 68); Patrick, May's husband, asks of the death of their fifteen-year-old daughter 'Who sees the sparrow fall?' and, refusing the consolation to be found in the gospel of Matthew (10:29), answers 'Nobody, it just falls' (p. 239); and Mark wonders (apropos a bigoted Catholic taxi driver) 'if that's what God was these days, and whether everybody now simply had a private god who sanctioned his or her own choices' (p. 145). Meanwhile, Anna, watching Wimbledon, fantasizes 'a new psychosis, Tennis Players Psychosis (TPP), where you went through life believing an audience was always watching you', thinks that 'everybody who still believed in God must share this feeling', and wonders whether those who don't (amongst whom she includes herself) 'were somehow less *there* in the world' (p. 8). While Berenice's punning description of her paper might suggest the type of atheist naturalism for which Richard Dawkins has become known, the general tone here is not so much one of militant secularism, as of a mournful post-secularism. What is marked in particular is the absence of the gaze of an all-seeing over-watching other. Eyes in the sky in this post-millenial context belong to micro-drones (p. 118) or CCTV cameras (p. 65). There is no benign regard in which all are held, the novel suggests, and many deaths go unwatched, uncounted, and unrecounted. And with this loss of an all-seeing eye comes the removal of any fantasy of a transcendental care-taker, and so of grace as a super-natural, salving gift.

This absence is of course marked in Smith's title, a truncated form of the idiomatic expression 'there but for the grace of God go I'. The phrase is often attributed to the Protestant martyr John Bradford, who is said to have uttered it upon seeing others led to execution. We see here the snag in the very idea of grace, of whatever theological hue. Insofar as, in both Catholic and Protestant traditions, grace is an unmerited gift from God, which means that my original sin need not be determining of my fate, it names a kind of unstinting beneficence. But the moment grace is accorded to some rather than to others, or is only intermittent, 'punctual' as well as 'actual', to borrow terms this time from the Catholic tradition, one thereby attributes a strange partiality or injustice to God.[21] Grace on the one hand, then, offers a way of thinking about gifts, or *give*, within an otherwise determining fate or economy, and so gestures towards hope and the possibility for invention and novelty beyond the prescribed or the calculable. But on the other hand, the very gratuity of grace also introduces problems of inequity, partiality, and preference. It is Brooke, Smith's fourth focalizing consciousness, who pursues this second set of questions as she reflects on:

> Amina, the girl in the year ahead of her at school who everyone knows came from a warzone and is way Christian, and says she became it and believed in God the very moment a bullet that was fired at her missed her. [...] From the moment it missed, she says, she has believed in God. Well duh. But what Brooke wants to know is what about the people who *were* hit by bullets and died? Does that mean that God didn't like them? Or that they didn't believe in Him or It? Or that they believed in the wrong God? Or that they did believe but that God just decided against them? (p. 330)

In the light of the broadly-speaking secular concerns of the novel as a whole, this brisk foray into questions of theology and theodicy nudges us towards a thinking of inequality and injustice, and so to a thinking of ethics and of how we conceive of responsibility to the other. If I am a finite being existing in a world of finite resources, with no infinite gift-giver to supplement these resources, then my gain always risks being another's loss.

For thinkers who eschew Kant's generalizing model of the categorical imperative, this situation describes the agony of the ethical *tout court*. And it is not only a question of *receiving* gifts but also of *bestowing* them. If I do good to some, others perforce suffer. In the second book he devotes to an exploration of the gift, *The Gift of Death*, Derrida finds this situation inscribed at the very beginning of Judeao-Christian scriptures.[22] He reads the story of Abraham and Isaac, emphasizing the fact that Abraham has to choose between his responsibility to God, and his responsibility to his son, choosing to sacrifice the claims of the latter to those of the former. This singular story manifests a general dilemma: 'I cannot respond to the call, the request, the obligation, or even the love of another, without sacrificing the other other, the other others.' And this situation, in which I am aboriginally, exorbitantly and, structurally guilty, is so frequent and banally quotidian that often it does not even provoke agonies of conscience. After all:

> How would you ever justify the fact that you sacrifice all the cats in the world to the cat that you feed at home every morning for years, whereas other cats die of hunger at every instant? Not to mention other people? (*GD*, pp. 70–71)

In the story of Abraham and Isaac, God intervenes and dissolves the ethical bind — just as in the Christian tradition his grace (bestowed through the sacrifice of his own son) salves original sin. But in a context in which 'the grace of God' is absent, or never arrives, what then?

It has long been the business of the novel to worry over this question, and to work out in narrative form the implications of the general structure of intersubjective involvement which engenders it. Think of the carefully orchestrated interpersonal economies in Eliot's *Daniel Deronda*, for example, and Deronda's explanation to Gwendolen Harleth of his dislike of gambling:

> There are enough inevitable turns of fortune which force us to see that our gain is another's loss: — that is one of the ugly aspects of life. One would like to reduce it as much as one could, not get amusement out of exaggerating it.[23]

Here the supernatural categories of fate and fortune are translated into a more material structure of profit and loss. In this context we might usefully recall one of the founding contentions of Ian Watt's influential *The Rise of the Novel*, namely that the genre is co-terminous with the advent of economic individualism.[24] But more recent critical interventions suggest that the alliance between a canonically-endorsed realism and liberal economics proposed by this account of the novel comes at the expense of the derogation of forms of writing (romance, gothic, the novel of sensibility etc.) which figure the individual subject and interpersonal relations differently, and as involved with, and traversed by, forces which they cannot simply own or wield.[25] Ali Smith's novel, with its central 'romantic' conceit, might be said to affiliate itself with strains of this counter-tradition. But what marks it out as a contemporary novel, is its situation of the ethical questions of justice and responsibility within the almost unthinkably vast contexts of global capitalism, and of global warming.[26] I want to suggest that these have implications both for its writing of character, and for its thinking of its own work, and of writing full stop.

Explicitly, contemporary global concerns come in to *There but for the* only through fleeting allusions. In the dinner party scene Hugo says complacently of 'the choice of toothpaste we have these days', 'it's great living in such a multivalent universe and having so much choice' (p. 147), while the erasure of the labour upon which such choice is predicated is slyly registered by another character's symptomatic mishearing of 'sweatshop' for 'sweatshirts' (p. 132). Meanwhile the more ethically-aware Anna thinks back to the summers of her childhood, and compares them with the present 'global warming summers' (p. 56) but does not pursue any further reflection on this. The novel's distinctly oblique treatment of its global contexts is hardly incidental. Such phenomena operate at a scale which transcends and subtends the levels of human character or narratable plot. It is perhaps for this reason that the adult character who appears to have grappled most thoughtfully with the ethical exigencies engendered by our global contexts is the one whose consciousness is so markedly withheld from readerly view. One of the things we do learn about Miles is that he is by profession an 'ethical consultant' who works with companies to 'make suggestions about where, depending on the brief, they could make themselves greener, or specifically help communities they're local to, or capitalize on what's already sound about themselves' (p. 129). But while the novel implies, and solicits, quite exceptional sympathy for him, we are made to understand that the ethical model his consultancy promotes is not without its complicities and bad faith. We infer that he makes a very decent personal profit from his business (his jacket is 'stylish, expensive, covetable', p. 48), and he reportedly tells Brooke that he is an 'ethic cleanser' (p. 129), a pun which suggests a world of self-disgust. In terms of character analysis, we might speculate that his decision to abjure society is in part a result of the intolerable subjective burden of the recognition that (as Mark thinks) 'more and more, the pressing human dilemma [is] how to walk a clean path between obscenities' (p. 159). But the formal point is perhaps rather that, however much the dilemma is experienced *by* humans, to render it solely in terms of the travails of an individual human consciousness and conscience risks re-inforcing the very individualism that is its cause.

It is here that the reflections of the child, Brooke, are accorded a certain privilege. Brooke is preternaturally sensitive to the hyperbolic ethical situation we have adumbrated, and she lives it in particular as a question of memory and recording — as a kind of responsibility to do justice to all that has taken place, as well as to the losses and sufferings of the world. She uses her Moleskine obsessively to archive for the future all the details and documents of her current situation. Meanwhile, she lies awake at night going through litanies of the dead and suffering across time, in a kind of *memoria passionis*:

> All the dead people from history line[d] up instead of sheep, looking with sad

long faces and queuing for miles and miles at a gate too high for them to jump over, so many there's no way you could count them. (p. 298).

But it isn't this hyperbolic memorializing which makes her most anxious, because here, at least, there are people 'to say sorry to' (p. 299). What frustrates the liberal-humanist adoption of a Christian ethic of confession and absolution, and of the piety of memorializing, is rather the always-present possibility of the unreliability or unintelligibility of recording and archiving itself. 'How do you know anything is true?' she wonders and answers herself, 'Duh, obviously, records and so on, but how do you know that the *records* are true?' (p. 289). A version of this problem gives her 'a different kind of not-sleeping from the kind where all the dead people from history line up' (p. 298). Coming upon a copy of *The Secret Agent* in which certain words have been circled by a previous reader, she becomes haunted by the impossibility of being 'able to know what the answer to why the words were chosen was' (p. 299), and it is this which keeps her awake three nights in a row. Her mother suggests that 'she would either just have to persuade herself [...] right now, to put up with the not-knowing, or she would have to make the active decision to rub out the circles', and promises her a 'special eraser from the office' to the latter end (pp. 299–300). But while erasure and a letting-go of the desire to know, like forgetting, are existential necessities, this realization does not mitigate the agony of the situation.

We can return here to the particular erased word which is our own guiding thread. Writing itself, Smith implies, is a form of grace, but by the same token, of ~~grace~~. Making good the lapses and deficiencies of human memory and attention, as divine grace supplements human error, it nevertheless only does so by confiding traces to a material support which is itself subject to loss and erasure, and which breaks with the contexts which might have made sense of them.[27] By way of recompense once more, this capacity to break with its context gives writing, too, a constitutively dative dimension, enabling itself to be offered as a gift to readers known or unknown. Such gift-writing is there in *There but for the* in the little texts which intersplice the four 'long short stor[ies]': Miles's and Brooke's short stories to each other, Miles's postcard to May, and his note to Mark. But, to sound the counter note, and to quote Derrida again, 'this does not imply that writing is *generous* or that the writing subject is a *giving subject*' (*GT*, p. 101). Writing's donation is a function of its repeatability and of its capacity to disseminate itself, in ways irrecuperable either by its scriptor or by any one of its readers.

It is in this context, I think, that we might read Smith's eschewal of the more recognizable forms of psychological realism. Dominic Head suggests that Smith 'circumvents an in-depth treatment of character' not because she subscribes to a belief in the 'instability of identity or the impossibility of the coherent subject' but because her 'method' 'might identify contexts in which the luxury of bourgeois identity formation cannot occur'.[28] I disagree. All her characters — however socially or otherwise marginalized — are, in the focalized rendition of their consciousness, accorded psychic interiority, the capacity for ethical choice (however circumscribed), and auto-affective inner conversation. In *There but for the*, for example, think of the internal monologue of the elderly, lower-middle-class May

Young ('incontinent, probable onset of mild dementia, danger to self', p. 213), as, in her final 'days of grace' she recollects some of the mis-steps of her past: 'Well, I wish, though, I really wish I hadn't done that thing to that rabbit. Out loud? No. That girl who was in the room, whoever she was, hadn't moved' (p. 213). The difference between an interior and exterior voice is here explicitly marked, as is May's capacity, even *in extremis*, for ethical reflection. The focalized narration marks and respects idiom, as it registers too the inward calculations of a subject. But while (Derrida again) 'a defined subject always calculates on returns and capitalizes' and 'one cannot discern the subject, except as the subject of this operation of capital' (*GT*, p. 101), the free indirect style that Smith here, as elsewhere, tends to favour, marks the exteriority of the writing to the inner life it simultaneously conjures. And the eschewal of depth psychology (along with the refusal of what James Joyce referred to as 'perverted commas' to mark off individuals' speech) in this case does not imply that certain characters cannot accede to the luxury of economic returns, but rather proffers the dream of a less restrictive, more generous, economy *tout court*. To this extent, we might suggest that the liberty of *style indirect libre* resembles the gratuity and the give of grace.[29]

Now, in using free indirect style, Smith is clearly not innovating but rather drawing on the gifts of a long novelistic tradition. What *is* singular, I think, is the way that she takes up the possibilities of such writing to reconceptualize the nature of the aesthetic, and of the 'work of art', at large. Here is where the novel's ethical concerns touch more nearly on its aesthetic ones, and the theological senses of grace start to blend with those connected with literature and art in general.

Artful

Art is at the heart of *There but for the* in a number of ways. Anna and Miles initially meet because they have both submitted winning entries to a short story competition. Miles and Mark encounter one another when they sit next to each other at a production of *A Winter's Tale* (a play which ghosts this novel) and strike up a conversation after the play has been interrupted by the ringing of a mobile phone. Brooke and Miles exchange stories, in a circuit which seems never quite to close. Beyond this, the fabric of the whole is threaded through with allusions to and discussions of plays, novels, poems, and short stories, to visual and installation art, and to music and song. (The particular focus on song perhaps nods towards the earliest Sanskrit origins of the word grace.)

But what model of art and of aesthetic experience and value does the novel itself propose? We might come at this question through looking at a critical (in both senses) response to it. Writing in the *London Review of Books* seven months after the publication of *There but for the*, and taking advantage of that lag to survey the novel's immediate critical reception, Theo Tait adopts a rather savagely sceptical position.[30] He kicks off with the furore around the 2010 Booker Prize, which espoused a controversially populist view of literary value, and for which Smith's novel wasn't shortlisted, and he suggests that the lamentations of the 'London literary world' over this omission were misplaced. His beefs are that Smith 'is sentimental about the basic purity and goodness of children', that (contra the received view that she 'punctur[es] middle-class philistinism and smugness') 'her characters are so stupidly tactless and frequently evil that their values come entirely pre-punctured', and that the novel as a whole is 'whimsical, tepidly experimental and desperately predictable in its sympathies'. The effect of the novel, finally, is 'to rain down simple pieties on the unfortunate reader'. And as if that weren't enough, he is also critical of what he facetiously calls Smith's 'gamesome wordplay'.

There are local details and evident misreadings in this review that can quite simply be countered — Tait misquotes, and muddles one character for another (both times in ways which make the novel appear simpler than it is). But these cavils aside, the larger aesthetic categories Tait deploys, in relation to which he finds Smith wanting, are perhaps worth consideration. He draws on the venerable categories of the satirical and the sentimental, and suggests that Smith is too sentimental and that this fault goes hand in hand with a lack of subtlety or complexity in her satire. The wrongness of these claims is interesting, touching as it does on the ways in which Smith conceives her own project, and the function of the aesthetic at large. Satire's ancient function is disclosive and corrective. It holds up for censure or mockery 'all the things which men do' (to borrow from Juvenal, *Satires* 2.1.80). There is certainly something of that taking place in the dinner party scene, in its rendition of casual racism and sexism, and of the structural solipsism and cruelty of liberal free-market economics and the privileged class which profits therefrom. But since, as we have suggested above, Smith's larger concern is with the ways in which we are all in a situation of general and structural complicity, the disclosure of either individual malice *or* beneficence is not quite the point. And this has implications too for its treatment of art.

Art in this novel (and as performed or enacted by it) is not, I would suggest, primarily disclosive or designed to 'puncture', but is, rather, reparative — in the sense given to this by Eve Sedgwick. Sedgwick discusses the idea of reparative practices and aesthetics in a 1997 essay entitled 'Paranoid Reading and Reparative Reading, or, You're so Paranoid, You Probably Think This Essay is About You', an essay which marks the beginning of a disciplinary 'turn' in literary studies towards the 'post-critical'.[31] Sedgwick's concern is with the stakes and implicit, performative claims of the forms of reading practice situated in the tradition of what Paul Ricœur famously dubbed the 'hermeneutics of suspicion': forms of reading (including, as she avows, many aspects of her own earlier practice) concerned with exposing hidden assumptions and structures at work in literary and cultural texts. Ricœur applies the term to Marx, Nietzsche, and Freud, and Sedgwick extends it to their successors and inheritors in the fields of 'New Historicist, deconstructive, feminist, queer, and psychoanalytic criticism', taking D. A. Miller's *The Novel and the Police* and Judith Butler's *Gender Trouble* as exemplary.[32] Her suggestion is that such forms of reading are structured in the same way that paranoia is, and that there are advantages and disadvantages to this way of relating to and knowing the world. As with paranoia, the hermeneutics of suspicion directs its energy to fending off bad surprises, by a microscopic forensic attention to the ideological and metaphysical complicities of every last element of the texts being read. In this aspiration to a panoptical purview, refusing to leave unexplicated any mystery in the objects of their attention, the hermeneuts become oddly mimetic of what they oppose, turning into the very police they abhor. And yet by the same token, they are oddly naive, placing an unexamined faith in the value of exposure itself, even though exposure doesn't necessarily lead to change. Conversely, Sedgwick suggests, reparative readings give up on any aspiration to a total accounting for a text, but rather help themselves to the bits they need, as they continue with the ongoing critical process of reading and writing and reflection and making. Reparation here is conceived as a form of continuation of and dialogue with the art work, and one that hooks up with an earliness in it, an ongoing conversation with its incompletion and 'still-to-be-madeness', with, as it were, the child in it. We might recall here the very opening vignette of *There but for the*, a magical story (which later turns out to have been written by Miles as a gift for Brooke) in which a young boy removes the 'grey bars' which cover the eyes of a man who is an older version of himself.

Smith's own explicit advocacy of a 'reparative' approach can be read in a moment in the novel in which art is not overtly at issue. Some drunken way into the dinner party, Hannah tells the story of a woman she knows who wakes one day in a field, wearing new clothes and with no idea of what has happened to her between Saturday and Tuesday. The guests respond pruriently:

> Had anything happened to her? You know, anything (she nods towards the child) — bad?
> That's the thing. It didn't seem to have, Hannah said. But she didn't know. She couldn't know for sure.
> Had anything good happened to her? the child says.
> Much more interesting, Miles says.
> Ha! Berenice says.
> Easy to go to the bad, Miles says. I'm always much more interested in things going to the good. (p. 142)

The prurient guests, like good practitioners of the hermeneutics of suspicion, fill the blanks with a horrified projection of sexual violence. But Smith underscores the possibility that the worst need not be the only truth — that in the unknown, and the breaks and gaps in memory and knowledge, there is possibility, and that possibility can always go either way. Of course this turning to the good is one name for the work of grace. But here, what is referred to is neither divine force, nor human flair, but rather simply the 'give' in a situation that means that the worst need not transpire.

My point is not to celebrate Smith's novel insofar as it corroborates the, reparative, post-critical, inclinations of contemporary theorists. It's rather that her thinking of grace itself, reparatively, allows for a fruitful continuation of the conversation. And it's here that the novel's more explicit discussions of art come in. *There but for the* is a novel which welcomes, as it theorizes, some of the more avant-garde possibilities of modern and contemporary art. The 'arty talk' (p. 151) at the dinner party names explicitly the work of Andy Warhol, Tracey Emin, and Damien Hirst, and alludes also to works by artists such as Cornelia Parker and Martin Creed (pp. 149, 152, 150). What connects these otherwise very different practitioners is their resistance to the humanist idea of the lone artist-genius, in whom long hours of training and practising and craftsmanship will one day find their apotheosis in the seemingly effortless grace of a beautiful work of art.[33] It is that model of art which Caroline wants to defend, when she says, 'I like to see a beautiful thing if I go to an art gallery as much as the next person. But contemporary art, I don't like it, and I don't understand it. Most of the time it's so pointless' (p. 149). She then reels off a list of 'pointless' works of contemporary art, culminating in 'that pointless artist who had the lights coming on and off in the room' (the allusion is to Martin Creed's Turner Prize-winning 'the lights going on and off') and concludes 'it doesn't make anything happen' (p. 150). But Miles, in what is his parting conversational gambit before absenting himself for good, demurs: 'Well, Miles says. It does. What does it make happen? Caroline says. It makes the lights go on and off, Miles says' (p. 150). While this might be taken as an account of the enlightening, epiphany-generating possibilities of artistic creation, its significance is perhaps simpler and more profound than this. Art, as a form of *techne*, participates in the most primitive sharing out, dividing up, partitioning, and shaping of the world, of the givens and gifts of *physis* or nature. It can refer to any form of mark-making, any drawing of a line or making of a distinction, by means of which more chiaroscuro effects might emerge. It's there at the origin of 'on and off' as it is in the distinction between light and dark.[34] Insofar as art, in this exorbitantly expanded sense, itself participates in the sharing out of 'natural' resources, it can neither wash its hands of a complicity with the worst injustices nor simply come to redeem them. But still, some artistic practices conjure with this situation more candidly, more helpfully, more generously, more inventively and more reparatively than others. The art work Miles explicitly defends, Creed's installation, eschews any metaphysical or humanist notion of grace. But it situates art as an on-going, democratically available, co-creation, in which the involvement of the gallery-goer — their structural involvement and essential 'complicity' — is foregrounded, and affirmed.[35] And Miles's defence of it resonates with and rewrites the nexus of material, ethical, and aesthetic questions and problems that ~~grace~~ in Smith's novel seems to name, situating art as ab-originally involved in the dispensation and shaping of the world's finite wealth.

Here we might return to the odd situation with which I began, of the paradoxical coming-into-its-own of grace, marked by its erasure in many works of contemporary fiction. Grace, as we have already said, is effaced or defaced in contemporary art because any dream of its coming from elsewhere (without or within) to save us, must be repudiated. But what we can now suggest is that it's for this very reason that ~~grace~~ is accorded a fundamental, an essential, a non-accidental role — as the very possibility of accident, or chance, as the give in any economy, however austere. Across her *œuvre* Smith has offered a series of 'defences' of art and literature, of which *Artful* is the most sustained, and Miles's one-sentence sally perhaps the most pithy. This revisiting of the genre of the defence itself is a mark of her contemporaneity: Rita Felski has suggested that 'the countless lamentations, perorations, jeremiads, diagnoses and defences of the humanities that have appeared in recent years [...] constitute a genre in their own right'.[36] The desacralizing of the arts and humanities, and the inextricable imbrication of art and literature in the global capitalist economies some of it might also seek to resist or criticize, renders such defences imperative, even while removing all of the grounds on which they have traditionally been made. ~~Grace~~, I suggest, names the groundless ground of one form of contemporary response to this situation.

What, then, of the novel as itself a 'work of art'? In its structure, *There but for the* offers a collection of loosely connected parts, which may be variously assembled, but without ever quite forming a whole. This is a feature of many of Smith's novels, including *Hotel World* and *The Accidental*. It is also perhaps *the* signature formal property of some of the most inventive Anglophone writing of the last few years — I'm thinking here of works such as Will Eaves's *The Absent Therapist* (2014), Claire-Louise Bennett's *Pond* (2015), Jenny Offill's *Dept. of Speculation* (2014), and Max Porter's *Grief is the Thing with Feathers* (2015), as well as of hybrid, 'creative-critical', texts, such as Maggie Nelson's *Bluets* (2009) and Joanna Walsh's *Hotel* (2015). In all these we see a marked inclination towards *part-writing*, in which pieces of prose are threaded together under a single title, and ask to be conceived in their inter-relation, while eschewing the kinds of connectedness ordinarily found in the novel or critical monograph. Once again, Smith's novel gives us the resources to think about a tendency in the larger field of contemporary writing, this time formally rather than thematically. The breaks which this writing at once marks and traverses refuse to posit a redeeming whole where there is none. But at the same time their patchworking doesn't simply bespeak an alienated fragmentation, but rather offers the open weave of a work that others can always take up. *There but for the*'s own parcelling out of its titular phrase, across each of the four main sections of the novel, is less a parsing than a sort of riffing, an exploration of the give and flexibility in the given-ness of the language we inherit. Its mode might be described not so much in terms of the broken figure of the aposiopesis found in its title, as via the rhetorical figure of anacoluthon offered in its opening sentence: 'the fact is, imagine' (p. 1). Here, the fracturing of grammar is not terminal, but gives on to unconventional new constructions, just as an interruption of the ostensibly given, the factual, demands and enables the work of imagination. In the gracelessness of a solecism, some new grace will be born.

We might find the figure of anacoluthon at work, too, in the novel's treatment of the performance of *The Winter's Tale*, interrupted in its closing scene by the ringing...

... but the 'gift of time' furnished by this Festschrift *has run its term. Others will have to continue the work of reading. Our revels now are ended. I hope, Ali and Roger, you have found some points of connection. Another of them, it occurs to me, might be your love of puns. I'm thinking, Roger, of that groansome moment in* Stendhal's Violin, *where you play on 'beau idéal' and 'ideal bow'.*[37] *Bad puns are the opposite of graceful. Forcing the issue, they cleave too closely to language's brute matter to achieve any beautiful synthesis of meaning, any epiphanic sublation of sound into sense, any effacement of their own clunky craft. But in their*

glee at the chancy — perhaps I should say Ali-atory — coincidences of language, they too are a kind of cherishing of the gifts of writing. And if you both, like Anna in There but for the, *agree that you'd never be friends with anyone if they weren't 'the sort to enjoy a bad pun' (p. 4) — well then perhaps this is no bad place to bring to a close my own poor contribution to* this *liber amicorum.*

Notes to Chapter 2

1. Let me mention in particular Ali Smith's *Artful* (London: Penguin, 2012) and Roger Pearson's *Unacknowledged Legislators: The Poet as Law-Giver in Post-revolutionary France: Chateaubriand, Staël, Lamartine, Hugo, Vigny* (Oxford: Oxford University Press, 2016).
2. Roger Pearson, 'Introduction', in *The Process of Art: Studies in Nineteenth-Century Literature and Art Offered to Alan Raitt*, ed. by Michael Freeman and others (Oxford: Clarendon Press, 1998), p. vii.
3. Ali Smith, *There but for the* (London: Penguin, 2012), p. 18. All page references to this work will henceforth be in the main text.
4. Pearson, 'Introduction', p. viii.
5. Smith, *Artful*, pp. 202–03.
6. Sophie Mackintosh, 'Grace', <http://www.thewhitereview.org/fiction/grace/> [accessed 19 July 2016].
7. Zadie Smith, *NW* (London: Hamish Hamilton, 2012), p. 102.
8. That Johncock intends some allegorical or symbolic significance to this name is suggested by the fact that while the surrounding characters are taken from real-life participants in the space race, and one of them is already called Grace, he nevertheless chooses this name for his central, fictional, heroine.
9. ' "*It is grace, again!*" ' thinks one of the characters later, as he finds his ill wife by the wreck of the ship: Sarah Perry, *The Essex Serpent* (London: Serpent's Tail, 2016), p. 406.
10. Jürgen Habermas and others, *An Awareness of What is Missing: Faith and Reason in a Post-Secular Age*, trans. by Ciaran Cronin (Cambridge: Polity, 2010).
11. The quotation from Vasari, along with most of my understanding of the Renaissance inheritance of the classical concept of 'grace', is taken from Ita Mac Carthy's essay 'Grace', in *Renaissance Keywords*, ed. by Mac Carthy (Oxford: Legenda, 2013), pp. 63–82 (p. 70).
12. Peter Fuller, *Theoria: Art, and the Absence of Grace* (London: Chatto & Windus, 1988). The quotation is from the book's blurb, and its claims are worked out across the book, in a detailed exploration of Ruskin's aesthetics, alongside an excoriating criticism of the violences and perversions of the ideas Ruskin espouses, in the work of late modernist and post-modern twentieth-century artists.
13. Friedrich Schiller, 'On Grace and Dignity' ('Ueber Anmuth and Würde') in *Schiller's 'On Grace and Dignity' in its Cultural Contexts*, ed. by Jane V. Curran and Christophe Fricker (Rochester, NY: Camden House, 2005), pp. 125 & 172.
14. Jonathan Tiplady, in his 'Good Air, My Only Friend, Believe', *Angelaki*, 12:2 (2007), 151–61, has a lovely footnote which captures something of the quality of Derrida's thinking of presence: 'whatever the deep questions deconstruction puts to it, presence does not just disappear after Derrida. In a certain way, it may even be able to appear more enigmatic, or is even thought *as such* for the first time' (p. 160).
15. Jacques Derrida, *Given Time: 1. Counterfeit Money*, trans. by Peggy Kamuf (Chicago, IL, & London: University of Chicago Press, 1992), p, 137. Subsequent references to this work will be given in the main text as *GT*.
16. For a helpful summary of this characterization of contemporary fiction, see Robert Eaglestone, *Contemporary Fiction: A Very Short Introduction* (Oxford: Oxford University Press, 2013), especially Chapter 2.
17. Timotheus Vermeulen and Robin van den Akker, 'Notes on Metamodernism', *Journal of Aesthetics and Culture*, 2:1 (2010), 1–14 (p. 2).

18. I'm thinking here of such important work as Isobel Armstrong's *The Radical Aesthetic* (Oxford: Blackwell, 2000) which positions itself as a corrective to the work of 'theorists from a tradition of a hermeneutics of suspicion [who] are mostly silent on the politics and poetics of beauty' (p. 2); and Simon Jarvis's 'An Undeleter for Criticism', *Diacritics* 32:1 (2002), 3–10 & 12–18, which explores the question of the existence, nature, and value of 'the experience of beauty', via a careful re-reading of the Third Critique.
19. Sianne Ngai, *Our Aesthetic Categories: Zany, Cute, Interesting* (Cambridge, MA: Harvard University Press, 2012), pp. 54 & p. 24.
20. The silence is of course not total. See, in particular, some suggestive comments on grace in Michael D. Snediker, *Queer Optimism: Lyric Personhood and Other Felicitous Persuasions* (Minneapolis: University of Minnesota Press, 2009), especially pp. 118–25. Snediker's thinking draws on Paul de Man's 'Aesthetic Formalisation in Kleist's Über das Marionettentheater' in *The Rhetoric of Romanticism* (New York: Columbia University Press, 1984), pp. 263–90.
21. See the helpful article on 'Actual Grace', in the *Catholic Encyclopedia*, <http://www.newadvent.org/cathen/06689x.htm> [accessed 25 July 2016].
22. Jacques Derrida, *The Gift of Death*, trans. by David Wills (Chicago, IL: University of Chicago Press, 1995), p. 69. References to this work will henceforth be given in the main text as GD.
23. George Eliot, *Daniel Deronda* [1876] (London: Penguin, 1995), p. 337.
24. See Ian Watt, *The Rise of the Novel: Studies in Defoe, Richardson and Fielding* [1957], 2nd edn (Berkeley: University of California Press, 2001), in particular Chapter 3, 'Robinson Crusoe, Individualism and the Novel', pp. 60–92.
25. See Nancy Armstrong, *How Novels Think: The Limits of Individualism 1719–1900* (New York: Columbia University Press, 2005).
26. For an extensive consideration of the relationship between contemporary fiction and globalization, see Peter Boxall, *Twenty-First Century Fiction* (Cambridge: Cambridge University Press, 2013), esp. pp. 165–209. And for a chilling and compelling account of the deformations of scale produced by the environmental crisis, and the corresponding problems this poses for literary representation, see Timothy Clark, *Ecocriticism on the Edge: The Anthropocene as a Threshold Concept* (London: Bloomsbury, 2015).
27. Mark Currie has written about Smith's treatment of the materiality of writing in this novel, in 'Ali Smith and the Philosophy of Grammar', in *Ali Smith: Contemporary Critical Perspectives*, ed. by Monica Germanà and Emily Horton (London: Bloomsbury, 2013), pp. 48–60.
28. Dominic Head, 'Idiosyncrasy and Currency: Ali Smith and the Contemporary Canon', in *Ali Smith*, ed. by Germanà and Horton, pp. 101–14 (p. 109).
29. I discuss the relation between free indirect discourse and grace more fully in my 'Without Grace (A Working Title)', *Oxford Literary Review*, 37:2 (2015), 197–216 (pp. 203–04). See also Honor Gavin's *Literature and Film, Dispositioned: Thought, Location, World* (Basingstoke: Palgrave Macmillan, 2014), which explores free indirect style in Henry James, James Joyce, Virginia Woolf, and Samuel Beckett, in relation to silent film.
30. Theo Tait, 'The Absolute End', *London Review of Books*, 34:2 (26 January 2012), <http://www.lrb.co.uk/v34/n02/theo-tait-the-absolute-end> [accessed 1 August 2016].
31. See for example Bruno Latour, 'Why Has Critique Run out of Steam? From Matters of Fact to Matters of Concern', *Critical Inquiry*, 30 (Winter 2004), 225–48; and Rita Felski, *The Limits of Critique* (Chicago, IL: University of Chicago Press, 2015).
32. Eve Sedgwick, 'Paranoid Reading and Reparative Reading, or, You're so Paranoid, You Probably Think This Essay is About You', in *Touching Feeling: Affect, Pedagogy, Performativity* (Durham, NC, & London: Duke University Press, 2003), pp. 123–52 (p. 125).
33. Here we might see Smith's novel as participating in a debate inaugurated by Kleiss's 'Über das Marionettentheater' (1810), as to whether 'grace' might in fact turn out to be more truly the property of the mechanical rather than the human and the conscious.
34. There's a real vibe between the idea that 'art makes the lights go on and off' and Jacques Ranciere's claim, in *The Politics of Aesthetics: The Distribution of the Sensible*, trans. by Gabriel Rockhill (London: Continuum, 2004), that aesthetics 'is a delimitation of spaces and times, of the visible and the invisible, of speech and noise, that simultaneously determines the place and the stakes of politics as a form of experience' (p. 13).

35. See Creed's comment in an interview with Laura Barnett in the *Guardian* (20 February 2010) that 'everything that everyone does is art, or at least a little creation', <https://www.theguardian.com/culture/2010/feb/22/martin-creed-artist> [accessed 1 November 2017].
36. Rita Felski, 'Introduction', *New Literary History*, 47:2 & 3 (2016), 215–29 (p. 215).
37. Roger Pearson, *Stendhal's Violin* (Oxford: Clarendon Press, 1988), p. 38.

— 2 —
Weight and Wit:
The Grace of Voltaire's Enlightenment

T. J. Reed

Virginia Woolf says somewhere that the steps between minds must be cut very shallow if people are to understand one another. If I understand her metaphor aright, someone has to be gently encouraged upwards by a step-cutter standing at a higher level who has a point to make.

Enlightenment writers had a number of points to make, as substantial as any in history and more fundamental than most, since they meant overturning the long-established beliefs, prejudices, and practices that together constituted pre-modern society. 'Weight' is not a bad term for the corpus of enlightened arguments, since the thing ultimately at issue was the weight of evidence, what we know as the 'burden of proof': for or against Jean Calas and his family, say, or for or against the notion that all is for the best in the best of all possible worlds.

The first of these issues was deadly serious and left no room for playfulness. Hence the powerful unadorned opening of Voltaire's *Traité sur la tolérance*: not the beginnings of an abstract discussion of the nature of tolerance, but a stark statement of the effects of *in*tolerance: 'Le meurtre de Calas...'.[1] The second issue, crucial to understanding the world, to knowing what to expect from it and how to act in it, might likewise have seemed to require systematic metaphysical — philosophical and theological — argument, spelling out at length the objections to a thesis that had itself been spelled out at length. But this was surely a case where weight needed to be lightened by wit. Might the audience not be given a spring-heeled start up those steps? A central problem of the Enlightenment was how to make its serious ideas palatable, attractive, entertaining... A straw in the wind is the way the sultanas in the dedicatory epistle to *Zadig* are *not* interested in ideas. Really? How can they possibly prefer the stories of the *Thousand and One Nights* 'qui sont sans raison et ne signifient rien?' 'C'est précisément pour cela que nous les aimons!' is the reply.[2] So it is not for nothing that *Zadig* itself comes in the guise of an oriental tale, albeit with an extreme rationality that at times anticipates Sherlock Holmes.[3]

A similarly light-hearted fiction is the means to draw the public into sympathy for the serially unfortunate Candide. His tragi-comic story will give them *en passant* an immediate feel for the realities of their own world. But what counts as wit in *Candide*? The text is not packed with distinct witticisms, as Voltaire elsewhere warns, 'l'empressement de montrer de l'esprit [...] est la plus sûre manière de n'en avoir point'.[4] Rather, the tale is told with a sustained cool irony that holds the disastrous events at arm's length as linked causes and effects, all proving the opposite of Pangloss's optimism. Each reiteration of his faith rings more hollow. The wit lies in the whole conception.

Care was needed. The ironies of Candide's career must not become irony at his expense. That could be read as heartlessness, putting the audience's sympathies for the argument at risk. This was Voltaire's effect on Schiller, a considerable literary critic, if with a tendency to moral severity. He contrasts Voltaire's effect with the 'Ernst der Empfindung' [seriousness of feeling] he finds in Christoph Martin Wieland:[5]

> Von der Voltairischen Satire läßt sich kein solches Urteil fällen. Zwar ist es auch bei diesem Schriftsteller einzig nur die Wahrheit und Simplizität der Natur, wodurch er uns zuweilen poetisch rührt; es sei nun, daß er sie in einem naiven Charakter wirklich erreiche, wie mehrmals in seinem 'Ingénu', oder daß er sie, wie in seinem 'Candide' u.a., suche und räche. Wo keines von beiden der Fall ist, da kann er uns zwar als witziger Kopf belustigen, aber gewiß nicht als Dichter bewegen. Aber seinem Spott liegt überall zu wenig Ernst zum Grunde, und dieses macht seinen Dichterberuf mit Recht verdächtig. Wir begegnen immer nur seinem Verstande, nicht seinem Gefühl. Es zeigt sich kein Ideal unter jener luftigen Hülle und kaum etwas absolut Festes in jener ewigen Bewegung.[6]

> [Of Voltaire's satire the same cannot be said. True, with this writer too it is only through the truth and simplicity of nature that he sometimes touches us poetically; whether because he really achieves it in a naïve character, as several times in *L'Ingénu*, or when he seeks and avenges nature in his *Candide*. Where neither is the case, he can admittedly amuse us as a wit, but decidedly not move as a poet. But his mockery has in general too little seriousness at its base, and that rightly makes his calling as a poet suspect. We encounter only his understanding, not his emotions. We cannot make out any ideal under that airy exterior, and hardly anything absolutely firm in that eternal movement.]

And Schiller goes on: precisely Voltaire's rich variety of forms shows that he 'never found a *single* form on which his heart could be imprinted', and it was perhaps a poverty of the heart, 'die Armut des Herzens', that determined his satirical calling.[7] Schiller's view is echoed down to our time. Isaiah Berlin calls Voltaire 'genuinely heartless'.[8]

'Too little seriousness', 'poverty of the heart', 'genuinely heartless'! These extraordinary judgements, which claim to go to the genetic root of Voltaire's writing, fail to see the emotional substance beneath the textual surface. True, Voltaire does not wear his heart on his sleeve, but to the less superficial eye there is a clear substrate of feeling that motivates the light-hearted play and is part of the rational commitment. 'Il invoque la raison, mais *il tire au cœur*', wrote Valéry.[9] It hardly needs to be said that feeling, indeed passion, motivates the eloquence of Voltaire's great public polemics, for the Calas, for the Sirvens, for De la Barre. (How can Isaiah Berlin have missed seeing that?)

For the rest, Schiller lumps Voltaire together with salacious French writers — Crébillon, Marmontel, Laclos — whose effects he finds morally inexcusable in contrast to the healthy frank sexuality of 'the German Propertius', i.e. his friend and literary partner Goethe, whose erotic *Roman Elegies* he is busy defending against charges of impropriety.[10] This is part of the image he presents of Goethe as in a higher sense 'naive', from where, ironically, a line runs back to Goethe's early days in Weimar, when his unlicked, non-courtly naturalness gained him the nickname of 'the Huron', borrowed from Voltaire's *Ingénu*.

The 'wit of the whole conception' applies equally to other stories. Where it is lacking, as in say *Le Monde comme il va*, the result is simply a dull spelling-out, with a banal compromise at its close. But elsewhere Voltaire is endlessly ingenious, not least in defiantly making delight out of ideas whose author meant them to make mankind cower down. For where *Candide* took off from Leibniz, *Micromégas* takes off from Voltaire's old enemy Pascal. Voltaire dismisses him early in the text with a direct shaft: the mathematical childhood prodigy, who worked out for himself thirty-two theorems of Euclid, later became 'un géometre assez médiocre et un fort mauvais métaphysicien'.[11] But the dropped name also serves as a clue to the structuring of the story on Pascal's 'deux infinis'.[12] Only Voltaire could have brought these designedly alarming conceptions alive, (super-)humanizing them in extra-terrestrial beings almost inconceivably immense yet benevolent towards the minute 'atomes intelligents' they discover on the 'tas de boue', the earth. The 'deux infinis' are contained in the title, already declaring a *Verfremdungseffekt* that cosmically outstrips the visitor viewpoint of Montesquieu's *Lettres persanes*.[13] One distinct witticism is then the metaphorical bringing together of the two infinitudes, as far apart literally as it is possible to be, when the benevolent Sirian is chagrined to observe 'que les infiniment petits eussent un orgueil presque infiniment grand'.[14] Among the human beings the story incidentally cuts down to size is 'quelque capitaine des grands grenadiers', who, if he were to read this work, would no doubt raise his soldiers' bonnets by two feet — but it would be no good, since he and they would remain infinitely small.[15] The addressee here must surely be Frederick the Great of Prussia, who famously collected ultra-tall recruits for his guards regiment.

All this is of course far from exhausting Voltaire's humorous means. There are numbers of asides and subordinate phrases, small barbs easy to miss in a too rhythmic reading. Thus, baptizing a fully conscious Huron male of twenty-two is not as straightforward as doing it to 'un enfant qu'on régénère sans qu'il en sache rien'.[16] With an eye fixed on the problem of adult immersion, the reader barely stops to reflect on the term of comparison, with its burden of preposterous theology. And when the first paragraph of *Jeannot et Colin* lists the taxes (they take up two full lines of print) that mean Colin's ploughman father is not 'puissamment riche' at year's end, it reads as just part of the preliminaries needed to get the story under way.[17] Po-faced acceptance becomes itself a weapon of satire. After all, 'Y a-t-il rien de plus respectable qu'un ancien abus?'[18] We have to stay alert to every detail. Including one that concerns all of us: 'Pour parler, il faut penser, ou à peu près'.[19]

One could go on cataloguing Voltaire's means — but it has surely long been done, and would go far beyond the scope of this brief tribute to his biographer. So, to conclude simply: Defenders of reason against attack by the armies of the *Infâme* and its ilk throughout human history have often had to argue that, if there was indeed a Creator, he also created our reason, and must have meant us to use it. By the same token, wit too deserves to be seen as a gift from on high, meant for use, easing every kind of *pesanteur* — another form of divine *grâce*.

Notes to Chapter 3

1. Voltaire, *Traité sur la tolérance*, in *Mélanges*, ed. by Jacques van den Heuvel, Bibliothèque de la Pléiade (Paris: Gallimard, 1961), p. 563.
2. Voltaire, *Romans et Contes*, ed. by René Groos, Bibliothèque de la Pléiade (Paris: Gallimard, 1954), p. 4. In ironic symmetry, the prophet Mohammed from his opposite ideological standpoint condemned the *Thousand and One Nights* as 'games of a frivolous imagination' with 'no moral purpose', leading Man 'not back to himself but out into absolute freedom'. According to Goethe at least, in his *Noten und Abhandlungen zu besserem Verständnis des 'West-Östlichen Divans'* (in *Werke*, ed. by Erich Trunz, 14 vols (Munich: Beck, 1988), II, 145–46.
3. That is, in Zadig's precise inferences about the animals he has not seen: *Romans et contes*, p. 9 ff.
4. Ibid., p. 13.
5. Wieland wrote philosophical-didactic novels with plentiful titillating episodes, fairy-tale verse narratives, and gentle satires: small-town small-mindedness is pilloried, at some length, by a court case over whether the hirer of an ass had the right to sit in its shadow without further payment. (Voltaire might have placed it in the 'genre ennuyeux'.) Wieland's subtlest is *Der goldene Spiegel* (1772), a variation on the 'mirror for princes' which sets the didactic narrative in the framework of the problem the philosopher has getting the prince to listen to it.
6. Friedrich Schiller, 'Über naïve und sentimentalische Dichtung', in *Sämtliche Werke*, ed. by Gerhard Fricke and Herbert G. Göpfert, 5 vols (Munich: Hanser, 1959), V, 694–780 (p. 727).
7. Ibid.
8. Isaiah Berlin, *The Crooked Timber of Humanity* (London: Murray, 1990), p. 159. Quoted in Roger Pearson, *The Fables of Reason: A Study of Voltaire's 'Contes philosophiques'* (Oxford: Oxford University Press, 1993), p. 242. On the flaws in Berlin's damaging and unduly influential treatment of the Enlightenment and its legacy, see my essay 'Sympathy and Empathy — Isaiah's Dilemma, or, How He Let the Enlightenment Down', in *Isaiah Berlin and the Enlightenment*, ed. by Laurence Brockliss and Ritchie Robertson (Oxford: Legenda, 2016), pp. 113–20.
9. Paul Valéry, *Œuvres*, ed. by Jean Hytier, 2 vols, Bibliothèque de la Pléiade (Paris: Gallimard, 1957–60), I, 524 ff. Quoted in Pearson, *The Fables of Reason*, p. 241.
10. Schiller, 'Über naïve und sentimentalische Dichtung', p. 744.
11. Voltaire, *Romans et contes*, p. 106.
12. Blaise Pascal, 'Disproportion de l'homme', in *Pensées*, ed. by Louis Lafuma (Paris: Delmas, 1952), p. 214.
13. Though it is not clear why the eponymous central figure, with his vast dimensions, bears a name that embraces the infinitely small as well as the infinitely large.
14. Voltaire, *Micromégas*, in *Romans et Contes*, p. 123
15. Ibid., p. 115.
16. Voltaire, *L'Ingénu*, in *Romans et Contes*, p. 246.
17. Voltaire, *Jeannot et Colin*, in *Romans et contes*, p. 140.
18. Voltaire, *Zadig*, in *Romans et contes*, p. 34.
19. Voltaire, *Micromégas*, in *Romans et contes*, p. 116.

— 3 —

Gravity, Grace, and Gore: French Gloves in the Nineteenth Century[1]

Anne Green

'Gloves are the emblem of faith', wrote Sir Walter Scott, and indeed for centuries gloves functioned as symbolic objects that lent gravity to solemn ceremonies of church and state.[2] Their ritualized role in coronations, in the celebration of pontifical masses or in the granting of fiefs signified the dignity of a sacred trust. In nineteenth-century France, however, gloves took on an extraordinary range of social and cultural meanings that eclipsed their ancient ceremonial role. Writers of the period soon recognized that gloves had figurative potential, and as they start to appear in works of literature their symbolic resonance undergoes a fascinating evolution that echoes the changing circumstances of nineteenth-century France.

At the beginning of the nineteenth century leather gloves were made entirely by hand, as they had been for centuries. Carefully prepared skins were cut up with shears and the pieces hand-stitched with needle and thread. But the French glove industry was in serious decline, undermined first by the trade embargoes of the Napoleonic wars, then by high export tariffs and a shortage of fine leather.[3] Not even the introduction in 1816 of the *mécanique* — a toothed clamp that held the pieces of skin together to facilitate stitching — could ensure its recovery. The astonishing resurgence of glove-production was largely due to Xavier Jouvin, the inventive son of a Grenoble glove-maker. After spending years studying different shapes and sizes of hand at the town's hospital, Jouvin devised a mathematical system for sizing gloves that guaranteed a good fit for any hand. As a result, gloves could be sold more quickly and efficiently; glove-fitting was no longer a lengthy process of trial and error. Soon after, Jouvin invented his *main de fer*, a calibrated mechanical cutter that stamped out precisely-measured glove pieces from six layers of skin at a time. He took out French patents on his inventions in 1834 and 1838, and as well-fitting Jouvin gloves became increasingly sought-after at home and abroad, Grenoble's glove-industry prospered.[4] When these patents expired in 1849, freeing other centres to adopt the new technology, the national output of leather gloves suddenly more than doubled: from a value of 20 million francs in 1847 it had jumped to 47 million francs by 1851, making the glove industry one of the most important in France.[5]

But demand for gloves kept increasing. By 1867 France was producing about 48 million leather gloves a year.[6] A shortage of skilled needlewomen meant that what had once been an urban industry spread to the surrounding countryside as country girls were recruited to this relatively well-paid work during the winter months when they were not needed in the fields. Although the seasonal nature of their output inconvenienced the manufacturers, these women's new source of income helped regenerate depressed rural areas, as happens when Gérard de Nerval's Sylvie exchanges her lace bobbins for a glove-maker's *mécanique* and dismays the narrator by adopting urban tastes and manners.[7] But even with these new recruits, demand for gloves still outstripped supply, and when the universal exhibition of 1878 displayed recently-invented machinery for sewing glove leather, the exhibition report commented that only by use of machine-stitching could glove-makers hope to keep up with the ever-increasing demand. The majority of gloves sold that year were indeed sewn by machine.[8]

How can we account for the phenomenal increase in demand for gloves in nineteenth-century France? As Mary Douglas and Baron Isherwood observe, demand can never be explained by looking only at the physical properties of goods: 'Man needs goods for communicating with others and for making sense of what is going on around him'.[9] During a period of rapid social change gloves fulfilled that function admirably. For Georges Guenot-Lecointe, the author of a *Physiologie du gant* published in 1841, the remarkable changes he had seen in glove-manufacturing even by that date were emblematic of France's evolution from barbarism to civilization: the old days of badly stitched gloves before the introduction of the *mécanique* evoked for him the 'premiers siècles de la barbarie', whereas a well-made straw-coloured glove was 'l'expression la plus avancée de la civilisation moderne'.[10] At the beginning of the century, however, a gloved hand had relatively little significance. As Guenot-Lecointe explains, in the early 1800s 'le gant n'avait joué qu'un rôle très-mesquin dans nos mœurs; on en parlait à peine, et [...] on ne s'[en] occupait guère'.[11] By the time he published his *Physiologie*, however, the glove had 'envahi toutes les classes'.[12] More and more people shared Guenot-Lecointe's conviction that 'le gant seul indique le rang que nous occupons sur l'échelle de Jacob' and enlisted gloves in their attempts to best position themselves within a rapidly evolving social hierarchy.[13] No longer solely the province of the upper class, by the 1840s glove-wearing had been adopted as a social marker by an aspiring bourgeoisie, while to the lower classes gloves were an enviable emblem of luxury and leisure. Madame de Girardin describes how happy little girls were to be given old gloves to play with, because 'de vieux gants, c'est de l'orgueil; les gants sont une dignité chez les enfants du peuple; c'est le luxe par excellence, c'est un symptôme d'oisiveté!'.[14] Although serving little practical purpose, the wearing of gloves had become increasingly indispensable to an expanding middle class, causing Gustave Flaubert to observe in 1846 that people would rather go out without a purse than without gloves.[15]

While some contemporary commentators fancied that gloves' new ubiquity was evidence of a new egalitarianism, most recognized that that was an illusion and that subtle variations indicated crucial social difference. Madame de Girardin tartly observed that despite what many people seemed to think, wearing white gloves and a black coat did not suddenly qualify a man to marry an heiress.[16] Simply wearing gloves was not enough. Knowing which gloves to wear, and when and how to wear them, was an essential indication of where one stood on the social ladder. And so as glove production grew, so too did the number of publications offering advice on an increasingly elaborate set of prescriptions and prohibitions surrounding glove-wearing and the presentation of a graceful hand.

The elaborate glove-wearing rituals of upper-class men, for example, were described by the writer and illustrator Bertall:

> Les hommes de haute élégance changent de gants quatre ou cinq fois par jour. Gant de cheval, le matin, gant de demi-toilette pour aller déjeuner, gant de toilette pour visite, chevreau ou peau de suède, gants de peau de chien pour conduire au Bois, gants pour aller dîner en ville, gants pour aller au bal, au théâtre, ou au club le soir.[17]

Although Bertall admitted that few could afford to fulfil all these so-called 'obligations', other commentators issued similarly nuanced decrees. Whereas a gentleman must remain barehanded when presented to a sovereign or head of state or when swearing an oath or signing a legal document, gloves were always to be worn in the street, on walks, in church, on journeys, at clubs, soirées, balls, and theatres. If invited to dinner, one removed one's gloves only when seated at the dining table. Valets and male servants waiting at table should wear white cotton gloves, but only when in livery or *habit noir*, and never when serving lunch; gloves should not be worn by chambermaids.[18] When in mourning, only black knitted or fabric gloves were to be worn — never leather.[19] In church, gloves must be removed when going to confession, taking communion, or taking holy water (a rule that Emma Bovary fails to observe in Rouen cathedral);[20] before baptisms it was customary for the godfather to send the godmother six pairs of gloves;[21] and during marriage ceremonies the bride and groom should wear white gloves which they remove only when the priest blesses the rings.[22] Men forming part of the wedding cortege wear putty coloured gloves, but those who have been invited only to the wedding mass wear suede gloves.[23] Even the language surrounding these culturally loaded items was caught up in social distinctions: the middle class *porte des gants*, whereas the upper class *se gante*.[24]

Choice of leather and colour were crucial, for as one commentator wrote, 'La couleur des gants est un indice presque certain des mœurs intimes de leur propriétaire'.[25] Certain basic rules pertained: darker gloves during the day, paler ones in the evening, when to be seen in dark gloves was considered to be 'une énormité'.[26] (The vicomte de Marennes reported, nevertheless, that after the death of Charles X in 1836 opportunists took both black and yellow gloves to the theatre or opera so that they could extend a hand in mourning if they met a Legitimist but appear conventionally gloved for an Orleanist.)[27] For Guenot-Lecointe, it was yellow gloves, particularly favoured by dandies and earning them their nickname of *gants jaunes*, that represented the acme of modern civilization, and yellow gloves remained fashionable throughout the century — maize or straw coloured for the morning, paler cream for evening.[28] Neutral colours such as pearl-grey or putty were also acceptable for men and women, although Charles Blanc advised against tones such as steel-grey, bronze or slate, colours associated with hard materials which might detract from the glove's essential quality of suppleness.[29] On the other hand brighter tones such as *sang de bœuf*, violet, poppy, or green (especially green) were a distinct sign of vulgarity or petit bourgeois provincialism.[30]

A glove's fit was another indicator of distinction. Although Madame Celnart told her readers in 1833 that 'il est disgracieux et commun d'avoir des gants trop larges', later in the century a more frequent transgression was for women to squeeze their hands into gloves that were too tight in an attempt to make them look smaller.[31] Commentators warned that this had the opposite effect.[32] Having one's gloves split or tear in these circumstances was clearly distasteful, although split seams were not only forgivable but possibly admirable if caused by applauding enthusiastically at the theatre.[33] On the other hand, wearing faded or soiled gloves was beyond the pale. Baroness Staffe told her readers that there was no uglier sight than a soiled glove, and reminded them that well-bred ladies spoke of 'des gants souillés' and never 'des gants sales', for the latter was a 'naturalist' term that evoked far too unpleasant an image.[34] Although nineteenth-century manuals of *savoir-vivre* offered extensive advice on glove-cleaning using substances ranging from toast crumbs to cyanide, in the best circles wearing gloves that had been cleaned rather than discarded was unthinkable.[35] 'Un gant décrassé ressemble à un dîner échauffé; il ne vaut jamais rien', declared Guenot-Lecointe.[36] The pressure to conform to these strictures is evident from constant textual references to 'des gants irréprochables'. The freshness of one's gloves was an indication of one's moral virtue, and gloves, like their wearers, must be beyond reproach.[37]

By the 1880s glove-wearing as a mark of social distinction had almost come full circle. Baroness Staffe records that certain gentlemen, exasperated by the lower classes' adoption of gloves, chose to signal their superiority by appearing in public barehanded and claiming that it took five centuries of leisured ancestry to breed a graceful, shapely hand. Staffe dismissed such protests as pretentious nonsense, however,[38] believing like most other commentators that a gloved hand revealed everything about a person; whereas style might be deceptive, gloves never were.[39] As Madame de Girardin declared, 'Les gants d'une femme trahissent tout son caractère'.[40] The formula that crops up repeatedly in such texts is 'Montrez-moi votre gant, je dirai qui vous êtes'.[41] Gloves could not lie.

If Guenot-Lecointe recognized that 'le gant est un symbole', so did writers of fiction.[42] Balzac was probably the first to exploit gloves' cultural significance and for him, too, they told the truth. As early as 1830, in his *Étude de mœurs par les gants*, a countess claims to her friends that she can determine their character and actions simply by inspecting their gloves the morning after a ball. For example a colonel's crumpled but perfectly clean gloves reveal that instead of dancing he spent the evening at the gaming tables, twisting and tearing his gloves in his anxiety about losing, while another man's discoloured gloves betray the fact that he danced too often with the same partner, for the dye of her gloves has transferred itself to his.[43] Gloves in nineteenth-century fiction frequently offer clues or shed light on mysteries, for they were felt to retain physical and mental traces of their wearers. In the first half of the century, however, they function mainly as convenient markers of class or social aspiration, or as shortcut indicators of character. Thus in *Eugénie Grandet* the contrast between Monsieur Grandet's stiff, solid pair that lasts him a year and a half and Charles's beautiful gloves of fine white leather neatly sums up the difference between the provincial miser and his foppish Parisian nephew.[44]

Offering opportunities for wry comment on a society in flux, gloves were quickly welcomed by realist writers concerned to incorporate details from everyday life into their fiction. So there are countless instances of characters picking up their gloves to signal that a visit is at an end, or of a glove splitting because too large (and by implication too ill-bred) a hand has been forced into it. Gloves are a frequent source of shame or embarrassment for those fictional wearers who are aware of society's demands but unable to meet them,[45] while those who transgress the rules without a sense of shame are clearly shown to belong on the lower rungs of the social ladder.[46] And of course the disparity between individual behaviour and what society decrees provides a rich source of comedy for writers such as Eugène Labiche, who flatter and entertain their middle-class audiences by depicting lower-class individuals whose deficient and graceless glove-wearing habits merely emphasize their social inferiority.

Writers, however, gradually came to realize that gloves opened up possibilities that went beyond everyday realism or class commentary. Revealing or concealing flesh, mediating contact, layering skin upon skin, capable of being turned inside out, and hovering uneasily between human hand and artefact, gloves were flexible in more senses than one. Flaubert, who famously dismissed contemporary literature as 'barbarism in white gloves', was particularly alert to their metaphorical potential.[47] But above all he was sensitive to the unsettling, uncanny quality of this thing that was both like and unlike a hand, a sense he articulated in one of his notebooks under the heading 'Théorie du gant':

> C'est qu'il idéalise la main, en la privant de sa couleur, comme fait la poudre de riz pour le visage; il la rend inexpressive (voir le vilain effet des gants sur la scène), mais typique; la forme seule est conservée et plus accusée. Cette couleur factice, grise, blanche ou jaune, s'harmonise avec la manche du vêtement, et, [sans] donner l'idée d'une nature autre (puisque le dessin est conservé), met de la nouveauté dans le connu, et rapproche ainsi ce membre couvert, d'un membre de statue. Et cependant, cette chose anti-naturelle a du movement. [...] Rien n'est plus troublant qu'une main gantée.[48]

Although the truly unsettling qualities of gloves do not generally make themselves felt in literary texts until later in the century, during the Second Empire their metaphorical associations start to change. In an intriguing reversal of their earlier connotations, literary gloves begin to be associated not with truth and revelation, but with concealment. The propriety and grace with which they had been linked is increasingly seen as a deceptive veneer concealing something vile that implicates society itself. Gloves start to function as emblems of hypocrisy, providing a falsely decorous layer to mask corruption — as Larsonneau recognizes when, in Émile Zola's *La Curée*, he observes that 'les gants ont du bon [...] on touche à tout sans se salir'.[49] It is the hypocrisy of those who do wrong without dirtying their hands that causes the Goncourts' Renée Mauperin to exclaim that she would prefer out-and-out villains, since 'ils ne font pas des infamies avec des gants!'[50] This sense that the metaphorical glove may cover something other than a fair hand gave rise to a common trope in the literature of the 1850s and 60s: the image of a loathsome presence visible through a glove's split seams, or of something repellent piercing a glove from within, as in Émile Deschamps's striking use of a poisoned fingernail protruding from a glove to convey the Second Empire's thinly-veiled corruption.[51]

Gloves were of course a useful plot device, particularly when deliberately dropped by a woman as a flirtatious invitation. Standing metonymically for the woman herself, such gloves were, in Edmond de Goncourt's words, 'le moule et l'empreinte de sa main, un objet gardant un peu de la vie de ses doigts'.[52] To offer or acquire a glove as a love-token was one form of that identification between woman and glove, and a lady's glove, preserved and fetishized as a memento of an affair, features in many novels as an evocation of both her gloved and ungloved hand, and so, by extension, of her clothed and unclothed body.[53] In early drafts of *Madame Bovary*, Rodolphe's tin of old love letters includes a lady's glove, just as Flaubert himself had preserved one of Louise Colet's gloves with her letters and told her that its scent evoked the smell of her shoulder and the warmth of her bare arm.[54] As the century progressed, writers explored this erotic aspect of the glove's associations further, from the sensual delicacy of 'la petite main qui travaille' as it buttons or unbuttons a glove,[55] to the more knowingly erotic 'undressing' evoked by Maupassant in *Fort comme la mort* as he describes the act of peeling off a long glove to reveal the nudity beneath:

> Elle avait de longs gants, montant jusqu'au coude. Pour en ôter un, elle le prit tout en haut par le bord et vivement le fit glisser, en le retournant à la façon d'une peau de serpent qu'on arrache. Le bras apparut, pâle, gras, rond, dévêtu si vite qu'il fit surgir l'idée d'une nudité complète et hardie.[56]

In keeping with the old expression 'perdre ses gants', which implied the loss of a girl's virginity, the sexual connotations of gloves became even more graphic as writers realized that the innocent glove could be exploited to dramatize aspects of desire that could not be described explicitly. Early manuscript drafts of *Madame Bovary* offer particularly striking examples. In one, Léon creeps downstairs after everyone has retired for the night to retrieve a pale glove dropped by Emma and take it back to bed with him; the glove still bears her scent and retains the form of her hand — the imprints of her fingernails, creases over the joints, and the curve of the leather where it stretched across the fleshy base of her thumb. Léon sniffs it, kisses it, inserts his fingers into it, and eventually falls asleep with his face resting on it.[57] Flaubert makes his intention perfectly clear in a marginal note to himself: 'faire comprendre qu'il se branle avec ce gant'.[58] Not surprisingly, Flaubert omitted this from the final version. Yet even where the sexual innuendo is less explicit, gloves often feature in later literary texts in ways that are erotically transgressive. For example Barbey d'Aurevilly — a writer whose predilection for using red ink on white paper was echoed in the idiosyncratic scarlet *pointes* of his own white gloves — manages to imbue a glove with a disturbing and violent sexuality. In an extraordinary scene at a zoo where a strikingly graceful woman and a caged panther stare into each other's eyes in a silent power struggle, he dramatizes the tension between the civilized female and her dangerous sexual animality by means of a violet glove that is suddenly reabsorbed into its original animal state:

> La femme, l'inconnue, était comme une panthère humaine, dressée devant la panthère animale qu'elle éclipsait. [...] Aussi, défaisant sans mot dire les douze boutons du gant violet qui moulait son magnifique avant-bras, elle ôta ce gant, et, passant audacieusement sa main entre les barreaux de la cage, elle en fouetta le museau court de la panthère, qui ne fit qu'un mouvement... mais quel mouvement!... et d'un coup de dents, rapide comme l'éclair!... Un cri partit du groupe où nous étions. Nous avions cru le poignet emporté: ce n'était que le gant. La panthère l'avait englouti. [...]
> — Folle! — dit l'homme, en saisissant ce beau poignet, qui venait d'échapper à la plus coupante des morsures. [...] et il le baisa, ce poignet, avec emportement.[59]

The woman watches her naked wrist being kissed, then the couple move away from the panther's cage, 'leurs visages tournés l'un vers l'autre, se serrant flanc contre flanc, comme s'ils avaient voulu se pénétrer, entrer, lui dans elle, elle dans lui, et ne faire qu'un seul corps à eux deux'.[60] The swallowing of the glove thus prefigures and enacts this erotic union.

Although in 1841 Guenot-Lecointe saw gloves as graceful emblems of distinction and civilization, by the 1880s such prestige is rarely evident when they appear in works of literature. Reassessed, they take on deeply unsettling qualities, as Flaubert had already sensed, and as Pierre Loti's gloved hands seemed to the local women he encountered in Morocco. 'Oh! As-tu vu? il a des mains à deux peaux!', they exclaimed in astonishment, their external perspective stripping gloves of all their acquired cultural significance and reducing them to a baffling extra layer of skin.[61] Douglas and Isherwood have argued that the consumption of goods is a ritual that seeks to make sense of the flux of events, but in the troubled aftermath of the Franco-Prussian war and the Commune fictional gloves seem to epitomize chaos rather than making sense of it.[62] Breaking free of their associations with the proprieties of a ritualized social order, they frequently appear burst, torn, fragmented, lost, or abandoned. Increasingly found detached from their partners and from hands, they convey physical, moral, and social disarray, like the dust-coloured glove-fingers that emerge from a tangle of clothes in a room filled with 'un irrémédiable désordre' in Huysmans's *En ménage*, for example.[63] In Zola's *Au bonheur des dames*, gloves are further divorced from hand and function as they are constructed into a monstrous shop display in the incongruous form of a Swiss chalet whose ground floor is composed entirely of black gloves, with gloves of other colours edging the windows, picking out the balconies and forming the roof tiles. The store's glove counter in that novel is a focus for corruption, and customers shoplift gloves on a massive scale: one woman is caught with sixty pairs stuffed inside her clothing, while another is found to have stolen 248 pairs of pink gloves from stores all over Paris as gloves come to epitomize dishonesty and grotesque consumer excess.[64]

Divorced from their earlier associations with distinction, grace, and truth, gloves have been turned inside out, as it were. No longer suggestive of a healthy and vibrant society, they convey the opposite. Whereas they were once hailed as the perfect expression of French civilization, that civilization was now widely perceived as corrupt and moribund, and literary gloves reflect that shift. It seems apt, therefore, to find Edmond de Goncourt in *La Faustin* likening a pair of very tight-fitting gloves to casts taken from the hands of a corpse.[65] For Charles Blanc, too, gloves charted a slide from vitality to decay and death. In 1875 he recalled the day he gained access to a room in the empty Tuileries Palace which had remained locked for seven years, untouched since the sudden death in a carriage accident of its occupant, the eldest son of Louis-Philippe. The sight of the prince's many gloves still lying strewn about the room left a deep impression on Blanc: while their diversity conveyed the young man's varied and active life, for Blanc their stiff, shrivelled skin denoted mortality. The gloves, like their young owner and the monarchy to which he was heir, were dead:

> Ce qui me frappa le plus, ce fut de voir sur une table, jetés çà et là, des gants de toute couleur et de toute espèce. La vie de ce jeune homme, partagée entre le plaisir, la chasse et la guerre, se révélait dans la physionomie de ces gants épars, les uns froissés, les autres intacts, les uns essayés, les autres encore dans leur boîte. Il y en avait en chamois pour conduire, en castor pour monter à cheval, en peau de chien, en canepin blanc, en chevreau, et toutes ces variantes de la toilette avaient là une signification singulière et saisissante... Mais, depuis longtemps, les peaux de ces gants s'étaient retirées, le canepin s'était raidi, le chevreau s'était parcheminé, et ces objets inertes, qui racontaient si clairement les habitudes du jeune élégant qui les avait portés, disaient aussi sa mort.[66]

Villiers de l'Isle Adam was more explicit in linking gloves with the decline of French civilization. In his short story 'La Machine à gloire' he conveys the mechanical conformism of contemporary society and predicts its imminent collapse by picturing a huge mechanism built into a theatre auditorium with a pair of beautifully sculpted wooden hands folded away under every seat, each hand clad in an immaculate yellow calfskin glove.[67] The gloved hands produce artificial applause which the audience follow like sheep, in a mindless reaction that would be capable of bringing the house down, literally, if the machine's controls were turned up to maximum.

As they spiral ever further from their original associations, fictional gloves take on macabre forms that hover disturbingly between artefact and hand, like the nightmarish advertizing sign in the shape of a gigantic purple glove that looms over the Passage des Panoramas in Zola's *Nana*, described as looking like a bleeding severed hand suspended from a yellow cuff,[68] or the 'glove' of blood that forms on Auguste's hand in *Le Ventre de Paris* after he plunges it into a bucket of blood from the pig he has just slaughtered,[69] or — even more unsettling — the freshly-amputated left arm that rests on a cushion of violet silk in Villiers de l'Isle Adam's *L'Ève future*, a pearl-grey glove still grasped in its slim fingers. The severed limb turns out to be made of artificial flesh covered with artificial skin, smooth and supple, like the finest glove-leather. This idealized skin envelops the form to produce a disconcertingly faithful copy of the arm and hand of a beautiful young woman,[70] in what is perhaps the ultimate illustration of what Flaubert had already sensed: that in its juxtaposition of living and dead skin there was something unnervingly uncanny about 'cette chose anti-naturelle' that troubled the boundaries between hand and glove, between authenticity and falseness, between the living and the dead.

In their journey from artisanal to industrial mass-production, nineteenth-century French gloves map not only the nation's increasing prosperity and technological progress, but fundamental changes in social hierarchy and social cohesion. But as the century nears its end, those detached and gory gloves seem resonant with a sense of violence and disintegration. Gone is the gravity associated with solemn ceremonial, gone is the grace to which an emergent bourgeoisie aspired. Instead, in the unsettled aftermath of the Franco-Prussian war, gloves project a dystopian vision that displaces the distinction and integrity that had once caused French gloves to be seen as 'l'expression la plus avancée de la civilisation moderne'.

Notes to Chapter 4

1. Another version of this essay, 'Gloves in Nineteenth-Century France: Materiality and Metaphor', appears in *Fashion, Modernity, and Materiality in France: From Rousseau to Art Deco,* ed. by Heidi Brevik-Zender (New York: SUNY Press, 2018), pp. 57–83.
2. Walter Scott, *Chronicles of the Canongate,* in *The Prose Works,* 9 vols (Paris: Gallignani, 1827–34), VII, 251.
3. For example, in 1787 the Grenoble glove industry employed 6,254 people, but by 1807 the number had fallen to about 2,800. Britain's import ban lasted until 1826; until it was lifted French gloves entered the country only as contraband. See *Bulletin de la Société de statistique, des sciences naturelles et des arts industriels du département de l'Isère* (Grenoble: Maisonville, 1851), pp. 201–08.
4. Edouard Rey, *Xavier Jouvin* (Grenoble: Allier père et fils, 1868).
5. Ibid., p. 110.
6. *Exposition universelle de 1867: rapports du jury international,* 13 vols (Paris: Paul Dupont, 1868), IV, 330–31. About three quarters of these were exported, mainly to England, while most of England's own glove output was exported to America. See also *Visite à l'exposition universelle de Paris en 1855,* ed. by Henri Tresca (Paris: Hachette, 1855), p. 54.
7. Gérard de Nerval, *Sylvie,* in *Œuvres complètes,* ed. by J. Guillaume and C. Pichois, 3 vols, Bibliothèque de la Pléiade (Paris: Gallimard, 1993), III, 559. See also Jean-François Vallet d'Artois, *Manuel de fabriquant de gants, considéré dans ses rapports avec la mégisserie, la chamoiserie etc.,* 2nd edn (Paris: Boret, 1835), pp. 502–05. In his novel *Le Gouffre* (Paris: Dentu, 1872), Elie Berthet writes of the benefits to country women engaged in glove-making in the area around Grenoble, and observes that 'la population purement agricole y était comme noyée au milieu de cette population industrielle' (p. 57).
8. Eugène Lacroix, *Etudes sur l'exposition universelle de 1878: annales et archives de l'industrie au XIXe siècle,* 10 vols (Paris: E. Lacroix, 1878), IV, 341. In *Le Gouffre,* Berthet contrasts the income and working conditions of Grenoble girls who sew by machine and produce twelve gloves a day with those of a poor, sick, rural glove-stitcher who sews by hand for fourteen hours a day to earn only twenty sous (pp. 111–13).
9. Mary Douglas and Baron Isherwood, *The World of Goods: Towards an Anthropology of Consumption* (London: Penguin, 1980), p. 95.
10. G. Guenot-Lecointe, *Physiologie du gant* (Paris: Desloges, 1841), pp. 66, 84.
11. Ibid., p. 72.
12. Ibid., p. 84.
13. Ibid.
14. Delphine de Girardin, *Lettres parisiennes,* 4 vols (Paris: Michel Lévy frères, 1857), I, 150 (14 June 1837).

15. Gustave Flaubert, *Correspondance*, ed. by J. Bruneau and Y. Leclerc, 5 vols, Bibliothèque de la Pléiade (Paris: Gallimard, 1973–2007), I, 355.
16. Girardin, *Lettres parisiennes*, II, 261 (17 January 1840).
17. Bertall, *La Comédie de notre temps: études au crayon et à la plume; la civilité, les habitudes, les mœurs, les costumes, les manières et les manies de notre époque*, 3 vols (Paris: Plon, 1874–76), I, 58.
18. Blanche Staffe, *Usages du monde: règles du savoir-vivre dans la société moderne* [1889] (Paris: Victor Havard, 1891), pp. 336, 337, 161.
19. A. de La Fère, *Savoir vivre, savoir parler, savoir écrire, à l'usage des gens du monde*, 7th edn (Paris: Nouvelle librairie scientifique et littéraire, 1889), p. 153.
20. *Manuel de politesse à l'usage de la jeunesse: savoir-vivre, savoir-parler, savoir-écrire, savoir-travailler par F. G-M.* (Tours: A. Mame et fils, 1908), p. 29; Anon., *Les Usages du monde: le savoir-vivre et la politesse chez soi, en visite, en soirée, au théâtre* (Paris: T. Lefèvre, 1880), p. 98; Agathe-Pauline Caylac de Ceylan, comtesse de Bradi, *Du savoir-vivre en France au dix-neuvième siècle, ou instruction d'un père à ses enfants* (Strasbourg: Levrault, 1841), pp. 15–16.
21. Anon., *Les Usages du monde*, p. 148.
22. Anon., *Le Livre de la famille: les personnes et les choses, savoir-vivre et savoir-faire, morale, éducation, économie domestique, hygiene, soin aux enfants, etc.* (Avignon: Séguin frères, 1892), p. 99.
23. Louise d'Alq, *Le Maître et la maîtresse de maison* (Paris: Bureau des *Causeries familières*, 1887), p. 107.
24. Guenot-Lecointe, *Physiologie du gant*, p. 109.
25. Ibid., p. 85; cf. also p. 109: 'On reconnaît la distinction d'un homme à la nuance de ses gants.'
26. Bertall, *La Comédie de notre temps*, I, 58.
27. Vicomte de Marennes [Eugène Chapus], *Manuel de l'homme et de la femme comme il faut* (Paris: Librairie nouvelle, 1855), p. 70.
28. Guenot-Lecointe, *Physiologie du gant*, p. 86.
29. Charles Blanc, *L'Art dans la parure et dans le vêtement* (Paris: Renouard, 1875), p. 178.
30. Guenot-Lecointe, *Physiologie du gant*, pp. 85–86; Bertall, *La Comédie de notre temps*, I, 58.
31. Madame Celnart [Élisabeth-Félicie Bayle-Mouillard], *Manuel des dames, ou l'art de l'élégance, sous le rapport de la toilette, des honneurs de la maison, des plaisirs, des occupations agréables* (Paris: Roret, 1833), p. 222.
32. For example, Blanc, *L'Art dans la parure et dans le vêtement*, p. 259; Guenot-Lecointe, *Physiologie du gant*, p. 85.
33. See Champfleury's description of a performance of *Hamlet* in *Contes d'automne* (Paris: V. Lecou, 1854): 'Alors l'applaudissement est une dette sacrée; il n'y a plus de convenances à garder, on déchire ses gants, on crie, il faut que l'émotion sorte violemment' (p. 209). Cf. Théophile Gautier, 'La Diva', in *La Comédie de la mort* (Paris: Desessart, 1838): 'Toutes les voix criaient, toutes les mains frappaient, | A force d'applaudir les gants blancs se rompaient' (p. 155).
34. Blanche Staffe, *Mes secrets* (Paris: G. Havard, 1896), p. 131.
35. For example, Celnart, *Manuel des dames*, pp. 222–23; Clarisse Juranville, *Le Savoir-faire et le savoir-vivre dans les diverses circonstances de la vie: guide pratique de la vie usuelle à l'usage des jeunes filles* (Paris: A. Boyer, 1879), p. 175.
36. Guenot-Lecointe, *Physiologie du gant*, p. 111. The anonymous author of *Les Usages du monde* states that the only thing more repulsive than a torn glove is one that emits the disgusting smell of having been cleaned with benzene or ammonia (p. 71).
37. Marennes asserts that a glove 'résume et exprime une foule de dispositions morales' (*Manuel de l'homme et de la femme comme il faut*, p. 69).
38. Staffe, *Usages du monde*, p. 337. Cf. Bertall, *La Comédie de notre temps*, I, 58: 'Je connais un grand seigneur dont les mains sont admirables de forme, de couleur et d'élégance, qui tient toujours ses gants à la main, et ne les met jamais, prétendant que les gens difformes sont seuls forcés d'en mettre... Je le crois dans son tort.'
39. Octave Uzanne, *Les Ornements de la femme. L'éventail — L'ombrelle — Le gant — Le manchon* (Paris: Librairies-imprimeries réunies, 1892), p. 234.
40. Girardin, *Lettres parisiennes*, III, 157 (6 March 1841).
41. For example, Uzanne, *Les Ornements de la femme*, p. 226; Guenot-Lecointe, *Physiologie du gant*, p. 111.

42. Guenot-Lecointe, *Physiologie du gant*, p. 78. Cf. Marennes, *Manuel de l'homme et de la femme comme il faut*, p. 69: 'Aujourd'hui [les gants] jouent un grand rôle, rôle symbolique'.
43. Honoré de Balzac, *Étude de mœurs par les gants*, in *Œuvres complètes*, 24 vols (Paris: Michel Lévy, 1870), XX, 437–41.
44. Honoré de Balzac, *Eugénie Grandet*, in *Œuvres complètes*, III, 1058.
45. For example, in *L'Education sentimentale* Frédéric is always at pains to be 'irréprochablement ganté' when visiting Madame Arnoux, but when he can no longer afford decent gloves he fears he will be unable to see her again: 'Il ne pouvait [...] se présenter avec de pauvres gants noirs bleuis du bout [...] Non, non! Jamais!' (Gustave Flaubert, *L'Education sentimentale*, ed. by P. M. Wetherill (Paris: Garnier, 1984), pp. 59, 91).
46. For example, Louise Colet, *Les Cœurs brisés*, 2 vols (Paris: Berquet & Pétion, 1843), II, 359–60.
47. Flaubert, *Correspondance*, II, 538.
48. Gustave Flaubert, *Carnets de travail*, ed. by P. M. de Biasi (Paris: Balland, 1988), p. 234.
49. Émile Zola, *La Curée* (Paris: A. Lacroix, Verboeckhoven et cie, 1872), p. 269.
50. Edmond and Jules de Goncourt, *Renée Mauperin* (Paris: Charpentier, 1864), pp. 168–69.
51. Émile Deschamps, 'Sur les *Fleurs du mal*', in Charles Baudelaire, *Les Fleurs du mal* (Paris: Michel Levy frères, 1868), p. 403. Several writers, including Flaubert, Gautier, and Hippolyte Taine, use a pierced-glove image to indicate the class origins of a parvenu. For example, attributing the bad behaviour of a wealthy young man-about-town to his lower-class ancestry, Taine writes that 'la grosse main de son grand-père, le marchand de bœufs, perce encore sous son gant jaune' (*Notes sur Paris: vie et opinions de M. Frédéric Thomas Graindorge* (Paris: Hachette, 1867), p. 147).
52. Edmond de Goncourt, *Chérie* (Paris: Flammarion & Fasquelle, 1921), p. 165.
53. For example, in Georges Pradel's novel, *Le Gant de suède* (1883), the preserved glove of the fiancée he had jilted years before triggers memories in the protagonist, who eventually tracks her down and proposes marriage. (She refuses.) Etienne-Prosper Dubois-Guchan's poem 'La Paire de gants', published in *Les Caprices d'un homme sérieux, esquisses poétiques* (1868), offers a variant on the theme: the male protagonist has preserved his own gloves as a memento of the young woman who gave them to him many years earlier.
54. Flaubert, *Correspondance*, I, 298–99.
55. François Coppée, *Promenades et intérieurs*, in *Poésies complètes* (Paris: A. Lemerre, 1925), p. 15. In *Clothilde* (Paris: Bureaux du Siècle, 1865), p. 354, Alphonse Karr includes the seductive gesture of removing a glove to take holy water in his list of thirty-two infidelities a faithful wife can commit between home and church.
56. Guy de Maupassant, *Fort comme la mort* (Paris: Albin Michel, 1965), p. 14.
57. *Madame Bovary* manuscripts, 'Brouillons', vol. 2, fol. 161, Centre Flaubert, Université de Rouen, <http://flaubert.univ-rouen.fr/bovary/index.php> [accessed 29 October 2018].
58. *Madame Bovary* manuscripts, 'Plans et scénarios', fol. 19, Centre Flaubert, Université de Rouen, <http://flaubert.univ-rouen.fr/bovary/index.php> [accessed 29 October 2018].
59. Jules Amédée Barbey d'Aurevilly, 'Le Bonheur dans le crime', in *Les Diaboliques* (Paris: Garnier Flammarion, 1967), pp. 126–27. This is not the only text to associate passion with a swallowed glove. In Victor Hugo's *Les Misérables*, Vol. 1, Book 3, Chapter VI, a suitor declares his love by telling his sweetheart that he would eat her gloves if she cooked them as beignets. In Eugène Labiche's play *Le Plus Heureux des trois*, in *Théâtre complet*, 10 vols (Paris: Calmann Lévy, 1898), VI, 69–70, when a girl feeds a bun to an ostrich at the zoo it swallows most of her glove; her companion's valour in retrieving three of the fingers makes her decide she should marry him.
60. Barbey d'Aurevilly, 'Le Bonheur dans le crime', p. 127.
61. Pierre Loti, *Au Maroc*, in *Œuvres complètes*, 11 vols (Paris: Calmann-Lévy, 1893–1911), V, 181.
62. Douglas and Isherwood, *The World of Goods*, p. 65.
63. Joris-Karl Huysmans, *En ménage* (Paris: G. Charpentier, 1881), p. 16.
64. Cf. Edmond and Jules de Goncourt's *Germinie Lacerteux*, where the duplicitous Jupillon works as a glove-cutter.
65. Edmond de Goncourt, *La Faustin* (Paris: G. Charpentier, 1882), p. 225.
66. Blanc, *L'Art dans la parure et dans le vêtement*, p. 180.
67. Auguste Villiers de l'Isle Adam, 'La Machine à gloire', in *Contes cruels* (Paris: C. Lévy, 1883), pp. 61–85.

68. Émile Zola, *Nana*, in *Œuvres complètes illustrées*, 19 vols (Paris: E. Fasquelle, 1906), I, 193.
69. Émile Zola, *Le Ventre de Paris*, in *Œuvres complètes illustrées*, II, 117.
70. Auguste Villiers de l'Isle Adam, *L'Ève future* (Paris: Brunhoff, 1886), pp. 272–73.

— 4 —
'Marcher droit sur un cheveu': Tightrope Walking and Prose Poetry in Flaubert

Kate Rees

As Huysmans wrote to Mallarmé in 1882, Flaubert's Homais would have been horrified by the prose poem, and its apparent incoherence.[1] This article considers the idea of an Homais-shocking prose poetry in relation to Flaubert's own work, arguing that the terms 'gravity' and 'grace' offer a means of understanding the tensions associated with Flaubert's hybrid style, a combination of lyricism and materialism which inscribes both poetry and narrative, timelessness and temporality. Flaubert wrote that he hoped that *Madame Bovary* would show he had been capable 'd'avoir su marcher droit sur un cheveu, suspendu entre le double abîme du lyrisme et du vulgaire'.[2] The article will focus on the *Trois Contes*, and on 'Hérodias' in particular, a compressed unit of prose (poetry) which indicates such a blend of the lyrical and the vulgar. Discussion of prose poetry will focus on the metaphors of walking and dancing in the *Contes*, seen by Valéry as methods of movement which illustrate the differences between prose and poetry. The walk is prosaic in that it is based on direction, as compared to the dance, which, like the poem, is 'un système d'actes, mais qui ont leur fin en eux-mêmes. Elle ne va nulle part'.[3] The 'grace' of Salomé's dance in 'Hérodias' is set alongside the 'gravity' of walks in the tale which ground the characters in the real world; these are dances and walks which evoke ideas of prosaic and poetic form. In offering an evaluation of 'Hérodias' as a potential prose poem, the article will also suggest connections between Flaubert and Baudelaire, links between the 'mouvements', the 'ondulations' and the 'soubresauts' of Baudelaire's prose poems and the rhythms of Flaubert's tales.

Flaubert's desired hybrid model of poetry and prose is to be achieved through a form of movement, a precarious balancing act. The writer is envisaged as a walker-acrobat negotiating a tightrope stretched across the two realms of the lyrical and the vulgar. The image evokes two styles of writing, which will be merged by the movements of the acrobat, or the artist who will 'marcher droit' — *droit* in the dual sense of upright and undeviating. It also suggests Flaubert unfurling the 'cheveu' of his prose above the abyss, suspended in mid-air, between the ground and the sky. Such a compromise between being grounded by gravity and compelled towards grace is evoked in another well-known phrase from his letters, which sees him positioned between the image of the bird as an emblem of lyricism and a more earthy, land-based approach:

> Il y a, en moi, littérairement parlant, deux bonhommes distincts: un qui est épris de *gueulades*, de lyrisme, de grands vols d'aigle, de toutes les sonorités de la phrase et des sommets de l'idée; un autre qui fouille et creuse le vrai tant qu'il peut, qui aime à accuser le petit fait aussi puissamment que le grand, qui voudrait vous faire sentir presque *matériellement* les choses qu'il reproduit.[4]

Flaubert's vision of an amalgamation of poetry and prose, the lyrical and the material, is conceptualized in images suggesting movement: here, the eagle's flight and the 'bonhomme' who moves as if over land, excavating the truth. The juxtaposition of graceful flight and an encounter with the mud of the real world is detected, too, in the Baudelaire prose poem, 'Perte d'auréole', which sees the speaker describe the loss of his distinguishing halo, indicative of his capacity for angelic status and flight. While dodging traffic in the busy urban streets, he is forced to let his 'auréole' plunge into the filth of the gutter, 'la fange du macadam'.[5] The halo has been the marker symbolizing his superiority, as an artist, over the common crowd. The necessary and initially unwanted immersion into the bustling boulevards represents the poet's shift away from the spiritual connotations of privileged poetic destiny evoked in the verse poem 'Bénédiction', or the soaring sky-bound potential of the 'albatros', into a material world of mud and traffic. As his halo falls into the mud 'dans un mouvement brusque', so the pedestrian must adopt similar sudden, abrupt movements and twists, not only with his legs but also with his mind.[6] The 'mouvements brusques' which become necessary here echo the leaps and bounds of the prose poetry described by Baudelaire in his preface to *Le Spleen de Paris*, 'musicale sans rythme et sans rime, assez souple et assez heurtée pour s'adapter aux mouvements lyriques de l'âme, aux ondulations de la rêverie, aux soubresauts de la conscience'.[7]

Paul Valéry's distinction between poetry and prose relies, too, on images of movement. In 'Poésie et pensée abstraite', he makes links between the process of walking and the evocation of poetic rhythm: 'Il arriva que mon mouvement de marche se propagea à ma conscience par un système de rythmes assez savant, au lieu de provoquer en moi cette naissance d'images, de paroles intérieures et d'actes virtuels que l'on nomme *idées* (*PPA*, p. 1330). After setting out an explicit connection between walking and rhythm, however, Valéry goes on to contrast walking and dancing. The walk is prosaic in that it is based on direction, as compared to the dance, which, like the poem, aims to create 'un certain *état*, par un movement périodique qui peut s'exercer sur place; mouvement qui se désintéresse presque entièrement de la vue, mais qui s'excite et se règle par les rythmes auditifs' (p. 1330). Goal-directed walking, like utilitarian language, becomes as if negated once the point of destination has been reached; all that remains is the endpoint itself and the process which has led to it is no longer of importance. The poem, though, 'ne meurt pas pour avoir vécu: il est fait expressément pour renaître de ses cendres et redevenir indéfiniment ce qu'il vient d'être' (pp. 1330–31). The dance and the poem are alike in that both represent a secondary use of limbs or language, one which is valued for its strangeness and its mystery, as opposed to the walk or the prosaic text, which are functional. So while, for Valéry, the walk may be valuable in the process of poetic composition, and while prose and poetry 'se servent des mêmes formes et des mêmes sons ou timbres' (pp. 1330–31), as the body relies on its limbs and muscles for both walking and dancing, as a structural metaphor walking is distinguished from the dance by its 'sens', both direction and meaning. In contrast, the dance aims instead at the intangible: 'un objet idéal, un état, un ravissement, un fantôme de fleur, un extrême de vie, un sourire' (p. 1330).

Valéry's discussion of generic forms is helpful in discussing Flaubert's blend of prose and poetry, particularly when visualized using Flaubert's own metaphoric incorporation of images and forms of dancing and walking. Attempts to account for the formal properties of the prose poem often emphasize brevity and a resistance to narrative. Suzanne Bernard asserts that:

> Le poème aura pour nécessité vitale la brièveté, condition *sine qua non* de l'unité d'effet [...] cette définition du poème comme un *tout*, dont les caractères essentiels sont l'unité et la concentration, il semble qu'on puisse tout particulièrement l'appliquer au poème en prose [...]. Totalité d'effet, concentration, gratuité, intensité: autant d'expressions qui nous confirment dans l'idée que le poème est un monde clos, fermé sur soi, se suffisant à soi-même et en même temps une sorte de bloc irradiant, chargé, sous un faible volume, d'une infinité de suggestions et capable d'ébranler notre être en profondeur.[8]

Michel Beaujour, though, takes issue with the desire to categorize prose poetry as 'short': he prefers a more flexible approach which might enable a reader to see, for example, Nerval's *Les Nuits d'Octobre* as prose poetry. He argues against attempts to define the prose poem in terms of lexical, syntactical, or stylistic deviance from 'ordinary' prose, opposing such approaches to an ontological viewpoint:

> The focus on prose poems signals the poet's more or less conscious choice of a Poetics derived from the quasi-theological belief that 'poetic language' is ontologically — rather than formally — different from ordinary language. This ontological difference (and motivation) gives access, through an experience less aesthetic than visionary or epiphanic to a 'poetic universe' inhabiting, so to speak, the obverse of language, which can neither denote nor connote.[9]

Beaujour sees the prose poem as a question mark which throws light on the contradictions of modern aesthetics, such as the distinction between Literature (as 'utterances or texts that use language for persuasive, informative or entertaining purposes') and Poetry, which connotes concepts such as mystery and otherness and the idea of putting language to play. Beaujour concludes: 'In Mallarmé's theory, then, the prose poem becomes a red herring across the track leading to much more fundamental matters concerning the status and functions of literature (or poetry) in general'.[10] Beaujour's questioning approach enables a more flexible way of reading prose poetry, and suggests that Flaubert's comments on an aesthetic fusion of prose and poetry result in a probing of the nature of literature, which can be aligned with the subversions of both prose and verse found, for example, in Baudelaire's *Le Spleen de Paris*.[11]

Recent studies have re-emphasized the connections between the work of Flaubert and Baudelaire. Kathryn Oliver Mills focuses on the two writers' contributions to modernity, highlighting their 'reconfiguration of the generic boundaries between poetry and prose' as a key theme of comparison.[12] Elissa Marder examines the disorders of time and memory in *Les Fleurs du mal* and *Madame Bovary*, evoking the responses of Baudelaire and Flaubert to what is perceived as the overstimulation of modern life.[13] Time is, too, the central focus of Cheryl Krueger's study of Baudelaire's prose poetry, and her analysis of the more anecdotal poems in *Le Spleen de Paris* will be employed in this article as a means of connecting the subversions of both prose and poetry at work in Baudelaire and in Flaubert's 'Hérodias'. Krueger argues that in a narrative-driven prose poem such as 'Le Mauvais Vitrier', 'while recognizable storytelling devices ultimately ensure temporal order and narrative progression, they do so while constructing a network of false stories and narrative games, textual time-killers that constantly reveal the mechanics of Baudelaire's prose'.[14] The ways in which Baudelaire's anecdotal poems reflect and undermine the processes of storytelling — by incorporating, for instance, in 'Portraits de maîtresses', four miniature narratives which each lead nowhere — are perceived by Krueger as a means of resisting the tyranny of time. Doing so in prose, rather than in verse, is a particularly daring feat for Baudelaire:

> Verse and lyricism would at first seem to provide a more productive textual counterpart for the representation of timelessness than prose, which belongs to the contingent world of time. Yet perhaps by sabotaging prose itself, Baudelaire comes closer to testing the boundaries of time.[15]

That Flaubert's own narratives disrupt the practices of narrative and the processes of temporality is of course a familiar theme.[16] Yet this focus on 'Hérodias' as a text which not only frustrates linear readings and problematizes narrative, but also incorporates elements of lyricism and calls attention to poetic forms, will seek to show that this *conte* can also be read as a *poème en prose* which has affinities with the time-resistant anecdotes found in Baudelaire's collection of prose poems.

In citing the last questioning line of the prose poem 'Le Mauvais Vitrier', 'mais qu'importe l'éternité de la damnation à qui a trouvé dans une seconde l'infini de la jouissance?', Krueger notes that 'it is precisely this paradox — finding infinity in a second, finding timelessness in time — that Baudelaire represents on a textual level, by writing poetry in relentless prose'.[17] A similar paradox is emphasized in 'Hérodias'. A combination of poetry and prose, the timeless and the time-bound, is found in the juxtaposition of Salomé's dance and the trek across the desert with which the tale concludes. The dance evokes the infinite, as Salomé's open arms reach out towards 'quelqu'un qui s'enfuyait toujours',[18] and her undulating body juxtaposes at intervals immobility — the permanence of the statuesque — and unstopping motion: 'et son visage demeurait immobile, et ses pieds n'arrêtaient pas' (*H*, p. 275) Here the Flaubertian imperfect and the doubly-emphasized 'et' serve to reinforce the lyric immutability of the dance. Ideas of flight are also conjured: Salomé's slippers, adorned with hummingbird feathers, evoke the 'colibris [qui] eussent eparpillé leurs plumes' glimpsed by Emma Bovary in the forest following sex with Rodolphe; the dancer is also compared to a 'papillon', and to the butterfly-winged goddess Psyche, 'prête à s'envoler'.[19] The passages describing the dance evoke music and rhythm; alliteration and internal rhyme suggest the circularity of the performance itself, which becomes increasingly 'frénétique': 'elle *tou*rnait *tou*jours, les *ty*mpanons sonnaient à écla*ter*, la fou*l*e hurlait' (*H*, p. 275). Salomé's final flamboyant acrobatic position is indicative of Valéry's definition of the dance/poem, a contorted and creative stance which emphasizes the body's artistic endeavour, its deliberate renunciation of conventional goal-driven movement: 'sa nuque et ses vertèbres faisaient un angle droit. Les fourreaux de couleur qui enveloppaient ses jambes passant par-dessus l'épaule, comme des arcs-en-ciel accompagnaient sa figure' (p. 275). The sheaths of coloured cloth, likened to rainbows, also intimate the infinite and the ethereal; endless arcs of shimmering colour. And yet this dance, which seems to transcend time, in the way it interrupts the verbosity and gorging of the feast, in its emphasis on flight and unstopping motion, in the way Salomé transports Herod back in time in her resemblance to her mother ('c'était Hérodias, comme autrefois dans sa jeunesse', p. 274), is also, of course, a catalyst for moving time onwards. It is intended to bring about the death of John the Baptist, and his severed head, carried by the messengers from Jesus back across the terrain towards Galilee in the closing lines ('comme elle était très lourde, ils la portaient alternativement'), has been often noted by critics as Flaubert's underlining of the prosy materialism of his religious tale;[20] the positioning of 'alternativement' as the final word of this text is an example of the cumbersome placement of adverbs noted by Proust in his essay on Flaubert's style.[21] This final walk — destination-driven, exhausting, weighted down by the corporeal in the most graphic way possible — gives an ultimate pedestrian reading, in both meanings of the word, to the transcendence hinted at in Flaubert's representation of the dawning of Christianity.

Yet 'alternativement' could also be read as an indicator of the 'alternating' forces at work in this story-come-prose poem. This is a text which might end with the walk, and the 'vulgaire' aspect of Flaubert's tightrope-walking prose, but it is also a text which, in its amalgamation of dancing and walking, raises questions about both poetry and prose. The goal-directed progression of the final image is at odds with the structures of the tale itself, which incorporates a number of journeys and narratives which lead nowhere, or are abruptly end-stopped, echoing Krueger's analysis of the multiple subverted mini-narratives in Baudelaire's prose poems. Simultaneously, 'Hérodias' sets its climactic dance-poem alongside other examples of lyricism and verse in the text, threading commentaries on the poetic throughout this hybrid tale. Oliver Mills suggests affinities between Flaubert's tales and the idea of prose poetry, claiming that:

> In the *Trois Contes*, Flaubert lays the groundwork for the discovery of the sublime in the pedestrian with a form that fuses poetry and prose, as he had aimed to do in his letters about modern art. The accent on emotions and the imagination in 'Un Cœur Simple', the importance of recurrent signs in 'La Légende de Saint-Julien L'Hospitalier', the divine power of the Word invoked by 'Hérodias' and the importance of imagery and symbols throughout, all engage the language of poetry.[22]

Generic hybridity can be detected through an analysis of the patterns of movement evoked in 'Hérodias', which underscore duality: the amalgamation of walking and dancing, goal-directed movement and timeless, circular turning. Although, as in Oliver Mills's analysis, a case can be made for seeing aspects of prose poetry at work in both of Flaubert's other contes — she suggests the dualities associated with the emphasis on the 'crépuscule' in 'La Légende de Saint Julien l'Hospitalier', for example, as indicative of liminality in the work[23] — focus here will fall on 'Hérodias', as the text which most obviously suggests a meditation on the poetic through the image of the dance, through the incorporation of lines of verse, and through the notorious challenges presented by the story to the practice of interpretation.

Marie Maclean's discussion of Baudelaire's prose poems reminds the reader that 'the name "poems" attached to them seems to have blinded critics to their most obvious feature, that they are in the first instance a dazzling display of many varieties of narrative'.[24] 'Hérodias', too, incorporates 'varieties of narrative', setting its short-story format, its three chapters, alongside a sense of the novel, in its echoes of *Salammbô*, as well as the theatrical, in its dramatization of Iaokanann/John the Baptist's prophecy, declaimed in darkness by an unseen 'Voix'. It can also be read as an amalgamation of mini-narratives, indicated by its somewhat erroneous title: although Hérodias, wife of Herod-Antipas, is responsible for the outcome in that she sets up the dance of her daughter Salomé and so brings about the demand for the head of John the Baptist, the tale, which charts the death of the prophet and the incomprehension of Herod, is in fact more about the two men. And even beyond the narratives of Herod, his wife, her daughter and the anticipation of Christianity as themes, the tale incorporates a sense of multiplicity in its glimpses of alternative witnesses to events, such as the executioner and Samaritan Mannaëi, who hates the Jews and so despises John the Baptist, or Phanuel, who interprets the signs in the stars and argues that John must be set free; access is also given to a profusion of races, languages, and peoples. Flaubert also undermines the linearity of his prose in the complexity of information which is provided throughout the tale, and in the opening chapter in particular, which sees juxtaposing paragraphs setting out the nuanced and often cryptic details of the Tetrarch's affairs (the complexity enhanced by this additional title supplied for Herod/Antipas).[25] The gaps in the prose are reflected in the descriptions of the landscape surveyed by Antipas:

> Tous ces monts autour de lui, comme des étages de grands flots petrifiés, les gouffres noirs sur le flanc des falaises, l'immensité du ciel bleu, l'éclat violent du jour, la profondeur des abîmes le troublaient, — et une désolation l'envahissait au spectacle du désert, qui figure, dans le bouleversement de ses terrains, des amphithéâtres et des palais abattus. (*H*, p. 256)

The chasms and abysses which rupture the terrain reflect the fractures of coherence in the text itself; the image of the frozen waves evokes immobility and timelessness, to set alongside the notion of destruction and temporal change connoted by forces which have ravaged the amphitheatres and palaces. The dash here, and the characteristically subverted conjunction 'et' provide connection and disconnection, linking the Tetrarch's desolation with the vista of the material backdrop and the spiritual immensity of the sky, and yet failing to provide a full explanation either for what Vinken perceives as a Baudelairean splenetic gaze.[26]

The combination of linearity and fragmentation detected in the panorama of the desert landscape is found, too, in the repeated insistence on walking or journeying in this text. The *conte*, which will culminate in the poetry of Salomé's dance and the prose of the decapitated head being passed from messenger to messenger in the concluding walk to Galilee, is in fact composed of a number of earlier glimpses of journeys, which serve to remind the reader of the array of teleological pathways at work at the level of narrative, and of the disruption of those pathways. These are journeys, made on foot or by mule or camel, not just by the awaited Roman proconsul Vitellius, but also by representatives of other races and religions making their way towards Herod to beg favours or to take part in the feast. Early in the narrative, Herod surveys the terrain and notes the empty roads before him, but several pages later those roads have filled up. In the second chapter of the tale, the number of arriving travellers indicates the sense of multiplicity and confusion at work in the prose. Valéry observes that 'elle [la marche] est un acte dirigé vers quelque chose que notre but est de joindre' (*PPA*, p. 1330), but Flaubert's prose persistently disables the reader from making such links, and so from seeing the text as directed towards a clear goal:

> Un tumulte s'éleva sous la porte. On introduisait une file de mules blanches, montées par des personnages en costumes de prêtres. C'étaient des Sadducéens et des Pharisiens que la même ambition poussait à Machærous, les premiers voulant obtenir la sacrificature, et les autres la conserver [...]. Presque en même temps arrivèrent des soldats de l'avant-garde. (*H*, p. 261).

These priests, whose aims are both parallel and antithetical, and the soldiers whose precise allegiance is initially obscured, indicate the linguistic strangeness and chasms of comprehension evoked by a narrative which employs definite articles, 'des soldats de *l*'avant-garde', asserting places and names as familiar while deconstructing familiarity. The connection between such prosaic confusion and contradiction, and the image of pedestrian movement, is reinforced several paragraphs later, when the press of people around Herod intensifies:

> Alors ils entouraient le Proconsul, en implorant des réparations d'injustice [...] les plus voisins de la porte descendirent sur le sentier, d'autres le montaient, ils refluèrent; deux courants se croisaient dans cette masse d'hommes qui oscillait, comprimée par l'enceinte des murs. (*H*, p. 262).

The criss-crossing action which takes place here will be examined shortly as an indicator of the intersecting generic questions raised in 'Hérodias'. A further walk is described in the remainder of the second chapter, when Vitellius's desire to see the underground chambers of Herod's fortress leads to a tour of the bee-hive-like structure of the estate. This walk, too, emblematizes both movement and stasis; the Romans are keen to parade around as many of the chambers as possible, but their ambulatory circuit of the storerooms is punctuated by the list-like descriptions of the various weapons and tools which interrupt the flow of the narrative; certain of these provisions themselves evoke the potential for speed (arrows connoting arcs of movement, bells for the chests of camels, a fleet of imprisoned horses capable of a 'galop frénétique') but their stored status also suggests inertia, indicating again the ways in which Flaubert's prose halts and surges.

The simultaneous incorporation of devices which work to initiate and further narrative progression, but also to subvert it, is extended too to the temporal structures of 'Hérodias'. On one hand, the tale unfolds in the everyday, giving chronological coherence to the unfolding of the short story format by keeping the frame of its action within one twenty-four hour period, from sunrise to sunrise.[27] On the other, a mystical temporality evoked by Phanuel's reading of the heavens gives an alternative understanding of passing time and prophetic progression ('la constellation de Persée se trouvait au zénith. Agalah se montrait à peine, Algol brillait moins, Mira-Cœti avait disparu', H, p. 268), while Salomé's dance offers suggestions of infinity, and imagistic patterns in the text collapse temporal distinctions, as when the head of John the Baptist is placed directly opposite the head of the drowsing intoxicated Aulus: 'par l'ouverture de leurs cils, les prunelles mortes et les prunelles éteintes semblaient se dire quelque chose' (p. 271).[28] Juxtaposing tendencies are thus established at the core of the text. Just as it encodes narrative multiplicity and progression, but also ruptures such prosaic endeavour, so too 'Hérodias' suggests a form of poetry, but also undermines such lyricism. The text's inclusion of the dance conjures evocations of timelessness, musicality, and the body's resistance to conventional forms of movement. However, the lines of verse cited at the heart of a discussion about the identity of John the Baptist and the idea of everlasting life are employed ambiguously. In answer to Jacob's claims as to Christ's miraculous powers and the fact that Iaokanann can be seen as the prophet Elias, Jonathas, a Greek-speaking Sadducee, replies with the poetic excerpt from Lucretius, 'Nec crescit, nec post mortem durare videtur' (p. 272).[29] There is irony in that the lyric is asserted in this text not to induce a sense of the immutability traditionally associated with poetry, but to argue for time-boundedness and the decay of the corporeal. Jonathas's scornful citation is immediately followed by an image of the corpulent Aulus preparing to vomit: 'Mais Aulus était penché au bord du triclinium, le front en sueur, le visage vert, les poings sur l'estomac' (p. 272). Such a reminder of corporeal disgust and sickness adds, as is the tendency of the text, a glimpse of materiality to set alongside evocations of transcendence, in some respects contributing to Jonathas's Lucretian quotation about bodily putrefaction as proof of 'rien de plus sot que la prétention du corps à la vie éternelle' (p. 272). Yet as the typically ambiguous Flaubertian 'mais' at the beginning of this sentence suggests, Aulus's heaving stomach can also be read equivocally, as a satirical comment on the pomposity of Jonathas's words and the lyrical insertion, or in order to give the lie to the idea that the body 'nec [...] durare' since within the text at least, if not in an afterlife, the material endures. As is the case with the prosaic elements of 'Hérodias', glimpses of poetry are both incorporated and undermined.

The dance, and its evocations of poetry, end abruptly: 'Elle se jeta sur les mains, les talons en l'air, parcourut ainsi l'estrade comme un grand scarabée — et s'arrêta brusquement' (H, p. 275). The brusqueness of this finale, and these concluding acrobatics, bring to mind the 'mouvement brusque' of the literal and rhythmic fall of the poetic halo in Baudelaire's 'Perte d'auréole', connecting this prose poem with Flaubert's *Trois Contes* which also, in their representations of potential sainthood, investigate implicit haloes and lost haloes in their amalgamation of the sacred and the mundane. Salomé's dance, with its final contortions, evokes, too, the Baudelairean 'miracle d'un prose poétique' described in the letter to Houssaye: it is both 'souple' and 'heurtée'; it echoes the 'ondulations de la rêverie' in the way Salomé 'balançait son ventre avec des ondulations de houle'; it unites body and soul as Baudelaire's terminology connects the conscious mind, the 'soubresauts de la conscience', with the 'mouvements lyriques de l'âme'.[30] Todorov's reading of Baudelaire's prose poems emphasizes patterns of opposition. He finds a unity in *Le Spleen de Paris* which is composed entirely of the confrontation of opposites, whether brought about by antithesis, incongruity, or ambivalence.[31] Opposition, tension, jerkiness — the stylistic and thematic incorporation of 'soubresauts' — all such traits are manifest in Flaubert as well as in Baudelaire. Such oppositions are given particular representation in 'Hérodias' through images of criss-crossing. These can be seen in the quotation above, which describes the crowds swarming around Antipas, or in Mannaëi's early description of the messengers who come to pay a visit to Iaokanann, 'comme les voleurs le soir aux carrefours des routes' (*H*, p. 255). The anticipation of the Christian cross in this tale in particular is visualized as a recurrent image by Vinken in her analysis of Flaubert's biblical intertextuality: she perceives, for instance, the 'fortress's vertical line [...] crossed by the horizontal; its form is a cross'.[32] Robert Greer Cohn's discussion of the prose poem sees it, too, as a form of crossing, arguing for a manner of examining Aloysius Bertrand's founding prose poems 'through the cross-hair optic of a vertical (poetic) axis fusing with a horizontal (prose) axis', and extending such an evaluation to Baudelaire's prose poetry too.[33] The 'croisement' also pinpointed by Baudelaire in his letter to Houssaye ('c'est surtout de la fréquentation des villes énormes, c'est du croisement de leurs innombrables rapports que naît cet idéal obsédant')[34] indicates, for Greer Cohn, 'the spontaneous existence of at least potential vision — poetic and/or ideational — *within* the prose dimension of the city [...] the vertical and the horizontal *interpenetrate powerfully*'.[35] The vertical and the horizontal intersect, in 'Hérodias', through the descriptions of the landscape: the opening passage itself offers glimpses of the interpenetration of two axes, in the image of the citadel of Machærus rising vertically from the plane of the Dead Sea, or the zigzagging path connecting the horizontal town with the vertically ascending ramparts. And this text offers a persistent 'croisement': Vinken sees the final position of Salomé's dance itself indicative of the cross:

> Salomé's dance, performed with a face as motionless as a pantomime's, figures a cross that the governor Vitellius perceives without recognising. Her performance points the way to those carrying John's head to Galilee: "her neck and her spine were at right angles to each other". Christ's cross is inscribed onto the beheading of John by Salomé's pantomime.[36]

For Vinken, the persistence of crosses, not just in 'Hérodias' but throughout

Flaubert's texts, indicates the idea that for Flaubert, human history echoes the events of salvation history, from Babel, through the Crucifixion and Resurrection. Yet the result of such a thoroughgoing engagement with the Bible is that Flaubert's work becomes an anti-Gospel, a resolutely anti-Christian movement which revises a tradition of love whose primal scene is Christ's act of renunciation on the cross. Instead of embodying self-affirmation or self-transcendence, Vinken's evaluation of Flaubert's crossed-out Christianity sees the Crucifixion as an act of forsaking the self, and the suffering this entails. This reading of Flaubert's work reaches a pinnacle in 'Hérodias'. What is indeed crossed out in 'Hérodias' is the attempt to interpret the story simply. Vinken's brutal reading of it may itself be too straightforward; it reflects, as do the other two tales in the *Trois Contes*, a glimpse of transcendence even while rendering such transcendence brutal and material.[37] 'Hérodias' is, with its poetry-prose cross, the most notorious of Flaubert's texts for demonstrating the theme of interpretation and its breakdown. The presence of the Roman interpreters, whose task is rendered so challenging (the priests, for example, do not understand Aulus's sarcastic mockery of their beliefs, and Phinées, their Galilean interpreter, refuses to translate his words) has been read as indicating that 'the primordial theme [...] is thus interpretation itself, and its breakdown [...]. The figure of the translator stands prominently between Babel and Pentecost'.[38] Such a foregrounding of the problems of interpretation is found, too, in *Le Spleen de Paris*. Maria Scott notes that 'The problem of how to interpret is a core preoccupation of the prose poems [...] sometimes the texts actually thematise reading or (mis)interpretation', and that Baudelaire's prose poems 'often feature an interpreting character whose readings of the world around him are themselves narcissistic, and consequently prone to significant blind spots'.[39] The idea that the prose poem is, by its very nature, a challenge to interpretation, a riddle, is suggested by Michel Beaujour, who describes it in terms of 'polymorphism, indescribability and elusiveness'.[40] 'Hérodias' reinforces its claim to be included in the category of 'the prose poem, with its mystic overtones and its suggestiveness of another, esoteric and unintelligible language', through its foregrounding of the practice of the riddle.[41] Mannaëi describes Iaokanann walking in the dark of his pit-prison, 'en répétant: "Qu'importe! Pour qu'il grandisse, il faut que je diminue"' (*H*, p. 255). Such parallel but antithetical movement is finally interpreted by Phanuel as the prophetic announcement of the coming of Christ, although the practice of understanding itself ('l'Essénien comprenait maintenant ces paroles: "Pour qu'il croisse, il faut que je diminue"', p. 277) is rendered typically cryptic and unexplained in the context of the tale, which substitutes the original verb 'grandisse' in Iaokanann's prediction for 'croisse', with its echoes of *croisement* and the cross. Centred around this riddle, 'Hérodias' evokes the contradictory form of literature par excellence, the prose poem.

Danger is also a feature which connects 'Hérodias' with Baudelaire's practice of the prose poem. Baudelaire refers to the implicit danger of the genre in a passage from 'Religion, Histoire, Fantaisie' in his *Salon de 1859*: 'Fantaisie' is described as being 'autant plus dangereuse qu'elle est plus facile et plus ouverte; dangereuse comme la poésie en prose'.[42] Krueger links the 'danger' inherent in the prose poem with the dangerous practices at work in 'Le Mauvais Vitrier', in which the narrator ends up hurling a pot at the unsuspecting glazier. Danger is also at work in 'Perte d'auréole', as the poet-figure is forced to leap in order to avoid the perils of city traffic. In 'Hérodias', not only is the text about the dangers of the poem-dance, and the threat to John the Baptist thus incarnated, but, in a broader sense, danger is bound up with the expression and structure of the text; Vinken argues that in this tale, 'language threatens, curses, wounds, incriminates, leads to killing'.[43] The idea that Homais would have been appalled by the prose poem suggests an awareness of the dangers of the genre, of the threat represented by the prose poem towards conventional generic forms. Homais's inability to deal with nonconformity is evidenced in his desire to homogenize and harmonize the apparently afflicted figures in *Madame Bovary*, the blind beggar and the limping Hippolyte. Homais wants to apply progressive treatments to the pair to rid them of their ailments, but he fails to recognize that their difficulties are indicative of a certain way of moving, seeing, or singing which is necessarily incurable. As Florence Emptez outlines in a study of 'feet' in Flaubert, his works are full of limping figures whose disabilities suggest the difficulties of walking.[44] When walking is seen as a reflection of prose, then the impediments to walking can be read as indicative of the ways in which Flaubert's prose breaks down, rupturing the time-bound and goal-driven forms of narrative in favour of a contradictory means of expression. In the figure of the Aveugle, in *Madame Bovary*, in particular, there is an amalgamation of fractured lyricism and limping prose. The beggar is an example of a poet, or at least a songster in Flaubert, as he declaims his bawdy lines. He is an itinerant figure who becomes a figure for alienation, sordidness, and morbidity, invoking disharmony rather than unity. He is himself endangered — met with the lashes of the coachman Hivert's whip — and connotes the threat to Romantic verse. He mixes together bawdiness and Romantic cliché. His song about a girl encouraged by the sunshine to thoughts of love is summarized dismissively, 'il y avait dans tout le reste des oiseaux, du soleil et du feuillage', although the complete lyrics are provided later in the text, and pinpoint the song as a traditional working class tune.[45] The beggar's rhyming couplets incarnate an outdated lyricism; his limping feet reflect limping poetic metre. Nevertheless, the Aveugle sings with a raunchy energy, hurling the impact of his sung verse in the faces of listeners and readers. The beggar symbolizes disfigurement and the concomitant disfigurement of the lyric, but he cannot be ignored. He demands to be heard: 'sa voix, faible d'abord et vagissante, devenait aiguë', and his song unnerves Emma. The Aveugle also, like Baudelaire's halo-less pedestrian, takes his chances with the hazards of the traffic, 'vagabondant avec son bâton tout au milieu des diligences', clinging precariously but tenaciously to the *Hirondelle*, 'entre l'éclaboussure des roues'.[46] His risky, limping methods of advance combine practices of prose and poetry, fracturing both. Homais's attempts to cure him and ultimately to imprison him suggest both the danger associated with the blind beggar's limping verse and, in turn, the ways in which social conventionality, represented by Homais's sanitizing treatments, endangers the risks of prose poetry.

In his article on Flaubert and the idea of literary justice, Roger Pearson connects the practices of Flaubert and Baudelaire, seeing Pierre Bourdieu's view of Baudelaire as a 'nomothète' as applicable to Flaubert too; both are 'heroically trying to rewrite the rules' of art and 'to redraw the map of what is considered aesthetically and culturally appropriate'.[47] As part of his argument that Flaubert's pursuit of stylistic 'rightness' was not simply a withdrawal into a self-sufficient realm of aesthetic perfection but instead an ethical gesture, a politically motivated style forged as a means of creating an alternative moral universe set apart from socially accepted norms, Pearson describes Flaubert's preference for disorder over order, noting, following Tooke, that 'Flaubert's aesthetic ideal was the harmony of discordant entities'.[48] Discordance acts as a further connecting point between Baudelaire and Flaubert, as they produce their clashes or harmonies of prose and poetry. Baudelaire's vision of verse poetry, and of the seeming inadequacies of the poet, are encapsulated in the image of the 'cloche fêlée', the cracked bell of 'Spleen et idéal', aligned with the poet's soul, which can no longer create the musical 'carillons' which would inspire memory. The much-quoted line from *Madame Bovary* on the subject of linguistic inadequacy also conjures a cracked vessel, the 'chaudron fêlé' on which tunes are thrashed out for bears to dance to, an image at odds with the desired form of literary and communicative expression which would instead enable the articulation of emotion, and could 'attendrir les étoiles'.[49] Both the bell and the cauldron emit discordant, tinny sounds which evoke the writers' responses to lyricism. The cauldron, which already reads as a prose-poem substitution for the musical and religious connotations of the bell (echoing, for instance, the cooking pots found in the prose version of Baudelaire's 'L'Invitation au voyage', instead of the lullaby-like refrains of the verse poem of the same name), produces the accompaniment for a dance.[50] Yet rather than being the graceful poem-dance envisaged by Valéry, Flaubert's prose-dance is instead performed by the lumbering bear, whose feet are necessarily weighted by gravity. The bear's lolloping footfalls indicate, once again, the prose-poetry cross produced by Flaubert's narrative tightrope walks.

Notes to Chapter 5

1. Huysmans writes: 'Plus que la poésie peut-être, le poème en prose terrifie les Homais qui composent la majeure partie du public' (cited by Daniel Grojnowski, *'A rebours' de J. K. Huysmans* (Paris: Gallimard, Folio, 1996), p. 155.
2. Gustave Flaubert, *Correspondance*, ed. by Jean Bruneau and Yvan Leclerc, 5 vols, Bibliothèque de la Pléiade (Paris: Gallimard, 1973–2007), II, 57.
3. Paul Valéry, 'Poésie et pensée abstraite', in *Œuvres*, ed. by Jean Hytier, 2 vols, Bibliothèque de la Pléiade (Paris: Gallimard, 1957–60), I, 1314–39 (p. 1330); hereafter referred to as *PPA*.
4. Flaubert, *Correspondance*, II, 30.
5. Charles Baudelaire, 'Perte d'auréole', in *Œuvres complètes*, ed. by Claude Pichois and Jean Ziegler, 2 vols, Bibliothèque de la Pléiade (Paris: Gallimard, 1961), I, 299.
6. Marshall Berman argues for this prose poem as an indicator of Baudelairean modernity: 'one of the paradoxes of modernity is that its poets will become more deeply and authentically poetic by becoming more like ordinary men. If he throws himself into the moving chaos of everyday life in the modern world — a life of which the new traffic is a primary symbol — he can appropriate

this life for art. The "bad poet" in this world is the poet who hopes to keep his purity intact by keeping off the streets, free from the risks of traffic' (*All That is Solid Melts into Air: The Experience of Modernity* (London: Verso, 1983), p. 159).

7. Baudelaire, *Œuvres complètes*, I, 229–30.
8. Suzanne Bernard, *Le Poème en prose de Baudelaire jusqu'à nos jours* (Paris: Nizet, 1959), pp. 439–40. Bernard also cites on this page the claim, made by Athys in 1897, that 'le poème en prose [...] n'est ni le conte ni la nouvelle, ce conte fût-il de Flaubert, cette nouvelle de Gautier'.
9. Michel Beaujour, 'Short Epiphanies: Two Contextual Approaches to the French Prose Poem', in *The Prose Poem in France*, ed. by Mary Ann Caws and Hermine Riffaterre (New York: Columbia University Press, 1983), pp. 39–59 (p. 52).
10. Ibid., p. 56.
11. The collection of essays *The Prose Poem in France* ends with a prose poem by John Hollander entitled 'The Way We Walk Now: A Theory of the Prose Poem': 'But then it ceased to matter where we were. What had become necessary that we do by way of amble, or of hop, skip, and jump, had so taken over power from mere place that it generated the shapes of space through which it moved, like a lost, late arrival at the start of a quest which had set out nonetheless, dreaming each new region into which he landed'. Hollander's poem draws attention to the metaphoric connections between prose poetry and patterns of movement, which becomes not just ambling, but athletic leaping, and even skateboarding (*The Prose Poem in France*, ed. by Caws and Riffaterre, pp. 231–32).
12. Kathryn Oliver Mills, *Formal Revolution in the Work of Baudelaire and Flaubert* (Newark: University of Delaware Press, 2012), p. 2.
13. Elissa Marder, *Dead Time: Temporal Disorders in the Wake of Modernity (Baudelaire and Flaubert)* (Stanford, CA: Stanford University Press, 2001). These recent studies follow on from Timothy Unwin's earlier study of the two writers: *Flaubert et Baudelaire: affinités spirituelles et esthétiques* (Paris: Nizet, 1982).
14. Cheryl Krueger, *The Art of Procrastination: Baudelaire's Poetry in Prose* (Newark: University of Delaware Press, 2007), p. 41.
15. Ibid., p. 57.
16. As discussed by Peter Brooks, among others, in *Reading for the Plot: Design and Intention in Narrative* (Oxford: Clarendon Press, 1984).
17. Krueger, *The Art of Procrastination*, p. 52.
18. Gustave Flaubert, 'Hérodias', in *Œuvres complètes*, 16 vols (Paris: Club de l'Honnête Homme, 1972), IV, 251–77 (p. 274); hereafter referred to as *H*.
19. Gustave Flaubert, *Madame Bovary*, in *Œuvres complètes*, ed. by Claudine Gothot-Mersch, 3 vols, Bibliothèque de la Pléiade (Paris: Gallimard, 2001–13), III, 292.
20. Alan Raitt, for instance, notes that the departure from the claustrophobic enclosure of the fortress represents a hint at an indefinite future and 'overtones of the coming spread of Christianity', but also observes that 'the last page may be read as a statement of purely material fact: the men have a long way [to] go in the heat of the desert, the head is heavy, so they take turns in carrying it' (*Flaubert: Trois Contes* (London: Grant & Cutler, 1991), p. 65).
21. Marcel Proust, 'A propos du style de Flaubert', in *Sur Baudelaire, Flaubert et Morand* (Paris: Éditions Complexe, 1987), p. 77.
22. Oliver Mills, *Formal Revolution in the Work of Baudelaire and Flaubert*, p. 128. She also refers to links between lyricism and the *Trois Contes* in listing 'the lyric rhythm of its prose, with its frequent groups of three, the tight enchaînements between chapters, the space created between the lines for Félicité's emotions [and] the relatively short length of the tales' (p. 129). Oliver Mills is making the case for a comparison between Flaubert and Baudelaire based on their experimentation with literary genre, and emphasizes, in her introduction, her intention to focus discussion on *Le Spleen de Paris* and the *Trois Contes*: in the event, though, the discussion of Baudelaire's prose poems is blurred by her comparisons with Joseph de Maistre, and her chapter on the *Trois Contes* is very brief. Barbara Vinken also notes that the *Trois Contes* have been compared to prose poems 'by virtue of their compressed intertextuality and their immaculate composition' (*Flaubert Postsecular: Modernity Crossed Out* (Stanford, CA: Stanford University Press, 2015), p. 21). Such compression is a feature of the prose poems highlighted by J. A.

Hiddleston in his evaluation of *Le Spleen de Paris*; he refers to the 'concentration and intensity [of the prose poem] which, with only the appearance of a paradox, gives us a feeling of expansion' (*Baudelaire and Le Spleen de Paris* (Oxford: Clarendon Press, 1987), p. 87).

23. Oliver Mills, *Formal Revolution in the Work of Baudelaire and Flaubert*, p. 134.
24. Marie Maclean, *Narrative as Performance: The Baudelairean Experiment* (London: Routledge, 1988), p. 42.
25. 'The early part of the story is a jumbled mass of nuggets of information, each one of which looks as though it might be vital, and all of which are presented on more or less the same level' (Raitt, *Flaubert: Trois Contes*, p. 62).
26. Vinken also notes the narrative blanks at work in this tale: 'considerable blanks in the narrative increase the darkness emerging in the story of Herodias and obfuscate the familiar perspective of the Bible. It remains fragmented right up to the pensive mood of Herod [...] he has the look of a king who suffers from Baudelairean spleen' (*Flaubert Postsecular*, p. 344).
27. Vinken notes that the structure of 'Hérodias' adheres to the classical unities of time and place (*Flaubert Postsecular*, p. 339).
28. Oliver Mills argues, citing Baudelaire's reference to modernity as the amalgamation of the eternal and the transitory in 'Le Peintre de la vie moderne', that 'the story told in "Hérodias" represents the ultimate union of the eternal with the transitoire' (*Formal Revolution in the Work of Baudelaire and Flaubert*, p. 141).
29. 'It [the body] neither grows nor is seen surviving death'; in full: 'Praeterea corpus per se nec gignitur umquam | Nec crescit necque post mortem durare videtur' (Lucretius, *On the Nature of Things*, ed. by Martin Smith, Loeb Classical Library (Cambridge, MA: Harvard University Press, 1992), pp. 212–14).
30. Gérard Gengembre's notes on the text makes clear the union of body and soul in the dance: 'les deux aspects de la danse se distinguent comme l'âme et le corps, comme une recherche et l'épanouissement'('Au fil du text', in Gustave Flaubert, *Trois Contes* (Paris: Pocket 1998), p. X). For Baudelaire's letter to Houssaye, see *Œuvres complètes*, I, 275–76.
31. Tzvetan Todorov, 'Poetry without Verse', in *The Prose Poem in France*, ed. by Caws and Riffaterre, pp. 62–78.
32. Vinken, *Flaubert Postsecular*, p. 339.
33. Robert Greer Cohn, 'A Poetry-Prose Cross', in *The Prose Poem in France*, ed. by Caws and Riffaterre, pp. 135–62 (pp. 137–38).
34. Baudelaire, *Œuvres completes*, I, 276.
35. Greer Cohn, 'A Poetry-Prose Cross', p. 144.
36. Vinken, *Flaubert Postsecular*, p. 356.
37. Oliver Mills underscores this idea in her remarks on the closing lines of 'Hérodias': 'As Flaubert underlines the earthly nature of human understanding with the heaviness of the tale's final image, he also reminds us that — although this tale comes closer to it than his earlier novels — sacred meaning only flickers in the dead weight of matter' (*Formal Revolution in the Work of Baudelaire and Flaubert*, p. 134).
38. Vinken, *Flaubert Postsecular*, p. 343.
39. Maria Scott, *Baudelaire's 'Le Spleen de Paris': Shifting Perspectives* (Aldershot: Ashgate, 2005), p. 6.
40. Beaujour, 'Short Epiphanies', p. 49.
41. Ibid., p. 57.
42. Charles Baudelaire, *Salon de 1859*, in *Œuvres complètes*, II, 644.
43. Vinken, *Flaubert Postsecular*, p. 345.
44. Florence Emptez, *Aux pieds de Flaubert* (Paris: Grasset, 2002).
45. Flaubert, *Madame Bovary*, p. 386: 'Souvent la chaleur d'un beau jour | Fait rêver fillette à l'amour'.
46. Ibid.
47. Roger Pearson, 'Flaubert's Style and the Idea of Literary Justice', *Dix-Neuf*, 17.2 (2013), 156–82 (p. 158).
48. Ibid., p. 160. He cites Adrianne Tooke, *Flaubert and the Pictorial Arts: From Image to Text* (Oxford: Oxford University Press, 2000), pp. 29, 111–12, 192.
49. Flaubert, *Madame Bovary*, p. 319.

50. 'Tout est riche, propre et luisant [...] comme une magnifique batterie de cuisine' (Baudelaire, 'L'Invitation au voyage', in *Œuvres complètes*, I, 302).

— 5 —
Le Juste Milieu:
Political Pornography in Numa's 'pièce à porte'

Natasha Ryan

There is an enigmatic quality to the nineteenth-century lithographer Pierre Numa Bassaget, known commercially as 'Numa'. Although his name appears in a number of artistic directories that were published around the middle of the century, little biographical information about the artist is known.[1] Nonetheless, his lithographic output was considerable and he did not escape the attention of Baudelaire, who mentions him in 'Le Peintre de la vie moderne', and later Walter Benjamin, who alludes to Numa in the 'Interior/Trace' convolute of *The Arcades Project*.[2]

Given our lack of knowledge about the artist, it seems appropriate that a corresponding air of mystery is evident in his work, and particularly in the 'pièce à porte' that he produced for the satirical journal *La Caricature* in March 1832. This work was part of a series of lithographs, collectively referred to as 'images [or] pièces à porte', which were produced collaboratively by a number of artists working for the journal and published therein throughout the early 1830s. These lithographs depict pornographic scenes that are by turns erotic, by turns comic, and are accompanied by tongue-in-cheek captions. In this, they conform to the tradition of erotic lithography that was common in the early nineteenth century.[3] What distinguishes this series from other pornographic lithographs of the time, however, is their physical structure, for the 'pièces à porte' feature a folding or slide-out panel overlaid on the original page: typically, a voyeuristic figure will be shown eavesdropping or peering through the keyhole of a closed door, which the reader must move aside in order to access the pornographic scene behind. This essay will consider the gradual shift in tone of the 'pièces à porte', moving from a vulgar hybrid eroto-comedy to a more serious and realist political commentary: in other words, a series that is initially wholly lacking in both gravity and grace ultimately finds a convenient expression of what is gravest about contemporary politics through the deliberate eschewal of aesthetic grace.

Given that the 'pièces à porte' are the work of several artists, the style and genre of these images can vary considerably. There are some more straightforwardly erotic examples, such as the lithograph by Devéria which appeared in the issue of 2 December 1830. This depicts a maidservant leaning against a door, a cautionary hand held up, accompanied by the caption: 'On n'entre pas'. When the reader contravenes this instruction and opens the panel, it is to find a young woman in undergarments, coyly unlacing her corset and stating: 'Fermez donc la porte, Justine!'[4]

However, other examples take a more humorous approach, such as the lithograph which depicts three bourgeois types, their backs to the reader, listening at a door behind which two lovers are engaged in a passionate embrace. The accompanying caption belies any suggestion of eroticism in this scene: 'Sans doute elle est avec Monsieur Jules qui lui apprend à connaître l'histoire', the legend reads, the implication being, of course, that 'l'histoire' is certainly not what Monsieur Jules is teaching.[5] Similarly, one of the earliest examples of a 'pièce à porte' shows an overweight and grotesque husband (Fig. 5.1) returning home early to find his wife in a compromising position (Fig. 5.2). The blithe caption informs us: 'Ma femme ne m'attend pas... Va-t-elle être contente!!'[6]

These early examples are devised in a spirit of good humour and, in line with the general character of the journal in which they appear, they are politically neutral. In its original conception, *La Caricature* largely refrained from taking a political stance and was uncritical of the constitutional monarchy, as its founder and editor Charles Philipon believed that King Louis-Philippe would honour his promise to abolish censorship and guarantee freedom of the press.[7] As a result, early issues of the journal avoid controversy, even going so far as to gloss over the riots of December 1830, and the tone of their humour is low-brow and popular, without recourse to satirizing any particular individuals or social class.[8]

Accordingly, the early 'pièces à porte' lack any political angle and their purpose is purely to entertain, requiring little philosophical investment from the reader. This does not mean, however, that the reader is merely a passive witness to the erotic scene before them, for the fold-out panel changes the nature of our reading experience and throws the question of genre into doubt. These are not texts we can flip past, they cannot be simply glanced at: in order to fully appreciate the 'pièces à porte' we must physically embed ourselves in the text, and can only access the full scene once we have changed the structure of the page by moving the door panel aside. As a result, the act of reading a 'pièce à porte' is temporal, belying the more typically spatial apprehension of visual art where the spectator stands before a tableau and experiences an instant in time, a frozen scene.[9] The 'pièces à porte' are distinguished from other contemporaneous lithographs because they involve a process and, therefore, they are more akin to the way we experience narrative, that is, as a succession of events over time.

Indeed, the language of the captions reinforces the narrativity of these pieces. The ellipsis in the husband's naive statement, 'Ma femme ne m'attend pas...' lures us into the text and gestures towards the scene behind the door, which only he will be surprised by. Similarly, when the maid tells us 'On n'entre pas', the negative construction almost dares us to prove her wrong and 'enter' the text, while the sexual undertones of that verb foreshadow the undressing of the young woman. Even the 'Monsieur Jules' caption is suggestive of its own role in the narrative process as, we might imagine, we too are offered the chance to 'connaître l'histoire' — to discover the *story* behind the door. The captions operate as invitations into the narrative, seducing us into opening the door and participating in the penetration of the text. Any eroticism in the pieces stems from this narrativization: much like

Fig. 5.1. La Caricature, 2 December 1830

Fig. 5.2. La Caricature, 2 December 1830

in modern pornographic films, the story is more important than its conclusion, the process more gratifying than the end result.

This is not unlike the theory that Barthes puts forth in his essay on striptease: 'le strip-tease [...] est fondé sur une contradiction: désexualiser la femme dans le moment même où on la dénude. [...] Seule la durée du dévêtement constitue le public en voyeur'.[10] Striptease is only successful because it develops within time, because it *teases*: the central paradox is that, as soon as the process is complete, the woman ceases to be an object of sexual attraction. Thus, any eroticism in the 'pièces à porte' is embodied in the closed door. The captions are suggestive of the scenes behind that door, but the women are only sexualized while they remain hidden. Like a veil or a mask, the door leaves the reader's imagination to do the work. The text mirrors clothing, and the reader, aligned with the voyeuristic figures portrayed on the outside of the door, is complicit in its unwrapping.

The door, then, is the most erotic thing about these lithographs. And it may have been even more scintillating for the reader of the 1830s, for whom the door may have constituted an example of what Benjamin refers to as 'threshold magic'.[11] The nineteenth century is a period that is characterized by thresholds — literal, political, aesthetic —, the whole century being composed of points of transition from old regimes to new. This is reflected architecturally as threshold spaces became increasingly popular: intermediary environments that were neither inside nor out began to be built across Paris in the form of winter gardens, covered marketplaces, department stores, Universal Exhibition halls, and, as Benjamin points out, the arcades.[12] As a result, the distinction between interior and exterior, and between public and private, was shifting. Philippe Hamon, who traces the alignment of architectural developments with changing approaches to narrative, identifies the threshold as central to the production of meaning in the nineteenth-century text:

> Given its various thresholds, partitions, doors, floors, and discriminating interfaces, architecture is therefore primarily a twofold concretization of narratives and norms [...] rather than being merely the way of organizing pure space. After all, a wall, partition, or threshold always involves more than static material separations [...]; they incarnate the constraints laid down by social or technological norms [...] far more than merely reflecting a stylistic order.
>
> The building undoubtedly analyzes space and constructs a system of differences, but in producing distinctions between full and empty, opened and closed, movable and immovable, private and social it manifests and reactivates normative notions of prohibited and permitted, of private and public, of sacred and profane, or of mandatory and optional, and thereby manifests and reactivates not just value but meaning itself.[13]

Hamon's study refers primarily to literature but it is possible to see a similar logic in play in the 'pièces à porte'. Here, we have a literal threshold but it too is concerned with the distinction between public and private and between what is permitted and prohibited. There is a sense of rebellion in the act of opening the door and therein lies the thrill of it. The door is a symbol of the reader's contravention of both paginal and social norms: it is an act of trespass where we break both the page and acceptable social practices.

But the door is also a textual threshold, for the question of genre also hinges (if you will pardon the pun) on the door. Once the door is open, a shift occurs in our experience of the text and we move away from any suggestion of the erotic and firmly towards the comic. Some artists accentuate this more than others: Devéria, for example, stays closer to the erotic with his corset-clad maiden, but there is nonetheless a hint of comedy in her exasperated cry to Justine to close the door; Monnier, by contrast, is courting comedy from the outset with his pig-nosed husband, about whom the only seductive quality is his wilful willingness to be deceived. This can partly be explained simply by differences in style between the artists and it is worth noting that Devéria's more erotic lithograph is also more realist in tone (it is printed in black and white, his characters are more convincingly human) than Monnier's brightly-coloured and cartoonesque figures.

Yet, wherever their emphasis ultimately falls, the 'pièces à porte' hover on a threshold between the erotic and the comic. Although we are paralleled with the voyeurs in these scenes, as readers we have none of their naivety and can sense what lies behind the doors. Consequently, from the moment we encounter the lithographs the eroticism is undermined because the comedy is always latent. The motion of folding back the page reinforces the change in genre and we are aware that, as soon as we commit to opening the door, we are moving into humorous territory. The closed door, even as it promises eroticism, also sets up a joke and the scene behind it is the punchline, merely confirming our suspicion that this is comedy disguised as pornography. Once the door has been opened, comedy reveals itself once and for all. The 'pièces à porte' tread a fine line between the erotic and the comic, operating in a *juste milieu*, a grey area where neither genre is wholly committed to, yet neither is entirely dismissed.[14] These early examples are neither grave nor graceful: their subject matter privileges the trivial, and their tone is a balance of seduction and amusement — but this was soon to change.

While Philipon had allowed his artists free rein in the early issues of *La Caricature*, in the Spring of 1831 the tone of the journal changed dramatically. Philipon had once been a supporter of Louis-Philippe, and *La Caricature* initially refrained from criticism of the king who, in August 1830, had promised freedom of the press. In December of that year, however, the Chamber of Deputies voted to impose a *cautionnement* of 30,000 francs on all political newspapers and to uphold the stamp duty on the periodical press.[15] Moreover, Louis-Philippe, having stopped the December riots with the aid of Lafayette and the National Guard, grew more confident in his own agenda and dissociated himself from the July Revolution which had put him on the throne. He became increasingly politically conservative, failing to support revolutions that were taking place in Belgium, Italy, and Poland, and distancing himself from the working-class Parisian populace who had overthrown Charles X. In January 1831, Louis-Philippe articulated his moderate stance: 'Nous ne devons pas seulement chérir la paix, nous devons encore éviter tout ce qui pourrait provoquer la guerre. Quant à la politique intérieure, nous chercherons à nous tenir dans un juste milieu'.[16]

Philipon's reaction was swift and unambiguous: he converted the journal into an instrument of acerbic political commentary. On 23 December he added a new subtitle to the journal, so that it became *La Caricature morale, religieuse, littéraire et scénique*, thereby transforming the purpose of the publication from one of entertainment to moral and aesthetic prescription. By January, the journal was featuring articles which explicitly denounced the actions of the government (Philipon's piece of 27 January 1831 depicts the trial of Françoise Liberté before the Chamber of Deputies).[17] And in February, Philipon produced the infamous 'Mousse de juillet' caricature — popularly known as 'Les Bulles de savon' — which portrayed the king blowing soap bubbles labelled with his insubstantial promises ('Liberté de la presse', 'La Charte sera une vérité', 'Les Maires nommés par le peuple' etc.), all about to burst.[18] Philipon's change in attitude could not have been more drastic and, in 1846, he acknowledged the overt shift in *La Caricature* towards political satire:

> En 1830, j'ai cru naïvement à la liberté de la presse. 'La censure ne devait être rétablie. Il ne devait plus y avoir de procès faits aux journaux.' C'étaient les propres paroles du Roi-citoyen, du Prince libéral que nous avions choisi. J'éprouvai le besoin de prendre ma part à ce festin de l'intelligence; et je fondai *La Caricature morale, religieuse, littéraire et scénique*. Tu vois qu'elle ne se proposait pas de parler politique.
> En effet, à quoi bon traiter de politique! Nous étions en plein âge d'or. Les Français étaient tous frères, tous d'accord. Notre Roi-révolutionnaire ne voulait point de cour, point d'argent, point de blasons; ses fils étaient nos frères, nos camarades de collège, nous n'avions point de maîtres, la politique n'existait plus.
> L'âge d'or n'a pas duré longtemps; tu verras, après une douzaine de numéros, poindre la caricature politique, douce d'abord, peu agressive, et tu la verras revenir plus souvent — plus souvent encore, et plus vive jusqu'à ce qu'elle occupe seule le Journal et devienne sanglante, impitoyable.[19]

For Philipon, caricature became a powerful weapon of resistance, and *La Caricature* gained a reputation for its radical liberal stance and explicit criticism of the constitutional monarchy. Where, though, did that leave the light-hearted and socially unengaged 'pièces à porte'?

With the journal's newly politicized perspective, the lithographs published by *La Caricature* tended towards satirical caricature of recognizable governmental figures — ministers, clergymen, and eventually Louis-Philippe himself — rather than the impersonal and amusing figures such as are shown in the 'pièces à porte'. This would seem to signify the end of this series, as least in so far as its sponsorship by *La Caricature* was concerned. However, in the issue of 1 March 1832 a new 'pièce à porte' appeared, in a format that would have been familiar to regular readers of the journal but with a very different tone. This lithograph, which was created by Numa, depicts a policeman with his back to us, peering through a grille in a wooden door, which he is locking. Beside him stands a soldier in the uniform of the National Guard, who stares out towards us (Fig. 5.3). When the panel is folded back (Fig. 5.4), we encounter a woman in a dark prison cell, her feet bound, her hands shackled to the wall behind her, and her mouth gagged. This woman, whose breasts are bare and who wears a Phrygian cap, is unmistakeable: she is Lady Liberty. The

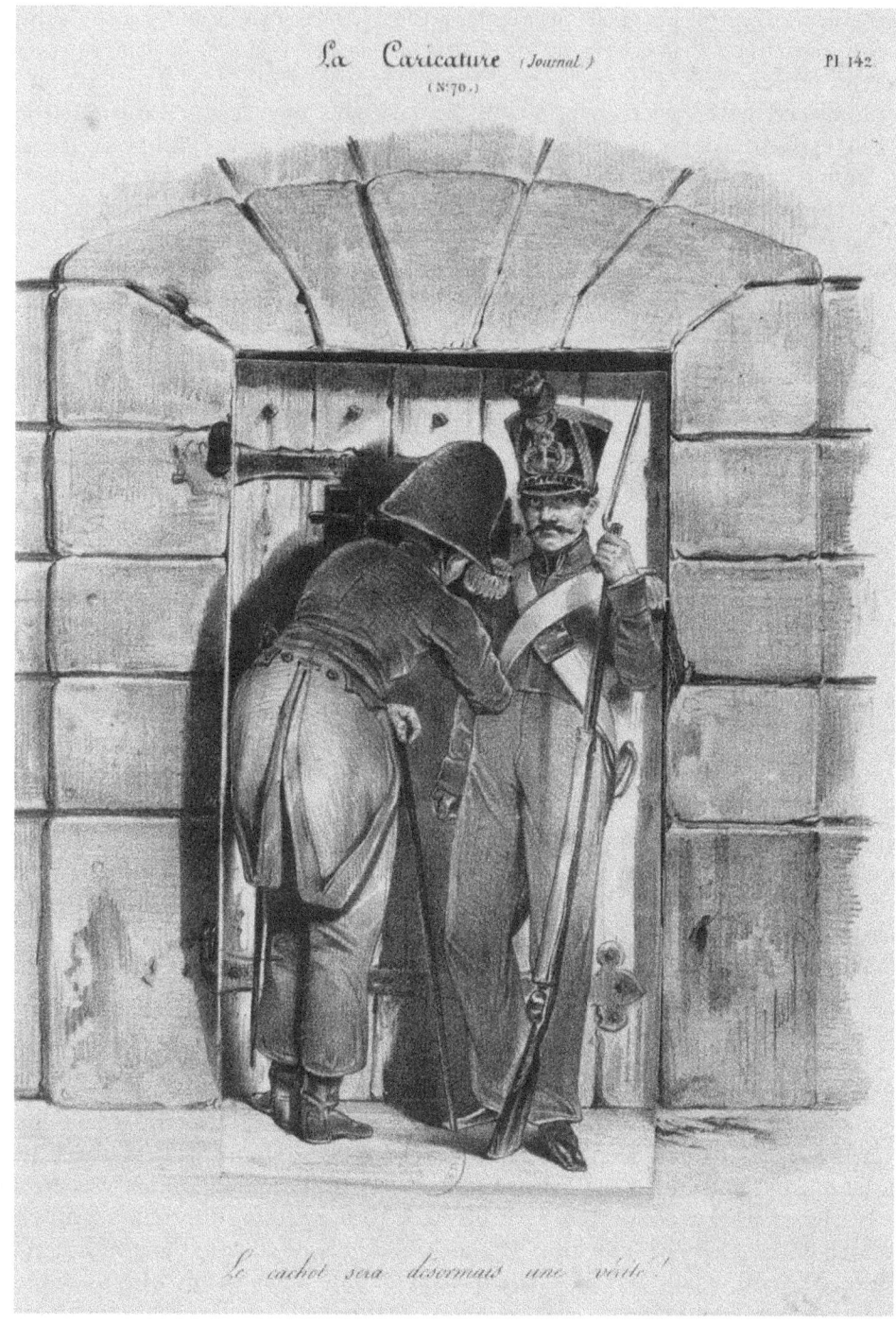

Fig. 5.3. La Caricature, 1 March 1832

Fig. 5.4. La Caricature, 1 March 1832

caption accompanying this image reads: 'Le cachot sera désormais une vérité!' Inside this issue of the journal we find the caption repeated with the added riposte: 'Ouvrez la porte, s'il vous plaît'.[20]

For a reader accustomed to the politics and style of La Caricature in 1832, this 'pièce à porte' was an open political statement. The image draws on a number of sources which would have been familiar to anyone well-versed in contemporary visual art, both the high-brow works exhibited in the Salons, and the less sophisticated, rapidly produced lithographs of the periodical press. First, and most obviously, the attire of Lady Liberty is a visual echo of Delacroix's famous 1830 painting, La Liberté guidant le peuple, which depicts Liberty atop a barricade, leading the July Revolution.[21] In a reverse move, however, Numa's lithograph portrays Liberty as a frightened prisoner, trussed up and immobile — a far cry from the confident revolutionary leader envisaged by Delacroix.[22]

Second, Numa's piece corresponds intertextually with a number of other lithographs produced by Philipon and his circle of trusted artists. In Spring 1831, Decamps produced two lithographs featuring Liberty: the first, 'La Liberté au poteau', shows her similarly dressed in cap and open robe, tied to a whipping post and about to be branded by government ministers with the letters 'T. R.' (timbre royal);[23] the second, subtitled 'Liberté (Françoise Désirée) fille du peuple, née a Paris le 27 Juillet 1830', depicts Liberty as a young girl being restrained with ropes by a group of juste milieu supporters, the king among them.[24] The image of Liberty captured and bound was a recurrent theme in the journal, and Numa's lithograph conforms to that tradition. What is more, a further visual precedent to Numa's depiction of a shackled prisoner had been produced by Philipon and Julien in 1831. Their lithograph entitled 'Le Juste Milieu: entre la guillotine et la Liberté' shows a man in a sparse prison cell, chained to the wall and gazing dolefully towards the reader while graffiti on the wall behind him includes the phrase 'liberté ou la mort' and a sketch of Lady Liberty's head. For Philipon, therefore — and by extension, for the artists who collaborated with him — there was an unequivocal association between the juste milieu government and the imprisonment or obstruction of liberty.

Moreover, the caption of Numa's piece is a deliberate echo of two phrases that were resonant in the public consciousness. The first was Louis-Philippe's declaration in the summer of 1830 that 'la Charte sera désormais une vérité', which effectively proclaimed his acceptance of the new Charter devised after the July Revolution. The second was a revision of this: 'la charge sera désormais une vérité!'. This was the caption that accompanied a lithograph produced by Philipon in 1831 entitled 'Le Juste Milieu', which depicted a pear-shaped headless figure in ancien régime costume, a tricolour cockade pinned to its hat. Where Philipon was concerned, the symbol of the pear was shorthand for the king himself, and this caricature unambiguously undercuts Louis-Philippe's supposed adherence to the Charter.[25] As a result, Numa's caption, which substitutes 'le cachot' for 'la Charte' or 'la charge', is a further response to the king's broken promise: not only is the charter removed from the phrase, but imprisonment is explicitly inserted in its place, implying that freedom of the press will henceforth be impossible.

* * * * *

Numa's 'pièce à porte', then, is part of a series of images of Liberty being restrained, and it draws on a number of Philipon and *La Caricature*'s recurring motifs. In fact, there is little evidence to inform us as to where Numa's personal political sympathies lay and it would not be unreasonable to assume that the germ of this piece came from Philipon himself. It was common practice among the artists and editors of *La Caricature* to share ideas and incorporate existing motifs into new designs. Furthermore, Philipon would sometimes dictate the content of the lithographs to other artists and it is difficult to say how far his influence spread.[26] The links between this 'pièce à porte' and other lithographs which appeared in *La Caricature* and elsewhere are characteristic of the journal's practices and, as David Kerr explains: 'Much of the newspapers' humour was based around a system of accumulation. Jokes from previous issues were constantly recycled and elaborated upon, while new characters and new symbols added constantly to the caricaturists' repertoire'.[27]

Consequently, the reader would come to Numa's lithograph with a wealth of background knowledge about the depictions of Liberty and would be fully aware of the history behind the caption. Indeed, they would even appreciate the humour of the caption, for it is not merely a statement about the incarceration of Liberty, but also a joke aimed at the artist himself. For Numa and Philipon the publication of this very lithograph was a risk in itself, and could have resulted in their prosecution and potential imprisonment for criticizing the July Monarchy.[28] The gag which binds Liberty's mouth is a clear emblem of the censorship of the press — *La Caricature* itself was shackled and rendered mute by a government of broken promises.

This 'pièce à porte' is just as ambiguous in terms of genre as the earlier, apolitical, lithographs in the series. Unlike the other examples we have seen, Numa's piece is inflected with a definite political gravity: its message is explicit and, once the door has been opened, the political angle of the work is as exposed as Lady Liberty's breasts.[29] Nonetheless, before the door opens and Liberty is revealed, there is still a trace of the eroto-comedy evident in the rest of the series, embodied in the voyeuristic policeman. The comedic element in particular is corroborated by the self-reflexivity of the caption. Thus, the characteristics that originally made the 'pièces à porte' successful as a form of entertainment are now used as a political weapon, and the ambiguity of the earlier pieces is exploited to further the expression of *La Caricature*'s political sympathies. Regular readers of the journal were accustomed to the comic nature of lithographs in this format and, consequently, to open the door and find Liberty bound and gagged would have been something of a shock. Our expectation is that the 'pièce à porte' will provoke laughter but, in fact, the very things that make this lithograph funny while the door is closed (the peeping policeman, the caption) set us up for the startling conclusion that there is nothing funny about the message behind it. The early 'pièces à porte' taught us that there is a correlation between an absence of gravity and an absence of grace; this later example subverts the correlation, harnessing the comic absence of grace as a means to express political gravity.

This lithograph is once again a threshold text, sitting in a middle-ground between serious political criticism and humour. And this is, in essence, the definition of satirical caricature. Philipon himself expressed the efficacy of disguising critique as comedy:

> Parler sérieusement m'ennuie; j'aime à attacher un petit grelot à mon idée; plus elle est sérieuse, plus je la crois sage, plus j'aime à la voir courir déguisée en folie. [...] il se trouve toujours par-ci, par-là, quelques braves gens que le bruit des grelots amuse, comme moi, et qui savent reconnaître la pensée sérieuse sous son masque de gaîté.[30]

Numa's 'pièce à porte' is perfectly in line with Philipon's preferred method. The lithographs of *La Caricature* occupied an aesthetic *juste milieu*, using vulgar comedic pornography to mask a serious message — their condemnation of the *juste milieu* king.[31]

But the additional layer operating in this text is that, as we have seen, it also enacts the threshold, embodying the space between the surface and the mask. If, as Albert Boime states, 'caricature's primary function is unmasking, the stripping away of the surface decorum just below which the individual's true agenda seethes', then the way it accomplishes this is by laying a mask of its own over its subject matter.[32] The 'pièce à porte' goes a step further and adds a physical mask in the form of the page of which it is constituted. Liberty herself may be half-naked but she is covered in textual clothing. 'Ouvrez la porte, s'il vous plaît', the journal commands, asking the government to uphold the values of the July Revolution and release Liberty. But this imperative is also an instruction to the reader, a request that we physically participate in the unmasking of the page, that we peel back the comedic layer of caricature to reveal the truth behind. It is the reader who must take part in the liberation of the press and of liberal, working-class values. A shift occurs from the early 'pièces à porte' to this one: where once we were complicit in our own gratification — erotic and/or comic — now we are complicit in the political protest. Numa encourages us to actively support the radical left and this is the real risk the lithograph takes because such an incitement to insurrection may very well be grounds for imprisonment. Numa's text is a criticism of a *juste milieu* government, which had one foot in republican values and the other in the more conservative agenda of the monarchy. The effectiveness of this text lies in the fact that it too embodies a *juste milieu* of its own. Hovering on a threshold between eroto-comedy and serious political critique, all the gravity of this 'pièce à porte' is masked by its abstention from grace. Ultimately, it is up to the reader to do the unmasking and cross the threshold symbolized by the unfolding door.

Notes to Chapter 6

1. Numa's name is listed in: the *Annuaire de l'industrie française* (Paris: Pagnerre & L. Mathias, 1851); the *Annuaire publié par la Gazette des beaux-arts: ouvrage contenant tous les renseignements indispensables aux artistes et aux amateurs* (Paris: Bureau de la Gazette des beaux-arts, 1870); the *Annuaire général du commerce, de l'industrie, de la magistrature et de l'administration ou almanach des 500.000 adresses de Paris, des départements et des pays étrangers* (Paris: Société des annuaires & Firmin-Didot frères,

1842); the *Annuaire des artistes français* (Paris: Guyot de Fère, 1836), and others. The records of the Bibliothèque nationale de France indicate that Numa died in 1872, and conjecture that he was born around 1802. We know also that he taught art classes at the 'École communale', rue Sainte-Élisabeth, in 1850–51. See *Annuaire de l'Industrie française*, p. 71.

2. Baudelaire describes Numa, along with a select number of other contemporary lithographers, as 'historiens des grâces interlopes de la Restauration', comparing these artists to novelists who capture the daily metamorphosis of life. See Charles Baudelaire, *Critique d'art suivi de Critique musicale*, ed. by Claude Pichois (Paris: Gallimard, 1992), pp. 346–47. Benjamin, meanwhile, associates Numa with the magic of thresholds in *The Arcades Project*, trans. by Howard Eiland and Kevin McLaughlin (Cambridge, MA, & London: Belknap Press of Harvard University Press, 1999), p. 214.
3. Lithography became a form of mass media in the aftermath of the French Revolution. Cheap and easy to produce, it constituted a new type of visual art that could be widely disseminated with little delay in the printing process. As such, it was an ideal vehicle for erotic imagery. Lithography was quickly associated with working-class ideals and, consequently, as Albert Boime explains, 'conservatives, both in politics and aesthetics, dismissed lithography as vulgar, pandering to the poorly educated masses' (*Art in an Age of Counterrevolution, 1815–1848* (Chicago: University of Chicago Press, 2004), p. 324).
4. *La Caricature*, 2 December 1830.
5. This lithograph is unsigned but it is possible that it was the work of Numa. See John Grand-Carteret, *Le Décolleté et le retroussé: un siècle de gauloiserie*, 2 vols (Paris: Édition photographique, 1910), II, 33.
6. *La Caricature*, 2 December 1830. This piece is also unsigned but Jules Brivois, who provides a list of all the lithographs that appeared in the first eleven issues of the journal (from 4 November 1830 to 13 January 1831), attributes this piece to Henri Monnier. See *Bibliographie des ouvrages illustrés du XIXe siècle, principalement des livres à gravures sur bois* (Paris: L. Conquet and P. Rouquette, 1883), p. 75. Many of the lithographs that were printed in *La Caricature* were unsigned, while others were misattributed, partly as a result of the collaborative nature of the journal and partly because the editor, Charles Philipon, would sometimes assume responsibility for more politically controversial pieces in order to protect his artists. For more detail, see David S. Kerr, *Caricature and French Political Culture, 1830–1848: Charles Philipon and the Illustrated Press* (Oxford: Clarendon Press, 2000), pp. 34–35.
7. The abolition of censorship was decreed in the revised Charter of 1830. See Kerr, *Caricature and French Political Culture, 1830–1848*, p. 81.
8. The trial of Charles X's former ministers occasioned riots in Paris in mid-December 1830 as working-class Parisians, students, and artisans protested against the fact that the ministers did not receive the death penalty. Kerr explains that *La Caricature* barely reported this and, in its early issues, the only group of people repeatedly critiqued in the journal was the clergy (*Caricature and French Political Culture, 1830–1848*, pp. 66–70).
9. In 1766, G. E. Lessing made a distinction between the way we experience painting and the way we experience literature, the former being spatial, and the latter temporal. Lessing states: 'if it is true that in its imitations painting uses completely different means or signs than does poetry, namely figures and colours in space rather than articulated sounds in time, and if these signs must indisputably bear a suitable relation to the things signified, then signs existing in space can express only objects whose wholes or parts coexist, while signs that follow one another can express only objects whose wholes or parts are consecutive' (*Laocoön: An Essay on the Limits of Painting and Poetry*, trans. by E. A. McCormick (Baltimore, MD: Johns Hopkins University Press, 1984), p. 78). This distinction dominated early nineteenth-century approaches to the *ut pictura poesis* tradition, although the distinction was later questioned with the emergence of new media, such as photography and cinema.
10. Roland Barthes, 'Strip-Tease', in *Mythologies* (Paris: Du Seuil, 1957), p. 165.
11. Benjamin points to the importance of the threshold in the nineteenth-century urban experience. For him, the *flâneur* is poised on a threshold, while the arcades and exhibition halls represent threshold spaces. He states: 'Nowhere, unless perhaps in dreams, can the phenomenon of the

boundary be experienced in a more originary way than in cities. [...] As threshold, the boundary stretches across streets; a new precinct begins like a step into the void' (*The Arcades Project*, p. 88).

12. Many scholars have analyzed the cultural impact of the Universal Exhibitions during the nineteenth century. For an account of how they influenced literary culture, see Anne Green, *Changing France: Literature and Material Culture in the Second Empire* (New York: Anthem Press, 2011), pp. 5–33. On the impact of department stores, see Alison M. K. Walls, *The Sentiment of Spending: Intimate Relationships and the Consumerist Environment in the Works of Zola, Rachilde, Maupassant, and Huysmans* (New York: Peter Lang, 2008). For a detailed account of the increasing popularity of winter gardens throughout the century see Bernard Marrey, *La Grande Histoire des serres & des jardins d'hiver: France 1780–1900* (Paris: Graphite, 1984). For a general conceptual overview of the use of thresholds in literature and visual art see *Thinking on Thresholds: The Poetics of Transitive Spaces*, ed. by Subha Mukherji (New York: Anthem Press, 2011).
13. Philippe Hamon, *Expositions: Literature and Architecture in Nineteenth-Century France*, trans. by Katia Sainson-Frank and Lisa Maguire, introduction by Richard Sieburth (Berkeley: University of California Press, 1992), p. 31.
14. In the history of visual art, the term 'juste milieu' first referred to a style of painting in the 1830s which married the Romanticist and Classicist tradition. Michael Marrinan sees this movement as closely connected with Louis-Philippe's official philosophy, see *Painting Politics for Louis-Philippe: Art and Ideology in Orléanist France, 1830–1848* (New Haven, CT: Yale University Press, 1987). Albert Boime subsequently applied the term to a group of artists in the 1880s whom he identified as reconciling Impressionism and 'l'art pompier' (official, academic art); see *The Academy and French Painting in the Nineteenth Century* (New Haven, CT, & London: Yale University Press, 1986). I am not using the term in either of these contexts, but merely to refer to a 'middle ground' between two genres of lithograph. As we shall see, the term 'juste milieu' had its roots in politics, referring to Louis-Philippe's reign. Robert Jensen notes that there was a trend in the nineteenth century of naming artistic movements or styles after political expressions: 'aesthetic tropes such as "avant-garde" and "juste milieu" are but the most notable examples of the tendency of the era to define styles as if they were points along a political spectrum' (*Marketing Modernism in Fin-de-Siècle Europe* (Princeton, NJ: Princeton University Press, 1994), p. 37).
15. See Kerr, *Caricature and French Political Culture, 1830–1848*, p. 71.
16. Quoted by Louis Blanc in *Histoire de dix ans: 1830–1840 (Révolution française)* (Paris: F. H. Jeanmaire, 1882), p. 293.
17. See Kerr, *Caricature and French Political Culture, 1830–1848*, pp. 71–72.
18. This piece did not appear in *La Caricature* but was published by La Maison Aubert, Philipon's publishing house.
19. Charles Philipon, letter to Roslje, 7 July 1846, reproduced in L. Carteret, *Le Trésor du bibliophile: époque romantique 1801–1875* (Paris: L. Carteret, 1927), p. 124.
20. *La Caricature*, 1 March 1832, column 557.
21. This painting was first exhibited at the 1831 Salon. For a detailed analysis of the way in which it embodies Delacroix's political views see Boime, *Art in an Age of Counterrevolution*, p. 242. Boime suggests that, although Delacroix appears to celebrate the role of the working class in the July Revolution, he also credits the king and National Guard with its success: 'it may be concluded that Delacroix located himself squarely on the side of the *juste milieu*'. Boime also sees the figure of Liberty in this painting less as the representation of working-class values than as an allegory of the 'dynamic idealism' that drove the Revolution which, if anything, is more representative of a bourgeois concept of freedom (p. 257).
22. Boime analyzes the significance of the Goddess of Liberty in July Monarchy art, with a particular focus on Delacroix (*Art in an Age of Counterrevolution*, pp. 253–63).
23. *La Caricature*, 27 January 1831.
24. *La Caricature*, 3 March 1831.
25. Pears became symbolic of Louis-Philippe and his regime thanks to a series of sketches created by Philipon while he was on trial for his caricature 'Le Replâtrage', which showed the king

plastering over the traces of the July Revolution. As part of his defence at trial, Philipon claimed that any object could be made to resemble the king, including a pear, and he produced a series of drawings in which the king's head gradually becomes increasingly similar to a pear. Subsequently, pears were used widely in criticism of the king and were particularly featured in *La Caricature*. See Kerr, *Caricature and French Political Culture, 1830–1848*, p. 83.

26. See Kerr, *Caricature and French Political Culture, 1830–1848*, pp. 35–38.
27. Ibid., pp. 44–45.
28. In reality, Numa probably had little to fear because lithographers themselves were rarely prosecuted for their caricatures and the only artist working for *La Caricature* to be imprisoned was Daumier (see Kerr, *Caricature and French Political Culture, 1830–1848*, p. 39). For Philipon, by contrast, the risk was more real: printers, editors, and publishers were targeted far more often than artists, and Philipon was prosecuted sixteen times between February 1831 and August 1832. As Kerr explains, the majority of these cases were acquitted and he was only convicted three times. He did, however, spend thirteen months in prison on account of his publications and was fined 10,000 francs (*Caricature and French Political Culture, 1830–1848*, p. 81).
29. Boime points out the significance of Liberty's partial nudity in Delacroix's painting: '[Liberty's] exposed breasts stem from the revolutionary visual vocabulary that identified partial nudity with candor and commitment' (*Art in an Age of Counterrevolution*, p. 256).
30. Philipon, *Le Journal amusant: journal illustré, journal d'images, journal comique, critique, satirique, etc.*, 28 September 1861, p. 7.
31. The use of pornography to express a political opinion was not new in France at this time and had enjoyed a particular vogue during the Revolution of the late eighteenth century, when Marie Antoinette was often the subject of such images. Lynn Hunt examines this in her chapter 'Pornography and the French Revolution', in *The Invention of Pornography: Obscenity and the Origins of Modernity, 1500–1800*, ed. by Lynn Hunt (New York: Zone Books, 1883), pp. 301–39, where she states: 'Politically motivated pornography helped to bring about the Revolution by undermining the legitimacy of the ancien regime as a social and political system' (p. 301).
32. Boime, *Art in an Age of Counterrevolution*, p. 324.

— 6 —

'Grâces sataniques':
Laughter, Redemption, and
Poetic Self-Awareness in *Les Fleurs du mal*

Kate Etheridge

In *Les Fleurs du mal*, Baudelaire's spiritual perspective is nearly always pessimistic.
From his opening poem, 'Au lecteur', Baudelaire presents evil as a force that penetrates the whole of human life, entering not only our souls but also our bodies. We cannot divorce ourselves from the crowd of demons that revels in our brains, 'serré, fourmillant, comme un million d'helminthes', nor avoid breathing in 'la Mort dans nos poumons' (ll. 21, 23).[1] Across the collection, it is equally impossible to divorce Baudelaire's religious preoccupations from his poetry as a whole.[2] However, as Jonathan Culler notes, literary criticism has tended to marginalize this aspect of Baudelaire's writing, particularly dismissing his interest in the devil and the demonic as 'something mistakenly appended to this quintessentially modern poetry'.[3] A more holistic approach to *Les Fleurs du mal* reveals the extent to which Baudelaire's ironic poetic perspective, a central tenet of his modernity, is intimately connected to his religious standpoint.

Baudelaire's religious pessimism cannot be fully reconciled with any traditional Christian narrative. Joseph Acquisto uses this premise to argue that Baudelaire's work establishes 'a continuum between Christianity and atheism'.[4] This echoes Damian Catani's contention that for Baudelaire evil has both secular and religious origins, at times resulting from 'human perversity' and at others from 'divine agency'.[5] For both Acquisto and Catani, Baudelaire interweaves two opposing perspectives on religion into his poetry. This form of doubling aptly reflects his position on the threshold separating tradition and modernity. Baudelaire neither strictly adheres to Catholicism, nor fully embraces secularism. Instead he adapts a Christian framework to suit the uncomfortable sense of disorder that characterizes modern life.

Acquisto suggests that Baudelaire achieves this 'shift away from traditional Christianity' not through 'an affirmation of secularism but rather [through] the removal of redemption [...] as a conceptual or actual possibility'.[6] In *Les Fleurs du mal*, the traditional Catholic notion of divine grace is never presented as an attainable reality. This is because evil is deeply embedded in Baudelaire's vision of human experience and, as a result of original sin, no human being can be elevated to a state of absolute purity. Even God is fallible. In *Journaux intimes*, Baudelaire asks: 'Qu'est-ce que la chute? Si c'est l'unité devenue dualité, c'est Dieu qui a chuté' (I, 688). The Fall, in destabilizing the coherent order and unity of Creation, thus represents not only man's downfall but also that of God. In poems such as 'Les Litanies de Satan' (I: 124–25), God appears as both wrathful and avaricious, banishing man from Paradise (ll. 43–44) and jealously hiding precious gems in secret corners of the earth (ll. 19–20). Jesus, meanwhile, is shown in 'Le Reniement de Saint-Pierre' to be so passive as to deserve St Peter's denial. Furthermore, he never appears to be capable of redeeming the sins of humanity.

With the possibility of redemption effectively precluded, Baudelaire instead suggests that humanity can find partial consolation in other quarters. The most striking example of this appears in 'L'Irrémédiable' (I: 79–80), where Baudelaire depicts humanity in the process of a never-ending fall into damnation. The final stanzas of the poem suggest that the only relief afforded to the individual in his otherwise relentless suffering is self-awareness:

> Un phare ironique, infernal
> Flambeau des grâces sataniques,
> Soulagement et gloire uniques,
> — La conscience dans le Mal! (ll. 37–40)

The idea of self-awareness as a form of consolation is central to both Baudelaire's poetry and the criticism that it has inspired. However, the terms used to describe it in this poem merit closer attention. Awareness is the Devil's beacon: Satan, and not God, is the sole bringer of light in 'L'Irrémédiable'. His is a torch of 'grâces sataniques', a phrase that Peter Broome describes as a 'troubling oxymoronic pairing', continuing the oppositions of darkness and light offered in the penultimate stanza but developing them 'on a plane more challenging and far-reaching than the merely visual'.[7] In his otherwise extensive analysis of the poem, Broome does not elaborate on the specific tensions at work here. Appearing at the climax of a poem that enumerates the various ways in which mankind has fallen from divine grace, the concept of satanic grace is blasphemous, ironic, and highly suggestive.

In a poetic universe that rejects the possibility of redemption, it can be argued that the satanic grace of 'la conscience dans le Mal' acts as the only means by which Baudelaire's poetic subject can seek solace, albeit of a partial, tainted kind. This disrupts the usual trajectory of grace, which facilitates the ascension of the soul to heaven, since it offers no movement towards a higher plane. Furthermore, satanic grace is predicated on the subject's sense of self rather than on the self-effacement necessary, in Simone Weil's estimation, for the entry of God's grace into the human soul.[8] Instead, the subject is given a privileged insight into his own wretchedness. By the grace of Satan, he is shown that he can never be saved. This restricted and perverse form of redemption leaves the subject in a position of stasis, for while it enables a self-reflexive worldview that raises him above the condition of bestial ignorance, it cannot ultimately reverse his fallen state. Like the 'navire pris dans le pôle | Comme en un piège de cristal' (ll. 25–26), Baudelaire's subject is trapped, frozen in the very act of falling. He is both too human ever to be redeemed and too conscious of the fact ever fully to be damned.

Within 'L'Irrémédiable', the broader effects of this satanic grace are deceptively ambiguous. Awareness within evil provides humanity with its 'soulagement et gloire uniques'; the adjective here encourages the reader to pair the two concepts, thus masking the important distinction between them. The idea that awareness is comforting suggests that it is a gift bestowed on man by a secondary party (in this instance, through Satan's grace). However, the competing notion that awareness is glorious suggests that it is a personal achievement of which man can be proud. The difference between the two concepts is of fundamental importance in our interpretation of 'la conscience dans le Mal': awareness is at once a faculty bestowed on man by Satan and an impressive product of human agency. Humanity may also feel pride at its achievement in developing awareness. In this case, the phrase invites further questions: does this sense of pride, in itself a sin, have satanic or human roots? The final stanza of 'L'Irrémédiable' questions the fundamental basis of human agency, highlighting ambiguities that have significant implications for our understanding of the rest of *Les Fleurs du mal* and its treatment of sin and self-awareness.

Baudelaire explores the themes of self-awareness, sin, and agency through numerous tropes. For instance, they are manifest in the recurrence of mirroring in his poetry, as well as in his broader treatment of seeing and blindness. They are also apparent in Baudelaire's conception of laughter, a theme that serves as a useful case study for exploring the concept of satanic grace, particularly given that it has received relatively little critical attention. This oversight has persisted despite both the numerous examples of laughter within the *œuvre* and the publication of Baudelaire's 'De l'essence du rire' two years before the first edition of *Les Fleurs du mal*. 'De l'essence du rire' explores the psychology of laughter and its place within the arts. Here, laughter is intimately connected with the corruption of postlapsarian humanity, since 'le comique' represents 'un des plus clairs signes sataniques de l'homme et un des nombreux pépins contenus dans la pomme symbolique' (II: 530). However, both in this essay and in Baudelaire's poetry, it becomes clear that although laughter symbolizes wretchedness, it is not without its own saving graces.

The theories of 'De l'essence du rire' interweave laughter with the notion of man's superiority, describing it as:

> À la fois signe d'une grandeur infinie et d'une misère infinie, misère infinie relativement à l'Être absolu dont il possède la conception, grandeur infinie relativement aux animaux. C'est du choc perpétuel de ces deux infinis que se dégage le rire. (II: 532)

In this Pascalian formulation, laughter is the sign of man's trapped position between the divine and the base. Although here humanity believes itself to be superior to animals, elsewhere in 'De l'essence du rire' Baudelaire extends this to include other human beings. Laughter, he argues, is an involuntary spasm provoked by 'la vue du malheur d'autrui', but it has deeper roots in 'un certain orgueil inconscient' in the mind of the laughing man. Humanity laughs because it believes that it would never find itself in the situation of its victim (II: 530, 531). However, an awareness of our shared condition as fallen sinners undercuts such a notion. This is 'la conscience dans le Mal', depicted as a guiding beacon for the fallen man in 'L'Irrémédiable'. In this poem, we observe precisely the tension between inexorable moral degradation and elevated awareness that produces laughter, which surges forth suddenly from the depths of the dichotomous split within man. 'L'Irrémédiable' and 'De l'essence du rire' expose doubled tensions between superiority and inferiority and between pride and humility, both of which play a crucial role in the aesthetic and moral structures underpinning Baudelaire's poetry.

In Baudelaire's poetic universe, laughter can be used to blur hierarchies of superiority, since all who laugh are also the potential target of mockery. This mockery at times acts as a spur to action on behalf of the maligned party, leading to further hierarchical reversals. Humanity grapples with itself in a constant, introspective struggle in which notions of superiority are shown to be subjective and perhaps fundamentally flawed.[9] However, the lingering ambiguity in 'De l'essence du rire' regarding the truth of this superiority complicates our understanding of it. Implicit in Baudelaire's thinking is the idea that aware human beings are superior to those who, either out of sheer ignorance or misguided piety, cannot detect their own bestial, fallen state.

This is paradoxical, since superiority would then emerge from an acknowledgement of one's own degraded position. James Hiddleston compares this paradox to that of the motivation behind philanthropic acts:

> Good deeds engender conceit and self-satisfaction, but my awareness of that can never free me totally from pride, since my admission that my motive is tinged with imperfection becomes in turn a cause of pride and superiority over those who are not similarly aware [...], and the process can repeat itself in an endless descending spiral of superiority and imperfection.[10]

The complexities and contradictions of this are inherent in the laughter of Baudelaire's poetic figures. Although laughter is the product of a sense of superiority, the laughing man's simultaneous awareness of his flaws triggers his pride, leading to a resurgence of his superiority in a subtle power play. The dual notions of pride and self-knowledge are intimately connected to Satan, both in his proud rebellion against God and in his temptation of Adam and Eve with the prospect of acquiring God's knowledge. If for Baudelaire pride is a curse that Satan inflicted on mankind, self-awareness seems to have been his gift, producing the ever-oscillating uncertainties that characterize human experience in *Les Fleurs du mal*.

Although all of humanity supposedly laughs out of some sense of awareness, this awareness does not seem to be evenly distributed. In 'La Fausse Monnaie', the speaker remarks that 'le plus irréparable des vices est de faire le mal par bêtise', whereas in 'Le Joueur généreux' we are told that 'la plus belle des ruses du diable est de vous persuader qu'il n'existe pas' (I: 324, 327). These examples suggest that humanity still suffers from a lack of awareness, as some individuals remain incapable of understanding either the malignity of their actions, or its potentially satanic root. It may be that all of humanity instinctively knows itself to be fallen, but for Baudelaire satanic grace gives only a select few the self-awareness truly to comprehend this on a conscious level. The contemptuous mockery of the less aware individual is a theme that recurs throughout *Les Fleurs du mal*. Baudelaire's use of laughter in this collection complicates the analyses that appear in 'De l'essence du rire' and further reinforces the ambiguities latent within it.

The ignorance of those who lack awareness is repeatedly lampooned throughout the *œuvre* by the nameless *je-poète*, the figure whose emotions and responses determine the tone of each section of the work. This speaking figure is in many ways Baudelaire's archetypal laughing man, deriding those he considers less aware than himself while also conscious of his own flaws, which make him the target of mockery. However, this is twisted somewhat by the reader's emotional investment in him throughout the collection, which skews the reception of his laughter and the laughter directed towards him. The alignment of the poet with the reader, established from the very first address in 'Au lecteur', arguably leads us to sympathize with his sense of artistic superiority, which seems to survive the frequent derision directed towards it. In 'De l'essence du rire', Baudelaire declares:

> Ce n'est point l'homme qui tombe qui rit de sa propre chute, à moins qu'il ne soit un philosophe, un homme qui ait acquis, par habitude, la force de se dédoubler rapidement et d'assister comme spectateur désintéressé aux phénomènes de son *moi*. (II: 532)

Baudelaire's poetry demonstrates that the speaking *je-poète* has attained a similar ability to view himself from the outside. As a result, he is subject to Hiddleston's 'endless descending spiral of superiority and imperfection'; the speaker is ultimately convinced of his own superior status as an aware artist, simultaneously proud of and anguished by the knowledge of his own fallibility. While at times it appears that the speaker uses laughter either to assert his superiority over others or to engage in processes of self-degradation, his ironic perspective and his references to other laughing figures mean that these self-assessments are frequently ambiguous. In order to interpret the speaker's relationship with sin, laughter, and self-awareness, it is necessary to examine some of the contexts in which laughter appears in *Les Fleurs du mal*.

The presumed superiority inherent in laughter means that its somewhat unhinged echoes can be felt throughout Baudelaire's satanic poetry. Debarati Sanyal suggests that for Baudelaire 'laughter signals a lucidity purchased at the cost of faith in all representations of absolute authority'.[11] The rejection of God's power is committed with laughter because it has its roots in the sin of pride, making it fundamentally satanic. Indeed, in 'L'Imprévu' (I: 172), Baudelaire shows Satan to be a laughing figure. Here, he ridicules mankind's bad faith and lack of awareness in assuming that it can continue its acts of evil and delay repentance until the final hour:

> Chacun de vous m'a fait un temple dans son cœur;
> Vous avez, en secret, baisé ma fesse immonde!
> Reconnaissez Satan à son rire vainqueur,
> Enorme et laid comme le monde! (ll. 25–28)

Through triumphant laughter, Satan, punished for the ultimate act of hubris, now reigns over humanity and mocks its never-ending conceit. However, despite vanquishing humanity with his laughter, through it Satan also emphasizes his connections with mankind's plight. While man's heart is dedicated to the worship of Satan, the world around him reflects satanic attributes in its ugliness and impurity. These shared flaws undermine Satan's sense of superiority, and yet his awareness of the fact gives him the upper hand. Satan is thus trapped in the same never-ending vortex as humanity, alternately elevated and degraded by his self-awareness and pride.

The dynamics of power in this poem become more complex when we consider that the speaking voice is shared between numerous different characters, including the Devil, the clock, Harpagon, Célimène, and various representations of human attitudes to virtue and sin. Because the poem's perspective is fractured, the *je-poète* of the text — the only first-person figure whose words do not appear as direct speech in *guillemets* — is relatively marginalized. However, his perspective influences the overall tenor of the poem. As the figure that brings together the other characters' snippets of speech, he directs the poem's moral argument. His sole appearance, in the fourth stanza of the text, is therefore particularly significant:

> Mieux que tous je connais certain voluptueux
> Qui bâille nuit et jour, et se lamente, et pleure,
> Répétant, l'impuissant et le fat, 'Oui, je veux
> Etre vertueux, dans une heure!' (ll. 13–16)

Although the stanza predominantly focuses on the description of people burdened by ennui and who continuously delay a life of virtue, its first line reveals the importance of awareness for the speaker. Claiming to know these people better than anyone else, he links himself with their fate while simultaneously highlighting the broader and more complex view of sin that elevates him above the rest of humanity. While such people are described as blind, deaf, and fragile, consumed by evil like a wall infested with an insect that hollows it out (ll. 19–20), the speaker is able to hear not only their excuses but also the warnings of the Devil and the ticking clock.

In this stanza, the speaker imitates Satan in reminding mankind of its hypocrisy while simultaneously demonstrating that he shares its plight. The speaker knows these sinners 'mieux que tous' partially because he is a fellow victim of ennui. Both Satan and, through his grace, the speaker are cursed with a level of pride and self-awareness that situates them above the common man without ultimately being able to transcend his fate. In their shared perspicacity, the speaker and the Devil perversely take on God-like powers of omniscience, an idea that is reinforced by references to the Black Mass and the 'ciboire' used for a satanic communion (ll. 22–24). The description of Satan as a kind of god continues in the eighth stanza, when he directly addresses the sinners, implicating the reader along with them by echoing the collection's opening poem, with its 'hypocrite lecteur':

> Avez-vous donc pu croire, hypocrites surpris,
> Qu'on se moque du maître, et qu'avec lui l'on triche,
> Et qu'il soit naturel de recevoir deux prix,
> D'aller au Ciel et d'être riche? (ll. 29–32)

The identity of the 'maître' here is uncertain. The Devil seems to refer to God, whom the sinners attempt to hoodwink in order to be rewarded both in heaven and on earth. However, the word might equally apply to Satan himself, who, like God, can see through humanity's ruses and has the power to punish those who attempt to evade him. The second of these theories seems more likely given that in the following stanzas the Devil tells the sinners that they must follow him towards a palace made of universal sin. He describes them as 'compagnons de [s]a triste joie' (l. 36), a paradoxical phrase that recalls the dual nature of laughter and also stresses the intimate bond between man and *maître*.

After this prolonged evocation of mankind's sin and damnation, the final stanzas of the poem appear to offer one of the rare examples of redemption in *Les Fleurs du mal*. As soon as the Devil has finished his triumphant speech, the poem undercuts his pride. From the depths of hell, the scene switches to the very highest point in the universe, where angels play trumpets to honour those who willingly accept God's punishment (ll. 43–44):

> Le son de la trompette est si délicieux,
> Dans ces soirs solennels de célestes vendanges,
> Qu'il s'infiltre comme une extase dans tous ceux
> Dont elle chante les louanges. (ll. 49–52)

In this closing stanza the sound of the trumpet, the symbol of Judgement Day, certainly brings comfort to those who believe that their torment is a just penalty imposed by a prudent God. However, on closer inspection, it is not certain that these self-aware sinners ever achieve full salvation. Instead, their reward, or perhaps their punishment, is simply to hear the glorious sound of praise infiltrating their minds, descending from a heaven that may remain forever inaccessible. The poem ends before these souls can be redeemed — indeed, the transcendence implied in the word 'extase' is deferred because it is contained within a simile — and we are left in a position of never-ending stasis. Trapped in limbo, these souls are unable fully to ascend to heaven and must eternally endure the pain that comes with their awareness of its unreachable existence.

At this stage of the poem, the speaker's viewpoint is uncertain. However, it is significant that his overview of the human spectrum of sin and hope ends so inconclusively, preventing the moment of salvation from taking place. This is reminiscent of 'Bénédiction' (I: 7–9), where the poet, the despised object of ridicule of the rest of humanity, declares his faith in God after a lifetime of punishment on earth. In both 'Bénédiction' and 'L'Imprévu', the declaration of faith hangs suspended at the end of the poem, since God never appears to reject or reward it in a decisive manner. Indeed, the very notion of faith relies on man's unwavering belief even when God's existence is unproven; the believer must dispel any doubts from his mind that he might be the victim of an elaborate cosmic joke.

This sense of doubt and even paranoia is present at numerous points in *Les Fleurs du mal*. In 'Les Sept Vieillards' (I: 88), the speaker suspects himself to be the victim of a cruel joke as seven spectral men move towards him: 'À quel complot infâme étais-je donc en butte, | Ou quel méchant hasard ainsi m'humiliait?' (ll. 33–34). Addressing the reader, he cautions anyone who laughs at his panic:

> Que celui-là qui rit de mon inquiétude
> Et qui n'est pas saisi d'un frisson fraternel
> Songe bien que malgré tant de décrépitude
> Ces sept monstres hideux avaient l'air éternel! (ll. 37–40)

In other words, the man mocking the speaker's distress may one day find himself in a similar situation, since these nightmarish figures are destined to haunt humanity eternally. Here, the reader is both the laughing man and the possible subject of this cruel cosmic joke. As the torturer and the potential victim, the reader is closer to the speaker in spirit than he might wish to be. However, his laughter is not fully self-aware until the speaker reminds him of his vulnerability. By turning the reader's laughter on its head and exposing the fragility of his position, the speaker takes on Satan's duties in revealing the hypocrisies of mankind.

The speaker's fear of a cruel and mocking cosmos is realized when Baudelaire explores the possibility of a vindictive God in 'Le Reniement de Saint Pierre' (I: 121–22). Here it is God and not Satan who meets suffering with laughter. In this blasphemous poem, God is depicted as a 'tyran gorgé de viande et de vins' (l. 3), listening to the cries of martyrs and torture victims with detached enjoyment but failing to intervene on their behalf. This includes Christ:

> — Ah! Jésus, souviens-toi du Jardin des Olives!
> Dans ta simplicité tu priais à genoux
> Celui qui dans son ciel riait au bruit des clous
> Que d'ignobles bourreaux plantaient dans tes chairs vives.
> (ll. 9–12)

Here, God has become a sadist. His piercing laughter reverberates in heaven and prefigures the nails that will penetrate Jesus's flesh during his crucifixion. The internal rhyme of 'priais' with 'riait' poignantly reveals how the supplication of the Son is met with the Father's derision, while the assonance of the stanza's third line evokes the connection between laughter and the infliction of pain. As Pierre Emmanuel notes, here Baudelaire portrays 'a fallen God, since he laughs. No more than man, God is not without loss: in the cosmic drama, Jesus alone is innocent, and thereby, precisely, absurd; he can save neither man, nor God'.[12] Indeed, this notion of Jesus's absurdity recalls his inability to laugh in 'De l'essence du rire': 'Aux yeux de Celui qui sait tout et qui peut tout, le comique n'est pas. Et pourtant le Verbe Incarné a connu la colère, il a même connu les pleurs' (II: 527). Laughter is established here as something beyond the framework of Jesus's comprehension.[13] The verb *connaître* and the ironic description of Jesus as all-knowing and all-powerful almost seem to suggest that humanity is in this sense superior to Him. Even though the speaker in 'Le Reniement de Saint Pierre' lauds his 'immense Humanité' (l. 16), Jesus's inability to laugh means that he is forever barred from a fundamental human experience. Of course, this also demonstrates how man's false sense of superiority pervades the speaking voice in 'De l'essence du rire' and produces paradoxes, for in this interpretation, man's fallen status would enable him to triumph over the divine.

God, meanwhile, takes on numerous human and even satanic attributes in 'Le

Reniement de Saint Pierre', seemingly suffering from the ennui that Baudelaire depicts as the cornerstone of evil in 'Au lecteur'. As a laughing figure, he both revels in his sense of superiority over Jesus and implicitly acknowledges that this perspective is flawed, perhaps because Jesus is God's own bodily manifestation on earth. Baudelaire's God is a self-torturer in a similar vein to the speaker in 'L'Héautontimorouménos'. His laughter also suggests that he senses both his 'grandeur infinie' and 'misère infinie' (II: 532), and yet to whom would God be inferior? If Baudelaire's laughing God has become an echo of mankind and Satan, with their many flaws, we are left with a ceaseless and unstable mirroring in which no party conclusively gains the moral upper hand. God, Satan, and man echo each other in their manic laughter, and, at the heart of religion, God's wholeness is irreparably fractured. His capacity to redeem mankind also seems weakened by his unwillingness or inability to intervene in earthly affairs.

In 'Le Reniement de Saint Pierre', God and Jesus are united by their inertia. Indeed, the speaker applauds St Peter's denial of Jesus because of his decline into this inactive state. Once capable of whipping the 'vils marchands' trading in God's temple (l. 26), Jesus is now the victim, like mankind, of what Acquisto calls 'the inoperativity of stasis'.[14] God also appears to be lethargic and passive. In his laughter, he reacts to the world but does not appear to shape it. As such, the poem implicitly calls for action from another quarter. In 'L'Imprévu', Satan plays this role as the active punisher of mankind, doing his duty in forcing humanity to understand its moral decrepitude. He also engages with humanity in 'Les Litanies de Satan', offering his teachings and words of comfort to those exiled from Paradise. In this sense he is analogous to the poet of *Les Fleurs du mal*, who, by satanic grace, is able to perceive and communicate to the reader the moral flaws that plague both mankind and God.

Although resigned to the same fate as the rest of humanity, both the poet and the Devil are able to seek solace in their ability to transcend and interpret their own condition. In this endeavour, the poet shows himself to be capable of self-mockery, a perspective that, as we have seen in 'De l'essence du rire', is the preserve of the philosopher. In certain poems, this self-mockery appears in the laughter of other figures, including the speaker's mistresses. In 'La Béatrice' (I: 116–17), the poet-speaker caricatures himself through the cruel laughter of his mistresses and of a troop of demons, who vividly depict him as a would-be Romantic and even explicitly refer to him as a caricature. The poem begins with a moment of self-mockery that pre-empts this depiction, as the speaker wanders through barren lands, making a complaint to nature and engaging in a process of introspection:

> Comme je me plaignais un jour à la nature,
> Et que de ma pensée, en vaguant au hasard,
> J'aiguisais lentement sur mon cœur le poignard,
> Je vis en plein midi descendre sur ma tête
> Un nuage funèbre et gros d'une tempête,
> Qui portait un troupeau de démons vicieux. (ll. 2–7)

It is significant that, immediately before the speaker sees the troupe of demons, he describes himself as whetting the knife of his thoughts on his heart. This ambiguous metaphor appears to suggest a form of cerebral sharpening at the expense of the speaker's emotions. In an act of self-torture, the speaker directs his thoughts inwards and exposes himself to the scathing critique that the demons are soon to unleash. Given that they descend on his head, we may interpret these demons as a purely mental manifestation of the speaker's self-awareness. In this scenario, the demons become the embodiment of satanic grace, enabling the speaker to adopt this self-reflexive position.

The demons' laughter strengthens this idea, since for Baudelaire laughter indicates a divided self. Shortly afterwards, the speaker reports the demons' speech:

> — 'Contemplons à loisir cette caricature
> Et cette ombre d'Hamlet imitant sa posture,
> Le regard indécis et les cheveux au vent.' (ll. 13–15)

The physical description of the speaker, offered here at one remove, provokes the laughter of beings that seem to believe that he is a second-rate poet. If we interpret this as the poet's view of himself, the description becomes a grotesque mirror image recalling the 'cœur devenu son miroir' in 'L'Irrémédiable' (l. 34). Within this verbal mirror, the speaker sees a doubled shadow reflecting his real self as a mere copy of a theatrical character. The demons also describe him as 'ce bon vivant, | Ce gueux, cet histrion en vacances, ce drôle' (ll. 16–17), designations that paint him as both a vaguely shambolic entertainer and an outright impostor.

Even as they torment him, the demons are amused by the poet's attempts to peddle his talents in order to move them to pity. They describe themselves as the 'auteurs de ces vieilles rubriques' (l. 21), a phrase that invites two possible readings: are the demons referring to their cruel caricature of the poet here, or are they describing themselves as the authors of his performative tricks? The latter interpretation reinforces the demons' role as representations of the speaker's consciousness. In this case, they would be closely connected to the poet's creative process, and therefore would be entertained by his attempts to hoodwink them, since they already know him to be a fraud. Both interpretations are possible, and together they reveal that trickery is the main connection between the speaker and the demons. Richard D. E. Burton comments that because of this 'the "spectators" [i.e., the demons] are themselves "actors," and ham-actors, charlatans, tricksters at that [...]. Everyone in "La Béatrice" is a fake, a fraud, a *saltimbanque*'.[15] Given this, we cannot take the demons' description to be wholly accurate, and yet the speaker's account of the scene has also been called into question. As representatives of the speaker's self-directed derision, the demons verbalize his doubts about his poetic worth and originality.

After the demons have finished their caricature, the speaker reasserts his pride in a manner that both contrasts with their contemptible view of him and simultaneously continues his self-parody through hyperbole:

> J'aurais pu (mon orgueil aussi haut que les monts
> Domine la nuée et le cri des démons)
> Détourner simplement ma tête souveraine. (ll. 23–25)

Here the speaker gives the impression that he believes himself to be superior to the demons, yet the statement in parentheses is more acutely self-aware. The same can be said when the speaker's mistress finally appears among the demons, and the poet complains that this outrage 'n'a pas fait chanceler le soleil' (l. 27). Referring back to his initial attempts to move the world by recounting his plight, here the poet comically emphasizes his inability to interest the vast, indifferent landscape in his individual fate.

The arrival of the speaker's mistress, with her laughter and humiliating sexual betrayal, represents a blow from which the poet cannot recover. He describes her, standing among the demons, as:

> La reine de mon cœur au regard nonpareil
> Qui riait avec eux de ma sombre détresse
> Et leur versait parfois quelque sale caresse. (ll. 28–30)

In these lines, the mistress confirms the truth of the speaker's self-doubt, which is embodied in the demons, by joining in with their laughter. The speaker might have been able to master his own self-criticism, but this betrayal — his beloved reflecting his darkest ideas about himself — ultimately provokes the erosion of his identity. Baudelaire indicates the power play between the mistress and the speaker by returning to the conflict between the head and the heart, the very dynamic that announces the demons' arrival in ll. 3–4. While earlier on in the poem, the heart suffered at the expense of the head, which tortured it in order to sharpen its perceptions and thoughts, here the heart takes its revenge. Before his mistress appeared, the poet would have turned his proud 'tête souveraine' away from the scene, but he is thwarted by the 'reine de [s]on cœur'. The poet's head, the locus of his intellect, is no longer the ruling power. Instead, the queen of his heart echoes his self-mockery and in doing so prevents him from remaining immune to its painful effects.

The mistress's echoed laughter instigates the implosion of the speaker's self-belief. It is therefore significant that the title of Baudelaire's poem links her with Dante's muse, a figure who often represents the promise of salvation.[16] Baudelaire's mistress is an ironically cruel copy of Dante's Beatrice. She is incapable of leading the poet to redemption in any traditional sense, instead colluding with his demons to facilitate the satanic grace of self-awareness. Seeing his myriad flaws reflected in her laughter, the poet is unable either to turn away or to continue to shape his own narrative. Like the damned man only partially redeemed by self-awareness, the speaker is frozen in a moment of contemplation, unable to act. As such, the poem's ending hangs in suspense, caught between movement and stasis.[17]

This agonizing immobility is a dominant feature of 'L'Héautontimorouménos' (I: 78–79), a poem that suspends the speaker between a series of opposing dualities. Unlike 'La Béatrice', this is a poem that initially attempts to assert the speaker's active dominance through his violent sadism directed towards an unspecified addressee. However, this violence is only ever potential; the speaker fantasizes about performing different acts in the future tense, but when describing himself in the present tense, he is singularly inactive. Although he is the passive object of exterior forces — most notably irony, which shakes and bites him — the speaker is only ever the subject of the verb *être* in the present tense. As such, he is defined by static modes of being that suggest no other movement than the oscillation between their internal contradictions. Like the poet in 'La Béatrice', the speaker in 'L'Héautontimorouménos' is frozen by self-inflicted torment.

In the poem's opening stanzas, Baudelaire introduces biblical references, comparing his desire to strike the addressee with Moses striking the rock (ll. 1–3). This is an intriguing parallel, particularly given that Moses strikes the rock on two separate occasions in the Bible (Exodus 17:5–6 and Numbers 20:8). On the first occasion, God instructs Moses to strike the rock at Horeb, causing water to flow from it to quench the thirst of the people. On the second occasion, God orders Moses to speak to the rock in order to make water flow, but instead Moses strikes it twice. After his second stroke, water does indeed flow, but God punishes Moses for his disobedience by preventing him from entering the Promised Land. As Johnson Lim Teng Kok argues, Moses's decision to strike the rock twice suggests his belief that human force, rather than divine grace, will bring forth the water. He also demonstrates a lack of faith in the power of the spoken word to perform the miracle. Furthermore, Moses speaks to the congregation before striking the rock in terms that suggest that the miracle is a human achievement rather than a gift from God: 'Et ayant assemblé le peuple devant la pierre, il leur dit: Ecoutez, rebelles et incrédules: Pourrons-nous faire sortir de l'eau de cette pierre?' (Numbers 20:10).[18] When Baudelaire associates his speaker's violent fantasies with Moses, we cannot be sure whether he is alluding to the smiting of the rock as an obedient or a disobedient act. The latter seems more in keeping with the tone of the poem, although the ambivalence between the two is important, since it contributes to the irony of the first stanza. Like Moses, the speaker is punished, although in this case he has not yet acted on his desires. In his imagined future, the speaker replaces the rock with a human body and strikes it in order to conjure forth tears that will perform the same healing and redeeming function as the water sent by God for the Israelites. However, for the speaker, just as for Moses, this presumption of control over his own fate and the manipulation of other people's suffering in order to bolster his sense of power ultimately preclude the possibility of redemption.

Indeed, after his description of his planned actions, the speaker asks:

> Ne suis-je pas un faux accord
> Dans la divine symphonie,
> Grâce à la vorace Ironie
> Qui me secoue et qui me mord? (ll. 13–16)

This reference to the divine symphony suggests the harmonious nature of God's creation, which clashes with the poet's desires. However, the fact that he refers to himself as a 'faux accord' rather than a false note indicates the inherent multiplicity of his identity, which jars with both the divine symphony and with itself. The speaker's sense of himself as a 'faux accord' is ostensibly the product of the disjunction between his violent intentions towards the unknown victim and the reality of his paralyzing self-mortification. Desiring sadistic action but unable to act, the speaker contravenes both God's teachings and his own wishes, even though they contradict each other.

The irony of the poet's situation is described as both an internal and an external phenomenon. Initially, it shakes and bites him, indicating its existence outside his body, but then it surges from within, in the poet's voice and as a black poison in his blood (ll. 15–18). Irony thus permeates the poet in the way that sin infects the human organs in 'Au lecteur'. Sin and irony are deeply connected, since to perceive the world ironically is to perceive disjunctions and mismatches within God's supposedly harmonious creation. This includes the splits and divisions within the speaker's psyche, which are a product of fallen humanity's pride and disobedience. The awareness of these divisions sparks the list of opposing dualities in the final stanzas:

> Je suis la plaie et le couteau!
> Je suis le soufflet et la joue!
> Je suis les membres et la roue,
> Et la victime et le bourreau!
>
> Je suis de mon cœur le vampire,
> — Un de ces grands abandonnés
> Au rire éternel condamnés
> Et qui ne peuvent plus sourire! (ll. 21–28)

Here Baudelaire continues to depict the ironic, self-aware sinner as a sadomasochist.

The tortuous tension between pleasure and pain inherent in the sadomasochist's experience is also inherent in the laughing man, who derives pleasure from the despair of others and yet in turn recognizes his own wretchedness. The poetic self is therefore not merely split: it is also aware of its duality. However, the poet goes one step further than his fellow men in verbally engaging with his own metaphysical condition, for he is also the analyzer of trauma through language.

The use of one masculine and one feminine noun in each line of the penultimate stanza highlights the disjointed, contradictory factions warring within the poetic self. The dash in l. 26 signifies a subtle change in perspective. The poet views himself with detachment, much like the philosopher in 'De l'essence du rire', and summarizes his own plight. The concept that he is 'un de ces grands abandonnés' connects him with the rest of the damned, yet the speaker distinguishes himself from the common herd of humanity by framing his tortured condition as one of grandiose tragedy. The idea that the rest of mankind shares the poet's fate is somewhat subordinate to the specifically individual nature of his complaint, seen also in the insistent anaphora of the penultimate stanza, with its repeated first person pronouns. Setting himself subtly above and beyond those who, as he is well aware, share his own condition, the poet asserts a superiority that is a paradoxical marker of his condemned hubris.

Satanic grace manifests itself in the speaker's laughter by facilitating a partial recuperation of his soul. The phrase 'grands abandonnés' suggests that the poet belongs to a group of people elevated to a state of glory even as they are abandoned and condemned. Indeed, Acquisto notes that the speaker's eternal laughter indicates the persistence of the subject's identity, which can never fully be eradicated. This is because 'the fall enacted and represented by this poem is not a fall *into* anything but rather an eternal fall'.[19] As a man condemned to eternal laughter, the speaker maintains his split selfhood throughout this never-ending fall, meaning that wholeness and purity are unobtainable. Baudelaire reiterates this in the distinction between laughter and joy, which echoes the discrepancy between the two in 'De l'essence du rire'. The poet is condemned to laugh forever — the hellish connotations of 'rire éternel' are suggestive of a maniacal laughter — and yet a smile, the sign of joyful innocence, is destined to remain out of his reach.

Laughter in *Les Fleurs du mal* is marked by these contradictions and power struggles. The poet's conscious wretchedness and his sense of superiority are prominent features of Baudelaire's verse, be it through sadism, Satanism, his disdain for humanity, or his knowing self-deprecation. An analysis of some of the instances of laughter in *Les Fleurs du mal* shows that the poet repeatedly establishes himself as existing in a sphere of isolation from the common man. Unlike the blind crowds that swarm around him, his eyes are open to the reality of the human condition, towards which he ceaselessly attempts to direct the reader. Underpinning this, however, is a second truth: namely, that the poet cannot ever truly divorce himself from his own humanity and, even as he laughingly criticizes the pride and hypocrisy of others, he himself becomes the victim of these essentially human traits. Laughter as a manifestation of satanic grace is, like many other concepts in Baudelaire's poetic universe, inherently tainted. Self-awareness is never fully attainable, pride can never fully be abandoned, and satanic grace impedes the poet's path to either divine redemption or total damnation. Art is perhaps the only way of capturing the complex contradictions in the eternal fall of the laughing man, even if it cannot facilitate the artist's transcendence. The laughter incorporated into Baudelaire's poetic universe is an expression of the poet's irreconcilable inner duality and his self-awareness, underpinning the fundamental thematic basis upon which *Les Fleurs du mal* is constructed. Through his subtle depictions of laughter, Baudelaire invites the 'hypocrite lecteur' to share in this self-awareness and to become a beneficiary of the same satanic grace that allows his poetic 'fleurs maladives' to flourish (I: 3).

Notes to Chapter 7

1. Charles Baudelaire, 'Au Lecteur', in *Œuvres complètes*, ed. by Claude Pichois, 2 vols, Bibliothèque de la Pléiade (Paris: Gallimard, 1975–76), I, 5. Further references to Baudelaire's poems and essays will be to this edition. Henceforth the volume number and page number will be given in the main body of the text.
2. See Marcel A. Ruff, *L'Esprit du mal et l'esthétique baudelairienne* (Paris: Librairie Armand Colin, 1955).
3. Jonathan Culler, 'Baudelaire's "Satanic Verses"', *Doing French Studies*, special issue of *Diacritics*, 28.3 (1998), 86–100 (p. 87).
4. Joseph Acquisto, *The Fall Out of Redemption: Writing and Thinking Beyond Salvation in Baudelaire, Cioran, Fondane, Agamben, and Nancy* (London: Bloomsbury, 2015), p. 4.
5. Damian Catani, 'Notions of Evil in Baudelaire', *The Modern Language Review*, 102.4 (2007), 990–1007 (p. 993).

6. Acquisto, *The Fall Out of Redemption*, pp. 4–5.
7. Peter Broome, *Baudelaire's Poetic Patterns: The Secret Language of 'Les Fleurs du mal'* (Amsterdam: Rodopi, 1999), pp. 447–48.
8. Simone Weil, *Gravity and Grace*, trans. by Emma Crawford and Mario von der Ruhr [1947] (London & New York: Routledge, 2004), p. 41.
9. See also Alain Vaillant, *Baudelaire: poète comique* (Rennes: Presses universitaires de Rennes, 2007), pp. 129–31.
10. J. A. Hiddleston, *Baudelaire and the Art of Memory* (Oxford: Clarendon Press, 1999), p. 111.
11. Debarati Sanyal, *The Violence of Modernity: Baudelaire, Irony, and the Politics of Form* (Baltimore, MD: John Hopkins University Press, 2006), p. 43.
12. Pierre Emmanuel, *Baudelaire: The Paradox of Redemptive Satanism*, trans. by Robert T. Cargo (Alabama: The University of Alabama Press, 1970), p. 143.
13. See also Peter L. Berger, *Redeeming Laughter: The Comic Dimension of Human Experience* (Berlin: Walter de Grutyer, 1997), p. 198.
14. Acquisto, *The Fall Out of Redemption*, p. 49.
15. Richard D. E. Burton, 'Baudelaire and Shakespeare: Literary Reference and Meaning in "Les Sept Vieillards" and "La Béatrice"', *Comparative Literature Studies*, 26.1 (1989), 1–27 (p. 15).
16. See, for instance, Charles Williams, *The Figure of Beatrice: A Study in Dante* [1943] (Cambridge: D. S. Brewer, 2000), pp. 7–8.
17. See Acquisto on the contemplation of evil as a cause of inaction in Baudelaire's poetry (*The Fall Out of Redemption*, p. 47).
18. See Johnson Lim Teng Kok, *The Sin of Moses and the Staff of God: A Narrative Approach* (Assen: Van Gorcum, 1997), pp. 146–48. All biblical quotations are taken from the 'Bible de Sacy' (*BLS*), as Baudelaire quotes from Lemaistre de Sacy's translation in *L'Art romantique*.
19. Acquisto, *The Fall Out of Redemption*, p. 111.

— 7 —
Quant au Livre de Mallarmé

Bertrand Marchal

Dire le Livre de Mallarmé est sans doute une tâche, sinon 'impossible' comme le Livre qui fit l'objet il y a quelques années d'une journée d'étude à la Bibliothèque nationale de France, du moins éminemment problématique.[1] C'est bien moins se donner un objet de discours que tenter une approche oblique, à la manière de la divagation mallarméenne (non pas 'Le Livre', mais 'Quant au Livre') en commençant par convoquer un faisceau de questions, ou d'ambiguïtés à peu près irréductibles.

Et d'abord de quoi parle-t-on quand on dit 'le Livre de Mallarmé'? Du Livre idéal dont la lettre autobiographique à Verlaine fit pour la première fois l'aveu en novembre 1885, et qui fit l'objet, en 1897, des trois divagations regroupées sous la rubrique 'Quant au livre', bref de ce livre purement virtuel rêvé comme la limite ou le point de fuite de la littérature universelle?[2] Ou du livre sinon réel, du moins partiellement réalisé, matérialisé par Jacques Scherer lorsqu'il publia en 1957, sous un titre pour le moins ambigu, *Le 'Livre' de Mallarmé*?[3]

Le 'Livre' de Mallarmé est-il donc le Livre de Mallarmé, le livre réel se confond-il avec le livre idéal? Peut-on, dans l'exposé, passer indifféremment de l'un à l'autre, quand on sait que le dossier publié par Jacques Scherer ne se compose que de deux centaines de notes préparatoires aussi sommaires que lacunaires, plus souvent numériques, en outre, que fictionnelles, alors que Mallarmé, dans sa lettre testamentaire rédigée la veille de sa mort, avait demandé à sa femme et à sa fille de brûler le 'monceau semi-séculaire de [s]es notes'?[4]

Ce Livre même, à supposer qu'il soit un, comment faut-il l'écrire? livre ou Livre? Est-ce, en d'autres termes, un livre peut-être suprême mais qui coexiste avec d'autres livres, ou le Livre unique et absolu dans lequel se fondraient idéalement tous les livres existants? On connaît la célèbre formule qui ouvre la divagation sur 'Le Livre, instrument spirituel': 'tout, au monde, existe pour aboutir à un livre',[5] quand, quelques années plus tôt, la lettre autobiographique à Verlaine faisait, non sans précaution rhétorique, le saut d'un livre au Livre:

> J'ai toujours rêvé et tenté autre chose, avec une patience d'alchimiste, prêt à y sacrifier toute vanité et toute satisfaction, comme on brûlait jadis son mobilier et les poutres de son toit, pour alimenter le fourneau du Grand Œuvre. Quoi? c'est difficile à dire: un livre, tout bonnement, en maints tomes, un livre qui soit un livre, architectural et prémédité, et non un recueil des inspirations de hazard, fussent-elles merveilleuses... J'irai plus loin, je dirai: le Livre persuadé qu'au fond il n'y en a qu'un, tenté à son insu par quiconque a écrit, même les Génies. L'explication orphique de la Terre, qui est le seul devoir du poëte et le

jeu littéraire par excellence: car le rythme même du livre alors impersonnel et vivant, jusque dans sa pagination, se juxtapose aux équations de ce rêve, ou Ode.[6]

Même saut, assorti de la même prudence rhétorique, dans 'Crise de vers':

> Plus ou moins, tous les livres, contiennent la fusion de quelques redites comptées: même il n'en serait qu'un — au monde, sa loi — bible comme la simulent des nations. La différence, d'un ouvrage à l'autre, offrant autant de leçons proposées dans un immense concours pour le texte véridique, entre les âges dits civilisés ou — lettrés.[7]

Cela n'empêche pas Mallarmé d'utiliser, sans qu'on puisse toujours y voir une intention marquée, tantôt la majuscule, tantôt la minuscule, tantôt l'article défini, tantôt l'indéfini, comme si l'idée même du livre ne pouvait, sans jamais se fixer, que se mouvoir dans cet entre-deux, qui est celui de l'idéal et du réel.

Cet objet instable ou fuyant du livre, comment peut-on tenter sinon de le fixer, du moins d'en rendre compte? Par l'analyse structurale sans doute, à laquelle invitent les notes publiées par Jacques Scherer, mais à condition de ne pas faire l'impasse sur la dimension historique ou généalogique. Le discours historique peut d'ailleurs lui-même être double, soit qu'il tente de replacer le rêve mallarméen du livre dans l'histoire de l'absolu littéraire de deux siècles de romantisme, soit, à une échelle beaucoup plus restreinte, qu'il étudie la genèse et l'évolution de l'idée du livre dans les seuls textes de Mallarmé. De ce dernier point de vue, le rêve du livre, ou plutôt de ce que Mallarmé appelle alors l'Œuvre ou le Grand Œuvre, fait son apparition en 1866 et procède par conséquent de la crise décisive du printemps de cette année-là, qui consacre la mort de Dieu et la découverte mallarméenne du néant. À cette époque, le Grand Œuvre se propose une échéance lointaine (dix ou vingt ans), mais possible. Vingt ans plus tard, quand Mallarmé fait pour la première fois, par l'intermédiaire de Verlaine, l'aveu public de son rêve, le Grand Œuvre s'appelle désormais le Livre, mais ce Livre n'est plus un projet réalisable, il n'est plus qu'une limite idéale en deçà de laquelle le poète ne peut que se tenir:

> Je réussirai peut-être; non pas à faire cet ouvrage dans son ensemble (il faudrait être je ne sais qui pour cela!) mais à en montrer un fragment d'exécuté, à en faire scintiller par une place l'authenticité glorieuse, en indiquant le reste tout entier auquel ne suffit pas une vie. Prouver par les portions faites que ce livre existe, et que j'ai connu ce que je n'aurai pu accomplir.[8]

Le 'Livre' de Mallarmé (ou bien faudrait-il dire le Livre de Jacques Scherer?) est-il un de ces fragments avortés du Livre impossible? Est-il Le Livre ou simplement un livre, ce livre avec le contenu duquel Mallarmé, à la fin de 1888, se proposait de 'jongler' dans ce qu'il appelait '[s]on grand projet mystérieux des Lectures'?[9]

À défaut de pouvoir jamais répondre avec certitude à toutes ces questions, on peut au moins postuler que les notes publiées par Jacques Scherer consonnent très évidemment avec les spéculations sur le Livre qui se lisent dans *Divagations*, ne serait-ce que parce que Le Livre, c'est-à-dire, au fond, la littérature, est sans doute le 'sujet de pensée, unique'[10] autour duquel tournent non seulement l'ensemble des 'Variations sur un sujet',[11] mais l'œuvre entière de Mallarmé, et qu'il importe peu, en fin de compte, que ces notes soient celles d'un livre ou du Livre, d'un simple fragment ou du tout, dans la mesure même où le rapport de la partie au tout, ou du livre au Livre, est pour Mallarmé un rapport d'homologie structurale.

De ce point de vue, le Livre de Mallarmé, qui inaugurait la journée susdite de la BnF sur le livre impossible sous la rubrique du 'livre total', aurait pu illustrer aussi justement chacune des autres rubriques convoquées: 'livre total', mais aussi 'livre inachevé', 'livre impossible', 'livre ruiné' (le Livre est le chef-d'œuvre inconnu, jusqu'au feu inclusivement, de Mallarmé, ce nouveau Frenhofer), 'livre sans fin', à quoi l'on pourrait d'ailleurs ajouter 'livre bombe' ou 'livre feu d'artifice': on connaît la réponse de Mallarmé au journaliste Paul Brulat qui l'interrogeait au soir de l'attentat d'Auguste Vaillant à la chambre des députés le 9 décembre 1893: 'Je ne sais pas d'autre bombe, qu'un livre'.[12]

Livre total donc, étant entendu que cette totalité n'est pas accumulative, ou encyclopédique, comme dans *La Comédie humaine* ou *La Bible de l'humanité*, mais se fonde sur une logique structurale qui se formule ainsi: le livre, 'expansion totale de la lettre', n'est rien d'autre que le 'pur ensemble groupé dans quelque circonstance fulgurante, des relations entre tout'.[13] C'est ce que Mallarmé, dans sa lettre autobiographique, appelle 'L'explication orphique de la Terre'. Cette totalité-là n'est donc pas exclusive de la brièveté, comme le suggère cette lettre à Octave Mirbeau qui n'est pas qu'une simple boutade:

> Alors, c'est embêtant, même à écrire, les articles pour la *Revue des Deux Mondes*, mon pauvre vieux cher ami: parbleu! tout ce qui ne tient pas en une phrase. L'explication de l'univers s'il y en a une, autre que l'occasion offerte de quelquefois vous serrer la main, Mirbeau, atteindrait tout juste les quarante pages d'un article de revue.[14]

Le corollaire de cette totalité structurale, c'est la logique combinatoire qui fait du Livre un objet impersonnel et mobile, un objet qui se construit dans des séances de lecture qui mettent en jeu un rituel liturgique ou théâtral, et qui se prête à une autre mobilité organisée, celle de la diffusion.

Il résulte de cette prise en compte de toutes les dimensions de l'objet livre que les notes publiées par Jacques Scherer peuvent se répartir en quatre catégories: les notes de contenu, ou notes fictionnelles; les notes concernant la structure du livre; les notes concernant le rituel des séances; les notes concernant la diffusion.

Or la logique du Livre est d'établir des correspondances entre ces quatre niveaux par des équations tantôt numériques, tantôt thématiques, tantôt génériques, de telle façon, par exemple, que les rares scénarios fictionnels ne font que thématiser les données structurales. La fable, ici, procède de la forme.

Au centre de ce dispositif apparaît celui que les notes nomment l'Opérateur, c'est-à-dire, au sens propre du mot, celui qui réalise l'œuvre (*opera*), étant entendu que l'œuvre, ici, ne préexiste pas à la lecture, n'a pas d'existence antérieure à l'opération qui la réalise. L'opérateur est donc ce mixte de l'auteur et du lecteur qui constitue l'œuvre dans le temps propre de chaque séance et sous le regard nécessaire des spectateurs. Quant à l'opération, elle joue de toutes les connotations possibles du mot: cette constitution de l'œuvre est à la fois une opération arithmétique, une opération financière, et une opération au sens chirurgical du mot.

S'il est facile de percevoir la dimension arithmétique ou la dimension financière de l'opération, la dimension chirurgicale est sans doute moins évidente, comme en témoigne ce petit relevé des occurrences du mot:

> opération
> — le Héros *dégage* — l'Hymne (maternel) qui le crée, et se restitue au Th que c'était — du Mystère où cet hymne enfoui (fol. 13 [4])
>
> *Idée*
> opérée supprimée (fol. 107 [85])
>
> Tout fonder ainsi sur une opération financière (fol. 171 [135])
>
> Défaire idée en livre
> son mécanisme opérateur là (fol. 177 [141])
>
> Le Héros dégage du Dr. l'Hymne en Mystère (Th. Idée)
> là est l'opération (fol. 206 [160])
>
> Le tout a duré trois quarts d'heure — un quart d'heure d'intervalle comme il fut d'attente au début (timbre de nouveau, lueur) et rentrée cette fois de l'opérateur rapportant le volume ainsi composé — c. à d. une opération inverse faite relativement à la deuxième partie de l'auditoire. (ff. 249 [194], 247 [192])

Pour suggérer, à défaut de montrer, l'équation qui s'établit entre les différentes dimensions de l'Opération, je me contenterai ici d'un minuscule exemple, qui aura en outre l'intérêt de rappeler une évidence trop souvent oubliée: si le Livre mallarméen est problématique, tous les commentaires qu'on a pu faire, qu'on fait et qu'on fera sont déterminés par la lecture elle-même problématique d'un manuscrit à la limite (parfois dépassée) de l'illisibilité.

Le feuillet le plus explicite sur ce que peut être, d'un point de vue non pas méta-poétique, comme dans les notes précitées, mais poétique, l'opération du Livre (au double sens, subjectif et objectif du génitif) est sans doute le feuillet 220 [169], l'un des très rares à présenter l'ébauche d'un scénario fictionnel. Voici, abstraction faite de la disposition spatiale, la lecture qu'en donne Jacques Scherer:

> Il se trouve dans un endroit-Cité-où L'exploit qui devait lui rapporter de la <u>gloire</u> <Th> dont il eût fait la fête — (noces) est un <u>crime</u> <Dr>: il s'arrête à temps en cette Opération; dont c'est un miracle que l'Invitation si bien comprise par lui, de celle qui la lui inspirait ait suffi à la dame qui la lui fit à son insu peut-être. lueur
> génie — farce
>
> mais laisser l'Invitation <ordre> sans y répondre fût-ce Non — on ne peut — alors qu'elle s'est à ce point livrée à lui est un <u>vol</u>. que cela pris
>
> et que la dame ait eu peur de ce qu'elle venait lui faire. À son insu peut-être. S'accorde. chapeau
> il la couvre en soi
> opération qui n'est
> [...]
> Invitation à <u>fête</u>
> à tout excepté au <u>repas</u> d'où sa faim. La loi se tait <mange — > n'ose se montrer telle

>   S'il est une loi c'est celle-là parce qu'on mourrait sans manger
>   elle se voile de +
>   + +
>   manger la dame
>   20 f. pour elle
>   [...]
>   Opération
>   crime   serment?
>   qui n'est ni. ni.
>   réclame suffrage
>   décoration   faillite
>   supplice
>   mais... on n'a jamais pu savoir que —
>   + chapeau éclate soleil
>   c'est clair comme le jour.

On notera que dans ce feuillet très elliptique, où l'opération s'apparente à un repas nuptial, plusieurs mots, signalés par le signe +, n'ont pu être lus par l'éditeur. Ces signes de l'échec de la lecture peuvent alors avoir un double effet: celui de jeter une suspicion généralisée sur la lisibilité de l'ensemble du feuillet, ou au contraire de créer l'illusion que, l'illisibilité étant strictement localisée, la lisibilité du reste s'en trouve en quelque sorte implicitement certifiée. Or il va de soi que les choses ne sont pas si simples, et que la frontière entre lisible et illisible est pour le moins incertaine. Pour le dire autrement, toute lecture d'un manuscrit comme celui du 'Livre' reste, pour une part non négligeable, conjecturale, avec tout ce que cela implique quant à la responsabilité de l'éditeur.

C'est pourtant une conjecture, donnée comme telle, même si je la crois certaine, que la nouvelle édition des *Œuvres complètes* de Mallarmé m'a permis de faire. Conjecture double qui concerne d'abord un même mot non lu deux fois: 'elle se voile de satin' et 'satin — chapeau éclate soleil'; qui concerne ensuite et surtout un autre mot une première fois mal lu, puis non lu: ce mot mal lu par Jacques Scherer lorsqu'il lit 'un vol. que cela pris', n'est pas un mot entier mais un mot abrégé: là où il lit 'que cela', il faut lire en fait 'pucel.' pour 'pucelage'. Le vol dont il est question est donc à lire ainsi: 'pucel[age] pris'. La même abréviation se retrouve quelques lignes plus bas, en dessous de 'elle se voile de satin': les deux mots non lus doivent se lire: 'n'est ni pucel.' Il apparaît, dans ces conditions, que cette opération n'est autre qu'une défloration symbolique, ce qui justifie la thématique nuptiale du scénario. On ne s'étonnera pas que le même mot identiquement abrégé se retrouve dans un autre ensemble de notes de Mallarmé, celui que son premier éditeur, Jean-Pierre Richard, a publié sous le titre d'*Épouser la notion*:

>   [d'un] regard il juge qu'elle n'existe pas —
>   c'est cela enlever le pucel.
>   il la veut vierge
>   non seulement vierge de tous mais vierge de lui.[15]

On ne s'étonnera pas davantage que le mot 'opération' apparaisse aussi dans *Épouser la notion*:

> il la sacrifiera [...]
> s'il le faut —
> lui ôtera
> tout — opération — [16]

rappelant ce qu'on lit sur le feuillet 107 [85] déjà cité du 'Livre': 'Idée/opérée supprimée'.

À partir du moment où le même mot d'"opération' vaut aussi bien pour la forme du livre que pour son contenu fictionnel, la même ambivalence caractérise l'abréviation du mot 'pucelage' qui apparaît non seulement dans le scénario poétique du feuillet 220 [169] mais aussi dans deux feuillets consécutifs (122 [99] et 123 [100]) qui évoquent cette fois la forme même du livre et le rituel de la lecture. Ces deux feuillets, où le mot était laissé en blanc par Jacques Scherer, se lisent ainsi:

> Les pages extérieures non jointes au milieu libre — sont les extrêmes, le plus loin qu'on puisse aller ou une feuille. elle ne peut donc pas être suivie d'une autre — elle ne peut s'il y en a d'autres que les recevoir à l'intérieur — correction — une fois tout défait — et, le pucel. même — une fois qu'on a joué sur ceci qu'il pouvait ne rien y avoir — [...]
>
> tout ce qu'il y a tiré de la feuille — en la développant — lumière ce qui en échappe — tout ce qu'il faut y voir sur ce blanc vierge en un clin d'œil. sans signe caractères
>
> on la développe — on s'arrête juste avant la grande ouverture intérieure, pucel. ou on va savoir si quelque chose (autre que tout ce qui est) ou rien.[17]

La lecture, en tant qu'elle consiste d'abord à ouvrir la feuille vierge — ce que Mallarmé appelle 'la grande ouverture intérieure' (et non 'la grande aventure intérieure' comme lisait Jacques Scherer) —, est donc proprement un dépucelage du Livre, et l'on conçoit que le scénario de noces idéales — qu'il s'agisse des *Noces d'Hérodiade*, de *L'Après-midi d'un faune*, du 'Nénuphar blanc' ou d'*Épouser la notion* — soit peut-être l'unique scénario mallarméen, avec sa double déclinaison poétique et méta-poétique, comme en témoigne cette définition de la lecture à la fin du 'Mystère dans les lettres':

> Lire —
>
> Cette pratique —
>
> Appuyer, selon la page, au blanc, qui l'inaugure son ingénuité, à soi, oublieuse même du titre qui parlerait trop haut: et, quand s'aligna, dans une brisure, la moindre, disséminée, le hasard vaincu mot par mot, indéfectiblement le blanc revient, tout à l'heure gratuit, certain maintenant, pour conclure que rien au-delà et authentiquer le silence —
>
> Virginité qui solitairement, devant une transparence du regard adéquat, elle-même s'est comme divisée en ses fragments de candeur, l'un et l'autre, preuves nuptiales de l'Idée.[18]

Cette division de la virginité, qui prélude au repli nuptial, appelle ainsi une figure privilégiée de l'hymen, celle de la déchirure du voile, qui, dans les notes du 'Livre', se réalise à deux niveaux: si dans les notes de contenu, où les noces idéales prennent la forme d'un scénario mythique, l'Idée joue les dames voilées, dans les notes de structure, qui renvoient au rituel théâtral des séances, le voile est le rideau de scène, un rideau que déchire symboliquement la musique: témoin le feuillet 33 [21], qui évoque le lieu théâtral des séances:

> l'arabesque électrique s'allume derrrière — et les deux voiles
> — sorte de déchirure sacrée du voile.[19]

En donnant à cette déchirure sexuelle et théâtrale du voile une dimension sacrée, Mallarmé rappelle évidemment que la déchirure du voile est dans le récit évangélique de la Passion le signe de la mort du Christ et plus largement, pour le XIXe siècle intellectuel, le signe de la mort de Dieu. Comparant la crise de vers à la Révolution déicide du siècle précédent, Mallarmé retrouve tout naturellement cette métaphore:

> On assiste, comme finale d'un siècle, pas ainsi que ce fut dans le dernier, à des bouleversements; mais, hors de la place publique, à une inquiétude du voile dans le temple avec des plis significatifs et un peu sa déchirure.[20]

Voilà bien la vérité moderne: derrière le voile, il n'y a plus de dieu; il n'y a rien, ou plutôt il y a ce 'Rien, qui est la vérité'.[21]

Défaire l'idée en livre, ou dépuceler la notion, c'est donc aussi, et peut-être surtout, rencontrer la mort de Dieu, et le Néant, ou ce Rien qui est la vérité. C'est d'ailleurs très exactement ce que dit Mallarmé, dans *La Musique et les lettres*, quand il avoue, au milieu de sa conférence, ne faire rien d'autre qu'*'opérer*, en public, le démontage impie de la fiction et conséquemment du mécanisme littéraire, pour étaler la pièce principale ou rien'.[22] Si la Bible est ce livre qui donne accès à Dieu, si l'Encyclopédie est ce livre qui donne accès au monde, le Livre mallarméen, auquel 'tout, au monde, existe pour aboutir', est aussi, d'une autre façon que le livre flaubertien, un livre sur rien.[23]

Notes to Chapter 8

1. 'Le Livre impossible', BnF, 23 mars 2001.
2. 'L'Action restreinte', 'Étalages', 'Le Livre, instrument spirituel'.
3. Jacques Scherer, *Le 'Livre' de Mallarmé: premières recherches sur des documents inédits* (Paris: Gallimard, 1957).
4. Stéphane Mallarmé, *Œuvres complètes*, éd. par Bertrand Marchal, 2 vols, Bibliothèque de la Pléiade (Paris: Gallimard, 1998–03), I, 821.
5. Ibid., II, 224.
6. Ibid., I, 788.
7. Ibid., II, 211–12.
8. Ibid., I, 788.
9. Ibid., I, 802.
10. Ibid., II, 82.
11. C'est le titre sous lequel furent publiées dans *La Revue blanche* en 1895 les articles qui seront repris dans *Divagations*.
12. Mallarmé, *Œuvres complètes*, II, 660 (réponse publiée dans le supplément gratuit du *Journal* du 10 décembre 1893).
13. Ibid., II, 226 et 224.
14. Ibid., I, 811.

15. Stéphane Mallarmé, *Épouser la notion*, éd. par Jean-Pierre Richard (Fontfroide: Bibliothèque artistique et littéraire, 1992), p. [40]; *Œuvres complètes*, I, 630 et 1066. On notera que le mot 'pucel.' était encore donné comme illisible dans la pré-originale de ces notes (Jean-Pierre Richard, 'Mallarmé et le rien d'après un fragment inédit', *Revue d'Histoire littéraire de la France* (oct.-déc. 1964), 639).
16. Richard, 'Mallarmé et le rien d'après un fragment inédit', p. 638; Mallarmé, *Épouser la notion*, p. [32]; *Œuvres complètes*, I, 629 et 1065.
17. Mallarmé, *Œuvres complètes*, I, 576.
18. Ibid., I, 279–80.
19. Scherer, *Le 'Livre' de Mallarmé*, p. 180.
20. Stéphane Mallarmé, 'Crise de vers', *Œuvres complètes*, II, 204–05.
21. Stéphane Mallarmé, lettre à Cazalis du 28 avril 1866, *Œuvres complètes*, I, 696.
22. Stéphane Mallarmé, *La Musique et les lettres*, *Œuvres complètes*, II, 67 (je souligne). Il s'agit bien ici, comme dans les Notes en vue du 'Livre', d'une *opération*.
23. Stéphane Mallarmé, 'Le Livre, instrument spirituel', *Œuvres complètes*, II, 224.

— 8 —

Gautier, Leconte, Mallarmé: Gravity Redeeming Grace?

Tim Farrant

Ô Poëtes, éducateurs des âmes, étrangers aux premiers rudiments de la vie réelle, non moins que de la vie idéale; en proie aux dédains instinctifs de la foule comme à l'indifférence des plus intelligents; moralistes sans principes communs, philosophes sans doctrine, rêveurs d'imitation et de parti pris, écrivains de hasard qui vous complaisez dans une radicale ignorance de l'homme et du monde, et dans un mépris naturel de tout travail sérieux; race inconsistante et fanfaronne, épris de vous-mêmes, dont la susceptibilité toujours éveillée ne s'irrite qu'au sujet d'une étroite personnalité et jamais au profit de principes éternels; ô Poëtes, que diriez-vous, qu'enseigneriez-vous? Qui vous a conféré le caractère et le langage de l'autorité? Quel dogme sanctionne votre apostolat? Allez! vous vous épuisez dans le vide, et votre heure est venue. Vous n'êtes plus écoutés, parce que vous ne reproduisez qu'une somme d'idées désormais insuffisantes; l'époque ne vous entend plus, parce que vous l'avez importunée de vos plaintes stériles, impuissants que vous étiez à exprimer autre chose que votre propre inanité. Instituteurs du genre humain, voici que votre disciple en sait instinctivement plus que vous. Il souffre d'un travail intérieur dont vous ne le guérirez pas, d'un désir religieux que vous n'exaucerez pas, si vous ne le guidez dans la recherche de ses traditions idéales. Aussi êtes-vous destinés, sous peine d'effacement définitif, à vous isoler d'heure en heure du monde de l'action, pour vous réfugier dans la vie contemplative et savante, comme en un sanctuaire de repos et de purification. Vous rentrerez ainsi, loin de vous en écarter, par le fait même de votre isolement apparent, dans la voie intelligente de l'époque.

Leconte de Lisle, 'Préface', Poèmes antiques

Chaque être crie en silence pour être lu autrement
Simone Weil, La Pesanteur et la grâce[1]

'Tel qu'en lui-même...'. For posterity, Leconte de Lisle has become fixed as leader of the Parnassians, midwife to Verlaine and Mallarmé, antibody to Rimbaud, a satellite which was once a planet. Roger calls him as a 'repressed sensualist',[2] hinting at something more interesting than previous commentators have done,[3] presenting him as a poet whose manner and language the young Mallarmé could try on, but as yet rarely emulate. This essay reconsiders the first half of Leconte's career, reactualizing hybrid and diverse elements in his apprenticeship, resituating his 1852 *Poèmes antiques* in the context of Gautier's contemporary *Émaux et camées*, and exploring how Leconte both reflects and builds on their adamantine exoticism, Orientalism, and craft. Leconte does more than 'merely' foreshadow Mallarmé in typography or language, belonging to a more scholarly and substantial *filiation*. As the preface to *Poèmes antiques* makes clear, Leconte identifies the voids and the shortfalls of Romanticism, poets' failure to relate to the intelligent, the masses, and the contemporary, along with the incoherence and lack of rigour he would reproach in Victor Hugo. But he also sees in these very failings and in poets' consequent isolation the forces which will make poetry central. Yet if we are tempted to read this as a kind of *ex post factem* justification of Mallarméan Olympianism and 'difficulty', other statements in Leconte's preface should give us pause. 'Inanité', under his pen, is just that, not gold. The people are ahead of the teacher:

> Instituteurs du genre humain, voici que votre disciple en sait instinctivement plus que vous. Il souffre d'un travail intérieur dont vous ne le guérirez pas, d'un désir religieux que vous n'exaucerez pas, si vous ne le guidez dans la recherche de ses traditions *idéales*.[4]

The 'travail intérieur' — to be understood in the English or archaic French sense of suffering, excessive labour, as much as merely work — expresses a tormenting modern predicament which leaders cannot recognize or address, unless they act as mentors in humanity's quest for its ideal, which, drawing on *idéal*'s etymological origins in the image as something seen,[5] we might gloss as 'visionary' traditions.[6]

Leconte thus sees, decades ahead of Mallarmé, the poet's paradoxically detached, yet central, relationship to society. And he also recognizes the centrality of the big, rather than the exiguous. Humanity's religious desire, its quest for ideal traditions, is explored, or rather, fought out, in Leconte's verse in a series of agonistic combats which take in conflicting, yet often complementary, belief-systems (Christianity and Paganism, classical and Celtic, Indian and Nordic mythology), where humanity's potential for the spiritual is always mediated by the material, by the real — something 'dur et rugueux', as Weil notes. 'On y trouve des joies, non de l'agrément.'[7] Leconte embodies the scholarly import and ideological presence of such myth- and belief-systems much like, perhaps, a Renan, treating them with a Renanian detachment and impassivity.[8] Yet if such positions seem agnostic, fatalistic, or nihilistic, they are also, and perhaps primarily, agonistic: the *travail* is work, both physical and spiritual, involving suffering as well as effort. Leconte's world-view is primarily violent and conflictual. His very pessimism, his apparent fealty to the base and the material, demands attention both in itself and as a gateway to Mallarméan, absolute poetic grace. Weil hints at the idea of gravity, material and intellectual, as the path to salvation — as the gap the spark must bridge, the abyss faith must leap, if the world itself is to be redressed.[9] If work leads, for Weil, ultimately to grace (*La Pesanteur et la grâce* closes with a 'Mystique du travail'), 'la grâce comble, mais elle ne peut entrer que là où il y a un vide pour la recevoir, et c'est elle qui fait ce vide'.[10]

* * * * *

There are three formative dichotomies in the first half of Leconte's career: between the 'exotic' and the metropolitan (oscillations between his native Ile Bourbon (Réunion), and Britanny, before his definitive move to Paris, aged 27);[11] between the Indian, and the classical (Graeco-Roman), and more recent (especially Fourierist) ideas of progress in the *Poèmes antiques* (1852);[12] between the latter and the Gallo-Celtic (perceived as more authentic) in the *Poèmes barbares* (1862); and, more widely in these collections as in his later work, between the Western and the oriental. Yet none of these dichotomies is in a straightforwardly antinomial relationship to the other. Leconte was, by origin and upbringing, both metropolitan French and colonial, and his work is both classically antique and 'ancient' — ethnically Breton, Celtic.[13] The terms 'antique' and 'barbare', designating Leconte's first two collections, are themselves ambiguous, and emblematic of the hybridity (but not syncretism) which characterizes his work throughout his career.[14] The *Poèmes antiques* (1852) evoke the classical and the Indian sub-continental antique; whilst the *Poèmes barbares* (1862) encompass the pagan Celtic, the Nordic, and also, more perturbingly, the biblical violent and antique. *Barbare* also, of course, denotes one who speaks an alien language.[15] It thereby resituates the Judaeo-Christian as the alien, typographically isolating individual poems in wide white space (in the *Poèmes barbares*, Leconte's second version), undermining conventional conceptions of the volume as an ensemble, still less an epic, inviting instead contemplation of its individual pieces and their relationship to each other, to silence, and to space, in an almost proto-Mallarméan way. In ways now largely forgotten, Leconte's poems synthesize, reduce, distil their invariably much more extensive sources, moving away from the heavy-weight epic which was a staple of canonical eighteenth- and nineteenth-century French poetry, and which Hugo was still constructing in *La Légende des siècles*, his multi-volume panorama of humanity's development from its origins to the modern.[16]

Such reflections might apply to a poem written the year after Leconte's *Poèmes barbares*, Mallarmé's 'Plainte d'automne'.[17] The *orgue de Barbarie* which the poet hears from his window is emblematic of a problematic relationship to the canonical and the popular,[18] as well as to poetry, music, and language.[19] The distinctive feature of the barrel-organ is, precisely, its cyclical repetition of melody: it is, in all senses of the word, canonical, employing a folkloric repetition and refrain that Leconte also exploits in his Burns rephrasings at the end of the *Poèmes antiques*. At the same time, *Barbarie*, with its echo of *barbare*, scrambles language, making the *orgue* instrumental, as a way towards reverie and *or*.[20] And Mallarmé's essay on Wagner could take the reverie further:

> Voici à la rampe intronisée la Légende.
> Avec une piété antérieure, un public, pour la seconde fois depuis les temps, hellénique d'abord, maintenant germain, considère le secret, représenté, d'origines. Quelque singulier Bonheur, neuf et barbare, l'assoit: devant le voile mouvant la subtilité de l'orchestration, à une magnificence qui décore sa genèse.
> Tout se retrempe au ruisseau primitif: pas jusqu'à la source.[21]

The 'légende', like the canonical barrel organ, embodies the cliché, the *poncif* expected 'avec une piété antérieure', 'le secret, représenté, d'origines': set-dressing masquerading as authenticity, 'une magnificence qui décore sa genèse'.[22] The 'ruisseau primitif' is a place of recycling, 'retrempe' as much as renewal, figuring the primitive but not the primal or primordial, precisely 'pas jusqu'à la source'. To this extent, it echoes the ongoing Romantic quest for authenticity and origins, a quest doomed to disappointment — as Flaubert knew better than any: 'Il faut s'en tenir aux sources,' he wrote in 1852, 'et Lamartine est un robinet'.[23] If Leconte adds a salutary and sobering historicism to sentimental Romantic (for example, *troubadour*) apprehensions of the past, Mallarmé *can* go one better.[24] Listening carefully, we hear 'une magnificence qui *dé-corps* sa genèse' and 'pas jusqu'à la source', a dis-embodiment of origin (as well as of the poet, the writing subject), and a step towards the well-spring, towards the virtual — ideas already implicit in Leconte's *désir religieux* and his *traditions idéales*.

Mallarmé sees the quest for origins as a movement from the Greek to the Teutonic, 'hellénique d'abord, maintenant germain'; for a modern reader (as indeed for Mallarmé's contemporaries) this might have geopolitical implications reaching far beyond Wagner. Such tensions, east-west rather than north-south, are emblematically apparent not only in Leconte's collections but in that other key production of the dawning Second Empire, Gautier's *Émaux et camées*, exactly contemporary with Flaubert's Lamartine-tap and the *Poèmes antiques*, and which opens with his 'Préface':

> Pendant les guerres de l'Empire
> Goethe, au bruit du canon brutal,
> Fit *Le divan occidental*,
> Fraîche oasis où l'art respire.
>
> Pour Nisami quittant Shakespeare,
> Il se parfuma de çantal,
> Et sur un mètre oriental,
> Nota le chant qu'Hudhud soupire.
>
> Comme Goethe sur son divan,
> A Weimar s'isolait des choses
> Et d'Hafiz effeuillait les roses,
>
> Sans prendre garde à l'ouragan,
> Qui fouettait mes vitres fermées,
> Moi, j'ai fait *Émaux et camées*.

Gautier's preface strikes a number of determinant chords, reminding us that a key impetus of nineteenth-century Western orientalism was not a first-hand experience of, or engagement, with the oriental, but one aestheticized and mediated by Goethe's *West-Östliche Divan* (1813), which Gautier knew through Henri Blaze's translation.[25] The preface ends on a comfort theme which goes right back to *Le Coin du feu* poems by Delille or the younger Gautier, or Baudelaire's *Le Soleil* and *Paysage*. Baudelaire's poems, and Gautier's preface, initiate the particular political nature of retreat from, precisely, the political, in the shape of the opening stanza, where

Goethe's creation of the *West-Östliche Divan* 'pendant les guerres de l'Empire', 'au bruit du canon brutal', and of the 'ouragan', anticipate Gautier's refuge from Second Republic troubles.[26] But *Émaux et camées* itself has none of the fraught engagement with the contemporary which would characterize Baudelaire's *Tableaux parisiens* and *Le Spleen de Paris*. Indeed, there is little serious evocation of the present, apart from a mention of 15 December 1849,[27] and a pawky courtesan 'se renversant dans son coupé', making the obelisk in the Place de la Concorde realize how far it is from home, 'pilier profane | Entre deux fontaines campé', compared to its luckier opposite number in Luxor ('Nostaligies d'obélisques', ll. 45–48).

Gautier's *grande horizontale* neatly references, and upsets, any earnest idea of Goethe's divan; yet the fundamental inspiration — and, arguably, aspiration — is Goethean: towards the oriental, and the aesthetic, from the *divan*, and from the *Künstlergedichte*.[28] If the oriental, and the antique, are comprehensively referenced in many mentions of classical and oriental places, persons, and objects, what strikes is that the places are chiefly evocative, the persons artists, and the objects artefacts, all enlisted in the celebration of the crafting of the artwork (painting, jewellery, especially sculpture) which stand as metaphors for the aesthetic, and for the poet's craft as an enterprise of art and desire. Also remarkable is the evisceration of history, hence of narrative, in favour of description. There are none of the stories which would characterize Goethe's *Ballades* or those of Hugo, and very little of their medievalism. With description comes reverie and reflection; whilst the fantastic, a feature of Goethe and Hugo, as well as Hoffmann, gives way to *fantaisie*.

Gautier's yoking of art and desire seems inspired by Goethe, perhaps in particular the *Künstlergedichte*, of which Blaze translates several.[29] But Gautier's desire primarily becomes metaphorized, as a trigger for reflection and, in due course, for the ideal. In 'Nostalgies d'obélisques', the 'Obélisque de Luxor' envies its Parisian counterpart in the midst of the living city:

> Là-bas, il voit à ses sculptures
> S'arrêter un peuple vivant,
> Hiératiques écritures,
> Que l'idée épelle en rêvant.
>
> Les fontaines juxtaposées
> Sur la poudre de son granit
> Jettent leurs brumes irisées;
> Il est vermeil, il rajeunit!
>
> Des veines roses de Syène
> Comme moi cependant il sort,
> Mais je reste à ma place ancienne
> Il est vivant et je suis mort! (ll. 133–44)

But, in Gautier's ethic, it is death which gets the better of life. In the first of these verses, it is impossible to determine whether the 'hiératiques écritures' are those on the obelisk (literally, the surface meaning) or the 'peuple vivant' which, in a reversal of scopic power-relations, watches the people, as well as being watched by them. Either way, it is the 'idée' — etymologically, as Roger has also reminded us, something seen[30] — which parses, or spells out, these writings, but also scriptures, 'en rêvant': reflecting, but also dreaming. These are instances of proto-Mallarméan undecidability *avant* (and/or, as in Mallarmé, *dans*) *la lettre*, as well as proto-Verlainian fusions in the vaporizing of the 'fontaines' not, as in ll. 49–50, framing the Parisian obelisk, but 'juxtaposées', their 'veines roses de Syène' (l. 141) suggesting, as elsewhere in *Émaux et camées* ('Rondalla', 'Coquetterie posthume') by their pinkness a half-way stage between the real and the ideal, life and death: simultaneous gravity and grace.

In *Émaux et camées*, then, can be found at once an austerely aesthetic, indeed almost marmoreal, celebration of art; a Verlainian solipsism and reverie; and proto-Mallarméan linguistic symbolism, which, in 'La Nue', will take us from a cloud to the Ideal via a naked woman, 'l'éternel féminin' and a 'vague fumée' (verses 5 and 7), ending in a Goethean celebration of desire:

> A l'Idéal ouvre ton âme!
> Mets dans ton cœur beaucoup de ciel,
> Aime une nue, aime une femme,
> Mais aime! — C'est l'essentiel! (ll. 33–36)

But this is to go far beyond the pivot at the centre of this article, and, in poetic terms, arguably of the century, between Gautier's *Émaux et camées* and Leconte's *Poèmes antiques*, both, let us remember, of 1852.[31] Gautier explores the void of the historic and the Gothic in 'Le Souper des armures', where the supper, symbol of conviviality and social congress, takes place between empty suits of armour connoting an heraldic medieval past — for Romantics like Chateaubriand and Hugo emblematic of coherence and unity, plenitude, by association also suggesting nobility (via the assonantial half-echo of 'armoiries', aristocratic *blasons* or achievements), their impotence confirmed by empty helmets.[32] The nothingness of this historic, aristocratic, implicitly religious value-system is apparent also, in Goethean form, in the questioning of the marmoreal (here, the architectural) which characterizes the portal, or rather pediment, poem of *Émaux et camées*, 'Affinités secrètes':

> Dans le fronton d'un temple antique,
> Deux blocs de marbre ont, trois mille ans,
> Sur le fond bleu du ciel attique
> Juxtaposé leurs rêves blancs;
>
> Dans la même nacre figées,
> Larmes des flots pleurant Vénus,
> Deux perles au gouffre plongés
> Se sont dit des mots inconnus;
>
> Au frais Généralife écloses,
> Sous le jet d'eau toujours en pleurs,
> Du temps de Boabdil deux roses
> Ensemble ont fait jaser leurs fleurs;
>
> Sur les coupoles de Venise
> Deux ramiers blancs aux pieds rosés,
> Au nid où l'amour s'éternise,
> Un soir de mai se sont posés.

> Marbre, perle, rose, colombe,
> Tout se dissout, tout se détruit;
> La perle fond, le marbre tombe,
> La fleur se fane et l'oiseau fuit. (ll. 1–20)

'Affinités secrètes' ends with a questioning of a future which is already a past, and in which the impersonal may become personal, 'l'inconnu devient l'amant', the material immaterial, the inanimate animate and human, and love universal, even if none of these outcomes is yet visible to man:

> Vous devant qui je brûle et tremble,
> Quel flot, quel fronton, quel rosier,
> Quel dôme nous connut ensemble,
> Perle ou marbre, fleur ou ramier? (ll. 61–64)

The poem's subverted Goethean title recalls universal laws. But in 'Affinités secrètes' a more overt affinity links the classical and the oriental exotic, the 'temple antique' of l. 1 and Boabdil, last Moorish king of Spain.[33] For Gautier, in such unelective affinities the void has the potential to be transcended, if only, yet crucially, in potential, as his poem's final verse suggests. Yet the 'faux temple antique' (of the National Assembly) and the 'générations futiles' which thrash and writhe in 'Nostalgie d'obélisques' are a more accurate expression of a political disappointment which Leconte would express, if not embody, in the apparently adamantine agnosticism which characterizes his *Poèmes antiques*.

The *Poèmes antiques*, Leconte's first collection, is both more objective and more monumental than *Émaux et camées*, and grows from an older, more exotic and diverse ecosystem. Leconte's colonial *Réunionnais* forbears and inheritance — his great-uncle was Évariste de Parny — arguably has its impact on this collection.[34] Its most famous poem, 'Midi', was not added until the final version, and even then, only in an appendix; but the earlier poems in order in the collection, far more prominent for contemporaries, present what for us seems an almost *Ben Hur*-like selection of archetypally classical events and situations. Archetypally classical, however, not as epic or heroic, but rather, individual and lyrical, hence apparently trivial and personal, even if through the long telescope of slow time. The collection presents little that is redemptive or developmental; there is no mention, or even implication, or progress. On the contrary: stasis is fated; decline, fall, and annihilation unavoidable. Ancient emotions and scenarios are worked out and exemplified by ancient instances, and by the same great mythological cast: Hylas, Paris, Helen, Niobe. It is the world of François Noël, pedagogic, inevitable, with no chance of learning from experience;[35] a world of violence and conflict, of insuperable oppositions, of barbarity, caught at the zenith of civilization; a world of absolutes yet no hope.[36] Pitching its 'antiquity' at the contemporary, as if to rear some Phoenix from the ashes of Romanticism, from the brave aspirations dashed by 1848 (not least, of course, for poets, including Leconte himself), *Poèmes antiques* reads, in the first full year of the Second Empire, as if the game were in some sense already up, or at least just marking time, beneath its finish and control.[37]

But in another sense — the sense in which, above all, Mallarmé would use it —

the game is hardly started. The *Poèmes antiques* hit us with different ethnicities from their first Hindu, Vedic pieces, and there are signs of other diversities in the five Burns translations which might surprise (though Burns, like his much more famous compatriot Scott, was mentioned in the *Revue de Paris* at least as early as 1830), and which may be explained both by Burns's egalitarianism, very close to Leconte's own (though little of this survives in their most famous expression, Debussy's setting of *La Fille aux cheveux de lin*).[38] And the *Poèmes antiques* present a classical sensuality delicately present in Banville,[39] whilst proffering also a more earthy ethnic exotic redolent of *Réunionnais* predecessors like Parny or Bertin.[40] With the Hindu exotic alterities of the first poems, the way is laid for the Verlaine of the *Poèmes saturniens* or the *Fêtes galantes* or even the Mallarmé of 'Prélude à l'après-midi d'un faune'.

The tension between an overarching and inevitably fatalistic trajectory, and something more ventilated and enabling, marks Leconte's next collection, *Poèmes barbares*. Composed over several years,[41] the *Poèmes barbares* rely on features which would be characteristically Symbolist, and which had already marked *Émaux et camées*,[42] notably the presentation of the poems as individual pieces, rather than as a collection, and a liberal, not to say profligate layout which makes the spaces between poems at least as important as the pieces themselves.[43] Somewhat uncharitably, Pich explains this layout largely by expedient, if not commercial, reasons, as a way of making the poems, and the collection, seem more substantial and significant than it is. Yet something much more absolute is at stake. If this well-ventilated layout suggests space for reflection and potential of a kind Mallarmé later exploits, gravity perhaps ceding to a grace, Leconte makes space only for desolation, for reflection on real oblivion as the inevitable end-point of creation: aesthetic, poetic, cosmic.

This cosmic trajectory is the collection's overarching *raison d'être*, far surpassing the 'anthology' or *recueil* characteristics stressed by scholarly emphasis on its genesis, its successive editions, or on its individual pieces. It becomes gradually more apparent as one reads one's way through, and links Leconte's project (there does not seem exactly to have been a scheme) in its overall pattern and destination to other, more overtly epic undertakings: Hugo's *Les Contemplations* and Baudelaire's *Les Fleurs du mal*, both composed concurrently with the earlier of the *Poèmes barbares*, and Hugo's *La Légende des siècles* (begun in 1859, during the composition of the *Poèmes barbares*, and finally completed in 1883, two years before Hugo's death) — not to mention the elephant outside the room, *Le Parnasse contemporain*, which can been seen as its own epic of the contemporary, proposing, recording the poetic output of its era, the Second Empire, in its three volumes of 1866, 1871, and 1876. Just as Baudelaire's 'Livre' (*Les Fleurs du mal*) had, he told his lawyer, 'une terrible moralité',[44] so Leconte's is, analogously, animated by a deep morale or ethic, unlike Baudelaire's, not set out in any preface (in the *Poèmes barbares* there is no equivalent even of 'Au lecteur'), but which pervades the volume and finally surfaces at the end.

The *propos* of *Poèmes barbares* is not indicated initially by anything other than its title, and most of the poems express a violence familiar from the *Poèmes antiques*. But the title nonetheless needs taking seriously, for it bespeaks an inspiration and purpose quite distinct from the earlier collection. The *Poèmes barbares*, unlike their 'antique' predecessors, draw on a heterogeneous diversity of inspiration in stark contrast to the more homogeneous (Greek or Roman classical, or Hindu) motivations of the *Poèmes antiques*, and far less neatly or rationally organized than in the undeniably admirable scholarly treatment of these collections by Alison Fairlie. The later collection presents a series of bloody, and landmark, conflicts more epic and national than personal (unlike the classical-inspired and mainly personal encounters of the *Poèmes antiques*), which really reads like some gruelling multi-poem *mémoire* (or *supplice*) *de guerre*. Modern readers, softened by the sonnet or the lyric, are insufficiently battle-hardened to cope with the long verse, the *in extenso* theatre of combat, the recurrent encounter with violence, brutality, and slaughter which is standard issue in Leconte. He gives us lyric as ordeal, clothed, it is true, on occasion in seemingly familiar, local, colours: the Hispanism of Don Iñigo, which takes us back beyond *Hernani* to the original *Le Cid*, or the Ossianism of Dom Guy.[45]

But what is really material here is that which goes beyond the implications of the canonical, as well as the material itself. Leconte's 'Ossianism' has substance, not just in the convincing geo-reality of its settings, as much topographies as landscapes, but also in its sublimes of violence: fists, more than mists, decimation, carnage, often more mimetically, memorably rendered than Leconte is given credit for, awe-inspiring examples of national stories. National stories recounted as verse epics, embodiments of the presence of history in the contemporary, presentations also of the national as patchwork, momentous *faits et gestes* of previous ages. Leconte is paradoxically exotic: he is what one might call an ethnic metropolitan, naturalized from the colonies, who inhabits and maps the diversities of France in a lengthy poetic perspective. One of the oddities of Leconte's landscapes, especially given his origins, is that they are chiefly metropolitan French. The metropolitan ethnic (the Breton, the Celtic, the Nordic) is botanized, naturalized, treated as a sample and an example, a patch of the national work. The properly foreign, that which has its origins and ongoing, current nineteenth-century being outside Europe and far from metropolitan France, is the province of the *Poèmes antiques*, and later, the *Derniers vers*; it is treated not as the exotic, or local colour, not held up for quaint, picturesque, anecdotal appreciation, but exists seemingly only to be appropriated, silently, uncommented by Leconte, as part of a heterogeneous, but not syncretic, selection of belief-systems, samples of a varied range of foreign, contemporary, not obsolete or historical religions, presented without explanation or pedagogy.[46] In the *Poèmes antiques*, many classical references would have been familiar to the first readers; but many others, Hindu, Vedic, unfamiliar names, and tales come out of the blue, like missiles, and are laid out as so many opaque and therefore perplexing geological specimens, *émaux et camées*, perhaps, but with little of the narrative, anecdotal, or cultural accessibility which Gautier's title implies. In this collection, Leconte's aim seems to be almost exactly the opposite of Mallarmé's later quest to 'donner un sens plus pur aux mots de la tribu'.[47] The *tribus* in the *Poèmes antiques* come from anywhere but round here, he seems to say, and hardly require a purer meaning, their virginity untried by anything as vulgar as familiarity. The *Poèmes antiques* seem simply to present what is, or what was, and for Leconte, still is — even if scholarly comparison with contemporary, especially epic, sources repeatedly confirms Leconte's remarkable ability to synthesize.

If the *Poèmes barbares* apparently do little that is different, they are more accessible and national; the bards are more important; and the bard is a creator, but also destroyer, and, most crucially, a decider: the one who makes, and rules, with words. 'La Vigne de Naboth' conjures up a vision of destruction only to destroy it, thereby asserting the power of the word in a proto-Mallarméan (but, in its setting in the Holy Land, also quasi-ethnic, indeed religious and sacramental) way. The poem turns the biblical story of the divine vengeance mediated by Elijah on Ahab for his fraudulent appropriation of Naboth's vineyard (1 Kings 21) into a nihilistic, aporetic parable. At its end, the agent of vengeance goes on his way, leaving only void in his wake. 'Le Massacre de Mona' takes this further. Shifting the theatre of action to prehistoric (Roman) Anglesey, the poem, like 'La Vigne de Naboth', allies violence and beauty, in a riveting account in which space, place, and the elements assume and subsume the human. The poem begins *in medias res*, yet less in terms of drama (although the poem is certainly dramatic) than of the middle of a legend or a lay:

> Or Mona, du milieu de la mer rude et haute
> Dressait rigidement les granits de sa côte
> Qui, massifs et baignés d'écume et pleins de bruit,
> Brisaient l'herbe furieuse en herbes dans la nuit. (ll. 1–4)

The wind and the rocks are personified:

> L'Esprit rauque du vent, au faîte noir des rocs,
> Tournait et soufflait dans ses cornes d'aurochs;
> Et c'était un fracas si vaste et si sauvage,
> Que la mer s'en taisait tout le long du rivage,
> Tant le son formidable, en cette immensité,
> Par coups de foudre et par rafales emporté,
> De cris et de sanglots, et de voix éperdues,
> Comblait le gouffre épais des mornes étendues.
> L'Esprit du vent soufflait dans ses clairons de fer,
> En aspergeant le ciel des baves de la mer;
> Il soufflait, hérissant comme une chevelure
> La noire nue éparse autour de l'île obscure,
> [...]
> L'Esprit de la tempête, avec ses mille bouches,
> Les appelant, soufflait dans ses trompes farouches.
>   (ll. 7–18, 25–26)

This is a drama of, and amongst, the elements, more than a human conflict; a cosmic joust in which man is principally a bit-player who takes whatever these forces throw at him. (There is scant naming or even concept of nature, still less Nature, in Leconte, save hostile, no doubt on account of its Romantic baggage.)[48] Bit-players apart, that is, from the actors who really matter, the Masters and the Bards:

> Ainsi les Maîtres, fils de Math, le très puissant,
> Volaient, impétueux essaims [...]
>
> Les Bardes sont debout dans leurs sayons rayés,
> Aux harpes de granit les deux bras appuyés
> A leurs reins pend la Rhote et luit le large glaive.
> La touffe de cheveux qu'une écorce relève,
> Flotte, signe héroique, au crâne large et rond,
> Avec la plume de l'aigle et celle du héron. (ll. 35–36, 55–60)

This is a whole fellowship — comprehensive, embodied, sages with status and agency, a sacerdotal function ('Chef sacerdotal', l. 89) firmly rooted in their domain. The story, or legend, which is related is of a previous bliss (Arcadian or pre-Lapsarian, except that these classical and biblical references are absolutely not evoked),[49] in which man was at one with the world, before the dragon Avank destroyed it and Mona (Anglesey) was rescued in an ark:

> Et l'homme était heureux sur la face du monde [...]
>
> Et la terre était bonne, et douce était la mort
> Car ceux qu'elle appelait la goûtaient sans remord.
> (ll. 179, 184–85)

We are at the opposite pole from the virtual, universal Master evoked by Mallarmé. This legend comes out of the elements, a yarn seemingly spun from the wind (here ubiquitous as a presence, yet without any hint of the Paraclete), which in due course finds its voice in a Bard:

> Il étendit les bras vers l'orage des cieux,
> Puis il resta debout, droit et silencieux;
> Et sur le front du cercle immobile, une haleine,
> Faible et triste, monta, qui murmurait à peine,
> Souffle respectueux de la foule. Et voilà
> Qu'une vibration soudaine s'exhala,
> Et qu'un Barde, ébranlant la harpe qu'il embrasse,
> Chanta sous le ciel noir l'histoire de sa race. (ll. 135–42)

And yet the Bard's high sacramental function — his deciding power of life and death, of all, and nothing; above all, his power of absolute creation and annihilation, the fact that the story is bodied forth and then destroyed — at the poem's end is effectively vaporized into the air, sea, and rocks from which it appeared, suggesting a proto-Mallarméan virtuality, or to put it perhaps more accurately, revealing the Parnassian feet of clay, or granite, from which the impersonal Master's air-castles are confected. To suggest this is, I hope, less to commit some crime of *lèse-Stéphane* (still less *lèse-Roger*), than to weigh a certain Parnassian gravity which is there in Mallarmé, but which has been lost sight of as Parnassianism has gone out of fashion, and as Mallarmé, along with Baudelaire, has taken the lead in posterity's great sweepstake. It is also to evoke a relationship with a writer for whom Leconte had much sympathy and admiration, but not now generally considered in the same breath: Flaubert.[50] For in Leconte, as in Flaubert, it is from violence that beauty comes. Sometimes it comes overtly, as in 'Le Conseil du Fakir':

> Or la Begum, riant comme les Bengalis,
> Et penchant vers l'époux son col plein d'indolence,
> Dit: — Le saint homme rêve! — Et puis elle lui lance
> Une bourse du bout de ses beaux doigts polis.
> Le filet, enrichi d'une opale de Pers,
> Sur le pavé de marbre incrusté de métal
> Sonnet jette un flot d'or qui roule et se disperse.
>
> Voici le prix du sang au meurtrier fatal,
> Dit le Fakir; maudit soit-il! Nabab, le glaive
> Est hors la gaine: agis avant qu'il ne se lève! (ll. 47–56)

And sometimes it comes less evidently. In the closing lines of 'Le Massacre de Mona', it is the weapons which make the music, even, or perhaps particularly, at the climax of annihilation:

> Meurs donc! cria Murdoc'h, meurs, selon ton envie.
> Mourrez tous, — Païens que le Démon convie,
> Vous qui du Seigneur Christ êtes les meurtriers
> Car la vengance a faim et soif! A moi, guerriers! —
>
> Et les flèches de cuivre à pointe dentelée
> Sifflèrent brusquement à travers l'assemblée.
> Et les harpes vibraient, sonores, et les voix,
> Tranquilles, vers le ciel résonnaient à la fois:
> Ne cessaient qu'à l'instant où l'âme ouvrait ses ailes.
> Les arcs tintaient, les traits s'enfonçaient dans les flancs,
> Sans trêve, hérissant les dos, les seins sanglants,
> Déchirant, furieux, la gorge des prêtresses
> Dont la torche fumant incendiait les tresses.
> Et tout fut dit. Quand l'aube en son berceau d'azur
> Dora les flots joyeux d'un regard frais et pur,
> L'Ile saint baignait dans une vapeur douce
> Ses hauts rochers vêtus de lichen et de mousse
> Et mêlant son cri rauque au doux bruit de la mer,
> Un long vol de corbeaux tourbillonnait dans l'air. (ll. 497–515)

The convergence of priests and warriors, the assonance of 'harpes' and 'arcs', link combat and poetry; the way in which the scene is bodied forth and then just as easily collapses, flat-packed by the Bard recalls Flaubert's narrator's ability to shrink a whole experience to a picture.[51] But Leconte also embodies a Mallarméan ethos in which *néant* can be *or*. Or to put it differently: Mallarmé might have denied that he was a Parnassian with perhaps as much justification as Flaubert declaring that he was not a realist.

The *Poèmes barbares* may be considered also in a different relationship to contemporary reality, ten years into the Second Empire; unlike the *Poèmes antiques*, no longer classical, sub-continental, southern, but Nordic, Gothic, modern. The *barbare* is both the brutal and uncouth, but also the unintelligible language of the Other. The theme of this multi- but not poly-glottism is an emerging constant throughout the collection. In its later poems, Babel is presented as a threat of incoherence close to the reality of disintegration Thiers sought to counter by his insistence that 'la République sera conservatrice ou elle ne sera pas'.[52] Some poems make their Republican sentiment explicit, in the very midst of contemporary brutality;[53] others propose a transcendent Olympian detachment and impersonality, 'Le Vœu suprême', for example, or most memorably, 'Les Montreurs'.[54] This poem — Leconte's answer to 'Les Mages', 'Le Vieux Saltimbanque', and 'Le Pitre châtié'[55] — begins with the visceral, the animal, the dust, and ends with silence and renunciation in the virtual. Yet it is in the very stones themselves that cosmic chaos is mirrored and ultimately redeemed, by the very language, the term *barbare*, which is the marker of the abjection of humanity and the world. The barbarous, in other words, becomes the route to poetry, gravity the way to grace.

These stones are, then, the very opposite of *bibelots*, or mere ornaments, even if they risk being abolished. On the contrary: *rochers* are a Bard's best friend. It is in the final pieces of the collection that the material really comes into its own, in 'L'Anathème', 'La Fin de l'Homme', and in an unwontedly short poem, the antepenultimate piece of the collection, 'Aux modernes'. Leconte, more impartial than impersonal, yet undeniably urgent, impassively navigates a cataclysmic series of disasters, which cumulate to form a terrifying vision of the fate awaiting humanity. If, for Leconte and his contemporaries, the vision was biblical and apocalyptic (as for example in the poems just mentioned or 'L'Ecclésiaste'), for the twenty-first century he appears above all eco-critical. The mines which are tunnelled out and exhausted in 'Aux modernes' may be redolent of the *Niebelungen*, but for us they foretell man's excessive impact on the earth:

> Vous vivez lâchement, sans rêve, sans dessin,
> Plus vieux, plus décrépits que la terre inféconde,
> Châtrés dès le berceau par le siècle assassin
> De toute passion vigoureuse et profonde.
>
> Votre cervelle est vide autant que votre sein,
> Et vous avez souillé ce misérable monde
> D'un sang si corrompu, d'un souffle si malsain,
> Que la mort germe seule en cette boue immonde.
>
> Hommes, tueurs des Dieux, les temps ne sont pas loin,
> Où, sur un grand tas d'or vautrés dans quelque coin,
> Ayant rongé le sol nourricier jusqu'aux roches,
>
> Ne sachant faire rien ni des jours ni des nuits,
> Noyés dans le néant des suprêmes ennuis,
> Vous mourrez bêtement en emplissant vos poches.

'Aux modernes' indeed: this makes Baudelairian *ennui* look cheerful, or at least interesting, perhaps above all because of the final line, which offers apparently no hope of redemption, or of any ethical or religious framework whatsoever: it is, irredeemably, earthbound.

The *rocs* and *rochers* littering these poems, and which, in a way, are their foundation, seem the abject opposite of the *monts*, locus of inspiration for Leconte as in the Bible. And yet the point of gravest despair is in fact the implicit annunciation of grace. 'Le Nazaréen', a piece which builds on Nerval's 'Le Christ aux oliviers' and 'Les

Fenêtres' in an apparently far more contentious and blasphemous manner, is but the prelude to the black despair which ends 'La Fin de l'homme', whose mood really is definitively post-lapsarian:[56] 'Salut, ô noirs rochers, cavernes où sommeille | Dans l'immobile nuit tout ce qui me fut cher' (ll. 60–61). The word *Grâce* recurs twice (ll. 45, 46, 67), but only as a plea for pity and release from the burden of living.

And yet this is not the end — or if it is, it is involuted and paradoxical. In the terms of this poem, men are God's sin, and he ought never to have allowed them to be born (l. 68), but, given this fact, Christ, the son of man, ought to save us, but to die in order to do so, or (and this is no doubt Leconte's ultimate interpretation): if God is really to abandon us, at that point man will also die. On one level this reads like an ultimate prophecy of eco-doom, as the final poem, 'Solvet seclum', begins: 'Tu te tairas, ô voix sinistre des vivants'. On another, it is an involuted, paradoxically deconstructionist conclusion ('La Fin de l'homme', l. 80: 'Meurs, nous vivrons!'), and as the end of 'Solvet seclum' suggests, grace will come at the moment of greatest gravity:

> D'un seul coup la nature interrompra ses bruits.
> Et ce ne sera point, sous les cieux magnifiques,
> Le bonheur reconquis des paradis antiques,
> Ni l'entretien d'Adam et d'Ève sur les fleurs,
> Ni le divin sommeil après tant de douleurs;
> Ce sera quand le Globe et tout ce qui l'habite,
> Bloc stérile arraché de son immense orbite,
> Stupide, aveugle, plein d'un dernier hurlement,
> Plus lourd, plus éperdu de moment en moment,
> Contre quelque univers immobile en sa force
> Défoncera sa vieille et misérable écorce,
> Et, laissant ruisseler, par mille trous béants,
> Sa flamme intérieure avec ses océans,
> Ira fertiliser de ses restes immondes
> Les sillons de l'espace où se fermentent les mondes. (ll. 14–28)

Grace will be in the dissemination, in the fertilization of the world's remains, in gravity turning into the virtual. It is an ending which, if it does not conform to current cosmic knowledge (whereby the sun, rather than the earth, will expand and effectively explode as a red giant), crystallizes a key dynamic in Leconte. Gravity, its nineteenth-century heaviness, so out of fashion in verse as in furniture, in fact enables grace. Heaviness is not past, but before us; but, as for Weil, that may be precisely what is redemptive. *Poésie(s)* come from the *barbare(s)*; indeed, the *barbare* may be precisely its precondition.

The last pieces of the *Poèmes barbares* take us to a nihilistic nadir, a point from which there is apparently no return. In merely material terms this is incontestable: the miners of 'Aux modernes' have hit bare rock. Hope flickers in the praise of freedom in certain *Poèmes barbares* which prefigure the collectivist millennium encapsulated in the *Catéchisme républicain* (1872) and the *Poèmes tragiques* (1883);[57] yet it is all but extinguished in Leconte's last collections, the *Poèmes tragiques* and the *Derniers vers*, and in his other writings, his translation of the *Iliad*, and his version of the *Oresteia*, which seem merely to circle around unchanging human situations and conundra, to represent absolute stasis, the opposite of all progress.

Leconte's despair is crystallized by 'L'Illusion suprême', the poem which, more than any other, seems to eliminate all hope. It is here, perhaps, that the force of gravity in his work is strongest. Yet the apparent abjection of this moment is, in Weilian terms, the one which is both furthest from, and therefore offers the greatest possibility of, grace. 'L'Illusion suprême' seemingly writes off God absolutely, yet also posits the opposite, the possibility of a transcendent, and redemptive illusion, and of a poetry surpassing abjection. 'L'Illusion suprême' thus embodies the agonistic combat with gravity which, for Weil, can lead to grace, yet also a Mallarméan aporia in which illusion is both *néant* and plenitudinous. In this, it seems to parallel, however unintentionally, 'le doute du Jeu suprême' which Mallarmé evokes in 'Une dentelle s'abolit' (1887). The doubt about the 'Jeu suprême' (poetry) seems like the shadow-side of Leconte, for whom the purpose and value of poetry is never in doubt, at least not his own, despite his misgivings about the direction of contemporary poetry, expressed as early as his preface to the *Poèmes antiques* with which we began. Yet the misgivings of Leconte and Mallarmé, however different in their nature, place both of them, by dint of their isolation, in 'la voie intelligente de l'époque', put both on the way to grace, and so make them the heirs (in Leconte's case, however reluctant) of Baudelaire.

Gautier and, following him, Leconte, came out of a rejection of the contemporary and a refuge in the aesthetic, and there is in both a desire to reappropriate classicism, the marmoreal, to take it away from the *scolaire* and the schoolbooks where for decades it had languished, and, in Leconte's case, to re-appropriate it as something both violent and recondite — violence being the marker of a sensuality and physicality insurgent beneath a surface which dare not speak its name. But this reappropriation also betokens a shifting of the aesthetic goalposts towards something new and visceral whose anti-Christian corporality is all the more compelling for being, precisely, not clothed but uncovered, incarnated yet contained in classical and pagan myth. The memorializing of *Les Dieux antiques*, consecrated by Mallarmé in his 1880 treatise, arguably occurs a generation earlier, in *Émaux et camées* and the *Poèmes antiques*. The titles of both suggest relics: exquisite, but highly resonant *bibelots* in the case of *Émaux et camées*; the *Poèmes antiques*, something modernity has left behind. Yet the death of these gods, accompanied by the death of the poet(s) whom Leconte so vilifies in his preface to the *Poèmes antiques*, also presages a Phoenix-like rebirth. Poetry will move from being cause, or *chose*, to *effet*, as Mallarmé would so comprehensively demonstrate. The real ideal of Leconte de Lisle is perhaps, in fact, closer to Mallarmé's *cri de cœur*: 'L'Idéal! L'Idéal! L'Idéal!' — a cry which is all the more real, and heartfelt, because it is not there — a grace which shines through, yet attests the presence of, gravity. What more fitting tribute could there be to Roger?

Notes to Chapter 9

1. Simone Weil, *La Pesanteur et la grâce* [1947] (Paris: Plon, 1988), p. 134.
2. Roger Pearson, *Unfolding Mallarmé: The Development of a Poetic Art* (Oxford: Oxford University Press, 1996), pp. 17–18. 'Repressed sensualist' suggests a bigger story, mixing institutional Classicism (hence repression, political, and sexual), traditionally associated by French readers with Leconte, with something more subversive, indeed virtually the reverse, which he (along with other forms of Hellenism, and apparently marmoreal writers such as Gautier) connoted for contemporary English acolytes like Swinburne. See Charlotte Ribeyrol, *Etrangeté, passion, couleur: l'hellénisme de Swinburne, Pater et Symonds, 1865–1880* (Grenoble: Ellug, 2013). Mallarmé's elimination of this inheritance (the absence of quotations or intertextual references to poetic predecessors in his verse, his submission of only one poem to Gautier's *Tombeau* where Swinburne presented five) says much about the contrasting conception and reception of Gautier and Leconte amongst English and French contemporaries. I thank Dr Ribeyrol for drawing these matters to my attention.
3. With the notable exception of Baudelaire, who deems the descriptions 'trop bien faites, trop enivrantes pour n'avoir pas été moulées sur des souvenirs d'enfance' not to reveal the poet's origins 'dans une de ces îles volcaniques et parfumées, où l'âme humaine, mollement bercée par toutes les voluptés de l'atmosphère, désapprend chaque jour l'exercice de la pensée' ('Réflexions sur quelques-uns de mes contemporains: IX Leconte de Lisle', in *Œuvres complètes*, ed. by Claude Pichois and Jean Ziegler, 2 vols, Bibliothèque de la Pléiade (Paris: Gallimard, 1975–76), II, 176).
4. Leconte de Lisle, 'Préface', *Poèmes antiques* (my emphasis).
5. Roger Pearson, 'Mallarmé's Homage to Villiers de L'Isle-Adam', in *The Process of Art: Studies in Nineteenth-Century Literature and Art Offered to Alan Raitt*, ed. by Michael Freeman and others (Oxford: Clarendon, 1998), pp. 135–53 (p. 138).
6. Cf. Seth Whidden, *Authority in Crisis* (Farnham: Ashgate, 2014), esp. pp. 155–56.
7. Weil, *La Pesanteur et la grâce*, p. 59.
8. 'Le seul poète auquel on pourrait, sans absurdité, comparer Leconte de Lisle, est Théophile Gautier' (Charles Baudelaire, 'Réflexions', in *Œuvres complètes*, II, 177. Leconte did not correspond with Gautier until 6 September 1865 (*Correspondance générale*, ed. by C. Lacoste-Veysseyre and P. Laubriet, 12 vols (Geneva: Droz, 1985–2000), IX, 108). Gautier's subsequent private mentions are flippant, if his public praise was fulsome: 'un poète de premier ordre, de race homérique [...] Ses rêves sont des rêves de Paros et d'azur'; painters, sculptors, and 'les élèves de l'école' should read his Illiad translation night and day, 'car elle contient toute la véritable antiquité' (4 November 1867).
9. The reductive, instrumental notion that poetry must somehow be traduced as 'useful' to be acceptable is the starting point of Seamus Heaney's *The Redress of Poetry* (London: Faber & Faber, 1995), p. 1.
10. Weil, *La Pesanteur et la grâce*, p. 18.
11. Jean Dornis, *Essai sur Leconte de Lisle* (Paris: Ollendorff, 1909), pp. 5–6.
12. Leconte's classical pieces in the *Poèmes antiques* in part derive from and converge with Fourierist doctrine of a new order via a return to the antique. See Alison Fairlie, *Leconte de Lisle's Poems on the Barbarian Races* (Cambridge: Cambridge University Press, 1947).
13. Dornis, adopting a then ostensibly respectable racism, denies any 'créolité' in Leconte, stressing instead mythic Celtic origins and inclinations towards mysticism and abstraction shared with Renan (*Essai sur Leconte de Lisle*, pp. 6–8).
14. As Fairlie persuasively demonstrates in *Leconte de Lisle's Poems on the Barbarian Races*, Leconte contextualizes his subjects, exploring how particular historical circumstances embody recurrent political and religious power-struggles between old and new orders. But he never ventures a syncretic synthesis, or unifying religious panacea, such dogmatic solutions being a feature of his early, pre-1848 years.
15. In Greek, one who literally stammers in a foreign tongue.
16. Joseph Vianey, *Les Sources de Leconte de Lisle* (Montpellier: Coulet, 1907), and Fairlie, *Leconte de Lisle's Poems on the Barbarian Races*, give multiple examples of Leconte's ability to synthesize even

unruly material such as the *Poema del Cid*. See also H. J. Hunt, *The Epic in Nineteenth-Century France: A Study in Heroic and Humanitarian Poetry from 'Les Martyrs' to 'Les Siècles Morts'* (Oxford: Blackwell, 1941).

17. Written in 1863 and first published in 1864; initially entitled 'L'Orgue de Barbarie'.
18. Or a 'mi-lieu' between verse and journalism (Roger Pearson, *Mallarmé and Circumstance: The Translation of Silence* (Oxford: Oxford University Press, 2004), p. 30).
19. See Helen Abbott, *Between Baudelaire and Mallarmé: Voice, Conversation and Music* (Farnham: Ashgate, 2009), pp. 196–99.
20. But not without its downside: 'or-gueux de Barbarie'. Cf. Pearson, *Unfolding Mallarmé*, p. 68.
21. Stéphane Mallarmé, 'Richard Wagner: rêverie d'un poète français', in *Œuvres complètes*, ed. by Bertrand Marchal, 2 vols, Bibliothèque de la Pléiade (Paris: Gallimard, 1998–2003), II, 156–57.
22. On Mallarmé's preference for fable over legend, see Pearson, *Mallarmé and Circumstance*, p. 60.
23. Gustave Flaubert, *Correspondance*, ed. by Jean Bruneau and others, 5 vols, Bibliothèque de la Pléiade (Paris: Gallimard, 1973–2007), III, 343.
24. Baudelaire wrote: 'Dans le poète comme dans le philosophe, je trouve cette ardente, mais impartiale curiosité des religions et ce même esprit d'amour universel, non pour l'humanité prise en elle-même, mais pour les différentes formes dont l'homme a, suivant les âges et les climats, revêtu la beauté et la vérité. [...] Peindre en beaux vers, d'une nature lumineuse et tranquille, les manières diverses suivant lesquelles l'homme a, jusqu'à présent, adoré Dieu et cherché le beau, tel a été [...] le but que Leconte de Lisle a assigné à sa poésie' (*Œuvres complètes*, II, 177–78).
25. J. W. von Goethe, *Poésies*, ed. and trans. by Henri Blaze (Paris: Charpentier, 1843; 1863). Charpentier would publish the 1863, 1866, and 1869 editions of *Émaux et camées*, succeeding Didier (1852, 1853) and Poulet-Malassis et de Broise (1858). Strikingly, Blaze relates that Beethoven was inspired to compose not only by the content of Goethe's verse, but also by its rhythm and craft: 'Là, chaque mot double de prix par la place qu'il occupe; la moindre syllable, le moindre chiffre a sa valeur, à peu près comme dans l'hiéroglyphe musical; et nulle part le maître [...] ne vous apparaît davantage que dans les pièces d'un fini sans exemple, contextures profondes où le travail ne se sent pas, bulles de savon taillées dans le cristal de roche et le diamant' (in Goethe, *Poésies*, pp. iii–iv). Such remarks suggest how the 'Le Parnasse allemand' might have inspired its French inheritor, via *L'Art pour l'art*, even if Blaze's translations are in prose.
26. Cf. 'Goethe, interrompu dans sa contemplation éternelle par les événements de 1811, ne trouva pas de plus sûr moyen d'y échapper que de se réfugier par la pensée en Orient' (Henri Blaze, in Goethe, *Poésies*, p. xxxii).
27. In the subtitle of 'Vieux de la vieille', and the date of a ceremony at the Invalides in their honour.
28. Blaze's edition of Goethe's *Poésies* contains, inter alia, 'Chant matinal de l'artiste', 'Chant du soir et [sic] l'artiste', 'Le Connaisseur et l'enthousiaste', 'Monologue de l'Amateur', 'Etudes', 'Antique', as well as numerous poems from the *West-Östliche Divan*.
29. Amongst others, 'Le Compagnon orfèvre' (in Goethe, *Poésies*, p. 39), 'Explication d'une ancienne vignette sur bois représentant la mission poétique de Hans Sachs' (p. 136), 'Chant matinal de l'artiste' (p. 159), Chant du soir de l'artiste (p. 163), and 'Le Connaisseur et l'enthousiaste' (p. 164), as well as 'Idéal' (p. 165) and nineteen poems of the *West-Östliche Divan*.
30. Pearson, 'Mallarmé's Homage to Villiers de L'Isle d'Adam', p. 138.
31. A more significant pivot might turn on *Les Contemplations* and *Les Fleurs du mal* in 1856 and 1857, together with Banville's *Odes funambulesques*.
32. Théophile Gautier, 'Le Souper des armures', ll. 53–54: 'Mais les casques ouverts sont vides | Comme les timbres du blason'.
33. Mentioned in, and subversively appropriated from, Chateaubriand's *Le Dernier Abencérage*.
34. The 'hasard heureux d'être né dans un pays merveilleusement beau et à moitié sauvage, riche de végétations étranges, sous un ciel éblouissant', together with 'cette sensibilité naissante d'un cœur et d'un corps vierges, attendrie par le sentiment inné de la nature, a suffi pour crée le poète que je suis devenu', even if 'l'oncle et le neveu ne se ressemblent guère' (Dornis, *Essai sur Leconte de Lisle*, pp. 3–4).

35. François Noël's *Dictionnaire de la fable, ou mythologie grecque, latine, égyptienne, celtique, persane, syriaque, indienne, chinoise, mahométane, scandinave, iconologique, etc.* (Paris: Le Normant, 1801; 4 edns. to 1823), and his *Leçons de littérature et de morale, ou recueil, en prose et en vers, des plus beaux morceaux de notre langue* (Paris: Le Normant, 1804; 29 edns. to 1862) were probably the first and most widely used pedagogic textbooks in nineteenth-century France (A. A. Cournot, *Des institutions d'instruction publique en France* [1864] (Paris: Vrin-CNRS, 1977), p. 230). For Bertrand Marchal, it is Mallarmé who moves myth definitively from embodied to metaphorical gods: 'Ni les poèmes mythologiques de Leconte de Lisle, trop visiblement appliqués à dresser le catalogue d'une mythologie de musée, ni ceux d'Hugo, même quand ils font un usage moderne des figures mythiques en les tirant vers le type ou le symbole [...] ne satisfont l'idéal mallarméen d'une liaison plus organique entre mythe et poésie [...]. Par le détour des *Dieux antiques* et de la fiction mythique, la poésie retrouve une nouvelle légitimité sous le signe de la métaphore, et devient le support de la réflexion anthropologique et religieuse de Mallarmé' (*La Religion de Mallarmé: poésie, mythologie et religion* (Paris: Corti, 1988), pp. 455–56). For John F. Desmond, Leconte expresses transcendence, if not redemption, through language, adducing Heaney's notion of 'poetry as grace' and his 'belief in the reality of a transcendent metaphysical order that is the ultimate source of meaning'; ideas Leconte might have viewed slightly more favourably than 'inclusive consciousness' or 'universal standards of value' (*Gravity and Grace: Seamus Heaney and the Force of Light* (Waco, TX: Baylor University Press, 2009), p. 3).
36. The post-1848 insurrection taste for violence in writings of the Second Empire, explored through the exotic, the barbaric, and the antique, evidenced most notably by Leconte and Flaubert's *Salammbô*, perhaps expresses disaffection with Romanticism's sentimental delicacies, disillusion with the idea of progress, and a desire for a more vigorous, decisive age: 'L'émeute de juin [...] montra subitement à la société épouvantée des formes monstrueuses et inconnues [...]. C'est une chose hideuse [...] que cette civilisation attaquée par le cynisme et se défendant par la barbarie' (Victor Hugo, *Choses vues 1830–1848*, ed. by Hubert Juin (Paris: Gallimard, 1997), p. 687 (25 June 1848)).
37. Leconte's foregrounding of the antique responds directly to his disappointment post-1848, his first work, *Les Ériynnyes*, taking an ancient Greek subject yet via unorthodox lexis (the *Érynnes* are the Furies), distancing itself from the institutional French Latinized classical. Leconte's unorthodox spelling of ancient Greek names (Klytemnestre for Clytemnestre, Phoibos-Apollôn for Phébus-Apollon etc.), much mocked by contemporaries, may be seen as an attempt to defamiliarize names and narratives institutional French culture had almost made second nature, akin to Flaubert's stratagem in *Salammbô* or *Hérodias*. Leconte's good intentions were not always welcomed: 'On n'y trouve pas la grâce ionienne [...] mais une beauté sévère, parfois un peu froide et presque éginétique, tellement le poète est rigoureux pour lui-même' (Théophile Gautier, *Histoire du romantisme*, cited by Fernand Desonay, *Le Rêve hellénique chez les poètes parnassiens* (Paris: Champion, 1928), pp. 264–77, 289–90. Desonay disagrees: 'c'est l'amour de la beauté qui a dirigé Leconte de Lisle vers telle conception philosophique de l'antiquité païenne: savoir, le panthéisme hellénique' (p. 298).
38. Number 8 of Debussy's *Préludes* (1910).
39. Cf. 'La Ville enchantée' or 'Académie royale de musique', from the *Odes funambulesques* (1857), which seem repeatedly to wonder what to do with the classical (as well as with much that has come since). Banville's answer in this collection is often to mock it — in 'L'Amour à Paris' 'Palmyre' was a *modiste*, whose ruins only remain — but this answer is never Leconte's. On Banville's delicacy, see David Evans, *Théodore de Banville: Constructing Poetic Value in Nineteenth-Century France* (Oxford: Legenda, 2014).
40. The elegies in Bertin's *Les Amours* (1780) have a delicately suggestive sensuality which would not be without similarities to Leconte, were they not in the first person; Parny's prose *Chansons madcéasses* (1787) are more frankly exotic and erotic and said to presage Baudelaire.
41. See Pich, 'Introduction' to *Poèmes barbares*, in *Leconte de Lisle et la création poétique*, pp. VII–XV.
42. Gautier's *Émaux et camées* were first published in 1852 by Eugène Didier, whose edition is only 108 pages long and generously laid out, with blank pages separating most of the poems.
43. The volume was published, like many Symbolist collections, by Lemerre.

44. Charles Baudelaire : 'Le Livre doit être jugé *dans son ensemble*, et alors il en ressort une terrible moralité' ('Notes pour mon avocat', in *Œuvres complètes*, II, 193).
45. Leconte de Lisle, *Poèmes barbares* LXX ('L'Accident de Don Iñigo') and LXVII ('Le Corbeau'); cf. Fairlie, *Leconte de Lisle's Poems on the Barbarian Races*, Chapter VIII.
46. Eclectic not in the contemporary, Cousinian sense, but simply in that of a heterogeneous collection.
47. Stéphane Mallarmé, 'Le Tombeau d'Edgar Poe', l. 6.
48. An exception is *Poèmes barbares* XLV, 'Ultra coelos': 'Nature! Immensité si tranquille et si belle | Majestueux abîme où dort l'oubli sacré' (ll. 25–26). For Weil, God's distance, perhaps akin to Leconte's 'oubli sacré', proves that God is there for man to strive towards through 'l'épaisseur infini du temps et de l'espace'. 'Pour que l'amour soit le plus grand possible, la distance est la plus grande possible. C'est pourquoi le mal peut aller jusqu'à l'extrême limite au-delà de laquelle la possibilité même du bien disparaîtrait. Il a licence de toucher cette limite. Il semble parfois qu'il la dépasse. / Cela est en un sens exactement le contraire de la pensée de Leibniz'. Weil, *La Pesanteur et la grâce*, p. 93.
49. Cf. Stéphane Mallarmé, 'Les Fenêtres', ll. 28–32: 'Je me mire et me vois ange! et je meurs, et j'aime | — Que la vitre soit l'art, soit la mysticité | A renaître, portant mon rêve en diadème, | Au ciel antérieur où fleurit la Beauté!' Mallarmé's 'encens' certainly seems 'fétide' (l. 2), compared to 'L'Esprit du vent' 'dans ses clairons de fer, | En aspergeant le ciel des baves de la mer' in 'Le Massacre de Mona'.
50. The admiration was mutual: 'J'aime beaucoup Delisle pour son volume [*Poèmes antiques*], pour son talent et aussi pour sa préface, pour ses aspirations. [...] Car c'est par là que nous valons quelque chose, l'*aspiration*. Une âme se mesure à la dimension de son désir, comme l'on juge d'avance des cathédrales à la hauteur de leurs clochers' (Gustave Flaubert, letter to Louise Colet, 21 May 1853, in *Correspondance*, ed. by Bruneau & others, II, 329). Further on he suggests parallels between his and Leconte's methods: 'Mouler la vie, n'est-ce pas l'idéaliser? Tant pis, si le moule est de bronze!' (p. 330). Whilst sympathizing with Leconte's impersonality in a letter of 26 August 1853 ('Un homme n'est pas plus qu'une puce. Nos joies, comme nos douleurs, doivent s'absorber dans notre œuvre. Les très belles œuvres sont [...] sereines d'aspect et incompréhensibles [...]. C'est l'éclat de la lumière, le sourire du soleil, et c'est calme! c'est calme! et c'est fort, ça a des fanons comme le *bœuf* de Leconte', p. 417), Flaubert was soon to question his admiration, detecting Leconte's vanity and labelling him a 'poseur taciturne' (7 April 1854, p. 546).
51. As, for example, at the end of *Salammbô* ('Et ainsi mourut la fille d'Hamilcar pour avoir touché au manteau de Tanit') or of *Saint Julien l'Hospitalier* ('Et voilà l'histoire de saint Julien l'Hospitalier, telle à peu près qu'on la trouve, sur un vitrail d'église, dans mon pays').
52. Adolphe Thiers, speech to the Assemblée nationale, 13 November 1872; Émile Zola, *La République et la littérature, Le Roman expérimental*, ed. by Aimé Guedj (Paris: Garnier-Flammarion, 1971), pp. 342–43; memorably reconfigured in Zola's declaration 'La République sera naturaliste ou elle ne sera pas'. Thiers was anxious to rally the support of monarchists.
53. For example, 'Le Soir d'une bataille', *Poèmes barbares* LII, l. 12 and end.
54. *Revue Contemporaine*, 37 (30 June 1862), 796.
55. Hugo, *Les Contemplations*, VI, 23; *Petits poèmes en prose*, XIV.
56. Cf. Leconte de Lisle, 'La Fin de l'homme', l. 51: 'jardin d'Iahvèh, Eden, lieu de délices'.
57. On this trajectory in Leconte, see Caroline De Mulder, *Leconte de Lisle: entre utopie et république* (Amsterdam: Rodopi, 2005).

— 9 —
Rediscovering Beckford's 'Satiric Gravity': Mallarmé's Rehabilitation of the 'French' *Vathek*

Damian Catani

Despite being born into the English establishment, William Beckford was unique in publishing his most famous work, *Vathek*, in French in 1786. In January 1836, a long-since forgotten review in the *Dublin University Magazine* of Schiller's English translations highlighted the case of *Vathek* as a cautionary tale of the significant damage to a work and author that a poor translation can inflict:

> So opposed may be the genius of the language, from which we translate, to that which supplies the new moulds into which the thought must be made to flow, that we do not know any where two volumes which produce an effect so wholly dissimilar as Beckford's English translation of his own French *Vathek* and the volume from which he translates. Every characteristic feature of the original is lost; and the English book, far from representing any of the liveliness, of the archness, of the orientalism, put forth with mock seriousness and *satiric gravity*, gives us something scarcely different in kind or degree from Dr. Hawkesworth's bloated extravaganzas of Almoran and Hamet, and the rest of our Western Orientalists.[1]

By bemoaning to an early nineteenth-century English-speaking readership the loss of that striking oxymoronic quality — the 'satiric gravity' — of William Beckford's most famous work, this quotation provides an apt starting-point for re-examining Mallarmé's own critique of this work, his 'Préface à Vathek', published forty years after this review, in 1876. For it points to the potentially serious cultural, as well as linguistic, repercussions for an author whose work has been 'lost in translation': in this instance, his work's singular ability — all the more remarkable for being in a language that was not his own — to redefine and modernize the hackneyed Western genre of the orientalist tale. This article argues that Mallarmé's return to Beckford's original French text offers a timely re-evaluation of the English author and the tale that first made him famous. This re-evaluation seeks to re-establish the reputation of both the man and his work, a reputation that had been dealt a blow first, by Beckford's 'scandalous' lifestyle, and secondly, by the confusion surrounding the translation and publication of *Vathek*. By adopting a more objective and pragmatic tone, Mallarmé's preface, it is argued, sheds valuable light on Beckford's innovative and radical modernization of the oriental tale, a modernization that was facilitated, to a significant degree, by the creative tension generated by his 'satiric gravity'.

Be that as it may, the irony facing Mallarmé scholars today is that his critical rehabilitation of *Vathek* is, itself, in need of critical reappraisal. In other words, despite the fact that his preface was first published in 1876 by Adolphe Labitte, slightly modified and republished with Perrin in 1893 (the version that is reproduced in the *Œuvres completes*), and subsequently abridged and reincorporated into *Divagations* in 1897, Mallarmé specialists, with the exception of Alfred Parreaux in the 1950s, have tended to give this article a wide berth.[2] They have preferred instead to focus on his other 'Quelques medaillons et portraits en pieds', such as those he devoted to Rimbaud, Verlaine, and Villiers. We can only speculate as to the reasons for this critical neglect. Can it be attributed to the difficulty and ambivalence of this famous preface, even by the exacting standards of a poet as notoriously hermetic as Mallarmé? Or could it stem from the elusive and eccentric reputation of the author of *Vathek*, the aristocratic dilettante William Beckford, who was born into a fabulously wealthy political family and led a scandalous and tormented life that has perhaps unjustly overshadowed his considerable literary talent? Or, as the *Dublin University Magazine* suggests, is it not simply the case that *Vathek*'s translation history is so complicated and protracted as to have alienated a whole host of potential readers and critics? Whatever the reasons for this oversight, it is especially ironic if we bear in mind that one of the most important themes in Mallarmé's preface is, precisely, the oblivion into which both Beckford and *Vathek* had fallen, almost a century after its initial publication in 1782. It is thus proposed in what follows to re-examine Mallarmé's preface, a preface that is itself a three-pronged attempt by the Symbolist poet to resurrect an author and work that remain relatively unknown, especially to French readers. First, he shows the extent to which Beckford was able to reinvigorate a literary genre — the oriental tale — whose importance and popularity, in 1782, was already on the wane. It was thanks to, among other qualities, his 'satiric gravity' that Beckford was able to give the oriental tale a new lease of life that was to sustain it well into Mallarmé's era: a testimony, according to the poet, to *Vathek*'s exceptional originality. Secondly, what also stood out, in the poet's estimation, was Beckford's personality, a personality that allowed him to escape the political career that had been mapped out for him in order to deploy his considerable imaginative powers not only to literature, as both author and bibliophile, but also to art and architecture, in his parallel role as an avid collector of decorative objects. Thirdly, Mallarmé homes in on the thorny question of *Vathek*'s literary identity, a question that is pertinently raised in the *Dublin University Magazine* review: namely, the fact that it was written in French by an Englishman, and the sheer proliferation of French editions and English translations that has generated so much confusion as to make it virtually impossible to establish a definitive version of the text. Mallarmé proposes a twofold solution to this problem: first, to give *Vathek* 'back' to France, as a work that belongs to the French literary canon, a solution that betrays a hint of jingoism on the part of the poet; secondly, to identify the type of reader who is most likely to ensure the survival of this text. In our present, post-Brexit era, where the sovereignty, cultural identity, and territorial rights of the individual nation state are perceived by many to be under threat, a closer examination of Mallarmé's subtle campaign to 'reclaim' *Vathek* as part of France's literary heritage seems especially timely and apposite.

Orientalism

Mallarmé gets straight to the heart of his subject-matter by expressing his regret and frustration that the oriental tale has lost its original dynamism, relevance, and imaginative power:

> Qui n'a regretté le manquement à une visée sublime de l'écrit en prose le plus riche et le plus agréable, travesti naguère comme par nous métamorphosé? Voile mis, pour les mieux faire apparaître, sur des abstractions politiques ou morales que les mousselines de l'Inde au XVIIIe siècle, quand régna le CONTE ORIENTAL; et maintenant, selon la science, un tel genre suscite de la cendre authentique de l'histoire les cités avec les hommes, éternisé par le *Roman de la Momie* et *Salammbô*.[3]

Here, Mallarmé makes an important distinction between two types of oriental tale that belong to two different historical and literary eras. The first, which is dominated by 'abstractions politiques ou morales' is the oriental tale that reigned supreme during the Enlightenment: namely, the satirical *contes* of Montesquieu and Voltaire that held up an imaginary Orient as a hyper-critical mirror to a West that had descended into corruption, decadence, and authoritarianism. The second type, which corresponds to Mallarmé's own era and is characterized by Gautier's Parnassian preciosity and Flaubert's sensual realism, is wedded to the notions of historical and scientific authenticity that underpin mid-nineteenth-century Positivism.

As we shall see, neither type of oriental tale is entirely satisfactory. The only contemporary exception to this rule, according to Mallarmé, is *La Tentation de Saint Antoine*, also written by Flaubert:

> Sauf en la *Tentation de saint Antoine*, un idéal mêlant époques et races dans une prodigieuse fête, comme l'éclair de l'Orient expiré, cherchez! Sur des bouquins hors de mode, aux feuillets desquels ne demeurent de toute synthèse qu'effacement et anachronisme, flotte la nuée de parfums qui n'a pas tonné.
> (II, 5)

Here, we can discern Mallarmé's attraction to an oriental tale 'mêlant époques et races', suggesting his preference for dynamic cultural and historical synthesis over the forgotten anachronisms of a particular period. This synthesis deconstructs the antithesis between the West and the Orient advanced by cultural critic Edward Said in his seminal book *Orientalism*, to which many Beckford critics are indebted.[4] *Orientalism* essentially denounces the West for conceiving of the Orient not as a genuine historical and geographical entity in its own right, enriched by a civilization that is worthy of equal respect, but as an imaginary and loosely defined space that the West fashions according to its own fantasies and, more cynically, its colonialist desire to dominate and control a people whom it considers to be its 'barbaric' inferior.[5] From the Western perspective, this fictional Orient, according to Said's powerful thesis, is both alluring and threatening: alluring, because it promises to satisfy, especially erotically speaking, the many desires that are repressed by an excessively rationalist and rigid West, but also threatening, because it is dominated by an excess of violence and irrationality.

Some of the stereotypes about this Orient — for instance, that of the voluptuous, adulterous women of the harem, or the tyrannical despot — had been established by *Les Milles et Une Nuits,* Antoine Galland's early eighteenth-century translation and adaptation of Arab folk tales. This work exerted a considerable influence on the oriental tale in both France and England.[6] Neverthless, with his customary perspicaciousness, Mallarmé is keen to highlight the richer, more nuanced and enlightened, multicultural Orient that is portrayed by Beckford, in comparison to Galland. Contrary to most authors of orientalist tales, Beckford possessed a profound knowledge of Arabic and Persian, as well as Islamic culture more generally. He was lucky enough, from his early adolescence, to have a private tutor, Alexander Cozens, a specialist in these languages who encouraged the young William to consult the vast library of orientalist works he had inherited from his father.[7] And even before publishing *Vathek*, he had already experimented with the genre of the oriental tale. He went to great lengths to perfect his Arabic and to translate an important collection of manuscripts of tales that had been acquired in Egypt in the 1760s and brought to Britain by Edward Wortley Montagu.[8] His appreciation of the Orient was thus serious, profound, and authentic, an authenticity emphasized by Mallarmé in his analysis of *Vathek*.

With remarkable concision, the Symbolist poet summarizes Caliphe Vathek's story: a moral descent into hell owing to his insatiable lust for knowledge and power that defies the authority of the religion, Islam, that he is meant to represent. In Beckford's tale, this unquenchable thirst is epitomized by the tower Vathek has built, with the help of genii, as a symbol of his absolute power and superiority over his people:

> L'histoire du Calife Vathek commence au faite d'une tour d'où se lit le firmament, pour finir bas dans un souterrain enchanté; tout le laps de tableaux graves ou riants et de prodiges séparant ces extrêmes. Architecture magistrale de la fable et de son concept non moins beau! Quelque chose de fatal ou comme d'inhérent à une loi hâte du pouvoir aux enfers la descente faite par un prince, accompagné de son royaume; seul, au bord du précipice: il a voulu nier la religion d'État à laquelle se lasse l'omnipotence d'être conjointe du fait de l'universelle génuflexion, pour des pratiques de magie, alliées au désir insatiable. (II, 6)

Beckford's more perceptive critics, including Mallarmé himself, have rightly praised the author's capacity to broaden and enrich the range of themes traditionally included in conventional orientalist literature, what Thomas Keymer refers to as his: 'expansion of the orientalist repertoire beyond the standard themes of despotism and decadence'. An example of this new repertoire is Beckford's description of the Hall of Eblis — the hell of the Koran — which is not only unique to orientalist literature but, according to Beckford, was also partly inspired by the Egyptian hall and Turkish boudoir of Splendens, where he grew up. No less a writer than Jorge Luis Borges was quick to credit Beckford's evocation of Eblis as: 'the first truly atrocious Hell in literature'.[9] But in the above paragraph, Mallarmé also perceptively identifies another crucial aspect of *Vathek*'s literary power: namely, the dramatic tension and moral complexity generated by its 'satiric gravity'. The French

Symbolist's words are remarkably similar to those of the *Dublin University Magazine* review: 'tout le laps de tableaux graves ou riants' refers to that oxymoronic quality — the oscillation between serious and satirical descriptions — that allows Beckford to hold in delicate equipoise the moral tension between heaven and hell.

'Satiric gravity' thus allows for a more morally nuanced portrayal of Vathek, one that is also reflected in his religious outlook. Beckford's decision to choose a ninth-century Caliphe named al-Wathiq as his historical model for Vathek is far from coincidental, for he was a significantly more multi-dimensional character than the usual oriental despot portrayed by Galland. In particular, Beckford was drawn to this Caliph's attempts to merge the Muslim faith with outside influences such as Zoroastrianism: 'With his Byzantine mother and his Zoroastrian wife [...] Beckford's anti-hero inhabits a world in which multiple traditions collide and mingle'.[10] Accordingly, *Vathek* ends with a Zoroastrian motif, consummation by fire, thereby also lending it a uniquely menacing, as well as multilayered quality.

This blending of cultures, this capacity to synthesize and assimilate seemingly disparate beliefs and practices, which is neatly encapsulated by Mallarmé, as we have seen, in the phrase 'mêlant époques et races' signals, according to some critics, not only Beckford's interest in religious syncretism, but also his blending of literary leitmotifs.[11] The Western myth of Christopher Marlowe's *Dr Faustus*, according to which the quest for omniscience and omnipotence leads to damnation, is recontextualized by Beckford in a distinctly orientalist setting.[12] Vathek, like Dr Faustus, persists, despite repeated warnings, in transgressing divine laws in his obsessive pursuit of absolute knowledge and power. For instance, not only does he defy Mohammed by building a tower that would allow him access to divine truths, but he also strives in vain to decipher the cryptic writing on sacred swords. Also indicative of this blending of orientalist and Western cultures is his insatiable thirst for knowledge that is forbidden by the prophet, a thirst that can be read as Beckford's latent satire of excessive Enlightenment rationalism. The caliph can thus be seen to embody the obsession, in the 'siècle des Lumières', with knowledge and collecting: 'Condemned for the age-old crime of unrestrained lust for knowledge and power — also, in the terminology of the novel, for something like the obsessive curiosity of an Enlightenment connoisseur and collector — Vathek ends with his companions in subterranean flames'.[13] If excessive reason, associated with the West, proves to be destructive, then the same cannot be said of its counterpart, the imagination, which positively thrives in the less restrictive environment of the Orient. With characteristic modesty and understatement, Mallarmé claims that no critical analysis, including his own, could possibly do justice to *Vathek*'s originality and visionary power. In accordance with his suggestive symbolism, which rejects mimetic realism, he prefers to allude to, rather than merely describe the emotional and psychological states that are triggered by this fusion of elements that belong to both Islamic and Western culture:

> Tant de nouveauté et la *couleur locale*, sur quoi se jette au passage le moderne goût pour faire comme, avec, une orgie, seraient peu, en raison de la grandeur des visions ouvertes par le sujet; où cent impressions, plus captivantes même

que des procédés, se dévoilent à leur tour. Les isoler par formules distinctes et brèves, le faut-il? Et j'ai peur de ne rien dire en énonçant *la tristesse de perspectives monumentales très vastes,* jointe *au mal d'un destin supérieur;* enfin *l'effroi* causé par *des arcanes* et *le vertige* par *l'exaggération orientale des nombres; le remords* qui s'installe *de crimes vagues ou inconnus; les langueurs virginales de l'innocence et de la prière; le blasphème, la méchanceté, la foule.* (II, 6–7)

Sadness, evil, fright, vertigo, remorse, langour: true to his notion of a suggestive poetry that incarnates his celebrated formula 'peindre non la chose, mais l'effet qu'elle produit', Mallarmé substitutes the subtle evocation of diverse emotions and psychological states for the straightforward description of concrete objects and physical beings. This is a process already set in motion in an earlier paragraph, in which the sentences, little by little, efface and 'vaporize' the typical literary Orient — an Orient of superficially exotic beings and concrete objects such as djinns, palaces, and so forth — in order to make way for imaginative dreams and more fleeting states of mind:

Peut-être qu'un songe serein et par notre fantaisie fait en vue de soi seul, atteint aux poèmes: or leur rythme le transportera au-delà des jardins, des royaumes, des salles; là où l'aile de péris et de djinns fondue en le climat ne laisse de tout évanouissement voir que pureté éparse et diamant, comme les étoiles à midi. (II, 5)

Mallarmé's implementation of his poetics of suggestion, however, is neither gratuitous nor narcissistic. It is simply a device that allows him to bring into sharp relief the authenticity and sophistication of Beckford's Orient: not Galland's decorative exoticism, but an Orient that is polyvalent, teeming with infinite possibilities and firmly rooted in its own, distinctive culture. Mallarmé highlights two examples of this: first, 'l'exaggération orientale du nombre' alludes to the Orient's taste for hyperbole and the infinite, as opposed to the Western notion of limits. Moreover, as critic John Garrett reminds us, what also distinguishes *Vathek* from *Les Mille et Une Nuits* is the remorse and sense of individual responsibility felt by its central protagonists. Whereas Ma'aruf, the shoemaker of one of Galland's tales becomes a wealthy man overnight, without the slightest moral repercussions, Vathek and his lover Nourinahar are forced to confront their crimes as soon as they enter Eblis.[14] Mallarmé aptly concludes his analysis of *Vathek* by confirming this clean break between Beckford's work and that of Galland: 'Bien: ce Conte, tout autre que des *Mille et Une Nuits,* qu'est-ce; ou quand brilla-t-il, du fait de qui donc?' (II, 7).

Beckford: The 'Depoliticized Aesthete'

Having praised the authenticity, originality, multicultural, and morally nuanced qualities of *Vathek,* qualities that are held in delicate balance by a 'satiric gravity' that reinvigorates and morally refines the oriental tale, Mallarmé shifts his focus to the biography and personality of its author Beckford. This he does, despite, as André Parreaux has convincingly shown, not having all the facts at his disposal, and choosing to omit some of them.¹⁵ It should be recalled at this juncture, however, that when it comes to literary biography, Mallarmé is far less concerned with strict fidelity to the historical truth about a given author, than using that author as a springboard to explore and refine aesthetic questions of a more universal import. According to this logic, what counts for him in Beckford's life, as is the case in his biographical portraits of Rimbaud and Verlaine, is his contribution to literature and art, and not extraneous 'scandalous' elements that would merely detract from an objective assessment of his literary reputation. This probably explains Mallarmé's almost complete silence on the so-called 'Powderham Scandal' of 1784 (to which he barely alludes with the word 'insinuations'), when Beckford was found in bed with the adolescent William Courtenay. Accused of pederasty and hounded by the English press and senior political figures, he was forced into exile in Switzerland, never fully to regain his former reputation. The critic Didier Girard, amongst others, has argued that this scandal largely explains why, upon his eventual return to England, Beckford practically cut himself off from English high society in order to take refuge in the architecturally and artistically splendid palace he had built at Fonthill, which included an enormous tower modelled on that of the Caliph Vathek.¹⁶

But to Mallarmé, such details are superfluous. Since his priority is to rescue an author and his work from critical neglect, he presents Beckford's literature and art as the direct consequences of his unique talent and genuine vocation and not as the regrettable by-products of destiny and misfortune. It was not scandal that forced Beckford to give up on the political career that was expected of him, nor was it scandal that condemned him to an intellectual life. On the contrary: it was entirely his choice to pursue his literary and artistic projects, a choice that allowed him to give full expression to his imaginative talents. Born into an extremely affluent political family, to an aristocratic mother and self-made father who acquired an immense fortune through the slave trade before entering politics (he was twice elected Mayor of London), Beckford was very much part of the English establishment. Brought up in the opulent surroundings of Fonthill Splendens Castle in Wiltshire, young William not only benefitted, as we have already seen, from private tutors, but also from the protection of high-ranking political figures:

> Sous la tutelle des lords Chatham et Littleton, anxieux d'en faire un homme politique marquant, étudiait, choyé par sa mère et banni d'auprès d'elle pour l'achèvement d'une éducation somptueuse, le fils de feu le lord-maire Beckford (de qui la fière adresse à George III se lit sur un monument érigé au Guildhall).
> (II, 7)

Mallarmé identifies in Beckford a talent and personality that allowed him to overcome a dilemma that both he himself, and the literary peers he sought to represent, faced throughout their own careers: namely, how to reconcile the demands of art and literature with those of economics and politics? How is it possible to retain artistic integrity and relevance in a society that is far more concerned with commercial and ideological imperatives?

Nevertheless, there remains the thorny topic of Beckford's undeniable elitism, not to mention his highly privileged background. Mallarmé quotes a paragraph by Beckford that leaves us in no doubt as to his feelings of intellectual superiority towards the masses:

> Les vérités importantes, sans en excepter une, ont été le résultat d'efforts isolés; — nulle n'a été découverte par la masse des gens, et on peut bien supposer qu'aucune ne le sera jamais; — toutes viennent du savoir, joint à la réflexion d'esprits hautement doués: les grands fleuves sortent de sources solitaires. (II,10)

Thanks to the studies of Bertrand Marchal and Jacques Rancière amongst others, we now know that the traditional image of Mallarmé as an elitist, ivory tower poet, who eschews all contact with society, is far too reductive.[17] A more practical and pragmatic side to Mallarmé has emerged that fully acknowledges the need for a mutually productive relationship between society and art, encapsulated in his celebrated formula: 'Tout se résume dans l'Esthétique et l'Économie politique' (II, 76).

How, then, do we explain his staunch defence of a man who, to all intents and purposes, seems to epitomize that same uncompromising elitism with which he himself was associated for so long? Perhaps, the question needs to be reformulated more subtly, as follows: if Beckford was, indeed, an elitist, then of what type of elitism, precisely, was he guilty? He had the courage and strength of character not to cave in to social expectations by taking the easy route towards the summit of the political and economic establishment. Instead, he decided, from an early age, to devote his life to literature and art, despite fierce opposition from his strict, Protestant mother. Arabic and Orientalism represented for him a liberating language and genre that subtly defied his conformist upbringing, the rigid rationalism of his century and the classical culture on which it was based. Courageous, too, was his bold decision to write *Vathek* in French, a language, like Arabic and Persian, that symbolized an act of resistance to his conventional political destiny, that was associated with English, Latin, and Greek:

> Le fait général du recours à un autre parler que le natal, pour se délivrer, par un écrit, de l'obsession régnant sur toute une jeunesse: renoncez à y voir mieux que l'espèce de solennité avec quoi il fallut s'asseoir à une tâche de caractère unique, elle, différente de tout ce que allait être la vie. (II, 8–9)

If Beckford was, indeed, elitist, then it was of a specifically aesthetic and literary nature, very deliberately chosen by him, and not the social and political elitism of his background, which he categorically rejected. According to Mallarmé, the first type of elitism is preferable to the second because it is associated with positive values: the imagination, which conjures up shared aesthetic experiences and rêveries, freedom of thought and expression, and individual strength of character. Conversely, however, the second type is linked to social oppression, namely: duty, reason, and hereditary power.

In order better to understand Mallarmé's admiration of this unique quality in Beckford, it is fruitful to compare him to Rimbaud, the subject of one of his other *Quelques médaillons et portraits en pied* (II, 120–28). Although there are certain obvious similarities between them — specifically, an exceptional precociousness and homosexual relationships that earned both of them a scandalous notoriety — both men were born into completely different backgrounds that separated them both socially and psychologically. Rimbaud came from peasant stock, was largely self-taught, and quickly abandoned poetry to embark on an ascetic and anonymous life of commerce in an Orient, East Africa, that was all too real and arid. By contrast, Beckford, as we now know, was a privately tutored aristocrat, destined for a political career, who looked with scorn upon his vast inheritance, but nevertheless spent it to rebuild from scratch a vast abode — Fonthill Abbey — that was overflowing with precious books and art objects, which were directly inspired by a rich, literary and artistic Orient. Rimbaud, in a sense, betrayed his poetic destiny for commerce, whereas Beckford betrayed his political destiny for art. The former became an arms dealer and ruthless businessman, the latter, a bibliophile, art collector, and, towards the end of his life, an acclaimed travel writer. In his portrait of Rimbaud, Mallarmé's acknowledgement of his poetic talent is qualified by a hint of disappointment and disapproval, whereas his admiration for Beckford is far more unequivocal: especially, the Englishman's total dedication to literature and art, despite the weight of family expectation and the many privileges from which he could so easily have benefitted.

But Mallarmé's praise of Beckford extends beyond that of his literary talents alone. He also claims that the power of his imagination was so vast that once *Vathek* had been written, this imagination had to be channeled into a new aesthetic endeavour: namely, the construction of an immense abode, Fonthill Abbey, right next to Fonthill House, where he had grown up. Thus literature naturally gravitated, via his imagination, towards architecture:

> Cette imagination aux vastes desseins, comme dépossédée de leur but spirituel rempli, et la même cependant, s'éprit d'abattre pierre à pierre le vieux Fonthill House, réfléchi dans le miroir d'un monotone bassin, pour édifier non loin Fonthill Abbey, au milieu de jardins acclamés les plus beaux de l'Angleterre. Résurrection à grand prix faite et de tout site et de tout temps, le seul rêve, invité à peupler le nouvel intérieur, eut, pour matériaux, ceux de l'art universel représenté là par ses merveilles: le ciel considérait d'immenses collections de fleurs. Points de faux soucis ni de démarche vers des honneurs sociaux: mais tendre uniquement autant que combler la magnifique construction ou de soies ou de vases, chaque meuble disposé d'après un goût jusqu'alors inconnu, voilà.
> (II, 9)

This impressively elaborate and uniquely imposing construction, which attracted painters of the calibre of William Turner from far and wide, was conceived by Beckford as a self-contained aesthetic space, a kind of theatrical spectacle that would immerse visitors into a world completely removed from the one they usually frequented.[18] It has been suggested that the intellectual influence behind this combination of gardens, ornaments, and buildings was philosopher Edmund Burke's notion of the sublime.[19] But the early seeds of Beckford's aesthetic ideas on the close connection between literature and architecture are to be found in the Fonthill Splendens of his childhood, which boasted an Egyptian interior inspired by Piranesi. As evidence of this childhood influence, Mallarmé includes from

Beckford's memoirs his nostalgic reference to this interior, as well as the Turkish boudoir, as the inspirations behind his Eblis. American critic Susan Sontag, who so admired *Vathek* that she wrote a novel that featured a semi-fictional Beckford, has argued that Beckford's Fonthill constituted a kind of homage to synaesthesia, a veritable feast of the senses that anticipated the theatre performances of the following two centuries:

> The mighty forerunner of all the aesthetic palaces of surfeit and synaesthesia and indoor theatrics of the next two centuries.... A cathedral of art [...] in which all the strong sensations our limited sensory organs crave will be amplified and all uplifting thoughts of which our slender spirit is capable will be awakened.[20]

Nor should we forget the famous spectacle organized at Fonthill House at Christmas time in 1781, shortly after Beckford's twenty-first birthday, an event to which he refers in an equally nostalgic tone in his memoirs as the catalyst behind *Vathek*. He employed the services of Philippe de Loutherbourg, an Alsatian artist and stage-designer who had London theatre audiences in raptures with his spectacular optical illusions. He invented the 'Eidophusikon', a proto-cinematographic creation that anticipated the phantasmagorical performances of the Romantic era:

> A visual and sensory space that integrates them [the spectators] in a perceptual and emotional relationship with the surrounding images. The idea is to create an illusion of being inside a total alternative world, unified in both time and space.[21]

Legend has it that this 1781 celebration featured a prototype of this famous 'Eidophusikon', a performance of Milton's *Paradise Lost*, in which Beelzebub and Moloch escape from a burning lake in order to occupy Pandemonium.[22]

Irrespective of what really took place, even if he does not mention Loutherbourg, Mallarmé seems fully to appreciate the extent to which Beckford conceived of Fonthill Abbey, not as some whimsical vanity project designed to enhance his social status, but as a serious commitment to creating a discrete, but spectacular enclave that stood apart (what Sontag calls an 'alternative world') in which each element — furniture, garden, building, ornaments, and so forth — would form part of a coherent and all-encompassing aesthetic whole. Mallarmé's association of Fonthill with 'l'art universel' perhaps also alludes to Wagner's notion of the *Gesamtkunstwerk* which began to filter into France in the 1860s, inspiring the poet's idea of 'le Livre'. What is more, his use of the word 'resurrection' to describe how Beckford replaced one construction with another, recalls the cosmic cycle of life and death that is figured in the 'drame solaire'.

In order to support his claim that Beckford's literature and aestheticism were genuine vocations and not the simple leisure pursuits of an obscenely rich and disabused dilettante, Mallarmé highlights two episodes — Beckford's lengthy stays in Paris during the French Revolution and Nelson's visit to Fonthill Abbey — which make it abundantly clear that he considered aesthetic imperatives to be far more important than political ones. In other words, Mallarmé seeks to 'depoliticize' Beckford in order to bring into sharper focus his talents as both aesthete and literary writer:

> Non que la personne du maître de Fonthill fut inconnue même cinq ou six ans plus tard, en plein changement politique: comparses des premières scènes révolutionnaires, nos estampes montrent un anglais à cheval qui partout assiste en curieux; lui. La chute de la Bastille une fois et encore la mort du Roi précédèrent de peu la rentrée à Londres ou dans ses domaines de cet étranger populaire: mais c'est sans allusion sûre à la gloire littéraire dont son insouciance privait le pays pour le porter autre part, que la Commune se fit un devoir d'inscrire à la suite du passeport cette mention: *Paris le voit s'en aller avec regret.*
> (II, 15)

This paragraph suggests the remarkably detached curiosity, encapsulated by the words 'curieux' and 'insouciance', Beckford felt about the French Revolution that was raging all around him. Recent biographies of Beckford, to which Mallarmé did not have access, reveal that he made a number of prolonged visits to Paris between 1786 and 1792. Three facts stand out: first, that at the beginning of the Revolution, before the Terror, he felt a certain sympathy and admiration for the revolutionary spirit of liberty and thus allegedly befriended certain high-ranking members of the Directoire; secondly, that he took advantage both of the mass exodus of French aristocrats and the devaluation of the French currency to acquire numerous valuable art objects at bargain prices, thereby boosting his vast collection at Fonthill; thirdly, during the Terror, when his life was in genuine danger as an English aristocrat, he is believed to have been saved by one Auguste Chardin, a Republican bookseller who sold Beckford rare books for his vast library. When England declared war on France in 1792 and Beckford found himself trapped in Paris as an enemy subject, he exploited his contacts in the Directoire to obtain a passport that would allow him to return to his homeland.[23] Despite the lack of accurate biographical information available to Mallarmé during his own lifetime, his assessment of Beckford as politically detached and pragmatic has subsequently been confirmed by the facts, especially Beckford's obsession with collecting art and books right in the midst of a revolutionary crisis. That the very real dangers he faced did not in the least deter him from his passion, certainly suggests an overwhelming urge on his part to prioritize art over politics.

A second key episode highlighted by Mallarmé is Admiral Nelson's visit to Fonthill at Christmas of 1800, a visit that was arranged through a family connection with Lady Hamilton, Nelson's lover: 'ce désir, cher à tout grand esprit même retiré, de donner des fêtes, une où Nelson, venu sur les pas de la seconde Lady Hamilton, applaudit sa sirène dans un divertissement tragique et sculptural' (II, 9). Even if Nelson and Beckford had very little in common and allegedly clashed, for Mallarmé, this episode has a deeper symbolic significance: namely, that Beckford was able to create a purely aesthetic space that neutralized political and military power, here epitomized by Nelson.[24] Mallarmé reorients his readers' perspective to aesthetic considerations that lie outside official history. In other words, Beckford's Nelson is not presented by Mallarmé as the great military hero who died for his country in the glorious English victory at Trafalgar, but as one man amongst many who took part in a shared aesthetic celebration. Mallarmé subtly suggests that the importance of art is equal, if not superior, to that of politics.

Literary Heritage and the Role of the Reader

Thus far, we have examined two arguments advanced by Mallarmé to justify his rehabilitation of *Vathek* and its author, Beckford: first, his original modernization of the oriental tale, a modernization that owes much to a morally nuanced 'satiric gravity' that Mallarmé neatly encapsulates in the phrase 'tableaux graves ou riants'; secondly, his ability to transcend his political background and destiny in order to create a shared aesthetic environment that is hermetically sealed off from external historical factors that could undermine it. Nevertheless, in order for this rehabilitation to be complete and definitive, there remains, according to Mallarmé, the thorny question of literary posterity: specifically, how to guarantee that this work captures a new readership and does not fall back into oblivion. If neither Beckford nor *Vathek* have received the attention they deserve, especially in France, how can this oversight be prevented from repeating itself? How can the future survival of this work be secured, both as material object published by reliable and influential publishers, and as a vehicle for ideas that make a lasting impression on its readers? These are questions, Mallarmé suggests, that can only satisfactorily be answered once two major obstacles have been overcome: first, establishing the national identity of the work, and secondly, determining the type of reader that would ensure its survival. Let us examine each of these in turn.

Why is the national identity of *Vathek* so important to Mallarmé, especially when this stance is so manifestly at odds with his usual staunch advocacy of an 'internationalist' outlook on literature? After all, his otherwise notoriously exclusive 'mardis' gatherings in the rue de Rome were renowned for their cosmopolitan inclusivity, welcoming such luminaries as Oscar Wilde, Arthur Symons, Stefan George, James Whistler, and many other non-French writers and artists to their ranks.[25] Moreover, as Marshall C. Olds reminds us, in the mid-1870s and the aftermath of the Paris Commune, Mallarmé was part of the international workers' movement as an elected Secretary of the Société internationale des poètes, which 'strove to foster cooperation among poets by overcoming the claustration of nationalisms, that parochialism advanced by the policies of the Second Empire'.[26] Be that as it may, Mallarmé argues that the very specific circumstances surrounding *Vathek* militate in favour of a more 'nationalist', or at the very least 'patriotic', stance that emphasizes its Frenchness. In today's parlance, Mallarmé comes across, at first blush, as the French literary equivalent of a Brexiteer, as opposed to a European. Nevertheless, he offers two plausible justifications for this approach. The first is the sheer proliferation of editions and translations of the work that have created a textual instability, a problem, as we have seen, that was presciently raised by the *Dublin University Magazine* in 1836; the second, is that it is written in French by an Englishman. The story behind the initial publication and translation of *Vathek* is so farcical as to be scarcely believable.[27] It all began very badly for Beckford. Having written his first version of *Vathek* in 1782, he entrusted the task of translating it into English to a certain Samuel Henley. In 1786, not only did Henley decide to publish his translation without Beckford's prior authorization, but he also had the gumption to present this version as his *own* adaptation of a manuscript written in Arabic. In response, an incensed Beckford rushed to have his own version published in French in Lausanne in November of that year and then again, the following year, in Paris. However, since Henley still had the original French manuscript in his possession, Beckford's subsequent versions were inferior and less idiomatic. This state of affairs prompted Borges to write, with a suitably caustic irony: 'The original is unfaithful to the translation'.[28] Further versions were later published in both languages: in French in 1815, in English in 1816; but by then, the situation had become so complicated that, according to critic Roger Lonsdale, 'no one text of *Vathek* in either French or English can be absolutely definitive'.[29] Mallarmé, therefore, meticulously retraces the constant back-and-forth of these various editions between the two countries, as well as his own efforts to get hold of them in the national libraries of Paris and London.

But Mallarmé identifies a further stumbling block: given that the original language in which this work is written does not correspond to its author's nationality, its identity has never definitively been established. Does this work belong to the French literary canon, because it is written in French; or to the British one, since it is written by an Englishman and translated into English? In short, which nation, France or Great Britain, has the more legitimate claim on 'ownership' of the work?

According to Mallarmé, the solution is simple: the work belongs to France, because it is written in French. Despite his criticism of Beckford's use of possessive and relative pronouns, not to mention his barely discernible 'anglicismes', Mallarmé praises Beckford's French for 'une certaine préciosité même agréable'. This preciosity is complemented by 'sa limpidité vive, avec un ondoiement large de périodes', and that same capacity for synthesis ('un idéal mêlant époques et races') to which Mallarmé had already alluded in his preface: namely, that Vathek successively bridges the gap between two quite distinctive literary eras, owing to a style that not only is reminiscent of Voltaire, but also prefigures the prose of Chateaubriand (II, 20). This is why, in a letter of 24 May 1876 to his friend the Irish poet Arthur O'Shaughnessy, who published the preface to *Vathek* as well as Mallarmé's famous *Gossips* in his review the *Athenaeum*, the French poet explains his determination to return *Vathek* to France, even if, as he acknowledges with a hint of irony, this is likely to incur the displeasure of the English:

> Le point de vue français dans cette affaire, est piquant et original, c'est que j'opère la restitution à la Littérature française d'un livre ignoré d'elle et que l'Angleterre croit le sien: livre, que, quant à sa date, je persiste à considérer comme un chef-d'œuvre, opinion, du reste, qu'a longtemps, n'est-ce pas? consacré[e] la critique anglaise. Londres, l'attitude, en face de cette restitution, doit peut-être se montrer différente; et un peu celle de gens me criant: 'Au Voleur!' Mais ceci nous regarde, regarde le journal, etc. (II, 769–70)

Whether or not it is justified to consider this 'return' of *Vathek* to France as a form of theft, Mallarmé is quite explicit about the opportunities missed by his homeland to reclaim ownership of this work. A combination of historical circumstances and personal failings has meant that *Vathek's* reputation is better in England than in

France. Mallarmé's comparison of Byron with Mérimée brings this difference into sharper focus. He gives full credit to Byron for reviving interest in *Vathek* and its author in his country of birth, even if Beckford himself was irritated at Byron's slightly patronizing description of *Vathek* as a youthful work.[30]

By contrast, in France, only Mérimée, whose literary style is not dissimilar to Beckford's, had been on the cusp of rehabilitating this unrecognized author, only to be prevented from doing so by his untimely death and historical crises that severely tested Anglo-French relations — the Revolution of 1789, the Napoleonic Wars and the Franco-Prussian War:

> Si, un homme du goût le plus sagace, maître en le récit (j'apprends ce fait tout en me relisant), Mérimée, avec les écrits duquel des morceaux un peu rapides du début de VATHEK et la simplicité volontaire d'expression qui en accompagne jusqu'au final grandiose ne sont pas sans de la resemblance, pensa de faire éditer pour les délicats, ses pareils, l'œuvre: compromis par la crise de 1870 comme par celle de 89 ou 1815, et aussi par la mort de l'académicien. (II, 16)

The implication is that Mallarmé intends to succeed where his fellow countryman failed: if Mérimée was unable to rescue Beckford from historical contingencies, then it is up to him to do so.

Mallarmé also regrets that Beckford himself was either unable or unwilling to penetrate French literary circles, circles that would have promoted the literary reputation of *Vathek* in France. Notwithstanding two brief encounters with Voltaire and Mme de Staël, two literary giants who represent two different eras, the Enlightenment and the pre-Romantic period, a combination of Beckford's pride and shyness prevented him from making his work well-known in France: 'Très fièrement timide, peut-être qu'attendait-il qu'on lui parlât d'abord de son livre de jeunesse' (II, 14).

Having thus outlined the reasons for the lack of interest in *Vathek* in France — political and historical contingencies, its author's timid personality — Mallarmé devotes himself to the task of ensuring the lasting appreciation of the work within his own era, an appreciation that demands the identification of an appropriate readership. This concern for the type of relationship that must exist between a literary work and its readers can be examined through the wider prism of the ideal, collective book Mallarmé envisioned for society. The studies of Jacques Scherer and Maurice Blanchot on his notes to 'le Livre', and, more recently, of Eric Benoit, have shown the extent to which Mallarmé conceived of 'le Livre' not only as a material object with a very specific format, lay-out, and affordable purchase price, but also in terms of its target readership.[31] In other words, Mallarmé seeks to reconcile form with content: the book's physical appearance, economic status, and survival as material entity go hand in hand with its capacity to disseminate important and lasting ideas in the minds of present and future readers. Aside from the issues of national identity examined thus far, Mallarmé poses serious questions about the type of reader that is targeted by *Vathek*, and, crucially, the type most likely to ensure the work's survival and prevent it from falling back into oblivion.

Mallarmé makes a crucial distinction between bibliophiles on the one hand, and readers who belong to 'la foule' on the other. His attitude towards the former, whose number corresponds to the limited amount of copies of the *Vathek* edition published by Labitte, is rather lukewarm. While he recognizes that these bibliophiles play an important role in guaranteeing the material survival of the work, he accuses them of egocentricity. Their main concern is not so much to preserve the book itself, nor to disseminate the ideas contained therein, but rather to delude themselves into thinking that they, and no one else, have discovered an antique object of rare value, preferably in the rarefied atmosphere of a library:

> Sagaces chercheurs d'objets rares, bibliophiles comptés par le chiffre même de la réimpression (cent et guère plus), ceux aux mains de qui elle echoit y tiennent aussi le sort de l'œuvre. Tout replacé juste où cela en devait être, comme si l'évocation semblait du néant et point de la poussière: se peut jouer le seul mauvais sort qu'il soit loisible d'abord, une indifférence étrange, point, mais la perte matérielle de l'édition. Solitairement, dussiez-vous, non coupés, feuillets de VATHEK, habiter dans la froide enveloppe du parchemin, au rayon illustre de bibliothèques, la lampe de la veillée suscitera avec recueillement et comme dans un premier honneur intime votre titre marqué en or. Plus se fera, chez de tels lecteurs, qui ambitionnent de n'ouvrir livres de jadis qu'à l'allure surannée et quand le sacra la sanction d'une hospitalité tranquille et riche: où flotte l'illusion de l'avoir, eux-mêmes, trouvé. (II, 19)

Mallarmé takes issue with that same attachment to old, dusty, and dated volumes that he discussed at the beginning of the article in relation to the oriental tale, a genre, which, as we have seen, he considered to have become obsolete. Bibliophilia fosters a mentality that perceives the book as an antique worthy of admiration, rather than a work containing ideas that are pertinent to contemporary society. Mallarmé's frustration with bibliophiles is confirmed in a more humorous and direct tone in that same letter of 1876 he wrote to Arthur O'Shaughnessy:

> Je regrette seulement qu'une édition populaire ou à tout le moins courante n'ait pas été faite par mon Éditeur immédiatement, car l'œuvre se serait ici acclimatée à coup sûr: au lieu que les bibliophiles pour qui est faite cette réimpression soignée et dispendieuse sont gens qui ne lisent point. Tant pis. (II, 769–70)

This, in a nutshell, is the crux of the problem: the bibliophile does not read; he merely collects. He is able to ensure the material survival of the work within a specialized and restricted milieu, but not the dissemination of the ideas it contains among a wider readership. Of course, Beckford, as Mallarmé tells us in his preface, was himself a renowned bibliophile: his book collection at Fonthill was as admired as its architecture and decor, numbering some six thousand works, including sixteenth-century esoteric literature.[32] But Beckford, as his biographers remind us, was a bibliophile who also *read*: he was perfectly capable, according to witness accounts, of devouring an entire book over breakfast.[33]

So if, with the exception of Beckford, the bibliophile is not the ideal reader, then who is? The answer, according to Mallarmé is 'la foule'. He calls for a popularized version of *Vathek* that could attract a wider public, a sentiment echoed in a paragraph of the first Labitte edition of the 'Préface à *Vathek*', that was later removed from the Perrin edition:

> Rien d'aisé comme de devancer, par voie d'abstraction et purement, des verdicts inclus dans l'avenir, lequel n'est que la lenteur à concevoir de la foule; et voici la fin de mes détours, à savoir si le conte oriental, réintégré en qualité d'offrande, va se joindre simplement aux archives, pour y dormir; ou tantôt nécessiter chez nous quelque mode de vulgarisation déjà projeté, peut-être même (comme de l'autre côté de la mer) sa réédition habituelle.[34]

Given the impossibility of predicting how future readers will judge the work, Mallarmé speculates whether it would not also be worth publishing a 'vulgar' version of it that is aimed at a broader readership. Indeed, the danger remains that even his own attempts at reviving the work — his preface to the edition of *Vathek* published by Adolphe Labitte, an edition of only 200 copies that will now doubt only be purchased by bibliophiles — will perhaps still not be enough to rescue this work from the oblivion into which it has already fallen in the past.

Despite his admiration for a writer who belongs to the British establishment, Mallarmé exhibits, here, a pragmatically anti-elitist attitude in his bid to preserve and disseminate *Vathek*, Beckford's most renowned work. Of course, there is undeniably a hint of jingoism in his proto-Brexit anxiety to 'take back control' of a work written in French by an Englishman. And yet, as we have seen, Mallarmé's attitude is more than justified by his desire to reacquaint his readers with that 'satiric gravity', the 'tableaux graves ou riants', of the French source text; only then, in his view, can this forgotten classic truly be appreciated by all those who admire and cherish great literature, irrespective of their nationality.

Notes to Chapter 10

1. See the article entitled 'Schiller', *Dublin University Magazine*, 37 (January 1836), 1–23 (p. 1, my emphasis).
2. André Parreaux, 'Le Tombeau de Beckford par Stéphane Mallarmé', *Revue de l'histoire littéraire de la France*, 3 (1955), 329–38.
3. Reference throughout this chapter is principally made to the 'Préface à *Vathek*' of 1876, using the following edition: Stéphane Mallarmé, *Œuvres complètes*, ed. by Bertrand Marchal, 2 vols, Bibliothèque de la Pléiade (Paris: Gallimard, 1998–2003), II, 5–20 (p. 5). Further references are included in the main text. The revised and abridged version of the 'Préface', entitled 'Beckford', was incorporated into *Quelques médaillons et portraits en pied*, in *Divagations* (1897) and is found at II, 129–37 of this same edition.
4. See, for example, John Garrett, 'Ending in Infinity: William Beckford's Arabian Tale,' *Eighteenth-Century Fiction*, 5.1 (1992), 15–34 (pp. 16–17).
5. Edward W. Said, *Orientalism* [1978] (London: Penguin, 2003).
6. On Oriental stereotypes influenced by Galland, see: *Three Oriental Tales: Frances Sheridan, 'History of Nourjahad'; William Beckford, 'Vathek'; Lord Byron, 'The Giaour'*, ed. by Alan Richardson (Boston, MA: Houghton Mifflin, 2002), pp. 1–10.
7. On Cozens's role as Beckford's 'spiritual father', see: *Vathek and Other Stories: A William Beckford Reader*, ed. by Malcolm Jack (London: Pickering, 1993), pp. x–xi; Didier Girard, *William Beckford: terroriste au palais de la raison* (Paris: Corti, 1993), pp. 20–26.
8. William Beckford, *Vathek*, ed. by Thomas Keymer (Oxford: Oxford University Press, 2013), p. xxxiii.
9. Jorge Luis Borges, *Other Inquisitions 1937–52*, trans. by Ruth L. C. Simms (Austin: University of Texas Press, 1964), p. 139.
10. Beckford, *Vathek*, p. xxv.

11. Keymer, in Beckford, *Vathek*, p. xxv. On the possible influence of Persian Sufism on Beckford's work, see Devendra P. Varma, 'Beckford's Treasures Rediscovered: The Mystic Glow of Persian Sufism in *Vathek*', in *Vathek and the Escape from Time*, ed. by K. W. Graham (New York: AMS Press, 1990), pp. 97–111.
12. On the parallels between Marlowe and Beckford, see Garrett, 'Ending in Infinity', pp. 26–27.
13. Keymer, in Beckford, *Vathek*, p. xxvi.
14. See Garrett, 'Ending in Infinity', p. 19.
15. Parreaux quite rightly reminds us that Mallarmé relies principally on Beckford's memoirs, recorded towards the end of his life by Cyrus Redding, *Memoirs of William Beckford, of Fonthill*, 2 vols (London: C. J. Skeet, 1859). Unfortunately, the content of these memoirs is often inaccurate or incomplete; see Parreaux, 'Le Tombeau de Beckford par Stéphane Mallarmé', pp. 331–32.
16. Girard, *William Beckford*, pp. 128, 147–48; see also James Lees-Milne, *William Beckford* (London: Century, 1990), p. xi.
17. See Bertrand Marchal, *La Religion de Mallarmé* (Paris: Corti, 1988); Jacques Rancière, *Mallarmé: la politique de la sirène* (Paris: Hachette, 1996); and my own analysis of Mallarmé's anti-élitism in: Damian Catani, *The Poet in Society: Art, Consumerism and Politics in Mallarmé* (New York: Peter Lang, 2003).
18. On the fascination Fonthill exerted on painters of the period, see James Lees-Milne, *William Beckford*, pp. 58–59.
19. Burke explains his notion of the sublime in *A Philosophical Enquiry into the Origin of Our Ideas of the Sublime and the Beautiful*. For Burke's influence on Beckford, notably on the architecture of Fonthill, see Sandro Jung, 'The Architectural Design of Beckford's *Vathek*,' *Eighteenth-Century Fiction*, 242 (2011–12), 301–23.
20. Susan Sontag, *The Volcano Lover: A Romance* (New York, 1995), pp. 324–25 (quoted by Keymer, in Beckford, *Vathek*, p. xx).
21. Iain McCalman, 'The Virtual Infernal: Philippe de Loutherbourg, William Beckford and the "Spectacle of the Sublime"', *Romanticism on the Net*, 46 (May 2007), 1–31 (p. 1).
22. McCalman, 'The Virtual Infernal', p. 28.
23. For a detailed, accurate account of Beckford's prolonged visits to Paris during the French Revolution, including his purchase of art objects and books and his political opinions and connections, see the biography by Brian Fothergill, *Beckford of Fonthill* (Stroud: Nonsuch, 2005), pp. 210–20.
24. The tense relationship between Beckford and Nelson is described by James Lees-Milne, *William Beckford*, pp. 53–54.
25. On the cosmopolitan ambiance of the 'mardis' see, for instance, Robert E. Norton, *Secret Germany: Stefan George and his Circle* (Ithaca, NY, & London: Cornell University Press, 2002), p. 148; also on the 'internationalism of the Symbolist movement', see Rosemary Lloyd, *Mallarmé: The Poet and his Circle* (Ithaca, NY, & London: Cornell University Press, 2005), pp. 166–67.
26. Marshall C. Olds, 'Mallarmé and Internationalism', in *Kaleidoscopes: Essays in Nineteenth-Century French Literature in Honor of Thomas H. Goetz*, ed. by Graham Falconer and Mary Donaldson-Evans (Toronto: Centre d'études romantiques Joseph Sablé, 1996), pp. 157–68 (p. 159).
27. On the complex history behind the translation of this text, see Keymer's comments in his edition of *Vathek*, pp. xxx–xxxi.
28. Borges, *Other Inquisitions*, p. 140.
29. William Beckford, *Vathek*, ed. by Roger Lonsdale (Oxford: Oxford University Press, 1983), p. xxxv.
30. See Keymer, in Beckford, *Vathek*, p. xv.
31. See Eric Benoit, *Mallarmé et le mystère du 'Livre'* (Paris: Champion, 1998); Maurice Blanchot, *Le Livre à venir* (Paris: Gallimard, 1959); and Jacques Scherer, *Le 'Livre' de Mallarmé: premières recherches sur des documents inédits* (Paris: Gallimard, 1957).
32. For a description of Beckford's library, which was reputed to house the largest collection in the whole of Europe, see Girard, *William Beckford*, pp. 184–86; also: Lees-Milne, who claims that, when he died, Beckford's collection had reached 9,837 books (*William Beckford*, p. 106).
33. Lees-Milne, *William Beckford*, p.105.

34. William Beckford, *Le 'Vathek' de Beckford, réimprimé sur l'édition française originale avec préface par Stéphane Mallarmé* (Paris: Librairie de la Bibliothèque nationale, 1876), p. xxxvii.

10

Literary Translation, Responsibility, and the Linguistic Lightness of Being

Clive Scott

Roger Pearson's distinguished career as a literary translator has, to date, inhabited the worlds of Maupassant and Zola, and has been informed by 'professional' ambitions: to avoid 'inaccuracy, infelicity and anachronism',[1] to find the right register, to match, where necessary, the author's painstaking research.[2] But declared and reassuring aims like these conceal both Roger's lively response to, say, Zola's 'economy of expression, [...] his carefully modulated use of tense and his knowingly arranged word-order',[3] and also a way with linguistic means which reveals his irrepressible inventiveness with tones, rhythms, and tempi, unerring in its ability expressively to 'landscape' narrative and to implicate and absorb the reader. One cannot but regret that his monumental, two-volume work on Mallarmé did not necessitate running translations of the poems and poetic extracts which might, in turn, have incorporated the tireless effervescence of his critical insights;[4] and one might say the same of the poets who people his recent *Unacknowledged Legislators*.[5] It is with the translation of poetry that this paper is concerned, and more particularly with the relationship — in its extremer forms it should be emphasized — between the potentially political implications of translational responsibility and a linguistic lightness of being in the translator, the spirit of which animates Roger's own translations.

What web of obligations does the literary translator assume as he/she confronts a source text? What balance sheet of commitments and freedoms? The translator has a range of approved skills (linguistic, cultural), skills acquired within a state apparatus, which authorize him/her to construct a version of the source text which keeps it intact, which endorses its being chosen, and thus endows it with a status. Qualification (having the skills) is the badge of entitlement. One version of democracy is precisely a political body constituted by entitlements (entitlement to vote, *civis romanus sum*). But the version of literary translation to be pursued in this paper relates more to the view expressed by Jacques Rancière: 'Democracy is the specific situation in which it is the absence of entitlement that entitles one to exercise the *arkhê* [power to act]'.[6] Are we then to argue that, if we wish translation to be a politically democratic act, a political act to further democracy, we must treat entitlement as an impediment? Does responsibility lie in a direction opposed to being properly qualified?

I should emphasize immediately that, in using the word 'political', I do not refer to the politics of the writer or translator, nor the representation of the political in a text, nor, then, to those kinds of interventionist translation which explicitly (seek to) shift particular ideologies, whether through re-gendering, say, or by using translation to critique or re-direct belief-systems. In fact, I want to avoid the idea that politics is necessarily about ideology. I want, instead, to ask in what senses translation as a general activity might be regarded as a political writing, or in what senses the mechanism of translational writing might be deemed political, and, more particularly, how writing might be made political by its very lightness of linguistic being, how political levitation might be conjoined with political gravitation.

But beyond this there are further implications: since we are addressing literary translation, then we must also consider the political repercussions involved in framing the literary, in linguistically transforming the literary, in manhandling the literary. Do some linguistic variants — dialects, creoles, pidgins — *naturally* step outside the accepted parameters of the literary? Do such variants have the required literary credentials, and what are these anyway? We may feel that we have all but eradicated linguistic discrimination, and have managed to assign to *all* languages a proper place in our concerns about biolingual diversity, cultural conservation, and so on; but, faced with translations of Baudelaire into Scots, say, we may still wonder whether Scots is 'qualified' to do justice to Baudelaire, or fear that Scots will remove Baudelaire's global currency.[7] But translation moves among languages precisely to remind us about the mobility of concepts and attitudes, to promote a readiness perceptually to adjust, to redistribute, our schemas of value. One of the tasks of literary translation is to generate and explore shifts in the location of the literary, in its modes of acting, and inevitably to insinuate that the literary is no less a political stake than human rights, that the literary is driven by implicit institutional prejudices, that the figures of poetics (metre, acoustic patterning, lineation) are discriminatory.

In the wake of Deleuze and Guattari, I might immediately argue that, inasmuch as the translation I wish to foster is by nature a minoritarian and deterritorializing writing, in so far as my vision of translation is a smooth-space, rather than a striated-space, vision, then it is set to undermine the state, the majoritarian, the world of procedures, borders, atavism, filiation. In other versions of political consciousness as manifest in translational language, translation might be either an 'imitation' of majoritarian language leavened with various kinds of Situationist *détournement*, or the corrosion of the majoritarian as *logos* by the majoritarian as *phone* (homophonic translation), or the development of those languages we have identified as variant (dialects, pidgins, creoles). These are all strategies within which the act of translation naturally sits. But if there is an inherent politics of translation, there is also a politics of reading, a politics both of reading to translate and of reading translations, a politics I will crudely split into a dual option: the accusative reading and the vocative reading.

Where reading enacts with a text an accusative relationship, it builds on the notion of that text as established or establishable, as a text fit to become a document, to achieve objecthood, fit, too, to be studied and interpreted, an institutional object. Reading, in this understanding, is a constitutive act: one reads through the text as a process of identification or recognition. And this constitutive reading tacitly endows the text with an author and thus with a certain authority. But as a further step, institutional textual studies seem to wish to get us out of the text into the text-transcendent, into the meta-textual, into the text-recuperative, to let text slip back into its writtenness, into its autonomy. The teleology of accusative reading is consensus, an agreed gamut of interpretations, the formation of the canonic, texts in the service of a discipline, or of a syllabus.

But when the text is read vocatively, or, more properly, nominatively/vocatively, then reading disestablishes the text, is forcibly text-immanent, a negotiated experience, interlocutory, with co-authorship always as a possible horizon. The pertinent question for the reader is not 'Do you understand it?', but 'What understanding have you come to with it?', 'What kind of reciprocity, or dialectical relationship, have you arrived at?' The vocative is the interposition into text of a prosody. Prosody is often referred to as the supra-segmental features, that is to say, those linguistic features which shape sequences of segments and which I shall lump together under the term 'paralinguistic', the vocal input: pitch, loudness, tempo, accentual intensity, tone, phrasing, pausing, mode of enunciation. Prosody is vocal experimentation with the text and thus equally self-experimentation; prosody is the variable pianistic 'touch' of vocal rhythm replacing the inert system of accent-relative-to-syllable that is metre. But prosody is also tied to the situation of speech, to a spatio-temporal situatedness, to a constantly self-modifying interlocutory relationship. In other words, linguistically speaking, it has to do with pragmatics. When we speak about experimentation and self-experimentation here we are referring to the play of expressive energies, the nature of the force of words, not to deliver a meaning enhanced by rhetorical devices (e.g. alliteration helps tie meanings together), but permutationally to weave together moving senses triggered by bodily sensation: vowels, for example, are voiced or unvoiced, rounded or unrounded, front or back, not pure, abstract sounds, as you find them in the International Phonetic Alphabet, but the complex physiology of laryngo-buccal articulations. Prosody is an investment of the body in language.

The distinction between meaning and sense is crucial to my case. Meaning is something which is seen to inhere in language by virtue of lexical and cultural embeddedness. It is something which, however ambiguous, however plural, must be respected and cannot be denied, something which has claims to make. But we must be careful, or else meaning will demand its dues overbearingly, and without right. Because meaning is, in fact, in a permanent state of obsolescence. Sense, on the other hand, has constantly to be made. But it is elusive; it multiplies, diversifies, escapes, or holds itself at a distance, just beyond our grasp. It is an integral part of any text's progress through time and space, a guarantee of that progress, and both sense and progress are dependent on the efforts that readers are prepared to make in pursuit of them. Translation, which for me is a particular version of reading, is not the retrieval of meaning from a text, in order to perpetuate it. Translation is an account of a sense-making of the source text by the translator, a sense-making which has written into it the activity of the readerly consciousness and the play of the readerly senses. In a word, then, translation does not recuperate meaning, but generates sense, as it generates the future of the source text.

Much critical energy has been expended, since antiquity, on classifying and rationalizing the figures of speech. There are dictionaries of such figures, not merely to ease the definition of rebarbative terms (asyndeton, anacoluthon, etc.), but also to suggest that, like other lexemes, these figures have not just structural but also functional signifieds. This is figures in the service of accusativity. For the vocative reader, such figures are: (i) text-generative or genetic impulses, peculiar to the text in question; that is, they are nonce sensations of the text, seeming to engender other, answering textual sensations, not the studied application of a system of accredited devices; (ii) they so thicken the text corporeally that they exceed the 'given' semantics; the (textual) texture encourages the constant re-projection of the text; (iii) the response of the reader is thus textually *inaugurative* and language becomes the bearer of a new epistemology.

The idea of a continuous movement towards understanding within the situational has two meanings — first, a pragmatics-related one: the reader, as we have seen, is in a vocative vis-à-vis with the text; reading as 'I' constantly involves a reversal, by the agency of text, into 'you'; if the target text is to be tested against the source text, then equally, by back-translation, the source text must be tested against the target text. The second meaning relates to the physical reading environment: the reader's perception of text is interfered with by ambience (ambient features, activities, noises), particularly when the reader looks up from the text; one might say that the text comes to an understanding *with* the environment. This seems to me important because it affirms that the text is a fact in our daily lives, that reading itself is a reconciliation of all the factors that participate in it, that reading is the cross-over point between imagination and perception, output and input, the internal and external. Is reading about getting something out of a text, or is it a mode of relating, the means by which I constitute myself in an environment, find my place? What is a text as an ecological force? Or do I mean: What is *reading* as a mode of ecological orientation?

One further point should be added: the vocative reading, and its practice through prosody, signal a rejection of the book, understood as a form of entombment, as the entropic epitome of the self-reflexive and narcissistic, as the merchandization of the canonical, as the singularization of text, as the policing of the institutional. Pragmatics or vocativity is the performance of language in all the space-times of the actual; it is the projection of text into social spaces, or the conversion of text into script, scenario, score, the text yet to be embodied.

If vocativity thrusts the text ('you') into time, the time of 'my' reading/speaking, then equally it delivers the text to lability, to textual volatility, to what I am calling 'linguistic lightness of being'. Translational reading, as an instrument of the vocative, has the capacity to make the already written unpredictable, or in other words, the vocative makes the source text a living *énonciation*, not an historical *énoncé*; the source text can, as it were, no longer be derived from a past. Why is this so? Because the vocative is an engagement with the becoming of the text, not with its 'message', a relationship of mutuality in making, rather than one text reading off the other. The time-boundedness of the relational, of I/you interaction, shifts the linguistic to the paralinguistic (verbal *and* visual), from segmented language to prosody as its vivifying force.[8]

The text read vocatively is, then, read for what it is capable of becoming, that is, within the 'aureola' or 'nimbus' of its possible variants and reformulations. Let us here remember Merleau-Ponty and his notion of a text read 'laterally':

> Elle [la parole] ne choisit pas seulement une signe pour une signification déjà définie, comme on va chercher un marteau pour enfoncer un clou ou une tenaille pour l'arracher. Elle tâtonne autour d'une intention de signifier qui ne dispose d'aucun texte pour se guider, qui justement est en train de l'écrire. Et si nous voulons saisir la parole dans son opération la plus propre, et de manière à lui rendre pleine justice, il nous faut évoquer toutes celles qui auraient pu venir à sa place, et qui ont été omises, sentir comme elles auraient autrement touché et ébranlé la chaîne du langage, à quel point celle-ci était vraiment la seule possible, si cette signification devait venir au monde.
>
> [Speech does not choose only one sign for one already defined signification, the way one reaches for a hammer to drive in a nail or pincers to pull one out. It gropes around an intention to signify which has at its disposal no text to guide it, for it is just being written. And if we want to grasp speech in its most authentic operation in order to do it full justice, we must evoke all those words that could have come in its place that have been omitted; to feel the different way they would have impinged on and rattled the chain of language, to know at what point this particular speech was the only one possible if this signification was to come into the world.][9]

A text always carries, in its very being, the possibility of becoming other; it never really supersedes the process of composition, of projective self-multiplication. Furthermore, it is inevitable that we should, as writers, as much be possessed by language as possess it; it is always in excess of any intention that the writer or translator may have, always reaching beyond its own textual borders. The reader, and indeed the translator, do not read off what is supposed to be there, transparently available, but participate in the capacitation of the work, in what it makes possible, the latent texts alongside.

This presupposes that we read not to hear 'exactly', but to hear vectorially as it were, both to trigger a verbal field which allows sense to circulate, to multiply, to test its flexibilities, and, at the same time, to play with formal properties, to feel for further formal configurations. Here it might help us to consider a French translation, by Philippe Mikriammos, of ll. 5–8 from the first stanza of Wilfred Owen's 'Dulce et decorum est':

> Men marched asleep. Many had lost their boots
> But limped on, blood-shod. All went lame; all blind;
> Drunk with fatigue; deaf even to the hoots
> Of tired, outstripped Five-Nines that dropped behind.
>
> [Les hommes dormaient en marchant. Beaucoup avaient perdu leurs
>   brodequins
> Mais, cahin-caha, chaussés de sang, ils allaient, boitant tous et tous aveugles;

> Ivres de fatigue, sourds même au hululement
> Des obus de 5,9 fatigués qui, distancés, tombaient dans notre dos.]¹⁰

A traditional critique of the French translation might remark that it sacrifices Owen's compression: where Owen's lines are underlyingly iambic pentameter, Mikriammos's (counted in the classical manner) are 18, 19, 13, 19 syllables long, partly perhaps because French compels participial constructions where English uses adverbial adjectives (asleep, lame), partly because French does not have compounds (blood-shod) at its disposal, but overall because Mikriammos has set a different pace, with more extended intonation-groups: in the second and third lines in particular he has avoided what is peremptory and uncompromising and jaggedly discontinuous in Owen's full-stop and semi-colons. But Mikriammos's syntax *is* episodic, and creates for these men a dreamier, more sleep-walking atmosphere, which Owen himself goes on to develop and thematize: 'If in some smothering dreams you too could pace' (l. 17). But we might admire the sudden directness and added pathos of Mikriammos's visual 'onomatopoeia' 'cahin-caha' (< *kahu kaha*), an alternative to 'clopin-clopant' or the verb 'clopiner'. This begins to loosen attitudes to the English as authoritative text. What kind of onomatopoeia might we use in English? How much is 'hoots', usually associated with owls or derision, compelled by 'boots'? Is *hululer* too uneven a sound, too lamentational? How would Owen's verse sound if it were blank verse? And if it were blank, how would you re-write it? What would these lines sound like if they had different rhythmic dispositions? What difference would there be if Mikriammos had used *bottes* rather than *brodequins*, or *manquer* rather than *perdre*? Can one hear anything of *se retirer* in 'dropped behind'? What differences in the distribution of the sensible are there in these two accounts, and what margins of redistribution still remain? As we read these texts together, we realize that it is not a critique of the translation that interests us so much as the reciprocal perturbations in a field of expressive energies; our attention shifts from what is there to what might be there, from questionable choices made to opportunities opened up, from nailing a detail to proliferation.

Does this mean that translation must be out of tune with the text it translates? No, because the dissensus it enacts is not a quarrel with the source text, but with the attitudes and language usually deemed appropriate to an account of the source text. The dissensus enacted in translation involves the source text and the target text's participating in a 'political' dialogue, a mutually reinforcing dissensus. Consensus, the re-assimilation of the source text into a parliamentary democracy of literary and linguistic understanding, in which translation might so easily connive, is the last thing that either party wants. But, it should be added, this dissensus politics is associated with contingency and precariousness. It cannot, of its very nature, wish the achievement of a stable state; it can only wish an act of the same nature repeated, that is to say, the generation of a multiplicity which expresses itself in heterogeneity.

I would like to exemplify this a little by considering a translation of Baudelaire's 'La Mort des pauvres':

C'est la Mort qui console, hélas! et qui fait vivre;
C'est le but de la vie, et c'est le seul espoir
Qui, comme un élixir, nous monte et nous enivre,
Et nous donne le cœur de marcher jusqu'au soir;

À travers la tempête, et la neige, et le givre,
C'est la clarté vibrante à notre horizon noir;
C'est l'auberge fameuse inscrite sur le livre,
Où l'on pourra manger, et dormir, et s'asseoir;

C'est un Ange qui tient dans ses doigts magnétiques
Le sommeil et le don des rêves extatiques,
Et qui refait le lit des gens pauvres et nus;

C'est la gloire des dieux, c'est le grenier mystique,
C'est la bourse du pauvre et sa patrie antique,
C'est le portique ouvert sur les Cieux inconnus![11]

My version runs:

        It's death that consoles
        Alas
        And keeps us going
        Life's goal and our only hope
        Which like an elixir
        Whips us to a peak and
        Sets our minds swimming and
        Gives us the strength
        To keep on the road
                              till nightfall

        Through storm snow
        And frost
        It's the glittering light on our dark horizon
        It's the four-star hotel you'll find in the Book
        Where you can eat and sleep and
        Take the weight off your feet

        It's an Angel with sleep
                              in its magnetic fingers
        And the gift of dreams
                            of ecstasy and
        Who's there
        To plump up the pillows of the poor
        And the naked

        It's the glory of gods it's the mystical garret
                            turned granary
        It's the poor man's bursting purse
                            and his ancestral home
        It's the gate that leads on
        To the unmapped
        Country
                            of the Skies.

Claude Pichois characterizes the 'politics' of this poem as 'un socialisme chrétien' [a Christian socialism] and 'une ardente charité' [an ardent charity].[12] This observation I would like to relate to a distinction between vocativity and impersonation. We might argue that the poet identifies with the poor, suggests that poverty is not a material state but a spiritual condition, shared by many more than those who live in abject penury. Images of physical well-being merely act as metaphors for spiritual longings, such that phrases like 'l'auberge fameuse', 'rêves extatiques', and 'grenier mystique' are suffused with pathos, rather than with, say, derisive condescension. But negative attitudes like this last are certainly allowed by the text. Is the 'auberge', then, Jacques Crépet's Samaritan's hostel of Luke 10:34–35 (but why then is 'livre' not capitalized?), or is the 'livre' Antoine Adam's 'guide de voyage, où l'auberge est signalée' [travel-guide, in which the ho[s]tel is given special mention]?[13] My own version concedes the guide-book recommendation but, equally, disambiguates the biblical presence. But both attitudes, the empathetic and condescending, are impersonations. The politics of the vocative, on the other hand, of the translator in ongoing dialogue with a text, is to release a less available politics, in two senses: first, as formal disclosure; and second, as an infinitely extendable and always speculative expressive formulation. Vocativity engages us in a dialogue which has no reason to end, nourished as it is by the dialectic of its own becoming.

Here, the translator is confronted by a structure of purposefulness (the sonnet) which is inhabited by a temporizing garrulousness ('Et/et', 'C'est/c'est': the 'waiting-for-Godot' syndrome). If the sonnet is the shape of death, a fixed and accelerative (quatrains > tercets) form, what understanding should we come to with it, in order that it begins to serve, rather than suppress, the poet/poor's self-perpetuating loquacity? How can the poor be prevented from speaking themselves to death, on the instruction, as it were, of a verse-form above their station, in the service of the elite? To begin with, I try to 'free' the text, but only to the degree that it still betrays its formal ancestry: a free-verse sonnet, then. I then try to inject the very loquacity of the poor with modal complexity, by, for example, exercising 'and' in line-initial and line-terminal positions. What is the psychology or rather *psychisme* of 'and'? Most obviously it is the instrument of conceptual automatism, as it occurs in collocations so common that they write themselves almost despite us. Deriving from this is the sense of 'and' as finding one's way home, of generating the conditions for closure ('x, y, and z'). But equally the 'and', particularly in narrative, may be the irrepressibility of invention, the forging of continuities. It is this kind of 'and' that is likely to gravitate towards a line-initial position, the position of the fallen upon, the re-motivating/re-motivated, a certain irrepressibility. The line-terminal 'and' is more likely to be connected with negative features, with the failure of invention, or the loss of a clear path, of impetus, the point at which discourse bends into the inconsequential or opens up on the incoherent, or on continuity for its own sake, unballasted. Then it becomes an attempt to show a resourcefulness which turns out to be only the *mechanism* of resource. In the first stanza of my translation, line-terminal 'and' is the carrier of redundancy, of that surplus which might be a source of self-persuasion. In the second stanza, it rounds off an enumeration with an element which is supernumerary and falls outside the logic of the preceding elements. And finally, in the third stanza, it again loses the thread and creates a continuation which is peculiarly haphazard, gratuitous.

But I also want to exploit the multiplication of margin that free verse allows. My hope is that the gradually increasing instances of the second margin in my translation introduces both a different kind of consciousness, self-aware, shading into 'What *am* I saying!!?', and a different kind of finality, something beyond garrulousness, when the voice is existentially alone with itself. In a sense, it hardly matters what the textual content of these second-margin fragments is: it is all a matter of tone and intonation, and perhaps of tempo and amplitude.

That other characteristic of the poem's loquacity, the repeated 'C'est', is a litany of minimal syntax and progressive self-intoxication, self-liberation, which reaches its most intense and insistent in the final stanza (4 instances). This intensity is endorsed by the repetition of syntactic structure in ll. 12 and 13 ('C'est' + def. art. + noun + genitive complement + 'c'est/et' + determiner + noun + adjective) and by the unusual repetition in the rhymes (the c and e rhymes are both in /tik/, plural for c, singular for e; this /tik/ is taken up line-internally, in the final line). Does this signal some achieved self-transcendence? If sonnet-structure is to be cast as the warp and weft of death, then perhaps we should imagine it reversed and architectural, a Pharaonic pyramid (or arrowhead?):

> Skies
> of the
> country
> unmapped
>
> leads on to the
> it's the gate that
> and his ancestral home
> the poor man's bursting purse
>
> mystical garret turned granary it's
> naked it's the glory of gods it's the
> there to plump up the pillows of the poor and
> fingers and the gift of dreams of ecstasy and who's
> weight off your feet it's an Angel with sleep in its magnetic
>
> you'll find in the Book where you can eat and sleep and take the
> and frost it's the glittering light on our dark horizon it's the four-star hotel
> and gives us the strength to keep on the road till nightfall through storm snow
> and our only hope which like an elixir whips us to a peak and sets our minds swimming
> THE DEATH OF THE POOR it's death that consoles alas and keeps us going life's goal

Such a design gives new point to 'whips us to a peak', and to 'Skies' as the final word; and the reversal of the direction of reading gives a certain impression of toiling against the tide, made increasingly easy the nearer one gets to the summit. Sonnet-structure, now dictated by architectural demands, is 5 + 5 + 4 + 4, a strangely careless or impertinent compliance. And the careful alignments of words which ensure the stability and shape of the building are affronts to the notion of linearity: this is a form of *Mittelachse* writing, in which the 'lines' are accidental outcomes of the pressures of symmetry from a notional centre. I have elsewhere made the case for tabularity as a political subversion of the linear, and while structure here does not allow the free disposition of verbal material, the layout does, like the tabular, demand a reading which is tentative, which must find its way.[14] Where the linear acts as a visual guarantee of a readability already arrived at and meriting a certain kind of submissive attention, this text guarantees nothing other than its own unfolding, with literary merit an open question. It quite literally compels us to read against the grain (upwards).

Translation here provides us with the opportunity to write, not against Baudelaire, but against a political tradition of text, against a political tradition of textual presentation which enjoins upon us to accept text as given, as the 'to-be-repeated', rather than as the source of readerly empowerment whereby a text becomes available for co-authoring, whereby it submits itself not to interpretation, but to re-imagining, reconfiguring, re-projecting. It is vital to us that all 'authoritative' forms of language have this vulnerability in translation.

Translation presents us with the safeguards of textual intervention and textual multiplication. If, in Gérard de Nerval's 'El Desdichado' sonnet-structure is again, in some sense, a death-structure, that is to say, a structure that must come to its *appointed* end, then the appointedness itself will represent, in the politics of forms, a capitulation:

> Je suis le ténébreux, — le veuf, — l'inconsolé,
> Le prince d'Aquitaine à la tour abolie:
> Ma seule *étoile* est morte, — et mon luth constellé
> Porte le *soleil noir* de la *Mélancolie*.
>
> Dans la nuit du tombeau, toi qui m'as consolé,
> Rends-moi le Pausilippe et la mer d'Italie,
> La *fleur* qui plaisait tant à mon cœur désolé,
> Et la treille où le pampre à la rose s'allie.
>
> Suis-je Amour ou Phébus?... Lusignan ou Biron?
> Mon front est rouge encore du baiser de la reine;
> J'ai rêvé dans la grotte où nage la sirène...
>
> Et j'ai deux fois vainqueur traversé l'Achéron:
> Modulant tour à tour sur la lyre d'Orphée
> Les soupirs de la sainte et les cris de la fée.[15]
>
> [Enshadowed, yes,
>   and disespoused, if that's the word;
>   disconsolate, inconsolable.
> Prince of Aquitaine whose tower's now
>   a ruined folly:
> As now a dead star
>   the *star* I steered by:
>   my music of the spheres
> Has for rosette
>   the *black Sun* of Dürer's *Melancholy*.

> In dark of death you gave me care
> Return to me Posilippo
> And Sea of Italy set fair
> In dark of death you gave me care
> The *flower* that brightened my despair
> Trellis where vine and roses grow
> In dark of death you gave me care
> Return to me Posilippo
>
> I'm Eros or Apollo... which?
> Either Lusignan... or Byron?
> The queen's embraces still bewitch
> I'm Eros or Apollo... which?
> My dreaming sings at perfect pitch
> In the grotto of the Siren
> I'm Eros or Apollo... which?
> Either Lusignan... or Byron.
>
> And twice, just twice,
>   with victory in my hands
> I've crossed the Acheron:
> Plucking the Orphic lyre and
>   alternating
>   turn by turn:
> The sighing of the saint
>   and the faerie's cries.]

But here the poet has seemingly outwitted that presumption, and part of the poet's ingenuity seems owed to his 'modulant tour à tour' Christian and pagan, and gender values: the rhymes of the octave are alternating, and the e-rhyme of the sestet (ll. 13–14) significantly transgenders the octave's a-rhyme to feminine (é > ée). The poem's paratactic syntax acts as a further mystification of motive and causality. But for the polyglot reader these observations are givens, elements of the poem's accusativity. When I shift to the vocative, I speak the poem, to hear what it says to me of its own 'concealed' expressiveness. And what I speak is thus an experimentation, an enquiry, which is above all concerned with paralanguage, with prosody, with what generates the suprasegmental, the interplay of rhythms, intonation, phrasing, tone, pausing, sequential quality of accent (intensity, duration, pitch). Prosody is what articulates and hears a vocal distribution, vocal and modal modulation, embodiment.

And what I hear grows from the presence of the colons (ll. 2, 12). These, it seems to me, are not signs of explanation or clarification, but of sedimentation, layers of recollection or self-confession, multiplying thresholds of insight, invested with dreaded discovery in the first stanza and hopeful expectation in the last. I have doubled these colons. Their incidence, at the same time suggests a structure of chiasmus interwoven with that of alternation, the journey of a voice that needs to sing itself back to Orphic capacity. Accordingly, I have created something akin to the 'enclosed' sonnet structure that one finds in, say, Baudelaire's 'L'Avertisseur', but my 'inner' stanzas are not tercets, but rather triolets, and my outer stanzas are still quatrain and tercet. This progression, into and out of the pair of triolets is accompanied by a shift from past participial forms in the first stanza to present participial ones in the final stanza, as the condemnation to loss is replaced by continuous or progressive states. The two-rhyme triolets themselves (ABaAabAB) are 'squared' forms, octosyllabic *huitains*/octaves, and present, through their circumscribed repetitions and progressions, collections of energies which cannot resolve themselves, which are as if caught in suspended interactivity, spaces of energetic turmoil, animated by a restlessly modulating paralanguage.

In the two versions following, 'El Desdichado2' and 'El Desdichado4', I use the computer to re-distribute the text in different, tri-columnar arrangements, having reduced the number of colons to two again. I have further introduced designs in graphite and enamel paint; the work in graphite is designed to capture something of the survival of the spirit of 'El Desdichado' in the work of Odilon Redon. These versions are intended as an interactive pair and they indeed have in common the disposition of the first three lines and the vertical, letter-by-letter spelling-out of '(m)y music of the spheres', in the space between the first and second columns:

In 'El Desdichado2', the 'centred' triolets are still visually recoverable, but their unusual margins mean that they now enjoy more 'assimilated', dispositional continuities with the other stanzas. The graphite images — black sun, fallen funerary column ('cippe' or 'stèle'), the baseball-bat shapes which are the beginnings of rotations, of other still invisible suns — provide a background for the spray of spots in black enamel, an accompaniment of the handwritten lines, the inky evidence of a writing that will never find its fair copy, a writing beset by 'mechanical' failure. In 'El Desdichado4', the graphite elements — black suns, tower — form a Cubist face, so that the text is more evidently inhabited by a presiding consciousness, but a consciousness haunted by peculiar dissociations: several of the rhymes of the triolets, to the left of the tower/nose have lost contact with their lines and go through the motions of rhyming as orphaned words, while the tracery of grey enamel paint, still besmirched by black drops, generates, in this frozen world, an animation, a potential dynamic, which has no cohesion, which is made of unfulfilled gestural impulses, but which nonetheless begets something like a concluding scribbled signature.

What is important in this associative doodling, this synaesthetic expansion, is the way it breaks open both this text and verbality itself. It is not just that the text is outstripped by what it generates in the reader, by the proliferation of sense and sensory activity, but that it fails to keep what it begets within its own jurisdiction. No language is sufficient to the human condition, no text can be permitted to become a *mot d'ordre*.[16] To reiterate: this is not to imply that translation necessarily subverts the source text, is in a relation of hostility to it; what prevents the source text from consolidating its authority is also a gift to it. This gift is the gift of the translator's linguistic lightness of being: to write in the vocative rather than the accusative, to write in the imaginary presence of all languages,[17] to write with a sense of inherent textual lability, to write within a stream of continuous variation, to write with the urgency of the situated, to write in linguistic excess, to write the reader out of aural/scriptural familiarity into a new distribution of the senses.[18]

El Desdichado2

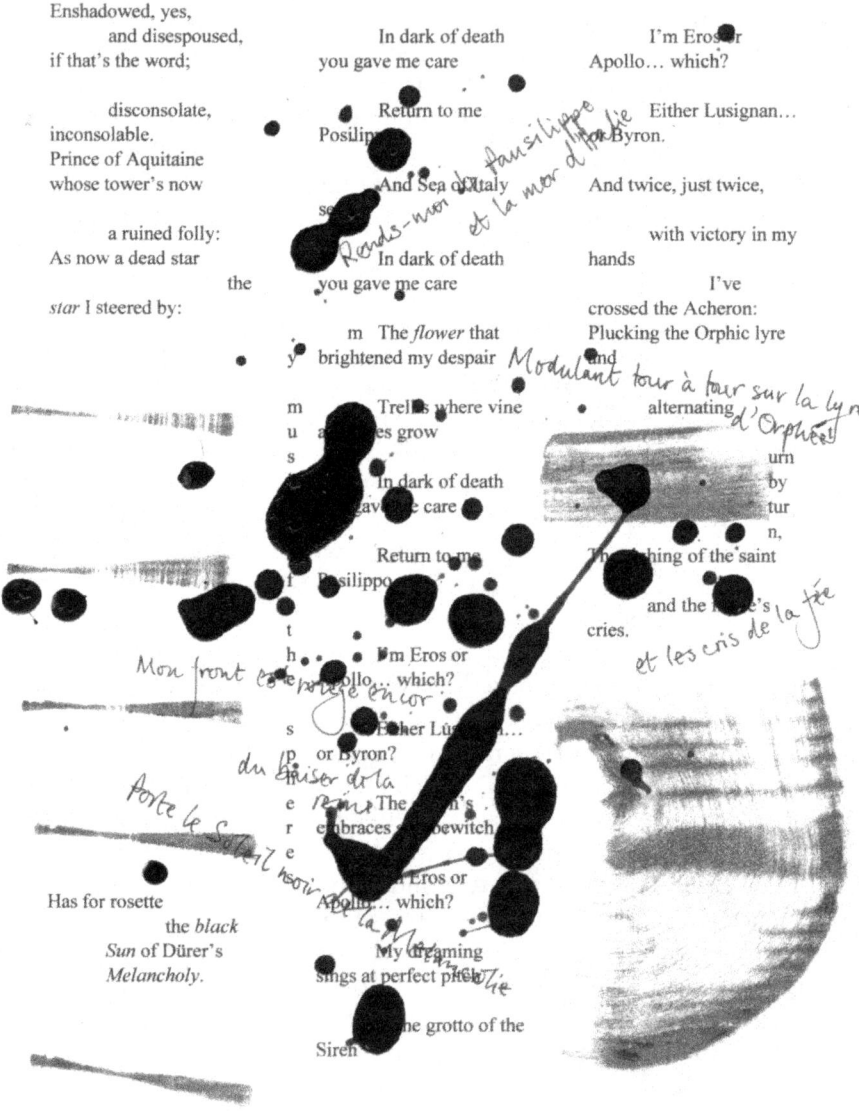

Enshadowed, yes,
    and disespoused,
if that's the word;

In dark of death
you gave me care

I'm Eros or
Apollo... which?

    disconsolate,
inconsolable.
Prince of Aquitaine
whose tower's now

    Return to me
Posilip...
And Sea of Italy

Either Lusignan...
or Byron.

And twice, just twice,

    a ruined folly:
As now a dead star
            the
star I steered by:

In dark of death
you gave me care

with victory in my
hands
    I've
crossed the Acheron:
Plucking the Orphic lyre
and

    m The *flower* that
  y brightened my despair

alternating

  m   Trellis where vine
  u   a   es grow
  s
            In dark of death
        ga   e care
            Return to me
        P silippo
    f
    t   I'm Eros or
    h   Apollo... which?
            Either Lusignan...
    s   or Byron?
    p
    e   The   's
    r   embraces   bewitch
    e
            I'm Eros or
            Apollo... which?

urn
by
tur
n,
Th   hing of the saint
and the   's
cries.

Has for rosette
    the *black*
Sun of Dürer's
Melancholy.

My dreaming
sings at perfect pitch
    e grotto of the
Siren

EL DESDICHADO[4]

Enshadowed, yes,
    and disespoused,
if that's the word;

    disconsolate,
inconsolable.
Prince of Aquitaine
whose tower's now

    a ruined folly:
As now a dead star
    the
star I steered by:

Has to soothe
    the *black Sun* of Dürer's melancholy.

care

care

my despair
grow
m
re
m
u
s
i
c
bewitch
o
f pitch
h
e
r
e
s

And twice, just twice

hucking the Orphic lyre and

The sighing of the saint

In dark of death you gave me

Return to me Posilippo
And Sea of Italy set fair
In dark of death you gave me

The *flower* that brightened

Trellis where vine and roses

In dark of death you gave me
Return to me Posilippo

I'm Eros or Apollo... which?
Either Lusignan... or Byron?
The queen's embraces still

I'm Eros or Apollo... which?
My dreaming legs at perfect

In the grotto of the siren
I'm Eros or Apollo... which?
Either Lusignan... or Byron.

with victory in my hands
I've crossed the Acheron:

alternating
turn by turn,

and the faerie's cries.

This gift is also the gift of an adaptability to a collectivity, but a collectivity of individuals, for whom the source text is a vehicle of a constantly self-diversifying self-affirmation. Translation is a socialization of language, not in the sense that it makes communally available a linguistic order already arrived at, but in the sense that it summons or invites the unpredictable inputs of all readers who come into contact with it.

We can thus easily imagine a translational ethos as a political ideal, and we can do so by taking account of Merleau-Ponty's opinion, expressed just after the war, in 'La Guerre a eu lieu' (June 1945):

> Or, cette tâche politique n'est incompatible avec aucune valeur de culture at aucune tâche littéraire, si culture et littérature se définissent, non comme des techniques hors du monde, mais comme la prise de conscience progressive de nos multiples rapports avec autrui et avec le monde.
>
> [This political task is not incompatible with any cultural value or literary task, if literature and culture are defined as the progressive awareness of our multiple relationships with other people and the world, rather than as extramundane techniques.][19]

The political task referred to here is the root-and-branch destruction of antisemitism and fascism, and the pursuit of an 'effective liberty'. It is, above all, translational writing's engagement with the multiple that one wishes to highlight here, in its operations across languages (verbal and visual), such that it cannot function without a readiness constantly to shift its perceptual position, to incorporate the dialogic 'you' and thus to increase the excess to be found in the work. Excess explodes authority in that it proposes a way of proceeding which thrives on the uncircumscribable, on an inability to prevent proliferation and the exploration of new experiential postures. This is a politics of the unpoliticizable; it is about creating a new translationese, not a translationese of the stylistically awkward or ponderous or over-punctilious, but a translationese of the floating world, a world of shifting contours, smooth space, undefined relations, of a syntax that is infinitely mutable, of an extended acousticity.

Notes to Chapter 11

1. Guy de Maupassant, *A Life*, ed. and trans. by Roger Pearson (Oxford: Oxford University Press, 1999), p. xxxi.
2. Émile Zola, *Germinal*, ed. and trans. by Roger Pearson (London: Penguin, 2004), p. xlv.
3. Émile Zola, *La Bête humaine*, ed. and trans. by Roger Pearson (Oxford: Oxford University Press, 1996), p. xlv.
4. Roger Pearson, *Unfolding Mallarmé: The Development of a Poetic Art* (Oxford: Clarendon Press, 1996) and *Mallarmé and Circumstance: The Translation of Silence* (Oxford: Oxford University Press, 2004).
5. Roger Pearson, *Unacknowledged Legislators: The Poet as Lawgiver in Post-Revolutionary France: Chateaubriand, Staël, Lamartine, Hugo, Vigny* (Oxford: Oxford University Press, 2016).
6. Jacques Rancière, *Dissensus: On Politics and Aesthetics*, ed. and trans. by Steven Corcoran (London: Bloomsbury, 2015), p. 39.
7. See, for example, Charles Baudelaire, *Fae the Flouers o Evil: Baudelaire in Scots*, trans. by James Robertson (Kingskettle: Kettilonia, 2001), and *Scottish Spleen: Baudelaire in Scots*, ed. by James

W. Underhill, Tom Hubbard, and Stewart Sanderson, trans. by Sheena Blackhall and others (Alford: Tapsalteerie, 2015).
8. By 'visual paralanguage' I mean visible features, such as layout, typography, punctuation, diacritical signs, which produce inflections in the voice or modalizations of tone or variations in tempo and amplitude.
9. Maurice Merleau-Ponty, 'La Science et l'expérience de l'expression', in *La Prose du monde*, ed. by Claude Lefort (Paris: Gallimard, 1969), pp. 15–65 (p. 64); 'Science and the Experience of Expression', in *The Prose of the World*, ed. by Claude Lefort, trans. by John O'Neill (Evanston, IL: Northwestern University Press, 1973), pp. 9–46 (p. 45).
10. *Anthologie bilingue de la poésie anglaise*, ed. by Paul Bensimon and others (Paris: Gallimard, 2005), pp. 1228–31.
11. Charles Baudelaire, 'La Mort des pauvres', in *Œuvres complètes*, ed. by Claude Pichois and Jean Ziegler, 2 vols, Bibliothèque de la Pléiade (Paris: Gallimard, 1975–76), I, 126–27.
12. Baudelaire, *Œuvres complètes*, I, 1089.
13. Charles Baudelaire, *Les Fleurs du mal*, ed. by Antoine Adam (Paris: Garnier Frères, 1961), p. 426. One might observe that Pichois supports the Crépet interpretation (Baudelaire, *Œuvres complètes*, I, 1089–90).
14. Clive Scott, *Translating Apollinaire* (Exeter: University of Exeter Press, 2014), pp. 249–50.
15. Gérard de Nerval, *Œuvres*, ed. by Henri Lemaitre (Paris: Garnier Frères, 1966), p. 693.
16. Gilles Deleuze and Félix Guattari, *Capitalisme et schizophrénie II: mille plateaux* (Paris: Minuit, 1980), pp. 95–97.
17. See Édouard Glissant, *L'Imaginaire des langues: entretiens avec Lise Gauvin (1991–2009)* (Paris: Gallimard, 2010), p. 14: 'On ne peut plus écrire une langue de manière monolingue. On est obligé de tenir compte des imaginaires des langues'.
18. The phrase 'the distribution of the sensible' refers to Jacques Rancière's 'le partage du sensible' (Jacques Rancière, *Le Partage du sensible: esthétique et politique* (Paris: La Fabrique, 2000)), that 'reconfiguration of the given perceptual forms' that defines an aesthetic politics (Jacques Rancière, *The Politics of Aesthetics: The Distribution of the Sensible*, ed. and trans. by Gabriel Rockhill, afterword by Slavoj Žižek (London: Continuum, 2006), p. 63).
19. Maurice Merleau-Ponty, *Sens et non-sens*, 5th edn (Paris: Nagel, 1966), p. 269; *Sense and Non-Sense*, ed. and trans. by Hubert L. Dreyfus and Patricia Allen Dreyfus (Evanston, IL: Northwestern University Press, 1964), p. 152.

— 11 —
Fighting Against the Fall: Gravity and Grace in Beckett's *Nouvelles*

Adam Watt

The comfort of home, or even the reassurance of familiarity, are experiences that are in short supply in the writing of Samuel Beckett. Consider 'neither', a text written and published in English in 1979, which opens 'to and fro in shadow from inner to outershadow | from impenetrable self to impenetrable unself by way of neither' and closes 'then no sound | then gently light unfading on that unheeded neither | unspeakable home'.[1] Home for Beckett is not a question of comfort, longing, nostalgia, or wistfulness. Some of these traits colour the words spoken by his characters but most of those we encounter in the pages of Beckett's texts are perpetually adrift: his protagonists experience what Ludovic Janvier terms 'une sensation presque totale de non-appartenance'.[2] For Adorno, Beckett's characters are 'flies twitching after the fly swatter has half-squashed them'; they are 'subjects thrown completely back upon their own resources, worldlessness become flesh, they consist of nothing but the wretched realities of their world, which has shrivelled to bare necessity'.[3] More recently, Paul Davies has argued that:

> Just as the word *homeless* has the ghost of home in it, so the people of Beckett's lost world faintly hear the breath of the pleroma and feel its unseen immensity. Their isolation is not that of never having been or never having had, but the isolation of separation — the *lessening* of contact, the *weakening* of musculature, the *wandering* of mind, the *fading* of destination.[4]

When we think of the citizens of Beckett's world, the terms 'wretched' and 'shrivelled', 'weakening', wandering', and so on may indeed seem much closer to the mark than any vocabulary of grace or salvation. What I would like to do in this essay is to suggest that there *are* elements of what we might call grace, fleeting promises of something beyond the horror of the here and now, to be found in Beckett's *Nouvelles*, the short narrative texts entitled 'L'Expulsé', 'Le Calmant' and 'La Fin', that the author wrote in the immediate aftermath of the Second World War.[5] In a piece for radio written in June 1946, precisely the period during which he composed the *Nouvelles*, Beckett wrote of his contemporary moment as 'this universe become provisional', describing this time as 'a vision [...] of humanity in ruins'.[6] Whilst concurring with Janvier, Adorno and Davies, I will suggest that in the world of the *Nouvelles*, a harsh and troubled world where succour of any sort is exceedingly scant, a form of grace may be afforded by recollections, on the part of the wandering, isolated protagonists, of what we might call alternative narrative homes, from authors ranging from Dante and Voltaire to Flaubert, Proust and Rilke.

Grace — whether in the sense of smooth, fluid movement or comportment, or in the religious sense of being favoured or blessed by God — is a rarity in Beckett's *Nouvelles*. The narrators of 'L'Expulsé' and 'La Fin' are cast out into the world from their dwelling places (for reasons never revealed) and abandoned to a painful life of wandering, while the protagonist of 'Le Calmant', more troublingly still, begins his narrative 'Je ne sais plus quand je suis mort', continuing 'j'ai trop peur ce soir pour m'écouter pourrir, pour attendre les grandes chutes rouges du cœur, les torsions du caecum sans issue et que s'accomplissent dans ma tête les longs assassinats, l'assaut aux piliers inébranlables, l'amour avec les cadavres' ('Le Calmant', p. 39). These are individuals whose movements of body and of mind are the antithesis of grace. The narrator of 'L'Expulsé' mentions that he is in the habit, when he finds himself in a difficult position, of raising his eyes to the sky, 'd'où nous vient le fameux secours' ('L'Expulsé', p. 18), though there is scant evidence in that story of it ever doing him any good. By contrast the narrator of 'Le Calmant' notes that for his part 'Je n'avais qu'à baisser la tête et à regarder à terre sous mes pieds, devant mes pieds, car c'est dans cette attitude que j'ai toujours puisé la force de, comment dire, je ne sais pas, et c'est de la terre plutôt que du ciel, pourtant mieux coté, que m'est venu le secours, dans les instants difficiles' ('Le Calmant', pp. 48–49). His hesitation here ('la force de, comment dire, je ne sais pas') is characteristic of the narrators of all of the *Nouvelles*, who demonstrate profoundly limited agency, together with an acute awareness of that limitation and an unerring will candidly to hold forth about it.

Here, for example, is how the eponymous 'expulsé' describes his movement:

> Je me mis en route. Quelle allure. Raideur des membres inférieurs, comme si la nature m'avait refusé des genoux, écart extraordinaire des pieds de part et d'autre de l'axe de la marche. Le tronc, en revanche, comme par l'effet d'un mécanisme compensatoire, avait la mollesse d'un sac négligemment rempli de chiffes et ballottait éperdument selon les imprévisibles saccades du bassin. ('L'Expulsé', p. 19)

The reason for this exceptional carriage is given no less candidly: in his childhood, the narrator tells us 'J'avais donc la fâcheuse habitude, ayant compissé ma culotte, ou l'ayant conchiée, ce qui m'arrivait assez régulièrement au début de la matinée [...] de vouloir absolument continuer et achever ma journée, comme si de rien n'était. [...] [J]usqu'à mon coucher je me traînais, avec entre mes petites cuisses, ou plaqué à mes fesses, brûlant, croustillant et puant, le résultat de mes débordements' ('L'Expulsé', p. 20). Similarly, though without the same graphic explanations, the narrator of 'Le Calmant' explains that he is someone 'que d'habitude les parkinsoniens distançaient' ('Le Calmant', p. 52), before elaborating that his is a 'démarche lente, raide, et qui à chaque pas semblait résoudre un problème statodynamique sans précédent' ('Le Calmant', p. 66). It is not only in their gait, however, that Beckett's bodies lack grace.

Roger Pearson writes of Mallarmé's notion of the poet as a writer 'employing an everyday medium to transmute the hopes and fears of the human soul into a golden treasury of sound and meaning'.[7] The remark is pertinent for Beckett, with the caveat that his characters tend to produce a rather less glittering array of 'sound and meaning'. The narrators of each of the *Nouvelles* have great difficulty in communicating verbally with the individuals they encounter. In 'Le Calmant', for example, the narrator tries to speak to a young boy he meets: 'je pris le parti de lui adresser la parole. Je préparais donc ma phrase et ouvris la bouche, croyant que j'allais l'entendre, mais je n'entendis qu'une sorte de râle, inintelligible même pour moi qui connaissais mes intentions' ('Le Calmant', pp. 49–50). In 'La Fin', when the narrator protests his eviction from the hospice, the orderly overseeing the process cajoles him: 'Allons, allons, dit-il, d'ailleurs on ne comprend pas le dixième de ce que vous dites' ('La Fin', p. 75). Later on he admits to having 'un accent bizarre [...] à force d'assimiler les voyelles et de supprimer les consonnes' (p. 81).[8] These characters are not silent, however. The narrator in 'La Fin' discourses at length on his flatulence: 'Je pétais, c'est une affaire entendue,' writes Beckett, with characteristic playfulness on the double sense of 'entendue', but even this mode of self-expression is physically curtailed: 'Je pétais, c'est une affaire entendue, mais difficilement sec, cela sortait avec un bruit de pompe, se fondait dans le grand jamais' (pp. 107–08). If this wasn't graceless enough, it accompanies an even lengthier (and graphic) discussion of the relative merits of scratching oneself and masturbation ('Le vrai grattage est supérieur au branlage, à mon avis', p. 100). The same character acknowledges that he stinks (p. 88) and sleeps rough amongst discarded condoms, vomit and cowpats (pp. 93–94). In the *Nouvelles*, then, rather than a golden treasury, we find humanity in ruins, humankind at perhaps its lowest ebb. 'On devient sauvage,' remarks the narrator of 'La Fin', 'c'est forcé' (p. 108).

And yet, these tales are much more than simple catalogues of ailments, suffering and brutality. They have literary qualities — rhythms, structuring devices, reflexivity — that play with genre and readerly expectation.[9] As Steven Connor puts it, in these texts, 'all that we have are relationships, and especially relationships of repetition, resemblance and recall'.[10] A nameless individual, old and physically weak, is variously ejected from a place of shelter, thrown down a set of steps, awakes alone in a field or finds himself wandering, adrift. Although Beckett's protagonists are 'homeless, friendless and loveless',[11] in each of these stories momentum, morale — and hope — are sustained through the act of story-telling itself. Rather than seeking to reconstruct a picture of a life and a sense of self via the work of recollection and reminiscence, telling stories for Beckett's narrators in the novellas is more simply a palliative for the punishing fact of existence. This point is plainly and darkly made in 'Le Calmant', in which the narrator, having explained his fears ('j'ai trop peur ce soir, [etc]', as quoted above), intimates: 'Je vais donc me raconter une histoire, je vais donc essayer de me raconter une histoire, pour essayer de me calmer' ('Le Calmant', pp. 39–40).

Narrative itself, then, is a 'calmative', and tortured, nightmarish existence is rendered tolerable, just, by the telling of stories. Following the horrors of the Second World War, during which Beckett's ties with his adopted home of France were most enduringly established, he turns to story-telling to come to terms with what he has experienced, and in the *Nouvelles* writes of world-less subjects whose primary succour comes from the telling of stories. The role of story-telling for the protagonists of Beckett's novellas is very close to the position articulated by Ali Smith in her 2012 Weidenfeld lectures: 'Even if we were to find ourselves homeless, in a strange land, with nothing of ourselves left', writes Smith, ' — say we lost everything — we'd still have another kind of home, in aesthetic form itself, in the familiarity, the unchanging assurance that a known rhythm, a recognized line, the familiar shape of a story, a tune, a line or phrase or sentence gives us every time, even long after we've forgotten we even know it'.[12] In what follows, I would like to suggest that sewn into Beckett's tales of desolation are moments like those identified by Smith, when a rhythm, a line, a shape or a phrase, offers succour or grace amidst the ruins.

While Beckett's narrators in the *Nouvelles* are vagabond and worldless as Adorno suggests, they do nevertheless construct a space for themselves in language. The home that they construct is not just in story-telling but in the recollection of and the return to other writers, other narrative homes, as it were. Firstly, let us consider a passage from 'La Fin', a story in which the narrator is expelled from a sort of sanatorium, dressed in the clothes of a dead man, and sent out into the world, in which he seeks refuge, successively in a basement room he shares with rats (where he is swindled and evicted to make way for a pig); then in a cave by the sea; a cabin in the mountains; and finally a boat he finds abandoned in a shed and that serves as his final, coffin-like resting place. Each of the physical spaces he inhabits is less conventionally welcoming than the last. Here is the narrator's account of finding himself in the street, before he manages to find the basement room:

> Dans la rue j'étais perdu. Il y avait longtemps que je n'avais mis les pieds dans cette partie de la ville et elle me semblait bien changée. Des bâtiments entiers avaient disparu, les palissades avaient changé de place et de toutes parts je voyais en grandes lettres des noms de commerçants que je n'avais jamais vus nulle part et que j'aurais été même en peine de prononcer. Il y avait des rues là où je ne me rappelais pas en avoir vu, plusieurs parmi celles que je me rappelais avaient disparu et d'autres enfin avaient complètement changé de nom. L'impression générale était la même qu'autrefois. Il est vrai que je connaissais la ville très mal. C'était peut-être une tout autre ville. Je ne savais pas où j'étais censé aller. ('La Fin', pp. 77–78)

Beckett's narrator cannot gain any purchase on his surroundings and as the passage progresses, the prevailing confusion and uncertainty only increase. He may be rudderless, disconcerted and alone, but he is not alone in experiencing this stark, uneasy sense of physical and communicative dislocation. Intriguingly, the text here bears a marked similarity in structure and lexis to a passage by another great wanderer of the European tradition, Rainer Maria Rilke. In his *Notebooks of Malte Laurids Brigge*, initially published in German in 1910, Rilke offers a narrative of a Danish intellectual living in Paris, who spends a good deal of time alone, pondering poverty, illness, good and bad fortune; he is, in many ways, a kindred spirit to Beckett's narrators. Here, in Herter Norton's translation, is one of his wanderings through Paris:

> I cannot recall how I got out through the numerous courtyards. It was evening, and I lost my way in this strange neighbourhood and went up boulevards with interminable walls in one direction until I reached some square or other. Thence I began to walk along a street, and other streets came that I had never seen before, and still other streets. Electric cars would come racing up and past, too brilliantly lit and with harsh, beating clang of bells. But on their signboards stood names I did not know. I did not know in what city I was or whether I had a lodging somewhere here or what I must do in order not to have to go on walking.[13]

Although there is no copy of *The Notebooks of Malte Laurids Brigge* in Beckett's library, he does open his (distinctly frosty) 1934 review of J. B. Leishmann's translation of Rilke's selected poems with the observation that 'Malte Laurids Brigge was a kind of deficient Edmond Teste', which suggests a familiarity with the novel (and with Valéry, though none of his works figure among Beckett's books either).[14] Given Beckett's resistance to the Rilke of the poems — he is denigrated for 'breathless petulance' and 'self-deception'[15] — recognizing the proximity between their two texts here is perhaps not so much a matter of influence, as a question of something more nuanced: a shared sensitivity to place, exile and homelessness.[16]

Let us take another example, this time from 'L'Expulsé', whose narrator, in the story's *in medias res* opening, is cast down a flight of steps into the street, only for the door to open a second time so that his hat, one of his very few belongings, can be thrown out after him. This leads to the following vignette:

> Comment décrire ce chapeau? Et pourquoi? Lorsque ma tête eut atteint ses dimensions je ne dirai pas définitives, mais maxima, mon père me dit, Viens, mon fils, nous allons acheter ton chapeau, comme s'il préexistait depuis l'éternité, dans un endroit déterminé. Il alla droit au chapeau. Moi je n'avais pas voix au chapitre, le chapelier non plus. Je me suis souvent demandé si mon père n'avait pas pour dessein de m'humilier, s'il n'était pas jaloux de moi qui étais jeune et beau, enfin, frais, alors que lui était déjà vieux et tout gonflé et violacé. Il ne m'était plus permis, à partir de ce jour-là, de sortir tête-nue, mes jolis cheveux marron au vent. Quelquefois, dans une rue écartée, je l'ôtais et le tenais à la main, mais en tremblant. Je devais le brosser matin et soir. Les jeunes gens de mon âge, avec qui j'étais malgré tout obligé de frayer de temps en temps, se moquaient de moi. Mais je me disais, Le chapeau n'y est pas pour grand'chose, ils ne font qu'y accrocher leurs saillies, comme au ridicule le plus saillant, car ils ne sont pas fins. J'ai toujours été étonné du peu de finesse de mes contemporains, moi dont l'âme se tordait du matin au soir, rien qu'à se chercher. Mais c'était peut-être de la gentillesse, genre celle qui raille le bossu sur son grand nez. A la mort de mon père j'aurais pu me délivrer de ce chapeau, rien ne s'y opposait plus, mais je n'en fis rien. Mais comment le décrire ? Une autre fois, une autre fois. ('L'Expulsé', p. 15)

In this instance, we have a story based upon a memory of the narrator's childhood. The story itself is a failure to the extent that the hat itself is never described, but is revelatory of a number of underlying issues that point towards reasons for the nature of the narrator's adult character. Despite the sad tenor of the story, certain elements can be identified that suggest a measure of enjoyment being taken in the act of narration: the insistent repetition of 'chapeau'; the sound play between 'chapeau', 'chapitre' and 'chapelier'; the self-deprecating concessions ('jeune et beau, enfin, frais'); and the likely allusion to Hugo's *Notre Dame de Paris*.[17] The lengthy disquisition on a boy's hat, found in a text that is particularly preoccupied with the potential and the limitations of narrative itself, however, surely also alludes to that Ur-scene of realist narration that exceeds its own possibilities — the description of young Charles's cap in Flaubert's *Madame Bovary*:

> C'était une de ces coiffures d'ordre composite, où l'on retrouve les éléments du bonnet à poil, du chapska, du chapeau rond, de la casquette de loutre et du bonnet de coton, une de ces pauvres choses enfin dont la laideur muette a des profondeurs d'expression, comme le visage d'un imbécile. Ovoïde et renflée de baleine, elle commençait par trois boudins circulaires; puis s'alternaient, séparés par une bande rouge, des losanges de velours et de poil de lapin; venait ensuite une façon de sac, qui se terminait par un polygone cartonné, couvert d'une broderie en soutache compliquée et d'où pendait, au bout d'un long cordon trop mince, un petit croisillon de fils d'or, en manière de gland. Elle était neuve; la visière brillait.[18]

In this well-known scene, with which Flaubert's masterpiece opens, the description of a hat, by which the central personage is identified, leads to revelations about his awkwardness of character, his inability clearly to make himself understood, his lack of grace and gracefulness, all traits shared by Beckett's stumbling, stuttering protagonists. Beckett's narrator tremblingly clutching his hat directly recalls Charles, who is mercilessly mocked by his young classmates, just as Beckett's narrator is the butt of the jokes of the 'jeunes gens' with whom he is obliged to associate; and Beckett's mention of the 'grand nez [du bossu]' chimes with Flaubert's allusion to the 'visage d'un imbécile'. When Flaubert embarks on the description of the hat, however, his narrative runs away with itself and a highly unlikely catalogue of feats of millinery accumulates before the reader's eyes. Scarcely a page into the novel, readers are destabilized by a verbal medium that resists the logic of the material world it purports to describe. Flaubert's text verbally constructs an impossible hat (pieced together in a sketch by Vladimir Nabokov in the margins of his reading notes[19]), whilst Beckett's homage gives us no hat at all.

We find a practice closely related to the Flaubertian technique at work on a number of occasions in Beckett's *Nouvelles*, where detailed descriptions are successively provided of objects, processes or events, the importance of which readers have little or no ability to determine. In 'Le Calmant', for example, the narrator takes shelter in a church; trying to leave, he finds himself in front of a door:

> au lieu d'être rendu à la nuit je me trouvai au pied d'un escalier à vis que je me mis à gravir à toute jambes, oublieux de mon cœur, comme celui que serre de près un maniaque homicide. Cet escalier faiblement éclairé, je ne sais par quoi, par des soupiraux peut-être, je le montai en haletant jusqu'à la plate-forme en saillie à laquelle il aboutissait et qui, flanquée du côté du vide d'un garde-fou cynique, courait autour d'un mur lisse et rond surmonté d'un petit dôme recouvert de plomb, ou de cuivre verdi, ouf, pourvu que ce soit clair.
> ('Le Calmant', pp. 53–54)

This passage is reflexive in a number of beguiling ways: like the stairway itself, we are somewhat in the dark about what is taking shape before our eyes, and like the 'escalier à vis', the passage spirals around as detail is layered on detail. And when the narrator acknowledges the troublesome nature of his task ('ouf'), we recognize for sure, if we hadn't already, that Beckett here is experimenting, having his narrator attempt to construct through language something coherent in a world that makes little sense. The tripartite structure of 'escalier', 'plate-forme' and 'dôme' in fact recalls the three-part structure of that other bewildering word-object in Flaubert's novel, the wedding cake 'pièce montée' whose base is 'portiques, colonnades et statuettes', and which displays 'au second étage un donjon', and on the 'plate-forme supérieure' supports, finally, 'une prairie verte où il y avait des rochers avec des lacs de confiture'.[20] The sense we might take from identifying these borrowings and echoes is that while the narrators of Beckett's stories may be hobbling through a life that is at times breath-taking in its brutality, a degree of grace or comfort is retained via the inter-textual allusions that connect them back to a wider history of tellers of tales.[21] As Beckett's narrators recall earlier narrative constructions they provide the sort of reassurance Ali Smith alludes to in the lines quoted above: in a cruel and unforgiving world, the existence of a textual elsewhere that can be recalled and, after a fashion, rebuilt, might be seen as a sort of coping mechanism for the narrators. And for Beckett's readers, these allusions provide a semblance of context or of prehistory to stories that might otherwise appear to be quite dislocated from any recognizable reality.

In addition to the allusions to Flaubert and Rilke I have already indicated, in the *Nouvelles* there are also many echoes of Proust, on whom Beckett had of course published a short monograph in 1931.[22] The narrators of 'L'Expulsé' (p. 14) and 'La Fin' (p. 91) both notice hawthorns as they trudge onward ('très onirique' remarks 'l'expulsé'). Like the narrator of Proust's *A la recherche du temps perdu*, the protagonist of 'La Fin' is struck by the noises that invade his living space: 'ce qui m'écorchait le plus c'était les cris des vendeurs de journaux', he remarks (p. 84), recalling the Proustian set-piece on the 'cris de Paris' in *La Prisonnière*.[23] And just as Proust's narrator listens to the strains of Albertine's song, heard through the partition wall as she performs her ablutions, so each evening Beckett's narrator in 'La Fin' hears the singing of 'une petite fille, à moins que ce ne fût un petit garçon' (p. 84). While Proust's narrator takes solace from the sound of singing, evidence of Albertine's proximity, in 'La Fin' the scenario is rather less straightforward. Does he hear a young girl or a young boy? 'Pendant longtemps', he informs us, 'je n'arrivais pas à saisir les paroles', indicating yet further interpretive uncertainty, of a sort that we have come to expect on the part of the narrators of the *Nouvelles*. The oddity continues, however: he is visited at times by 'une filette [sic]', of whom he says, 'Elle avait de longs cheveux rouges qui pendaient en deux nattes. Je ne savais pas qui c'était. Elle traînait un peu dans la chambre, puis elle s'en allait sans m'avoir rien dit' (pp. 84–85). The result is perhaps predictable: society cannot countenance the narrator's aloofness: 'Un jour je reçus la visite d'un agent de police. Il dit que j'étais à surveiller, sans m'expliquer pourquoi' (p. 85). This may seem like just another of Beckett's perturbing vignettes, communicative of the ways in which his protagonists live at odds with the world in which they find themselves. It takes on another colouring, perhaps, when we realize that Proust's protagonist goes through the same succession of experiences: to console himself after Albertine's departure, he has a 'petite fille' come to his room and soon receives a summons to the police headquarters when the girl's parents make a claim against him for 'détournement d'un mineur' (*RTP*, IV, 27). A little later we learn that 'un inspecteur était venu s'informer si je n'avais pas l'habitude d'avoir des jeunes filles chez moi'; assuming this is in reference to Albertine, we learn, 'le concierge [...] avait répondu que si' and from that moment on, 'la maison semblait surveillée' (*RTP*, IV, 30).[24]

A further Proustian echo is found enfolded in another curious vignette in 'La Fin'. In this case the narrator explains quite out of the blue that he has a pair of dark glasses 'que mon précepteur m'avait données'. This is the first mention of the glasses or of the 'précepteur' (to whom we shall return below). The narrator continues: 'Il m'avait donné l'*Ethique* de Geulincz. C'étaient des lunettes d'homme, j'étais un enfant. On le trouva mort, écroulé dans les W.-C., les vêtements dans un désordre terrible, foudroyé par un infarctus' ('La Fin', pp. 96–97). These are challenging lines for a reader of the *Nouvelles* — their motivation at this point in the narrative is not clear. We are left to guess how an individual whose childhood was sufficiently privileged to afford him a private tutor might have ended up in such dire straits. And we are given no pointers as to why this specific philosophical text (or indeed the glasses) should be bequeathed to the narrator. Here Beckett's jumps in logic and narrative cohesion point towards his rejection of what he identified and condemned in Balzac's novels — an unwavering 'enchaînement mécanique, fatal, de circonstances', without any element of 'imprévu', narrative that functioned like the movement of the balls on a pool table, 'sent in one direction or another according to a very precise strategy'.[25] A reader familiar with Proust's biography, as Beckett certainly was, will be struck, however, by the peculiar parallels between the apparently random details of the demise of the mysterious 'précepteur' and that of Proust's father, Professor Adrien Proust. This latter had to be somewhat ignominiously pulled, unconscious, from a lavatory stall in the Faculty of Medicine in Paris, having suffered a massive heart attack that ultimately killed him.[26] As Jean-Yves Tadié puts it, alluding to preoccupations that are decidedly Beckettian in nature: 'Lorsque Montaigne souligne que nous naissons dans l'ignominie, comme les excréments, et mourons en pleine gloire, d'une mort religieuse et théâtrale, il définit ce qui a manqué à Marcel et à son père'.[27] The narrator of 'La Fin' indicates that the gift of the glasses was instrumental to his survival: 'mes yeux n'étaient pas tout à fait éteints, grâce peut-être aux lunettes noires que mon précepteur m'avait données' (pp. 96–97). If the volume of Geulincz represents a gift of wisdom in parallel to this 'gift of sight', we might surmise that the undignified death of a man capable of such selfless acts of kindness would be considered by the narrator of 'La Fin' as cruel or iniquitous. But no such judgement comes: Beckett offers no explanations and his protagonists tend not to expend their limited energies on protesting injustice.

A final instance of a Proustian presence in the *Nouvelles* comes from a moment in 'Le Calmant' that takes the notion of home-coming or achieving some kind of solace or succour, denies its possibility in one movement, while offering a whisper of resolution via an allusion to a high-point of Proust's protagonist's development in *A la recherche du temps perdu*. Beckett's narrator looks at a row of houses:

> Cela me rappela que les maisons étaient pleines de gens, d'assiégés, non, je ne sais pas. Ayant reculé pour regarder les fenêtres je pus me rendre compte, malgré les volets, stores et mystères, que de nombreuses pièces étaient éclairées. C'était une lumière si faible, en regard de celle qui inondait le boulevard, qu'à moins d'être averti du contraire, ou de le soupçonner, on aurait pu supposer que tout le monde dormait. La rumeur n'était pas continue, mais entrecoupée de silences sans doute consternés. J'envisageai de sonner à la porte et de demander abri et protection jusqu'au matin. Mais me revoilà en marche. Mais peu à peu, d'une chute à la fois vive et douce, le noir se fit autour de moi. Je vis s'éteindre, dans une ravissante cascade de tons lavés, une énorme masse de fleurs éclatantes. Je me surpris à admirer, tout le long des façades, le lent épanouissement des carrés et de rectangles barrés et unis, jaunes, verts, roses, selon les rideaux et les stores, à trouver cela joli. ('Le Calmant', p. 68)

To be outside, homeless, weak and alone, without the succour of basic comforts — light, heat, a place to rest — Beckett's protagonist here might be forgiven some rancour. But there is none: instead, he finds beauty not in the grandeur and spiritual drama of a sunset, but in the more prosaic shifting colours of indoor lights contrasting with the growing gloom of nightfall. These lights are indicative of homeliness and warmth, vestiges of belonging and safety that he cannot share, yet he is not dismayed or down-hearted. He carries on, his journey continuing into the night like that of Proust's traveller on the opening page of 'Combray'.[28] And a comparison with the Proustian traveller is instructive here, I think. At the beginning of the second part of *A l'ombre des jeunes filles en fleurs*, Proust's protagonist, during a journey from Paris to Balbec, finds himself confronted not with nightfall, but with sunrise. The nascent artist in him sees it in exuberant terms of painterly enthusiasm, dashing from one side of the train to the other, trying to gather in dark and light, blue, pink and red in an attempt to 'rentoiler les fragments intermittents et opposites de mon beau matin écarlate et versatile et en avoir une vue totale et un tableau continu' (*RTP*, II, 15–16). These sorts of 'moments bienheureux', what Henry Miller describes as the moments Proust identifies when one needs an instant to 'pause to recover from the shock which one experiences when the habitual grey of the world is rent asunder and the colour of life splashes forth'[29] are of course immensely rare in Beckett. In the passage quoted from 'Le Calmant', the light of day and of hope recedes suddenly ('d'une chute à la fois vive et douce') and although a variety of barriers ('volets, stores et mystères') remain interposed between the interior world of comfort and the external world of provisionality in which the protagonist is stranded, what emerges is a scene in which an unexpected glimmer of beauty is found ('à trouver ça joli', he says, with marked absence of Proustian *longueur*). In the Proust passage, a natural phenomenon is observed, framed through a window, and accounted for using the language of art:

dans le carreau de la fenêtre, je vis des nuages échancrés dont le doux duvet était d'un rose fixe, mort, qui ne changera plus, comme celui qui teint les plumes de l'aile qui l'a assimilé ou le pastel sur lequel l'a déposé la fantaisie du peintre. Mais je sentais qu'au contraire cette couleur n'était ni inertie, ni caprice, mais nécessité et vie. (*RTP*, II, 15)

In 'Le Calmant', it is the mundane, man-made phenomenon of electric lights glowing behind window-blinds that takes the place of the breath-taking beauty of the natural world. The romantic tradition is mocked when light-bulbs, shades and shutters become in Beckett's hands 'une ravissante cascade de tons lavés, une énorme masse de fleurs éclatantes'. A moment of grace is permitted by dint of his being an outsider and thus in a position to observe the 'épanouissement des carrés et rectangles barrés et unis' from without, a sort of fractured, cubist landscape of light and dark. In a small, fleeting way, there is a sense of hope here in a denatured world, hope which is shored up by the echo of Proust, a reminder of a literary *lieu de mémoire* that is evoked, re-visioned, and surpassed.

The recollection of earlier narrative models brings a wide range of tonal qualities to the *Nouvelles*. As noted above, when in 'Le Calmant' the narrator tries to speak to a young boy, yet can marshal no sound, we read this: 'je n'entendis qu'une sorte de râle, inintelligible même pour moi qui connaissais mes intentions. Mais ce n'était rien, rien que l'aphonie due au long silence, comme dans le bosquet où s'ouvrent les enfers, vous rappelez-vous, moi tout juste' (p. 50). The allusion here, of course, is to Dante's *Divine Comedy*, whose *incipit*, just like the image from Proust's opening pages mentioned above, depicts a traveller who finds himself on a path, but in this case lost on an unknown path: 'Nel mezzo del cammin di nostra vita | mi retrovai per una selva oscura, | ché la diritta via era smarrita'. And Clive James' recent translation of Dante underlines the proximity of the Beckettian rasp to the fear struck in Dante's pilgrim: 'The keening sound | I still make shows how hard it is to say | How harsh and bitter that place felt to me'.[30] Beckett's protagonist has scarcely any purchase on the world through which he moves, his memories are weak and unreliable, and here, though he is so un-worded as to be unable to communicate to the human subject he finds before him, his literary recollection — albeit of the daunting entry into Dante's *Inferno* — gives him a point of reference he can share with the reader ('vous rappelez-vous'), and thus effectively a second opportunity to communicate after his initial failure with the young boy.

We might wonder how Beckett's protagonists come by their learning, learning that persists in shimmers and echoes in the monologues of these 'shuffling moribunds'.[31] One possible explanation comes from the protagonist of 'La Fin', who remarks in passing, as we have seen, on his having had a 'précepteur' as a child. This remark, and the word 'précepteur' itself, indeed, bear the marks of yet another literary source, and another figure who, like Beckett's protagonists, can be classified variously as an outcast, a *homeloose* wanderer upon whom unthinkable suffering and hardship are visited: Voltaire's Candide. Beckett read Voltaire's polemical tale in 1926 during his final year at Trinity College Dublin, at a time of 'growing introspection, depression and withdrawal', when he was acutely aware [...] of the poverty, pain and suffering that were visible almost everywhere around him [...]. He began to wander around the streets, observing how wretched the lives of so many of his fellow men could be: beggars, tramps, ex-soldiers wounded or gassed in the First World War.[32]

The visibility and injustice of poverty, pain and suffering are key motivating factors in Voltaire's *Candide*. In his poem on the Lisbon earthquake of 1755, Voltaire anticipates this (and Beckett's vision of 'humanity in ruins' at Saint Lô), though his focus is on the capacity for a loving God to allow such devastation rather than humankind's capacity to bring it on itself:

> Accourez, contemplez ces ruines affreuses,
> Ces débris, ces lambeaux, ces cendres malheureuses
> [...]
> Lisbonne, qui n'est plus, eut-elle plus de vices
> Que Londres, que Paris, plongés dans les délices?
> Lisbonne est abîmée, et l'on danse à Paris.[33]

He goes on to describe the fallen state of man, caught in the unresponsive world, which resonates powerfully with the figures we encounter in Beckett's *Nouvelles*:

> Il rampe, il souffre, il meurt; tout ce qui naît expire;
> De la destruction la nature est l'empire.[34]

Candide follows in the wake of this poem, and draws additionally on Voltaire's horror at the then-ongoing Seven Years War, expanding the compass of suffering further still, though the Lisbon earthquake is one of the 'atrocities and disasters of which the story provides such a seemingly inexhaustible catalogue'.[35] Crucially, for our purposes, the eponymous hero of the tale as well as being expelled from his dwelling place and cast out into the world (like Beckett's protagonists), has a tutor — 'le précepteur Pangloss' — who instructs Candide in matters of 'métaphysico-théologo-cosmolonigologie' yet is incapable of seeing the brutal and iniquitous realities of the world for what they are.[36] Pangloss, as is well known, instead preaches a blinkered version of Leibnizian Optimism, according to which 'Tout est pour le mieux dans le meilleur des mondes possibles'. The most explicit trace of Voltaire's tale in the *Nouvelles* comes in 'La Fin', when, living rough in the devastated cabin in the mountains, disappointed that he has failed to befriend a cow, the protagonist berates himself: 'Plus maître de moi j'aurais pu en faire une amie. Elle serait venue tous les jours suivie peut-être par d'autres vaches. J'aurais appris à faire du beurre, du fromage. Mais je me dis, Non, tout est pour le mieux' (p. 95). There are in fact a great many parallels and points of contact between the *Nouvelles* and Voltaire's story. They are thematically similar, though as is the general tendency with Beckett's writings, there is much less geographical specificity in his stories and the sites and locations through which their action moves are far less concrete than those — Westphalia, Lisbon, Paraguay, Constantinople — of *Candide*.[37] The protagonist of 'L'Expulsé' is literally thrown out of his dwelling place, whilst the Baron in Voltaire's story 'chassa Candide du château à grands coups de pied dans le derrière'.[38] Once ejected, 'Candide, chassé du paradis terrestre, marcha longtemps sans savoir où, pleurant, levant les yeux au ciel, les tournant souvent vers le plus beau des châteaux'[39], acts echoed, as we have seen, in both 'L'Expulsé' and 'La Fin'. In the latter story the imagery of expulsion from an earthly paradise is emphasized early on: 'Maintenant j'avançais à travers le jardin' (p. 76), the narrator tells us. Candide, we read, 'se coucha sans souper au milieu des champs entre deux sillons', then 'tout transi, [il] se traîna le lendemain vers la ville voisine'[40], whilst in 'La Fin' the protagonist sinks further still: 'La nuit fut froide. Je marchai longuement dans les champs', he intimates, continuing 'Je finis par trouver un tas de fumier. Le lendemain je repris le chemin de la cité' (p. 87). Famously, having survived many lifetimes' travails and hardships, Candide comes to the conclusion that 'il faut cultiver notre jardin'.[41] In a characteristically brutal recollection of this, during his short-lived stay in the basement room, the protagonist in 'La Fin' attempts to cultivate a plant of his own, a crocus:

> Je laissais le pot dehors, attaché à une ficelle qui passait par la fenêtre. Le soir, quand il faisait beau, un filet de lumière grimpait le long du mur. Alors je m'installais devant la fenêtre et je tirais sur la ficelle, pour maintenir le pot dans la lumière, et dans la chaleur. Cela ne devait pas être commode, je ne vois pas très bien comment je m'y prenais. Ce n'était pas ce qu'il fallait probablement. Je le fumais comme je pouvais et je pissais dessus quand il faisait sec. Ce n'était peut-être pas ce qu'il fallait. Il verdit, mais il n'y eut jamais de fleur, rien qu'une tige flasque garnie de feuilles chlorotiques. (p. 83)

These lines are full of pathos; a man with almost nothing, amid repeated negations and avowals of ignorance ('Ce n'était pas ce qu'il fallait probablement'), seeks — after a fashion — to cultivate his garden, to add a measure of colour and beauty to his existence, but in the broken world of the *Nouvelles*, this pitiful undertaking yields none of the hoped-for results. All the same, in stark tension with the lifelessness of the adjectives 'flasque' and 'chlorotiques', an unmistakable measure of consolation or promise comes here in 'verdit', the tiniest whisper of life and hope, like that which underpins Candide's apothegm or the unexpected 'espérance' that closes the Lisbon poem.[42]

Beckett's *Nouvelles* plunge us into a damaged, uncertain universe; as I have shown, woven into these narratives of wandering and hardship are glimmers of other textual worlds, which might be read as the memory traces of Beckett's narrators and equally might be thought of as moments of grace, temporary release from the travails of the here and now for protagonist and reader alike. In Beckett's early texts in French he is concurrently coming to terms with a world in ruins and determining his relation to a literary heritage stretching from Dante to Joyce. As his own mature aesthetic develops, in Beckett's prose fiction the physical locations shrink back from the discernable town-and-country backdrop of the *Nouvelles* into more austere spaces (such as the mud of *Comment c'est*) or abstract ones (such as the niches and ladders of *Le Dépeupleur* or the perplexing closed space of *Bing*).[43] Pared back in terms of syntax and lexis and progressively moving away from conventionally determinable narrating subjects, these later writings become increasingly inimical to the sorts of intertextual relations I have pursued in this essay. As Pascale Casanova has it, 'à partir de *Comment c'est* [...] Beckett attaque les "convention périmées" de la littérature sur tous les fronts. Il déleste progressivement ses textes de tous les éléments externes qui pourraient encore les rattacher à la tradition littéraire'.[44] Accordingly, then, to study the *Nouvelles* in relation to earlier texts they evoke and echo is to offer an account of Beckett's literary development, his path to aesthetic maturity. Between the early writings in English of the 1930s (*More Pricks than Kicks* and *Murphy*) and the extraordinary outpouring in French of the late 1940s and early 1950s (*Molloy*, *Malone meurt*, *L'Innommable* and *En attendant Godot*), the *Nouvelles* are a key staging post in Beckett's artistic development. Whilst his later texts at times defy existing categories and challenge conventional interpretive approaches, in the *Nouvelles* we find links and connections that place Beckett within a constellation of European, humanistic literary writers seeking, in a variety of ways across a number of centuries, to understand the place of the individual human subject in a world blighted by conflict and suffering.

Notes to Chapter 12

1. Samuel Beckett, 'neither', in *The Complete Short Prose: 1929–89*, ed. by S. E. Gontarski (New York: Grove Press, 1995), p. 258.
2. Ludovic Janvier, 'Les Nouvelles', in *Pour Samuel Beckett* (Paris: Minuit, 1966), p. 45.
3. Theodor W. Adorno, *Notes to Literature*, trans. by Shierry Weber Nicholsen, 2 vols (New York: Columbia University Press, 1991–92), I, 251.
4. Paul Davies, 'Three Novels and Four *Nouvelles*: Giving up the Ghost be Born at Last', in *The Cambridge Companion to Beckett*, ed. by John Pilling (Cambridge: Cambridge University Press, 1994), pp. 43–66 (p. 46).
5. Samuel Beckett, *Nouvelles et textes pour rien* (Paris: Minuit, 1958). Subsequent references to the *Nouvelles* will be incorporated in the text, giving the title of the story in question and page references from this edition.
6. Samuel Beckett, 'The Capital of the Ruins', in *The Complete Short Prose: 1929–1989*, ed. by S. E. Gontarski (New York: Grove Press, 1995), pp. 275–78 (p. 278). Marjorie Perloff has read the *Nouvelles* through the lens of Beckett's biographical experiences during the war: see ' "In Love with Hiding": Samuel Beckett's War', *Iowa Review*, 35.2 (2005), 76–103; see also Andrew Gibson's excellent article 'Beckett, Vichy, Maurras, and the Body: *Premier amour* and *Nouvelles*', *Irish University Review*, 45.2 (2015), 281–301. For a recent survey of Beckett's writings in relation to the historical events of his time, see Seán Kennedy, 'Humanity in Ruins: Beckett and History', in *The New Cambridge Companion to Samuel Beckett*, ed. by Dirk Van Hulle (Cambridge: Cambridge University Press, 2015), pp. 185–200.
7. Roger Pearson, *Unfolding Mallarmé: The Development of a Poetic Art* (Oxford: Clarendon Press, 1996), p. 301.
8. Gibson sets this point of detail in the context of the suspicion, exclusion, and persecution of those marked by perceptible 'otherness' during the Vichy regime ('Beckett, Vichy, Maurras, and the Body', p. 294). We might additionally note that though his French was fluent, Beckett retained a marked Irish accent when speaking the language: see for example Pascale Casanova, *Beckett l'abstracteur: anatomie d'une revolution littéraire* (Paris: Seuil, 1997), p. 131.
9. Perloff characterizes them as 'strange, lyrical fictions' (' "In Love with Hiding" ', p. 77).
10. Steven Connor, *Samuel Beckett: Repetition, Theory and Text* (Oxford: Blackwell, 1988), p. 87.
11. Perloff, ' "In Love with Hiding" ', p. 79.
12. Ali Smith, 'On Form', in *Artful* (London: Hamish Hamilton, 2012), pp. 47–92 (pp. 73–74).
13. Rainer Maria Rilke, *The Notebooks of Malte Laurids Brigge*, trans. by M. D. Herter Norton [1964] (New York & London: Norton, 1992), p. 59.
14. Dirk van Hulle and Mark Nixon, *Samuel Beckett's Library* (Cambridge: Cambridge University Press, 2013), pp. 100–02. For the review of Leishmann, published in T. S. Eliot's *The Criterion* in July 1934, see 'Poems by Rainer Maria Rilke', in Samuel Beckett, *Disjecta: Miscellaneous Writings*

and a Dramatic Fragment, ed. by Ruby Cohn (London: Calder, 1983), pp. 66–67. James Knowlson notes that a volume of selected poems of Rilke in the original German was among the books loaned to Beckett during his stay in Germany in 1936–37 (*Damned to Fame: The Life of Samuel Beckett* (London: Bloomsbury, 1996), p. 749, n. 21).
15. Beckett, *Disjecta*, pp. 66–67.
16. Germane here is the experience written about recently by James Wood, what he calls 'homelooseness': 'in which the ties that bind one to Home have been loosened, perhaps happily, perhaps unhappily, perhaps only temporarily'. 'Exile,' Wood writes, 'is acute, massive, transformative, but homelooseness, because it moves along its axis of departure and return, can be banal, welcome, necessary, continuous. There is the movement of the provincial to the metropolis, or the journey out of one social class into another' (*The Nearest Thing to Life* (London: Cape, 2015), pp. 105–06, 112–13).
17. Fifteen years after composing the *Nouvelles*, Beckett turned to Hugo without much success: 'J'essaie de lire *Notre-D. de Paris*. Impossible' (letter to Mania Peron, 18 September 1951, in *The Letters of Samuel Beckett, vol. II: 1941–1956*, ed. by George Craig and others (Cambridge: Cambridge University Press, 2011), p. 297.
18. Gustave Flaubert, *Madame Bovary*, ed. by Thierry Laget (Paris: Gallimard, 2001), p. 48.
19. Vladimir Nabokov, *Lectures on Literature*, ed. by Fredson Bowers (London: Picador, 1983), p. 131.
20. Flaubert, *Madame Bovary*, p. 77. Nabokov discusses the relations between the cap and the cake: see *Lectures on Literature*, pp. 128–32.
21. On Beckett's admiration for Flaubert and his innovations as a novelist, see Brigitte Le Juez, *Beckett Before Beckett: Samuel Beckett's Lectures on French Literature* (London: Souvenir Press, 2008), pp. 23–32; on Beckett's relation to Flaubert, see Hugh Kenner, *Flaubert, Joyce and Beckett: The Stoic Comedians* (Boston, MA: Beacon Press, 1962); and for a more recent critical appraisal of Beckett's Flaubertian borrowings, see Kate Rees, 'Double-Seater Desks, Broken Bicycles, Mating Dogs: The Dynamic of the Duo in Flaubert's *Bouvard et Pécuchet* and Beckett's *Mercier et Camier*', in *Flaubert: Shifting Perspectives*, ed. by Mary Orr, Anne Green, and Tim Unwin, special issue of *Dix-Neuf*, 15 (2011), 104–14.
22. Samuel Beckett, *Proust and Three Dialogues with Georges Duthuit* (London: Calder & Boyars, 1965).
23. See *La Prisonnière* in Marcel Proust, *A la recherche du temps perdu*, ed. by Jean-Yves Tadié, 4 vols (Paris: Gallimard, 1987–89), III, 623–30. Hereafter references to this edition will be incorporated in the text as *RTP*, followed by a volume number and page reference. For a brilliant analysis of these pages, see Léo Spitzer, 'Étymologie d'un "cri de Paris"', in *Études de style* (Paris: Gallimard, 1970), pp. 474–81. For a more recent engagement, see Daniel Karlin, 'Traduire les cris de Paris dans La Prisonnière' in *Son et traduction dans l'oeuvre de Proust*, ed. by Emily Eells and Naomi Toth (Paris: Honoré Champion, 2018), pp. 105–22.
24. Andrew Gibson associates the theme of surveillance and externally imposed controls on movement and activity that are found in the *Nouvelles* with the political climate of the Vichy period: see 'Beckett, Vichy, Maurras and the Body', pp. 294–95.
25. Le Juez, *Beckett before Beckett*, p. 28. The words in French are quoted from Rachel Burrows's notes on Beckett's lectures; the words quoted in English are Le Juez's paraphrase of Burrows's notes.
26. See Adam Watt, *Marcel Proust* (London: Reaktion Books, 2013), pp. 94–95, and William C. Carter, *Marcel Proust: A Life* (New Haven, CT, & London: Yale University Press, 2000), pp. 353–58. Beckett's father was also killed by a heart attack, though not in a public convenience.
27. Jean-Yves Tadié, *Marcel Proust: biographie* (Paris: Gallimard, 1996), p. 510, n. 2.
28. Here Proust's narrator proffers an image of a traveller to illustrate the effect of the sound he hears when waking in the night (the 'sifflement des trains'): this sound, he suggests, 'me décrivait l'étendue de la campagne déserte où le voyageur se hâte vers la station prochaine; et le petit chemin qu'il suit va être gravé dans son souvenir par l'excitation qu'il doit à des lieux nouveaux, à des actes inaccoutumés, à la causerie récente et aux adieux sous la lampe étrangère qui le suivent encore dans le silence de la nuit, à la douceur prochaine du retour' (*RTP*, I: 3–4).

29. Henry Miller, *Tropic of Cancer* [1934] (London: Penguin Modern Classics, 2015), p. 131.
30. Dante Alighieri, *The Divine Comedy*, trans. by Clive James (London: Picador, 2013), p. 3.
31. The phrase is Steven Connor's (*Samuel Beckett*, p. 1).
32. Knowlson, *Damned to Fame*, pp. 66–67. In 1937 Beckett visited Voltaire's quarters at Sanssouci in Potsdam, writing, intriguingly, to Thomas McGreevy: 'Voltaire's room is altogether charming and comic [...] and yet somehow full of exile and loneliness' (*The Letters of Samuel Beckett, vol. I: 1929–1940*, ed. by Martha Dow Fehsenfeld and Lois More Overbeck (Cambridge: Cambridge University Press, 2009), p. 432).
33. Voltaire, 'Poème sur le désastre de Lisbonne en 1755 ou examen de cet axiome "Tout est bien"', in *Contes en vers et poésies divers* (Paris: Nelson, 1936), pp. 105–11 (p. 105).
34. Voltaire, 'Poème sur le désastre de Lisbonne', p. 110. Fewer than twenty lines later in the poem we find the following couplet, which uncannily anticipates the *incipit* of *L'Innommable*. Voltaire writes: 'L'homme, étranger à soi, de l'homme est ignoré. | Que suis-je, où suis-je, où vais-je, et d'où suis-je tiré ?'; *L'Innommable* famously begins 'Où maintenant? Quand maintenant? Qui maintenant? Sans me le demander. Dire je. Sans le penser' (Samuel Beckett, *L'Innommable* (Paris: Minuit, 1953), p. 7).
35. Roger Pearson, 'Introduction', in Voltaire, *Candide and Other Stories*, trans. by Roger Pearson (Oxford: Oxford University Press, 1990), p. xx.
36. Voltaire, *Candide*, in *Romans et contes*, ed. by René Pomeau (Paris: Flammarion, 1966), pp. 179–259 (pp. 180–81).
37. In this, Beckett approaches what Dorrit Cohn has called 'non-referential narrative' ('Focus on Fiction', in *The Distinction of Fiction* (Baltimore, MD, & London: Johns Hopkins University Press, 1999), pp. 1–17 (pp. 9–17)).
38. Voltaire, *Candide*, p. 181.
39. Ibid.
40. Ibid.
41. Ibid., p. 259.
42. Voltaire, 'Poème sur le désastre de Lisbonne', p. 111.
43. Samuel Beckett, *Comment c'est* (Paris: Minuit, 1961); *Le Dépeupleur* (Paris: Minuit, 1970); *Bing* (Paris: Minuit, 1966). The first publication of *Bing* was a limited edition; it was subsequently included in *Têtes mortes* (Paris: Minuit, 1967).
44. Casanova, *Beckett l'abstracteur*, p. 143.

— 12 —

Gravity and Grace: Bonnefoy's and Bergson's 'Monde-images'

Emily McLaughlin

> But all the story of the night told over,
> And all their minds transfigured so together,
> More witnesseth than fancy's images,
> And grows to something of great constancy,
> But, howsoever, strange and admirable.
> (William Shakespeare, *A Midsummer Night's Dream*,
> V.1.23–27)

In many of his talks and essays, Yves Bonnefoy explains his conception of the poetic act using the image of a falling leaf. In the essays 'Poésie et liberté' and 'Le Degré zéro de l'écriture', the poet describes walking along a path, lost in conversation or thought, when, out of the corner of one eye, he sees a leaf fall from a tree and hesitate as it descends towards the long grass.[1] Bonnefoy describes the profoundly transformative effect that this hesitant motion has on his perception, not only of the leaf, but of the world around him, and his participation in it. The poet becomes aware of the way that his mind has been anticipating the trajectory of the leaf's descent, mapping it in linear terms before it has even unfurled. But as the leaf hesitates, the poet suggests that 'la ligne et ses points' dissolve (*SP*, p. 177). He no longer perceives the leaf as a discrete body nor the space that surrounds it as empty. And nor does he perceive himself as a distant observer detached from the scene that is unfurling before him. The leaf's descent exposes 'le pur acte d'être' (*E*, p. 315), what Bonnefoy, using a distinctly Bergsonian terminology, describes as 'un fragment de la durée' (*SP*, p. 177). It is perceived as 'moins une partie que le tout, ce tout étant le monde qui nous entoure, et dont rien nous montre qu'il est plus ou moins, ou autre, que la feuille qui se dissipe dans son sein qui n'est pas l'espace' (*SP*, p. 177). The notion of vacant and static 'outside' space that surrounds stable objects and the poet's own body reveals itself to be an illusion. The poet becomes attuned to the concrete temporal and spatial force by which the whole world evolves and he feels his own body moving, evolving, and falling with it. He observes: 'nous n'avons plus de réalité séparée en cet Un où notre propre durée de feuille qui tombe de l'arbre nous réinscrit. D'où un allègement de tout l'être. On pressent ce que pourrait être une divine gaieté' (*E*, p. 311).

This anecdote reveals much about the particular combination of gravity and grace that manifests itself in Bonnefoy's poetry. The term 'gravity' is particularly pertinent not only because of the importance that the poet attributes to the act of falling but also because of the seriousness of the poet's tone as he speaks of the descent of this leaf. Bonnefoy emphasizes just how much is at stake in the act of linguistic perception. He firmly believes that linguistic structures of representation shape our perception of existence in ways that do violence to it. In his essay *Le Lieu des herbes*, the poet argues that language deforms 'notre pratique de la réalité'.[2] In the act of perceiving and speaking about existence, the world hangs in the balance. The epigraph to his 1965 collection of poetry, *Pierre écrite*, uses a citation from Shakespeare's *A Winter's Tale* to suggest the precarity of this potential moment of loss or redemption: 'They look'd as they had heard of a world ransom'd, or one destroyed'.[3] In his anecdote about the leaf, Bonnefoy suggests that language represents existence in closed and coherent terms. Even as reality is unfurling, linguistic consciousness shows it to us retrospectively, as if the act were already complete. The leaf's descent is plotted in advance, as if it were a straight and coherent line, before it has even fallen. The unknown is conceived in terms of the known. And this is where the second sense of gravity — the physical law that we identify and predict — becomes pertinent. Bonnefoy suggests that language causes us to perceive material existence as if it simply obeys a finite series of preordained laws and and so causes us to think about existence and our actions in determinist terms.

The poet relishes the story about the leaf that hesitates momentarily in mid-air because this slight gesture reveals the unpredictability and creativity at the heart of material existence. It exposes all that our linguistic forms of perception tend to edit out; a diverse range of forces at play in the scene of perception (the leaf, the air, heat, moisture...) and the novel ways in which they combine. The act of falling, of succumbing to the dynamics of physical existence, is thus endowed with a new sense of potential, with a new grace. The poet attunes himself to a dynamic of renewal or redemption that does not reside in the pre-existent structures of the human mind or those of the physical world. He attends to the generative interactions of diverse worldly forces. The word 'grace' is fitting to describe this dynamic because it exposes a source of creativity and even beauty that is not given to the poet, either inwardly or outwardly, but that manifests itself in worldly processes of interaction that bring his structures of perception into being. This is the grace of the world's hesitant force of becoming, one that overtakes both the leaf and the poet, making them both tremble. The poet feels the diverse worldly forces that act in and through his body, that transport and transform him.

In his crucial essay on the image, 'La Présence et l'image' (1981), Bonnefoy argues that the representations of language distort our perception of existence because they suppress the temporal force of concrete existence.[4] He describes finitude as 'cet éternel censuré', suggesting that 'si nous savions l'écouter, il nous assignerait nos limites'. He argues that language appropriates the outer limits of existence, seizing hold of 'une réalité autonome, éprouvée substantielle, considérée suffisante' (*E*, p. 189), and suggests that the image makes us perceive 'un monde souvent cohérent, en apparence complet' (p. 189). The reader or viewer is drawn into an alternative world, one that seems more alluring and even more real than our lived existence for it gives us the impression of having acceded to 'une réalité enfin pleinement incarnée' (p. 189). And so, Bonnefoy argues that a self-reflexive study of the image allows us to perceive to what extent we can become caught up in processes of symbolic representation and reduce the world to 'un monde-image' (p. 191). This self-critical practice can alert us, not only to language's circumscription of the scene of sensual perception, but also to existence's insubordination in the face of such circumscription. We can attune ourselves to the perpetual motion by which finitude continually overturns the limits imposed by linguistic consciousness. We can become aware of the embodied activities of thinking, perceiving, and living that distribute and disperse linguistic structures. Reflecting 'sur ce qui réclôt sa parole', Bonnefoy argues that the task of poetry is to 'rétablir l'*ouvert*' (p. 199).

An early sequence of Bonnefoy's poetry, *L'Été de nuit*, published in *Pierre écrite* in 1965, offers a sustained meditation on the ways that the closed forms of language can limit the subject's perception of the physical world. The poems trace the vagaries of a dreaming mind over the course of one luminous midsummer's night. The title *L'Été de nuit* alludes to Shakespeare's *A Midsummer Night's Dream* (*Un Songe d'une nuit d'été*), inviting us to compare the fluctuations of the poet's thoughts to the successive enchantments that Shakespeare's characters undergo at the hands of Oberon and Titania. *L'Été de nuit* begins with a reworking of the Edenic myth, a scene within a starlit summer garden in which the poet feels that he has not been cast out of a realm of eternal essences but locked within it. A series of eight reveries follow that all spring from this 'original' fancy and that all explore how the representations of language give rise to a compulsive desire for coherence and closure. Dramatizing a voyage upon an open sea, reflecting on the contingency of material existence, the poet nonetheless explores how the images that he uses to understand the scene before him immobilize material existence, fixing its outer limits and reducing it to a static spatial plane. From one poem to the next, however, Bonnefoy uses the diachronic motion of the sequence as a whole to resist this stasis. Each new poem projects a new image, critiquing and contesting the validity of those that have gone before. The poet explores how the fluid motion of dream contests the coherence and sufficiency of these 'monde-images', deconstructing their closed forms, exploring how they are continually brought into and out of being by affective and embodied forces that cannot be delimited or mastered.

The divagations of the dreaming mind that are charted across the poems of *L'Été de nuit* also serve to dramatize the history of thought itself. From one poem to the next, Bonnefoy explores the changing nature of Western practices of representation, from Christianity, to idealism, to realism. The manner in which Bonnefoy traces the evolution of the Western world's image-practice is heavily influenced by one historical figure in particular, Henri Bergson, and his conception of the evolution of reflexive consciousness. Bergson argues that language is a biological adaptation that has allowed humanity to thrive because it has given us the capacity to objectify reality, to throw a static spatial net over the forms of the world, and to edit out the complex and heterogeneous flow of material reality. The series of enchantments that Bonnefoy depicts in *L'Été de nuit* are redolent of the linguistic transpositions that Bergson describes in his *Essai sur les données immédiates de la conscience* when he analyzes how the subject recuperates time symbolically, converting it into space, into 'un milieu indifférent', and projecting itself and other forms into this milieu.[5] Crucially, Bergson suggests that the linguistic subject has a remarkable capacity to confuse its own symbolic schema for reality itself, perceiving coherence and definition where there is only continuity and dynamism.[6] Present realities are perceived as fully realized forms, an ongoing action as an 'opération achévée'.[7] In *Matière et mémoire*, Bergson argues that both idealist and realist conceptions of the act of representation are guilty of this form of spatial recuperation. He contends that idealist thought simply figures the structures of the human mind as the external limit of this spatial configuration, and realist thought the laws of material process.[8] But he argues that both forms of thought presume — in very different ways — the correlation or 'adéquation' of consciousness and matter and conceive of the relationship between them in spatial terms. The philosopher asserts that only a properly temporal understanding of the image allows us to perceive, not the spatial opposition that separates matter and consciousness, but the continuous physical dynamics by which processes of action and representation, matter and memory, continually interact.[9]

The history of the poetic image that Bonnefoy charts in *L'Été de nuit* is thus also a reflection on Bergson's writings on symbolic consciousness and 'la durée'. Bonnefoy explores how a Bergsonian understanding of the interplay between memory and perception, action and reflection opens up the possibility of a finite thinking of the act of representation. The poet publishes *L'Été de nuit* in 1965 and, as the century progresses, other thinkers use Bergson's work to rethink the Western metaphysical conception of the image. In *Logique du sens* in 1969, Gilles Deleuze presents the image as a means of overcoming Platonism, conceiving of thought as becoming, and existence as a continual process of imaging.[10] In *Le Poids d'une pensée* in 1991, Jean-Luc Nancy suggests that the image deconstructs its own act of representation by foregrounding the concrete force of its own gesture of presentation and its refusal to be circumscribed by structures of comprehension.[11] Bonnefoy's *L'Été de nuit* anticipates these developments. It uses Bergson's inherently temporal understanding of the physical and mental activities by which an image is actualized to draw linguistic consciousness into more intimate forms of relation with the material world.

The first poem of *L'Été de nuit* presents a vision of a star-filled sky that seems to grow larger and to draw closer to humanity. As the poet describes how the light spills down from the night sky into the dark foliage in the garden, the use of wordplay in this first poem becomes more and more intricate. The reflections of light in the garden are associated with the patterns that emerge between the linguistic structures. Opening with the words 'Il me semble, ce soir', Bonnefoy signals from the outset that this sequence will present a series of 'seemings', a succession of various different perceptions of or impressions about existence. The poet describes the starlight using an insistent sibilant alliteration. It sounds out in the self-reflexive verbs, as if to suggest that this light spills forth towards us eagerly, of its own accord: 'Il me semble, ce soir, | Que le ciel étoilé, s'élargissant, | Se rapproche de nous'. As the sky swells, all things become brighter and more intimate. Even the night itself seems to be illuminated: 'la nuit, | Derrière tant de feux, est moins obscure' (P, p. 185). As we move into the second stanza, and as the starlight spills down onto the plants in the garden, the word 'feu' appears twice homophonically in the word 'feuillage'. The doubling of the same element here makes the foliage seem deeper and more abundant: 'Et le feuillage aussi brille sous le feuillage'. It creates the impression of what Mary-Ann Caws describes as an 'interior infinite': 'The original perception opens out on the inside in a deliberate creation of profundity, a sort of *mise-en-abyme* of contemplation'.[12]

The green and the orange-colour of the ripe fruit intensify in the second stanza: 'Le vert, et l'orangé des fruits mûrs, s'est accru, | Lampe d'un ange proche'. The alexandrine's metrical structure (2/4/3/3) accentuates the words 'vert' and 'orangé' and the assonance between 'mûrs' and 'accru'. The word 'l'orangé' harbours, homophonically, 'or' and 'ange', the precious metal pursued by alchemists and an angelic figure. And with the intercession of the phrase 'Lampe d'un ange proche', the poet invites us to perceive this growing light in metaphysical terms. There is 'un battement | De lumière cachée'. Just as an angelic presence was hidden earlier within 'le feuillage' and 'l'orangé des fruits mûrs', here too an angel appears and does not appear. There is a luminous fluttering, a veiled shimmer. Once this presence alights, however, it overtakes the form before us. The tree whose foliage was so dense and rich at the start of the poem now becomes 'l'arbre universel'. Perceived in essential or metaphysical terms, it becomes a universal or generic tree, 'l'arbre de la connaissance'.

This opening poem is an abbreviated sonnet, with two quatrains and one tercet, and so it moves very rapidly towards a conclusion after the *volta*. Once we perceive the tree in generic or linguistic terms, it is as if we suddenly cross a threshold and find ourselves in the Garden of Eden, this realm of eternal essences. As we do so, the penultimate line moves swiftly forwards in an enjambment and then the poem closes on a final decasyllable: 'Il me semble, ce soir, | Que nous sommes entrés dans le jardin, dont l'ange | A refermé les portes sans retour'. The poem clicks shut like a box (to use Yeats's phrase) and the doors of this Edenic paradise close firmly behind us.[13] Reworking the Edenic story, Bonnefoy suggests that we are not cast out of the garden but locked within it. He presents this accession — or fall — as irremediable. Haven eaten of the tree of knowledge and become prey to its 'seemings', we are locked within a realm of essences.

The reverie with which *L'Été de nuit* opens launches a diverse series of meditations. In the eight poems that follow, the poet uses an imagery of voyaging upon the open sea to explore the contingency of material existence and to trace how, over time, in endlessly different contexts, the Edenic dream resurfaces. The second poem of the sequence begins with an address to a mysterious figure who, seated at the prow of a boat, unfolds painted cloths and murmurs to herself:

> Navire d'un été,
> Et toi comme à la proue, comme le temps s'achève,
> Dépliant des étoffes peintes, parlant bas. (P, p. 186)

This female figure is perhaps the muse: the one who unfolds the central images of the tradition, the maps or cosmographies that humanity has used to understand the world and to orient itself within it. We hear echoes of Mallarmé's conception of the poem as a means to 'déplier' various different 'explications' of existence.[14] Given the constant references that Bonnefoy makes to Shakespeare's *A Midsummer Night's Dream* in the sequence, we might also suggest that these 'étoffes peintes' that are steadily uncovered are theatre cloths. Our navigator will be a busy stagehand who, from one poem to the next, will uncover new backdrops and plunge us into different worlds.

Strikingly, these images are unfolded 'comme le temps s'achève'. In this most contingent and mutable of landscapes, the open sea, the poet feels time draw to a halt. He remembers the dream of Eden: 'Dans ce rêve de mai, | L'éternité montait parmi les fruits de l'arbre'. The poet imagines being able to capture the physical plenitude of existence at its zenith, to offer to his companion 'le fruit qui illimite l'arbre | Sans angoisse ni mort, d'un monde partagé'. The fruit that is shared — 'le fruit qui illimite l'arbre' — seems to be an essential or idealized one, like 'l'arbre universel'. It is a form that is shared without destruction, without lapsing into a world of contingency and decay. The third stanza presents a vision of finitude that threatens this ideal: 'Vaguent au loin les morts au désert de l'écume'. Finitude is no sooner evoked, however, than it is redeemed. The balanced hemistichs of the next line stage this movement from perdition to salvation: 'Il n'est plus de désert | puisque tout est en nous'. The poet suggests that insubstantial and fleeting forms of material existence are saved from oblivion by human consciousness. Like Plato looking at the shadows in the cave, or like Kant envisaging his Copernican revolution, the poet affirms that 'tout est en nous'. Humanity is perceived, not as the plaything of the world, a spirit that blows through '[le] désert de l'écume', but as the reflexive consciousness that brings being to its full mode of articulation. The stanza thus ends with the image of the poet as Narcissus. He bends down and kisses his own image, without drowning. With this gesture, he vanquishes death: 'Et il n'est plus de mort puisque mes lèvres touchent | L'eau d'une ressemblance éparse sur la mer'. He performs an act of representation that gives existence order and meaning. Reflexive consciousness facilitates a tender embrace or communion between the subject and material reality. It harmonizes dualities of existence — interiority and exteriority, essence and existence, eternity and finitude — and delivers us to 'un monde partagé'.

The first poem of the sequence presents linguistic consciousness as a force that uncovers divine forces latent in the physical world. The second explores how this form of perception is translated into secular and idealist terms, as the act of representation itself comes to be perceived as the gesture by which the humanity *lends* the world form and meaning. Aligning the scene of Eve's temptation with the scene of Narcissus's seduction, Bonnefoy suggests that the human subject is seduced by the self-reflexive structures of its own thought. The dynamics of the physical world are given fullness and coherence; transience is redeemed by human perception. As we move into the third poem of the sequence, however, Bonnefoy proposes that this communion is achieved at the expense of movement in the third poem of the sequence. Immobility comes to be perceived as an originary and full state and motion as secondary and aberrant. The poem becomes a journey through a static space, 'dans l'immobilité', in the murky half-light of the gently moving underwater vegetation (*P*, p. 187). The figurehead that directs the poet's craft is lost in a state of rapture. 'Heureuse, indifférente', 'les yeux à demi clos', she directs the poet and 'le navire de vivre'. The poet's muse thus resembles a medium or a conduit. Leaning out over the prow, she pursues a distant *telos*. She explores the world whilst remaining strangely absent from it, engaging in processes of discovery that are largely internal. She pursues a transcendental ideal. The poem ends with the words: 'A jamais le reflet d'une étoile immobile | Dans le geste mortel'. This vision finds itself rapidly overturned, however, as, in the very next poem of the sequence, the 'figure de proue' lies on the ocean floor, stained with blood, rigging protruding from the seabed. The sequence moves into free verse as it evokes this process of destruction. Line lengths jut out irregularly like the fragments of the broken vessel and the poet's conception of the perfectly sufficient or autonomous nature of poetic language is shattered. The dynamic forces of material existence have exhausted poetry's attempts to maintain coherence: 'L'étoile, l'eau, le sommeil | Ont usé cette épaule nue' (*P*, p. 187). The stanza ends with a reference to painting, 'L'huile méditante', and to the practice of representation that once 'reigned over' the shadows of existence.[15] Now, the poet suggests, this queen 'ploie sa nuque | Comme on pèse l'âme des morts'. The image offers itself up in a sacrificial gesture, offering proof only of the sovereignty of material finitude.

Throughout the course of the sequence, the image of the journey serves to dramatize the dialectics that continually transform the poet's conception of the act of representation. From one poem to the next, images contest and supplant each other. The poetic quest assumes many different guises. The peaceful and self-sufficient 'figure de proue' of the third poem is obliterated by the contingency of material existence in the fourth. The human imagination has the capacity to redeem fleeting human actions in the third poem but it is matter that reveals its own immutable laws in the fifth. This poem presents another vision of a frozen landscape bathed in starlight. Bonnefoy writes: 'Voici presque l'instant | Où il n'est plus de jour, plus de nuit, tant l'étoile | A grandi' (*P*, p. 189). We drift once again into a luminous but static realm. Bonnefoy suggests that this light swells: 'pour bénir ce corps brun, souriant, | Illimité, une eau qui sans chimère bouge'. The poet now strips away the illusions of idealism and presents the image as purely sensory and empirical reflexion. He suggests that the image shows us the forms of the physical world 'sans chimère'. Playing with the image of 'la table' in the final line of the poem, Bonnefoy observes: 'La clarté protégée reposera | Sur la table des eaux'. He presents 'la clarté' as a force that will no longer be cultivated and discovered by human design (on the surface of the table or the page). Clarity or lucidity will be safeguarded by the inherently intelligible structures of material reality itself, 'la table des eaux'.

The poems of *L'Été de nuit* explore how the structures of reflexive consciousness critique and contest themselves and continually find new means to reassert their authority, presenting either the human mind or the material world as the structure that yields an immutable knowledge of existence. The series of images that the poet turns over explore how humanity's understanding of the relationship between consciousness and matter is steadily refigured. In spite of all this variation, Bonnefoy suggests that one factor remains constant. All these images present a timeless vision of reality. The relationship between human consciousness and reality is conceived in static, spatial terms. The sixth poem of the sequence reflects directly on this condition of atemporality. It bears a slightly different roman numeral to all the other poems, one preceded by an ellipsis, '… VI', as if to signal the poet's preoccupation with the question of suspension. It begins with the words: 'Longtemps ce fut l'été. Une étoile immobile | Dominait les soleils tournants' (*P*, p. 190). The Edenic summer evoked in the first poem never fades. Using the adverb 'Longtemps' in conjunction with the past historic tense 'ce fut', Bonnefoy suggests that one instant of time is prolonged indefinitely. Playing on the homophony between 'l'été' and 'l'étoile', repeating 'l'été' three times and 'l'étoile' twice, the poet uses these repetitions to suggest the static nature of this summer. As he reflects on this strange temporal state, he is perhaps playing with the double function of 'l'été' too which can serve both as a noun and as past participle. This summer, dominated by 'une étoile immobile', is a time that 'has been'. The world is perceived in static spatial terms as a series of realised and coherent forms. As the stanza progresses, night takes day hostage, bathing everything in an unchanging starlight: 'L'été de nuit | Portait l'été de jour dans ses mains de lumière'. Existence is muted and the poet and his companion talk in low voices, 'en feuillage de nuit'. Summer is lived, not in the present, but in the half-light — or half-life — of a static past.

The second stanza reflects on the effect that this static form of perception has on the human subject's relationship with the material world. It opens with another pair of alliterative nouns: 'L'étoile indifférente; et l'étrave'. The poet counterpoints the star and the prow, summoning up the archetypal image that has been used to suggest human desire and questing from Homer to Joyce. The juxtaposition of the two nouns — star and prow, object and subject — isolates them within space. The relationship between them is then figured in linear terms, 'et le clair | Chemin de l'une à l'autre en eaux et ciels tranquilles'. The poet traces a straight line between one form and another, as if plotting a course across the sea or drawing his trajectory on a map. The enjambment from one line to the next suggests the way that this 'chemin' cuts through space. Figuring the human subject as an 'étrave', Bonnefoy suggests that it has become an endlessly questing entity that continually contends with the distance that separates it from the physical world. The subject is always moving towards a *telos*, an indifferent star, that is given in advance. And material reality is 'indifférente', which is to say, cold and detached, indifferent to the poet's fate but, also, void of difference, immobile and immutable.

The image that Bonnefoy uses here recalls the spatial images, and even the visual diagrams, that Bergson uses as he explores how symbolic representation converts temporal realities into static spatial ones in *Essai sur les données immédiates de la conscience.* Bergson writes, 'on projette le temps dans l'espace, et on raisonne, consciemment ou inconsciemment, sur cette figure géometrique. Mais cette figure représente une *chose*, et non pas un progrès'.[16] This spatial form of recuperation profoundly distorts the human experience of time, Bergson argues. The linear trajectory that we figure in our heads between one form and another, he suggests, 'correspond, dans son inertie, au souvenir en quelque sorte figé de la délibération toute entière et de la décision finale que l'on a prise'.[17] The linear path that we represent in language takes the place of the fluid and dynamic physical process, the steady and incremental progression of states, through which we live. Bergson observes: 'cette ligne symbolise, non pas le temps qui s'écoule, mais le temps écoulé'.[18] The human subject no longer perceives present realities but only retrospective ones, finished and complete forms. As the geometric nature of the 'chemin' that Bonnefoy traces between two pre-given forms suggests, the subject conceives of its relationship to the physical world in a closed and determinist manner. In *Matière et mémoire*, Bergson describes this form of spatial mapping as 'l'illusion qui accompagne et recouvre la perception du mouvement réel'.[19] In the final lines of poem '...VI', Bonnefoy too suggests that this form of spatial figuration distances the subject from the dynamics of embodied and material existence. There is an immense swooning motion as the course the poet charts breaks entirely free of the forms of the material world and drifts off into empty space: 'Tout ce qui est bougeait comme un vaisseau qui tourne | Et glisse, et ne sait plus son âme dans la nuit'. The poet suggests that symbolic consciousness results, not in knowledge of the physical world, but in endless reverie. We lose all knowledge of ourselves and of the world as we endlessly sift through what Shakespeare describes as 'fancy's images' in *A Midsummer Night's Dream* (V.1.24). Language cuts its moorings, drifts off into oblivion, and the world 'ne sait plus son âme dans la nuit'.[20]

The central poems of Bonnefoy's sequence call into question the image practice that, throughout most of Western history, has allowed humanity to produce coherent visions of reality. It challenges the symbolic order that has dominated Christian, idealist, or realist visions of the world. This line of questioning is summed up in the seventh poem of the sequence, which poses one long question. It asks whether the poet has become fixated with the conception of poetry as a form of spatial quest: 'N'avions-nous pas l'été à franchir, comme un large | Océan immobile, et moi simple, couché | Sur les yeux et la bouche et l'âme de l'étrave' (*P*, p. 191). The poet is figured as a lover who is so deeply lost in reverie that he is unable to perceive anything other than the object of his desire. Like the muse whose eyes were half-closed in the third poem, he is draped over the prow of the boat, loving nothing except 'l'été': what 'has been' and, paradoxically, what is always yet to be appropriated. As the poet evokes this state, he questions whether he has been pursuing reality or just a linguistic fantasy. He asks whether, by seeking to enclose being, he has grasped nothing at all. Has he merely been tracing superficial patterns on the surface of existence, across 'un large | Océan immobile'? Has he imagined his way forward, 'N'étais-je pas le rêve aux prunelles absentes [...]?'

Throughout *L'Été de nuit*, Bonnefoy suggests that no single act of representation can capture the reality of lived existence. He continually suggests, however, that the movement from one poem to another, as the poetic sequence unfolds, can restore some form of dynamism to the poetic image. Each image is contested and deconstructed by another. And this motion makes us aware of their temporal existence, of the embodied processes of thinking, dreaming, or writing that give rise to them and disperse them. The final two poems of the sequence urge us to conceive of the image and the act of representation that it performs in this temporal and processual manner. The penultimate poem begins with an image of a constellation of stars, the Mallarmean emblem of text's static spatial configuration. It falls downwards, tearing its shoulder on the horizon as it reaches towards the running waters of earth: 'Mais ton épaule se déchire dans les arbres, | Ciel étoilé' (P, p. 192). As it falls, it seeks to embrace the running and breathing waters of the earth: 'et ta bouche recherche | Les fleuves respirants de la terre pour vivre | Parmi nous ta soucieuse et désirante nuit'. We are reminded of the figure of Narcissus who, in the second poem, bent down to kiss his own reflection on the surface of the water. Now Bonnefoy foregrounds, not the reflection of an image, but simply the act of embrace, the gesture of relation itself. The constellation seeks not to redeem the finitude of worldly existence but to share in it, to experience the anxiety and the desire of ephemeral existence. The poet apostrophizes the constellation in the second stanza: 'Ô notre image encor'. He suggests that the representation we project of our own form in the night sky brings us both light and suffering: 'Tu portes près du cœur une même blessure, | Une même lumière où bouge un même fer'. Our image — or our self-image — is wounded at its very core. And yet, whereas the previous poems have all sought to overcome this split, this poem simply affirms that this spatial division cleaves the image and the human subject in two. It does not call for this wound to be healed. Bonnefoy's third address to the image urges it to expose the reality of this schism: 'Divise-toi, qui es l'absence et ses marées'. He suggests, paradoxically, that this very division has the capacity to restore humanity to, and to mix it back within, a finite material world. He urges in the same breath: 'Accueille-nous, qui avons goût de fruits qui tombent, | Mêle-nous sur tes plages vides dans l'écume | Avec les bois d'épave de la mort'. Returning to the image of the tree, 'l'arbre universel' with which the sequence opened, he extols the divided nature of the image once more: 'Arbre aux rameaux de nuit doubles, doubles toujours'.

Strikingly, as the poet addresses the image here, he uses two prominent temporal adverbs. The image is 'Notre image *encor*' and the 'Arbre aux rameaux de nuit doubles, doubles *toujours*' (my emphasis). These adverbs could be both described, like Bonnefoy's image, as cleft forms. They are both temporally ambiguous forms that can designate that an action is 'still' being performed and 'always' being performed, or 'still' being performed and being performed 'again'. '[N]otre image encor' reaches towards existence in its immediacy 'still' but it encloses upon the past and is always destined to reach 'again'. Bonnefoy suggests that the image, like these temporal adverbs, is an unstable threshold across which we feel time migrate, from the openness of the present to the closure of the past. He argues that language does not close upon itself, absenting itself from the physical world, but that 'l'absence et ses marées' ebbs and flows all through it. The closure of representation is always interrupted by the openness of the act of relation. Language reaches 'encor', 'toujours' towards the physical world.

The eighth and penultimate poem of the sequence suggests that a temporal thinking of the image does not simply heal division but encourages us to conceive of it differently, to think it in temporal rather than spatial terms. This is the departure that Bergson makes in *Matière et mémoire* when he insists that 'la distinction du corps et de l'esprit ne doit pas s'établir en fonction de l'espace, mais du temps'.[21] He argues that the spatial opposition we forge between consciousness and matter is an artificial linguistic construction that fails to attend to the fluid processes of interaction by which these forces come into being. Critiquing the way that Western philosophy often thinks of the human body in closed terms, as if it were a container for perceptions or ideas, he insists that the body must be thought instead as a centre for action. He equates perception with action and he insists that pure memory is entirely virtual: the latter becomes actualized in the moment of perception, as it interacts with the scene before us and fixes its contours. Bergson thus presents the image as a form that arises from the continual interaction of perception and memory, action and representation, present and past.[22] He insists that it is not contained within the human body but that it happens 'parmi les choses'. It bears a relation to human consciousness but it also exceeds this relation. The process by which it comes into existence thus allows us to perceive 'une infinité de degrés entre la matière et la conscience'.[23] In the eighth poem of *L'Été de nuit*, Bonnefoy does not explore the relationship between matter and memory but relation and representation. He suggests that the division between these processes is like a tide or a rhythm. To become aware of this tide is, he suggests, to become aware of the interactions that are continually occurring between linguistic and material, cerebral and embodied processes. It is to become aware that one's body is the threshold across which these interactions occur and to find oneself drawn into a world of material process, mixed 'dans l'écume | Avec les bois d'épave de la mort'.

And so, in the final poem of the sequence, Bonnefoy suggests that this night of apparently infinite dreaming is drawing to a close. He addresses the immersive forms of reverie that language's structures of representation have inspired over the course of the sequence with the words: 'Eaux du dormeur, arbre d'absence, heures sans rives, | Dans votre éternité une nuit va finir' (*P*, p. 193). The poet sets three highly evocative noun clauses in apposition. 'Eaux du dormeur' suggests the endless fluidity and dynamism of dream; 'arbre d'absence', the abstract forms of perception into which the 'universal' forms of language plunge us; 'heures sans rives', a material world evacuated of its temporal force. Between one formulation and another, endless connotations proliferate. From one end of the alexandrine to the other, the words 'Eaux [...] sans rives' reach out to one another. The poet suggests that language's oneiric forms are always threatening to overtake us, to draw us into their labyrinthine structures.

Confronting this boundless linguistic reality, the poet pledges: 'Dans votre éternité une nuit va finir'. The poet envisages an act of closure, the imposition of a limit. This is not the spatial boundary envisaged by language or geometry, however, but a temporal boundary. And so, the very next lines of the poem read: 'Comment nommerons-nous cet autre jour, mon âme, | Ce plus bas rougeoiement mêlé de sable noir?' As night ends, day is simultaneously beginning. The thinnest red streak of light is starting to edge over the horizon, still dotted with grains of unlit sand. The poet suggests the coterminous nature of beginning and ending, dissipation and emergence, the perceptible and the imperceptible. He suggests that all physical existence, exposed at its own limits, at once withdraws and manifests itself. Addressing this final question to himself, to 'mon âme', the poet suggests that his own subjectivity unfurls on this mobile or trembling horizon. He greets the emergent and unknown reality that is coming towards him with a question. He asks what name it *could* be given. He is acutely aware of the way that linguistic consciousness tries to find a way of recognizing and remembering that which has not yet come into being. He suggests that his own subjectivity unfurls in this tension between perception and memory, the given and the virtual.

The final stanza of the sequence ends with a series of immersive images. Language is no longer perceived as an instrument of pure knowledge, as the transparent medium through which we see the world and its forms distinctly. The limpidity that we associate with clear-sightedness grows blurry: 'Dans les eaux du dormeur les lumières se troublent'. As the waters cloud, a form starts to emerge: 'Un langage se fait, qui partage le clair | Buissonnement d'étoiles dans l'écume'. Language no longer circumscribes the ideal or material realities of existence but is perceived as an emergent form. It emerges from the interaction of perceptual and material processes, like some form of distillate coming out of solution. Bonnefoy plays on the double meaning of the verb 'partager', suggesting that this language 'shares' in the stars' shimmering and clustering motion but that it also 'divides it up' and gives it a form. Language makes itself in this moment from a scene of perception and participation. It does not draw upon some pre-existing template, material, or ideal but its virtual reality is *actualized* by the clustering of the stars. This scene of sharing and division is also — as the use of the verb *partager* suggests — a scene of parturition. And so, the temporality of the image, of the act of representation, is no longer retrospective and recuperative but prospective and futural. It is a nascent form that is emerging from the 'buissonnement' of a material universe. The final line of the poem reads: 'Et c'est presque l'éveil, déjà le souvenir'. As soon as its prospective force is actualized, it becomes a memory, a bounded and finished thing. It is already slipping away from us. Bonnefoy suggests that all things emerge on this threshold between 'presque' and 'déjà', 'l'éveil' and 'le souvenir'. Our experience is born of a steady opening and closing motion, the ebb and flow of absence and presence. It is this motion that steadily grounds and ungrounds our existence. It immerses us in a processual physical world that we circumscribe for brief instants, in quick snapshots, before we discover that our projections have grown too solid, too rigid, and that other images are being actualized.

The poems of *L'Été de nuit* align the vagaries of the dreaming mind on one midsummer's night and the historical process by which the image evolves throughout the Western tradition. They foreground the temporal nature of thought, its sustained pursuits and its sudden reversals, its triumphs and crises. Refuting any conception of the universal or preeminent nature of symbolic consciousness, the sequence depicts its repeated attempts to grasp the essential structure of worldly existence as a series of chimeras or dreams. We are perhaps reminded of the way that the surrealist poet transcribes the wanderings of the unconscious mind. And yet, whereas the surrealist sought to tap into the wellsprings of human creativity by trusting the automatic reflexes of the mind, Bonnefoy offers a powerful critique of these automatic reflexes. He suggests that language colonizes the scene of perception, automating the human subject's responses to the physical world, immobilizing and flattening the concretely creative material world in which it finds itself immersed. The act of representation is presented as an act that bewitches the one who performs it, trapping the speaker within its closed forms, its eternal Edenic garden. As Bergson writes, 'la conscience, tourmentée d'un insatiable désir de distinguer, substitue le symbole à la réalité, on n'aperçoit la réalité qu'à travers le symbole'.[24] The poems of *L'Été de nuit* explore the manifold ways in which reflexive consciousness distorts our sensory impressions of the world as it recuperates intelligible forms from the flux of material existence, only allowing us to perceive reality 'à travers le symbole'. They reflect on Bergson's account of symbolic consciousness as a purely spatial and geometric mapping of existence. Bergson writes that 'nous tendons instinctivement à solidifier nos impressions, pour les exprimer par le langage' and that, in doing so, we end up confusing that which is 'une perpétuel devenir' with 'le mot qui exprime cet objet'.[25] He argues that this object 'se fixe par sa projection dans l'espace homogène', gaining 'les contours précis et l'immobilité'.[26] He never ceases to describe these processes of isolation and objectification as 'illusions'.[27]

Like Bergson's writings, Bonnefoy's poems explore the remarkable capacity that the linguistic imagination has to re-engineer the world of concrete temporal processes in which we find ourselves. It takes us on a kaleidoscopic journey through the various different 'pratiques de la réalité' to which the structures of linguistic consciousness give rise, exploring how the mind can endow the world with contours of its own choosing. He dramatizes the process by which we come to reside in a world in which 'le temps s'achève', drifting into 'l'immobilité', a realm 'où il n'est plus de jour, plus de nuit' (as he phrases in the fifth poem of *L'Été de nuit*). He never ceases to marvel at the discrepancy between the forms that language projects and the dynamic physical reality in which we live. Like Bergson's *Essai*, Bonnefoy's sequence demonstrates how — for all their apparent differences — the idealist and the realist image structure reality in the same way, 'l'une comme l'équivalent de l'autre' (to use Bergson's phrase).[28] As Suzanne Guerlac writes, the idealist and the realist image are 'duplicates of one another, two translations of a principle that remains mysterious'.[29] Discursive consciousness imposes its structures upon lived existence. We perceive its representations of time as if they were time itself, as if it were a form and not a force, and we reduce a world of concrete material forces to a homogeneous spatial plane. And human action fares no better. It is captured before it has even unfolded, locking the human subject into spatial schema, encouraging it to reason — consciously or unconsciously — in ways that are geometric. The subject progresses towards 'une étoile immobile', towards an object that is always already given in advance. And Bonnefoy suggests that it is our presupposition of the equivalence of discursive and perceptual consciousness that keeps inciting us to contrive 'une nouvelle organisation de l'ensemble', to use Bergson's phrase, to resurrect Eden again and again, in idealist or realist terms, in endlessly different guises.[30] It is with bitter irony that Bonnefoy observes that we are locked within a prison of our own making: the determinist structures of our own systems of thought.

The poetic subject of Bonnefoy's sequence is thus a dreamer and a besotted lover, 'couché sur l'étrave', lost in 'le rêve aux prunelles absentes'. There is something of the sleepwalker, or even the automaton, about him. His will has been commandeered by other forces, like the characters of Shakespeare's *A Midsummer Night's Dream*. Even as he interacts with the world, his mind, heart, and senses are no longer quite his own, for language always already dictates his thoughts and actions. The poems of *L'Été de nuit* offer a sustained exploration of how this form of automatism can become a kind of self-justifying compulsion, an all-consuming love affair, and of how, in the same gesture, it can insulate the human subject from outside influences and cause it to drift into a kind of half-life. Our lives, our physical reality, our world become static and homogeneous. And yet, the sequence also never ceases to remind us that these structures of representation are of our own making. It reassures us that we do not have to contrive any form of elaborate gesture to free ourselves from these structures. The final poem suggests very simply that, if we let it, time will break the spell: the night will end, day will break, and time's passing will reveal the fluid motion of dream, 'les eaux du dormeur'. As we see various images rise and fall, time makes us aware of the embodied and situated nature of consciousness. As Bergson suggests in *Matière et mémoire*, time reveals the subject to be, not a subject of knowledge or consciousness, not a container for ideas or perceptions, but a subject of action. It allows us to perceive representation as a contingent process. We recognize that representation promotes the consolidation of our impressions, collecting and organizing a fluid stream of sensory impressions, but that it emerges from a richly heterogeneous series of embodied and material processes.

And so, rather than insisting upon the correlation of the structures of language and reality, consciousness and matter, the poet insists upon their difference, their division. He insists that this division is not the spatial disjuncture between distinct processes that we encounter in dualist systems of thought: Christianity, idealism, realism. On the contrary, it is the temporal division that runs through all apparently distinct or autonomous forms, the rhythm of interaction that brings all processes into being. Bonnefoy suggests that, in the interaction of the body and the mind, relation and representation, perception and memory, an image comes into being. He addresses this image directly, as if to remind us of the dialogic nature of the processes that have given rise to it. Like Bergson in *Matière et mémoire*, he suggests that it is only by exploring how these processes continually interpenetrate in the movement forwards — as sensual perception actualizes memory and calls linguistic forms into being — that we can conceive of language's force in its virtuality, its creativity. He suggests that these processes allow us to conceive of the self as a temporal horizon across which distinct forces play. They alert us to the interplay of gesture and form, movement and appropriation, that brings us into being. The temporal threshold is, he insists, always a place of partition *and* participation. The oscillation between these two very different dynamics gives existence its nascent force.

The story of the falling leaf is the parable that Bonnefoy uses to explain this nascent force. The leaf that falls surrenders to the force of gravity and to the processes of physical existence. And the poet insists that its falling motion is quite the opposite of a mechanistic movement. Its trajectory is predetermined, he argues, only by the patterns with which we overlay its movement, by the laws and systems that we construct around its motion. Only symbolic consciousness perceives gravity as a law, a perfectly closed and predetermined system, the sterile repetition of the same, rather than as an interactive and unpredictable force. And yet, Bonnefoy insists, in reality, the leaf does not fall in a straight line. It hesitates. It exposes the unpredictable nature of its activity, the diverse material and immaterial forces that act in and through it and keep it in motion. Gravity is no longer conceived as an exterior force that acts on an isolated body but, in far more intimate terms, as one of many physical forces that brings the leaf's or the poet's existence into being. It is perceived as one of the many dynamics by which our interactive processual material world continually opens itself up anew, distributing itself in singular and surprising configurations. And Bonnefoy suggests that the grace of existence — like its creativity and its beauty — is to be understood in these terms. The grace of existence is exposed to us in the endlessly productive series of processes of exchange in which we are immersed. It is a force that is endlessly available to us but not controlled by us. Like the religious conception of grace, it thus requires a certain degree of humility and receptivity. It is the very force that brings us into being and that plays through us. Our power resides only in our capacity to inflect its hesitant force of its becoming. We can facilitate its opening, its processes of renewal. And in doing so, Bonnefoy suggests, we fall, alongside the leaf, back into the physical world. We realize that 'nous n'avons plus de réalité séparée en cet Un où notre propre durée de feuille qui tombe de l'arbre nous réinscrit'.

Notes to Chapter 13

1. This anecdote appears in Bonnefoy's essays 'Poésie et liberté', first published in 1989, and then published in the volume of essays *Entretiens sur la poésie (1972–1990)* (Paris: Mercure de France, 1992), pp. 308–31 (p. 311), and 'Le Degré zéro de l'écriture', first published in 2000, and then published in the volume of essays *Le Siècle où la parole a été victime* (Paris: Mercure de France, 2010), pp. 167–90 (p. 177). All subsequent references to these two texts will appear within the text, using the abbreviations *E* and *SP*.
2. Yves Bonnefoy, *Le Lieu d'herbes, le lac au loin* (Paris: Galilée, 2010), p. 15.

3. Yves Bonnefoy, *Poèmes* (Paris: Gallimard, 1982), p. 251. All subsequent references to this text will appear within the text, using the abbreviation *P*.
4. Yves Bonnefoy, 'La Présence et l'image', in *Entretiens sur la poésie*, pp. 179–202.
5. Henri Bergson, *Essai sur les données immédiates de la conscience*, in *Œuvres*, ed. by Jean-Louis Vieillard-Baron, 2 vols, La Pocothèque (Paris: Librairie générale française, 2015), I, 149–319 (p. 315).
6. Ibid., p. 240.
7. Ibid., p. 285.
8. In *Matière et mémoire*, Bergson suggests that we tend to conceive of the human mind as 'une unité pur' that confronts 'une multiplicité essentiellement divisible'. An opposition is forged between 'l'inextension' and 'l'étendue', between 'la qualité' and 'la quantité'. He writes: 'Nous avons répudié le matérialisme, qui prétend faire dériver le premier terme du second; mais nous n'acceptons pas davantage l'idéalisme, qui veut que le second soit simplement une construction du premier. Nous soutenons contre le matérialisme que la percéption dépasse infiniment l'état cérébral; mais nous avons essayé d'établir contre l'idéalisme que la matière déborde de tous côtés la représentation que nous avons d'elle, représentation que l'esprit y a pour ainsi dire cueillie par un choix intelligent' (Bergson, *Matière et mémoire*, in *Œuvres*, ed. by Vieillard-Baron, I, 349–576 (p. 511)).
9. Bonnefoy's engagement with Bergson allows the poet to juxtapose two models of linguistic perception: one static, abstract, and spatial; the other dynamic, temporal, and concrete. Throughout the sequence, there are subtle suggestions that Bonnefoy associates the first of these two models with Mallarmé's poetry. If so, it could be argued that Bonnefoy is using Bergson's critique of the spatialization of linguistic perception in order to critique Mallarmé's poetics of spatial relationships between words.
10. Gilles Deleuze, *Logique du sens* (Paris: Éditions de Minuit, 1969).
11. Jean-Luc Nancy, *Le Poids d'une pensée* (Sainte-Foy: Le Griffon d'argile, 1991), p. 19.
12. Mary-Ann Caws, *The Inner Theatre of Recent French Poetry* (Princeton, NJ: Princeton University Press, 1972), pp. 161–62.
13. W. B. Yeats, *Letters on Poetry from W. B. Yeats to Dorothy Wellesley* (London: Oxford University Press, 1964), p. 22.
14. We might also note that, in Bonnefoy's poem 'Le Tombeau de Stéphane Mallarmé', the poet corrects the humble gesture that Mallarmé makes in 'Salut' when he stations himself at the stern of the boat and situates Mallarmé instead 'à la proue' (in Yves Bonnefoy, *La Longue Chaîne de l'ancre* (Paris: Mercure de France, 2008), p. 119).
15. This poem about a shipwreck contains echoes of Mallarmé's sonnet 'A la nue accablante tu' which evokes a 'sépulcral naufrage', 'le mât dévêtu'. Just as Bonnefoy's poem cultivates patterns between a series of words that begin with the letter 'e', 'étoile', 'eau', 'épaule', Mallarmé's poem plays on homophonies between 'échos esclaves', 'écume', and 'épaves' (Stéphane Mallarmé, *Poésies* (Paris: Gallimard, 1992), p. 71). Bonnefoy's echo of Mallarmé's poem at this stage in the sequence suggests his awareness of the way that Mallarmé too critiques both idealist and realist accounts of the transparency of the act of representation and uses the image of shipwreck to dramatize the demise of a logics of representation.
16. Bergson, *Essai sur les données immédiates de la conscience*, pp. 278–79.
17. Ibid., p. 279.
18. Ibid.
19. Ibid., p. 519.
20. In this poem in particular, one might also suggest that Bonnefoy is critiquing Mallarmé's conception of the poem as a spatial entity. Bonnefoy reflects critically on the way that patterns are engineered between homophonic nouns, the way that physical existence is perceived as if it were a geometric space, and that connections are engendered between static forms within it. Bonnefoy is thus hinting that, although Mallarmé undoubtedly deconstructed a logic of representation and the vision of the world to which it gives rise, his poetry remains trapped within its spatialized mode of reasoning. Continuing to understand the relationship between subject and world in spatial terms, Bonnefoy suggests that the Mallarmean subject will always

find itself at a distance from the physical world that cannot be overcome.
21. Bergson, *Matière et mémoire*, p. 550.
22. Ibid., p. 551.
23. Ibid.
24. Bergson, *Essai sur les donnés immédiates de la conscience*, p. 240
25. Ibid., p. 241.
26. Ibid.
27. Bergson, *Matière et mémoire*, p. 520.
28. Bergson, *Essai sur les donnés immédiates de la conscience*, p. 237.
29. Suzanne Guerlac, *Thinking in Time: An Introduction to Henri Bergson* (Ithaca, NY: Cornell University Press, 2006), p. 169.
30. Bergson, *Essai sur les données immédiates de la conscience*, p. 237.

— 13 —
Grace and Gravity in Philippe Jaccottet

Charlie Louth

> Cette mystérieuse façon qu'a le langage quotidien
> de s'insinuer jusqu'à la plus haute poésie.
> (Jaccottet, letter to Gustave Roud, 17 May 1954)[1]

> Mais rendre la lumière
> Suppose d'ombre une morne moitié.
> (Valéry, 'Le Cimetière marin')[2]

Very often, when reflecting in his notebooks on what it is he wants to achieve in his writing, on what good writing should be (which he is always doing, as if defining the required mode might also be to enter into it, and certainly to prepare for it), Jaccottet thinks in terms of gravity and grace. This can be explicit, as in an entry from January 1964 which makes no secret of a debt to Simone Weil's title:

> La grande question pour qui s'entête à écrire: comment mettre les mots à l'épreuve, comment faire pour qu'ils contiennent le pire même quand ils sont lumineux, la pesanteur quand la grâce les porte? Je n'ai que trop tendance à dissocier l'un de l'autre.[3]

If Jaccottet has a tendency to separate gravity and grace, he is also always seeking to combine them, and is quite clear in his mind that words will only possess the heft and the lightness necessary if they manage to acknowledge 'le pire' while not falling foul of it, to achieve the lift and movement of a convincing rhythm without filtering out the reality of the world to which the words refer and which they have to remain part of. True words must oppose the materiality, the *pourriture* of the world, without denying it. 'On est pris entre le souci,' Jaccottet notes further in June 1964 in relation to the poems of *Airs* (published in 1967), 'de filtrer et de ne pas trop filtrer. La limite au-delà de laquelle purifier égale stériliser'.[4] The poetic word needs the soil and reek of the world, its weight, but it also needs its own detachment, its own music and shape, what makes us attend to it in its own right as a thing of beauty but also, precisely by virtue of that force of attention, prevents us from ignoring its attachment to the world from which it has sprung. The title *Airs* has this double-helix structure: it refers to the materiality of air and its movements and integrality to life, of which the collection's epigraph from Joubert reminds us: '*Notre vie est du vent tissé*', as well as to an attention to the world's surface, to the appearances of things; and it relates to the melodies of the poems themselves as they bring the nature of the world into focus, or catch it on the wing. But we are also made conscious that it is the substance of air, its 'souffle', to use a key term of Jaccottet's, that makes the 'tunes' possible and carries them.[5]

The Joubert epigraph seems an anticipation, in a less elegiac mode, of Rilke's famous lament in the second *Duino Elegy* that we, unlike the firmer existence that trees and houses have, 'ziehen allem vorbei wie ein luftiger Austausch', which Jaccottet translates as 'nous passons devant tout comme un commerce aérien'. There is no indication that Rilke ever came across Joubert, but it is quite possible that Jaccottet's choice of the phrase for his epigraph was prompted in part by the resonance, given that Rilke had once been his avowed 'poète préféré' and remains a bright star in the constellation of poets who accompany his work and give it its orientation.[6] In *Leçons*, the Rilke phrase is remembered again: 'Un homme — ce hasard aérien' (p. 458). The poems of *Airs*, to which we shall return, are in most respects as unlike the *Duino Elegies* as it is possible to be, yet they share an attention to the airiness of existence and to the point where the 'commerce aérien' of our lives becomes not (just) a thing to lament but a thing to elucidate and make sense of, and to live as a kind of opening. In an article on Joubert, written in 1966 when the finishing touches were being put to *Airs*, Jaccottet makes some remarks which while intended for Joubert, apply equally to the *Duino Elegies* and his own *Airs*:

> Ainsi procède-t-il à un rapprochement, par la douceur et la patience, du plus haut et du plus bas, ainsi tisse-t-il des liens ténus, mais forts, entre ciel et terre, et il nous semble, à le lire, que nous avons retrouvé une place dans le monde, à mi-chemin entre le plus léger et le plus lourd; du même coup, nous pourrions recommencer à croire que cette place est notre juste place, que nous sommes des notes nécessaires dans une vaste harmonie.[7]

Rilke seeks in his second *Elegy* to locate 'einen unseren Streifen Fruchtlands | zwischen Strom und Gestein' (Jaccottet: 'une bande à nous de bonne terre | entre fleuve et pierraille'). Joubert connects heaven and earth, as in an observation quoted by Jaccottet in his notebooks, *La Semaison* (for March 1966): 'Il n'y a que les eaux qui tombent du ciel qui puissent subsister en gouttes et briller comme les rosées' (p. 391). Jaccottet's airs circulate between the compact earth beneath his feet and the expanding universe above. All three are 'à mi-chemin entre le plus léger et le plus lourd'. The idea of in-betweenness is one Jaccottet's reflections cannot do without.

We have shifted from thinking of gravity as 'le pire', as the forces in the world which seem to deny the possibility of grace and make any artistic endeavour futile or misplaced, to thinking of it as materiality, the actual texture of reality, which poetry often cleaves to but necessarily works at a distance from. Perhaps this elision, which seems quite common in Jaccottet, is a revealing one: there are traces of a Christian sensibility in his work, despite his frequent disavowal of any ability to believe or even to comprehend the possibility of belief, expressed notably in respect of Simone Weil.[8] For all his allegiance to the everyday, and the supreme attentiveness to the surfaces of the natural world, his efforts to confront the horror *in* the world (in the notebooks: above all in the recounting of dreams) sometimes come close to being an expression of horror *at* the world as corrupt and unredeemable. When, in the quotation with which we started, he speaks of his tendency to dissociate gravity and grace, he is voicing a fear that (his) words might be (thought) empty. Though he dreams of a 'musique de paroles communes [...] déchirante non par ce qu'elle exprime, mais par sa beauté seule' (*La Semaison*, p. 339), a deep-rooted anxiety, a sort of ethical caution, makes him almost debilitatingly aware that such isolated beauty runs the risk of becoming mere ornament, of losing any relation to truth. And, in that case, ceasing to be beauty in the intended sense: note that Jaccottet's formulation doesn't actually envisage that the music of words would lose contact with 'ce qu'elle exprime', just that its force, its power to 'tear', would come only from its beauty, with the implication that true poetic beauty is always a product, the result of an interaction between language and the world: 'pas de beauté [...] dans les formes sans profondeur' (*La Semaison*, p. 354). To see this is also to acknowledge the possibility of a specious beauty, a gratuitous poetry, a form which is not true to the nature of things. Jaccottet's distrust of images stems from this, and his desire to leave them behind ('dépassement des images', p. 127); here, in *La Promenade sous les arbres*, he dreams of a 'poésie *sans images*' (p. 137). But in *Chants d'en bas* he recognizes that he cannot do without them:

> J'aurais voulu parler sans images, simplement
> pousser la porte...
>   J'ai trop de crainte
> pour cela, d'incertitude, parfois de pitié:
> on ne vit pas longtemps comme les oiseaux
> dans l'évidence du ciel,
>   et retombé à terre,
> on ne voit plus en eux précisément que des images
> ou des rêves. (p. 543)

We need images to be in the world, to inhabit the earth — they attach us to it by letting us see beyond it. And that is exactly why they are dangerous. Jaccottet's anxiety as to the legitimacy of his words is due to his awareness that an impulse in him pulls away from the reality of things towards 'l'insaisissable', a direction which makes it increasingly hard to distinguish the aesthetic from the religious.[9] (Perhaps it is better to say that the attention to phenomena, as it becomes more and more subtle, more and more precise, finds itself increasingly called to find ways to acknowledge what escapes it.) The word *pur*, which Jaccottet uses a good deal, is emblematic of this tendency. But so is the flickering suggestion that *pourriture* is endemic to the world: 'La merveille existe, la pourriture existe, l'horreur existe'; and the disgust that the notebooks so often register, particularly when recording dreams.[10] In perhaps its extremest version this sentiment appears in the words of the 'maître' in *L'Obscurité*: 'Voici sous nos yeux le pourissement du cadavre divin: prolifération, liquéfaction, vermine' (p. 191).

* * * * *

'Grâce' is also a word that appears frequently in Jaccottet's writings.[11] Its multiple and overlapping meanings and usages lend themselves to his apprehension of the world. When he talks of the rise and fall of canopies of eglantine as 'la grâce même' (*La Semaison*, p. 988), grace is a question not just of beauty and fluid movement but tilts into the sense of a gift or favour, something purely given. And when elsewhere he returns to particular effects of the light, produced in a certain place in early or late winter, at a certain time of day, and comments, 'Mais ce sont toujours des surprises, donc de l'inattendu, de l'immérité si l'on veut, des espèces de dons, ou mieux: une grâce du monde' (Taches de soleil, p. 179), 'grâce' encompasses the earlier meanings — beauty, gift — but has gone further to touch the theological: 'the free and unmerited favour of God as manifested in the salvation of sinners and the bestowing of blessings' (OED). Except that here, it is not 'grâce de Dieu', but 'grâce du monde', so a kind of secular grace, a grace which comes from the world we live in but which regenerates none the less. Grace emanating from the world rather than entering into it from outside; the world revealing itself perhaps.

Jaccottet's notes on dog-roses, those manifestations of grace, continue by way of a contrast with marguerites: 'À croire que certaines fleurs "donneraient sur" autre chose, et que d'autres seraient muettes, ou fermées. Tout cela n'est vraiment pas sérieux' (La Semaison, p. 990). Despite this self-mockery, the phenomenon of things 'giving onto' something beyond is a fundamental one for Jaccottet, and eglantines, like, as he goes on to say, 'les fleurs de l'amandier, du cognassier, du cerisier [...] déjà [...] trop sollicitées' (p. 991), are among the privileged flowers which seem to offer such a passage, so that he can call them, in their fragility and brevity, an 'image néanmoins de la seule obole valable pour passer sur l'autre rive' (p. 990). Grace is such a good word for thinking about Jaccottet's work because it hesitates between registering the mobile beauty of the world and not quite giving up the idea that in the apprehension of these moments a glimpse of some other world becomes possible, an 'autre monde' which may in fact be 'le nôtre' (La Semaison, p. 868), so that the world is as if given to us again. There are hundreds of reformulations of this thought or experience in Jaccottet's writing, an obsession with translating it into words is really what his work is, but in general terms he calls it an interweaving of 'le visible et l'invisible' (Truinas, p. 1209), or 'la limite et l'illimité' becoming 'visibles en même temps'. The latter formulation is offered as a definition of beauty, in full: 'Il se peut que la beauté naisse quand la limite et l'illimité deviennent visibles en même temps' (La Semaison, p. 354). Grace, according to a Hopkins poem which Jaccottet quotes part of in translation, is 'God's better beauty' — better because it opens towards something else — and it seems that Jaccottet, by quoting Hopkins without comment, agrees with him or is tempted to.[12]

Jaccottet's use of the word grâce often owes something to Simone Weil, whom he quotes at various points in his work and on whom he wrote two articles, 'Grandeur de Simone Weil' and 'La Géométrie et la foi', both for the Nouvelle revue de Lausanne, in 1950 and 1951.[13] There is evidence of Jaccottet returning to her writings periodically, for instance in 1959 when he quotes from Attente de Dieu (1950), a quotation worth giving here because it demonstrates the proximity between them so clearly:

> 'L'attention consiste à suspendre sa pensée, à la laisser disponible, vide et pénétrable à l'objet, à maintenir en soi-même, à proximité de la pensée, mais à un niveau inférieur et sans contact avec elle, les diverses connaissances acquises qu'on est forcé d'utiliser.'

> Plus loin: '*Les biens les plus précieux ne doivent pas être cherchés, mais attendus*'. (*La Semaison*, p. 343)[14]

Or again in 1970 in *Paysages avec figures absentes*, where he quotes at length from the same book (pp. 529–30); or in 1999 when he praises a well-known letter to Joë Bousquet (*Taches de soleil*, p. 177).

The idea of gravity is also essential to Jaccottet, often in more or less explicit relation to grace or to the idea of lightness. There is *pesanteur*, as in Weil's title, and many variations on *poids*; but there is also *gravité*, as when, quoting one of Hölderlin's letters, he remarks on 'ce que cache de gravité la poésie sous son masque de jeu' (*Taches de soleil*, p. 11), or when he speaks of 'la gravité légère' of Supervielle.[15] Gravity is a quality which poetry needs, and it is also a quality that poetry can bring to things to keep them from evanescence, as 'a makeweight in the unweighing of things'.[16] But it can be a danger too, as may be seen from Jaccottet's various comments on Yves Bonnefoy, whose poetry is always strongly associated with *gravité* and, Jaccottet implies, sometimes suffers from too much solemnity. An 'accent de *gravité enflammée*' Jaccottet sees as 'propre à l'éloquence qui se porte aux plus hauts objets, aux objets sacrés' and present in exemplary fashion in Bonnefoy.[17] But towards the end of the same essay, while admiring 'la gravité prenante d'un poète qui ne joue pas sur les mots', he suggests that there is an over-reliance on 'généralisation', a tendency to neglect the ordinariness and specificity of things in favour of what amounts to mere diction. Gravity here runs the paradoxical risk of lightness, of losing contact with the texture of the world. The same point is made more clearly in the notebooks, where in 1975, while still noting 'le pas à faire pour le rejoindre sur ces hauteurs un peu solennelles' he contrasts Bonnefoy's most recent collection, *Dans le leurre du seuil*, with his earlier work:

> Mieux qu'en aucun autre de ses recueils, il a su harmoniser son expérience quotidienne, sa culture et ses grands thèmes. La barque, l'étoile, le feu qui, dans *Hier régnant désert*, ne semblaient plus parfois que des mots, reviennent ici épaissis, alourdis, chaleureux. (*Taches de soleil*, p. 108)

The thickening and weighting of words, the treatment of them which prevents them from becoming or remaining 'que des mots', is here a process to counteract their 'gravity' in the sense of solemnity. Any extreme or excess bears a danger, and what is sought is an 'accord non pas paisible, mais vivant, légèreté et gravité, réalité et mystère, détail et espace' (note of October 1959, *La Semaison*, p. 341). For an example of such an 'accord', and to stick with Bonnefoy, we can quote a brief poem from *Du mouvement et de l'immobilité de Douve* (1953) which Jaccottet singles out more than once: 'Tu as pris une lampe et tu ouvres la porte, | Que faire d'une lampe, il pleut, le jour se lève'. Jaccottet records this in his notebooks as an example of how 'certains énoncés de faits parmi les plus simples' can attain 'la cime de la poésie', and offers a long commentary attempting to pinpoint the quality of the lines which at the same time expands their import dramatically:

> Il y a là deux éléments importants: ce ton parfaitement égal et pur, d'une part; de l'autre ces thèmes quotidiens, intérieurs, et non plus l'épopée. Une solennité pourtant comme hésitante et menacée. Pourquoi solennité? Parce

qu'il y a un respect nécessaire, une révérence devant la grandeur humaine — qui indéniablement existe — et de la gravité devant la souffrance. Pourquoi hésitante? À cause de notre faiblesse, de nos doutes, de nos craintes. La contradiction mystérieuse est celle-ci: l'extrême force à mes yeux du monde réel, sa présence obsédante, nourricière, émerveillante; [...] cette prodigalité folle, cette complexité à perte de vue, cette beauté aussi, dès qu'on prend un peu de recul, cet ordre en dépit de tout. Et, d'autre part: que toutes ces forces, que tout ce foisonnement, que cette réalité si présente, si puissante, si indubitable, ne soit plus que fumée à une autre échelle. [...] Voilà l'extraordinaire: tant de présence, tant d'intériorité dans tant d'abîme. (*Taches de soleil*, pp. 14–15)[18]

Bonnefoy's lines have an 'evenness' which acknowledges the weight of reality and the elements of which it is (here) composed, but also a fragility which is mostly dependent on the looseness of the syntax and on the contrast between the artifice of the lamp and the simple fact of day breaking. It is as if the words only just touch on what they name, bring it into the poem without confining it there. For Jaccottet, a balance has been found which lets reality seep into the poem, a form of words which catches both the prodigality and the fugitivity of the world, the density and the levity. The lines seem perfectly weighted and flighted, and in this balance it becomes impossible to separate out the part of gravity and the part of grace.

★ ★ ★ ★ ★

It's not surprising, given that questions of gravity and grace arise for Jaccottet out of the contradictory nature of reality, which presses on us with 'extrême force' and eludes us at every moment like smoke, that many of his reflections on the relationship crystallize around the work of Francis Ponge. As he says himself, Jaccottet has written more often on Ponge than on any other contemporary French writer, from his 'premier éloge' in 1946 to what at the time of writing is his most recent publication, *Ponge, pâturages, prairies* (2015), which begins with a meditation on Ponge's funeral originally published in the *Nouvelle Revue Française* in 1989 and adds a much longer continuation completed in early 1990. If, in his first piece wholly on Ponge, he underlines that 'les poèmes de Ponge naissent, comme tous les poèmes, d'une angoisse métaphysique', he does so to counter-act the impression that Ponge's work — 'cette encyclopédie à la recherche de définitions exactes' — is concerned only with recording and rendering the actual, the texture of things, somehow oblivious to any larger context they might be part of.[19] It may seem that Ponge restricts himself purely to what he can grasp cleanly in words, in a deliberately anti-philosophical and anti-metaphysical chasteness. As Jaccottet notes, but not definitively, Ponge's search for truth 'ne s'encombrait pas d'invisible, ayant assez à faire du visible'.[20]

This is not the place to go into the Ponge-Jaccottet relationship in detail, and much has been written on it already.[21] But the 'petit livre' *Ponge, pâturages, prairies* does allow us to pursue a bit further the meanings of gravity and grace. All of Jaccottet's writings on Ponge contain an uneasy mixture of admiration and reserve which derives partly from their friendship, which began in Paris after the war, and partly from the fact that, though Jaccottet learnt a great deal from Ponge, he likes him best when he defeats his own strictures, when his disciplined attachment to the visible, to surfaces, to the interlocking of word and world, exceeds itself, so that 'l'observation aiguë' conjoins with 'une vision élargie'.[22] Jaccottet's quarrel with Ponge — and in the end, despite some protestation to the contrary, the quarrel is quite a serious one — turns on his belief that Ponge tries too hard, that his *pursuit* of reality leads to his neglecting perhaps the most important aspects of reality, for all his regard for Ponge's 'hardiesse du regard et [...] hardiesse du langage'.[23] Reality, for Jaccottet, cannot in the end be pursued, it cannot be got at by work, certainly not work alone, but requires a lighter touch, even some inattention. The matter is complex, because Jaccottet's criticism of Ponge is also a form of self-criticism: when he calls Ponge 'le grand ouvrier de la langue' (*Ponge, pâturages, prairies*, p. 19) — words which are not immediately meant to carry any critical charge, but which advert to Ponge's working and reworking of language, his repeated attempts to render the nature of an orange or a shrimp — the phrase is also one which could be applied to Jaccottet, despite the great differences between them. In a prose such as 'Travaux au lieu dit l'Étang' (*Œuvres*, pp. 482–89), whose debt to Ponge is evident and which consciously makes the process of writing and approaching the 'secret', the 'inscription fugitive sur la page de la terre, qu'il faut saisir' (p. 483), part of its texture, the approach, the deliberation over how to go about the task, *becomes* the text; and this is only a more explicit form of how a great deal of Jaccottet's writing proceeds, especially the prose. Jaccottet too is an 'ouvrier', but one plagued by the thought that work is not enough. It is only exaggerating a little to say that all of his writing is a reworking of the one theme, a continued and renewed taking up of the task of responding to signs from the natural world: 'me voilà tâtonnant à nouveau, trébuchant, accueillant les images pour les écarter ensuite, cherchant à dépouiller le signe de tout ce qui ne lui serait pas rigoureusement intérieur' (pp. 483–84). But where Jaccottet is focused on the fugitivity of the phenomenon, which is actually taken as a kind of guarantee of its reality — 'plus le signe se dérobe, plus il y a des chances qu'il ne soit pas une illusion' (p. 484) — Ponge's objects, even if made to be destroyed, like a fruit crate, are never in doubt, and it is the text which needs to withdraw. Ponge's poem 'Le Cageot', from *Le Parti pris des choses*, ends: 'sur le sort duquel il convient toutefois de ne s'appesantir longuement'.[24] Still, it is this risk of dwelling too long, of weighing down the subject, that for Jaccottet Ponge runs and often succumbs to.

So Jaccottet draws our attention to those 'moments d'oubli' (*Ponge, pâturages, prairies*, p. 29) where Ponge seems to contradict, rather than consciously revise, his poetics. These are valuable moments for Jaccottet but not, it seems, indicative of what Ponge is engaged in most of the time; later, he makes a distinction between the kind of writing 'qu'il [Ponge] revendique, qu'il affiche' and 'celle qui parfois lui échappe' (*Ponge*, p. 55). He quotes a sentence of Ponge about truth — '*De façon générale, Elle ne me paraît pas chose à atteindre, mais à attendre*' (*Ponge*, p. 18) — which fits his own work much better than Ponge's and recalls a sentence quoted earlier from Simone Weil's *Attente de Dieu* (not a book Ponge is likely to have read).

Jaccottet brings out the difference between them precisely with reference to

'Travaux au lieu dit l'Étang', the difference between the attainer, whose 'prose toujours vigoureuse, exacte et tonique' (*Ponge*, p. 36) always hits the target, and the waiter, whose patient 'tâtonnements' open up a space in which something can appear that is perhaps hardly there. Having observed that in 'Travaux' he uses 'la méthode pongienne pour aller dans le sens opposé à celui où il marchait, lui, d'un pas si sûr', he makes the distinction in a startlingly literal way:

> Tout ce qui a donné lieu chez moi à un poème ou à une prose d'ordre poétique, l'a fait parce que, m'a-t-il semblé, une ouverture s'était produite dans le mur des apparences; [...]. Le but, ou plutôt le résultat étant ainsi d'ouvrir, de faire passer; de reculer la limite ou, au moins de l'aérer [...]. Les travaux de Ponge vont à fins contraires. Il boucherait plutôt ce genre d'interstices, pour en finir une bonne fois avec ce qu'ils semblent laisser passer; non, certes, par peur; par refus d'avoir peur de ce qu'il juge hors de portée, pour ne pas dire spectral.
> (*Ponge*, pp. 38–39)

Ponge, Jaccottet implies, is securing our knowledge of the world, making it fast against the threats of meaninglessness. He is silently drawing on words of Ponge's own which he quotes in his earliest piece on him: 'Chaque mot est pour moi,' Ponge writes, 'un trou vertigineux dont la profondeur nous menace en nous attirant. Écrire des poèmes, c'est essayer de refermer ces trous, c'est installer des *garde-fous* tout autour. Sinon, on sombrerait'.[25] But to fill in the holes rather than opening up a passage through them, is, Jaccottet thinks, while acknowledging that what passes may be 'effrayant', to neglect to 'rendre compte de l'être en son entier' (*Ponge*, p. 38); it is to make the world smaller than it is. Or, to put it another way as he then goes on to do, it could lead to the 'périlleux retournement de la poésie sur elle-même' (*Ponge*, p. 40), which since the closing pages of *L'Entretien des muses* in 1968 Jaccottet had been signalling the dangers of for contemporary verse.

In one of several attempts to get closer to what he means by 'ouverture', by the quality that both conveys and is an instance of 'ce qui tient, dans une certaine mesure, devant la mort' (*Ponge*, p. 40) — the reality of the death of a loved person, that is, not an abstract idea of death — Jaccottet has recourse, as often elsewhere, to a phrase of Hölderlin's from 'Der Rhein': 'Ein Rätsel ist Reinentsprungenes', which he translates (in pieces) as '*Est énigme ce qui sourd pur*', giving for 'Reinentsprungenes' also 'pur jailli' or 'jailli pur' (*Ponge*, pp. 39, 41).[26] This *jaillissement*, what springs up, when it occurs in a poem or a piece of music, Jaccottet compares to an 'inflexion' and adds, in brackets:

> (Et il m'est arrivé non pas de penser, là encore, mais de ressentir que la poésie, et la musique, dans leurs moments de magie, ou de grâce, semblent précisément infléchir le mouvement du monde, fléchir la rigueur du destin.) (*Ponge*, p. 42)

Again, 'grâce' is being used here in the overlapping sense of gracefulness and revelation, and it is strongly associated with movement: it is itself a movement, an inflexion, and it acts upon the movement of the world, effecting a small adjustment to things, or seeming to. And it achieves this, Jaccottet seems to imply, turning now to the meaning of 'pur' in 'jailli pur', by introducing something whose mystery or enigmaticness is that of the source, 'qui est l'énigme que l'on ne peut résoudre en autre chose qu'une énigme' (*Ponge*, p. 43). It is inexplicable, and for that reason real.

All this is enigmatic enough, and Jaccottet seeks in his next section to give two examples of the kind of 'inflexion' he means. One is a haiku by Buson:

> *En se rejoignant*
> *elles deviennent silencieuses*
> *les eaux de montagne.*[27]

The other is Goethe's 'Wanderers Nachtlied' (*'Über allen Gipfeln | ist Ruh'*).[28] By bringing in these two poems, Jaccottet is ostensibly illustrating what he means by 'jailli pur' in poetry. Both poems are intended as, and are, examples of a poetry made of a handful of elements whose arrangement:

> dans un mouvement et une sorte de métamorphose, permet au poète de susciter, autour de ce presque rien, un espace ouvert où la rencontre de ces éléments, dont chacun est lié pour nous à un nombre très élevé de correspondances intérieures, de souvenirs et de rêves, peut prendre sa plus large et plus profonde résonance. Et cela, de surcroît, sans avoir l'air d'y toucher. (*Ponge*, pp. 47–48).

Like the poems of *Airs*, they are filters. But they are also examples of lightness to set against Ponge's wrought density, and in the strange economy of *Ponge, patûrages, prairies*, they permit the balance to tilt from the critical to the poetic. The poems exemplify a certain aesthetic, but they also introduce a certain imagery. Both poems are written by 'voyageurs' (*Ponge*, p. 49), both invoke silence and mountains and a transition (actual in the Buson, anticipated in Goethe). These connections allow this penultimate section of Jaccottet's text to end on an image that, as he acknowledges ('une fois de plus'), occurs in many other places in his work, that of crossing a col.[29] These poems might help us, he suggests, to 'franchir le tout dernier col sans succomber au froid' (*Ponge*, p. 50). The book is a meditation on death, which begins 'au bord d'un gouffre froid' (*Ponge*, p. 19) at Ponge's ill-attended funeral and asks what can be set against it. It finds its answer in poems which are anchored in the world but seem barely to touch it, which use the elements of reality but also add something and allow them to breathe, in a delicate balance of gravity and grace.

The text doesn't end here though. A final section, with the title 'Pâtures et prairies', returns to the words of the psalm which were read at the funeral (fortuitously) alongside Ponge's poem 'Le Pré': '"L'Éternel est mon berger […] Il me conduit dans de verts pâturages"' (*Ponge*, p. 12); and with it to the idea of an archaic world where 'les choses […] étaient plus simples' — 'On avait deux espèces de soif, et deux espèces d'eau. Voir l'une jaillir vive ou couler avec tranquillité, c'était recevoir le rappel et la promesse de l'autre' (*Ponge*, p. 51). Words back then, and monuments and statues, had 'une grande force', the implication being that now, in our altered state, it is the lightness and insubstantiality, frailty even, of the haiku-like text which better equates to our relationship with death.

To his 'filet maillé de paroles' (*Œuvres*, p. 1208), as Jaccottet calls his text in a later, and similar meditation, this time occasioned by the death of André du Bouchet, to the 'tissu précieux' (*Ponge*, p. 53) of poems and pieces of music which risk a fragile structure of meaning in the face of death, he adds, having considered but discarded Dante (so having in fact of course briefly woven him in), 'la pastorale du *Conte d'hiver*' and its 'fusion suprêmement gracieuse des métaphores et des métamorphoses' (pp. 52–53). It is the scene in which Perdita, once 'lost' and now returned and 'grown in grace | Equal with wondering' (*The Winter's Tale*, IV.1.24–25), appears dressed as Flora and presides over a celebration of spring, that is, 'le printemps qui est aussi Perdita elle-même qui le fête, la grâce perdue et bientôt, par le pouvoir de l'amour, retrouvée' (*Ponge*, p. 53). Jaccottet had already written about *The Winter's Tale*, in Yves Bonnefoy's translation, in 1965, and there too it is 'la grâce de Perdita' on which he focuses.[30] Here he quotes some of the same lines again — part of an exchange between Perdita and Florizel in IV.4 — and in the same version:

> *Oh, que ceux-là*
> *Me manquent, pour vous en faire des guirlandes,*
> *Et, mon très doux ami,*
> *Pour l'en joncher sur tout, sur tout le corps.*
> *— Eh, comme un mort?*
> *— Non, comme un pré, pour les jeux de l'amour*
> *Et son repos. Un mort? Oui, pour l'ensevelir*
> *Bien vivant toujours dans mes bras. Allons, prenez vos fleurs.*
> *Je crois bien que je joue comme j'ai vu faire*
> *Aux pastorales de Pentecôte… Sûr que c'est cette robe*
> *Qui a changé mon esprit.*

This is followed by the question-comment: 'Jamais la pensée de la mort, surgie ici inopinément, et d'ailleurs par jeu, dans l'esprit de Florizel, aura-t-elle été plus tendrement enveloppée dans les mots, plus efficacement métamorphosée dans l'encens de la poésie?' (*Ponge*, p. 54). The use of this passage at this point depends on the translation, which has 'pré' for 'bank' ('like a bank for love to lie and play on') and turns the wrapping of death in words into a more pointed resurrection, in effect anticipating the scene at the end of the play when Hermione apparently comes back to life. Shakespeare's enveloping involves a play on words, with 'corpse' shifting from the normal sense to the obsolete 'living body of a person': 'Not like a corpse; or if, not to be buried, | But quick, and in mine arms'.[31] Perdita gracefully rejects the idea of death (not that kind of corpse, but this), though of course it has still been raised and thus enfolded. Bonnefoy's wording is subtly but unignorably different. The French Perdita accepts the idea of a corpse, but then, with a slight 'inflexion' of 'ensevelir', simply transforms it into a living body: 'bien vivant toujours'. The alchemy of translation has effected a change which is more miraculous in French, less founded, as if a loving embrace could bring someone back from the dead, an idea that, if not absent from the English, is only hovering at the margins as a metaphorical toning of the sense, whereas in the French it is central.

The inclusion of the pastoral from *The Winter's Tale* serves as a reflection on the grace of words, on their ability, as poetry, to take up and transform the gravity even of death. It is for Jaccottet a supreme instance, 'où la magie du théâtre s'exerce de la façon la plus insinuante' — where we can recall Roger Pearson's characteristically attentive exposition of the various senses of 'insinuation' in Mallarmé: not just 'an oblique speech-act', or penetration, but also 'a legal act of registration', an act which authenticates.[32] As Pearson reminds us, *insinuer* derives from *sinus*, a winding or turning, and it might evoke the twisting and weaving involved in constructing the poetic text, especially as practised by Jaccottet; and the legal sense suggests a process whereby words, without forfeiting their lightness, might gain some purchase on the arbitrariness of existence, might so structure silence and the idea of death that they achieve a credibility, even if only fleetingly. For Jaccottet the scene from *The Winter's Tale* is a kind of ritual which saves life from meaninglessness but in an almost intangible manner, its fragility a kind of guarantee.

'Dire cela peut paraître inacceptable; aussi grandiloquent qu'absurde, futile, inconvenant' (*Ponge*, p. 56). Jaccottet inserts many near-disclaimers into his text, he draws attention to its weaknesses in order to protect it from them, something that is also achieved by the hesitant, tentative syntax with its anticipations, qualifications, and doublings-back. But he has ventured similar movements and ideas before, and it is not a method he can or will give up on. He returns to the notion of the enigma and applies it to the grass, to the 'pâturages, prés, prairies' his thoughts have been circling round: 'la limpidité de l'herbe, des fleurs dans l'herbe, des prairies, est indéchiffrable, à jamais' (*Ponge*, p. 56). Perhaps it is a mistake to *want* to decipher them? But to speak of doing so is to express the intensity with which they seem to address him. Having taken leave of the language of the Bible (too symbolic), and also of that of Ponge (in a final mention of his name), neither of which seems sufficient to translate what cannot be translated, 'sa rumeur [...] aussi sourde qu'insistante' (*Ponge*, p. 55), he distinguishes the movement of his text from the 'prodigieuse ascension de Dante' in the *Paradiso*, and 'le superbe latin de saint Augustin', whose assurance and simplicity Jaccottet no longer thinks possible: '*Corpus pondere suo nititur ad locum suum. Pondus non ad ima tantum est, sed ad locum suum. Ignis sursum tendit, deorsum lapis*' (*Ponge*, p. 56).[33] Augustine, like Simone Weil, considers gravity as something that doesn't necessarily pull downwards.[34] But Jaccottet, instead of such movements of transcendence, prefers to hazard a different notion: 'mais qu'il y eût encore une "descension" (risquons le mot) possible, vers le plus humble de ce monde-ci'. The coinage 'descension' gestures towards a combination of gravity and grace, a falling movement that responds to the weight of the world but is not wholly bound by it. The 'verts pâturages', the 'pré', and the 'prairies' here become 'ces verdures basses [...] dont nous serons un jour, avec un peu de chance, revêtus' (*Ponge*, p. 57). (Perhaps all along somewhere Jaccottet has had one of Mallarmé's most beautiful lines in mind, from his 'Tombeau' for Verlaine: 'Verlaine? Il est caché parmi l'herbe, Verlaine' — the Ponge book is itself a kind of *tombeau*.)[35]

The text dwells a moment longer on the enigma of grass, on its quality 'à la fois plus près et plus loin de moi qu'un symbole, plus naïf et plus dérobé, plus faible et plus puissant', and acknowledging that the thought must seem 'inane et peu probant' suggests that 'parce que cette énigme est restée énigme et rayonne comme telle, elle équilibre, en quelque façon, l'autre (celle de l'orage infernal), elle l'absorbe, elle le rédime' (*Ponge*, pp. 58–59). The idea of 'équilibre' occurs once before in the book, where it is applied to Bach's 'Goldberg Variations'. And, as there, it leads to the thought of a limit, a frontier that while it cannot be crossed is somehow open. If there is an equilibrium, there is a relation across the fulcrum, even if on one side there is 'toujours un poids beaucoup plus lourd' and on the other 'presque rien que d'impondérable', as Jaccottet says of the 'oscillation' which he identifies as fundamental to his work in *À travers un verger* (p. 558). Elsewhere, Jaccottet remarks that 'la poésie [...] est au plus près d'elle-même dans la mise en rapport des contraires fondamentaux'.[36] Such a balance, when achieved, because it brings into relation so much, because it encompasses many contradictions, seems to need the extension, even if only in the imagination, beyond the visible, which does not seem sufficient to contain it on its own. *Ponge, patûrages, prairies* ends on the paradox of the border 'infranchissable, oui, mais parce qu'infranchissable, incompréhensiblement, ouverte' (p. 59). It crosses a border which cannot be crossed, and acknowledges the finality of death as an opening. Or at least it runs those possibilities together so that they interfere with each other: 'Un mur tellement mur qu'il ne barre plus le chemin. Une nuit tellement nuit qu'elle éclaire doucement les pas'. These are the closing words, and they pause on overt enigma, seeking speculative comfort in it just as the grass, and other 'signe[s] [qui] se dérob[ent]' (p. 484), have their force by virtue of not being decipherable.

Ponge has faded from view by this point, but not because he has been forgotten. If the text ends on death that is because it began at Ponge's grave, and the book is among other things (in other respects it is a typical Jaccottet prose, interrogating the world, trying to find a mode which corresponds to 'l'être en son entier') a reckoning with Ponge, a confrontation of two very different poetics in which only one is vindicated. The Jaccottet mode — conscious of the risks of doing so — opens out towards the 'invisible' in a way that Ponge has no interest in doing, and so the ending is also a demonstration of what Ponge lacks, of what he judges to be off limits.

The difference in their methods is clear enough: Ponge works and reworks the matter of language, scraping and applying it in layers like paint, giving it texture, thickness, and weight, covering the whole surface of the canvas. Jaccottet's work is more like a sketch, hinting at things, trying to bring out the essential traits, and soliciting the whiteness of the page.[37] He lightens, aerates, 'filters' the density of the world. If a Ponge text is like a fortress, self-contained, exits sealed, its stones fitted tightly together to endure, Jaccottet's is more like a spider's web, a 'réseau' (*Truinas*, p. 1203) that lets the light through, a fragile tracery made of spaces and tenuous connections, exposed to what passes and at risk of tearing. Like a spider, Jaccottet is always rebuilding his delicate structures, starting all over again, looking for new anchor points on which to fasten the slender threads of his syntax. Mallarmé does not appear very often in Jaccottet's work, although references and linkings to other writers are intrinsic to it, but there doesn't seem to be anything in Mallarmé's definition of poetry that he would disagree with: 'La Poésie est l'expression, par le langage humain ramené à son rythme essentiel, du sens mystérieux des aspects de l'existence: elle doue ainsi d'authenticité notre séjour et constitue la seule tâche spirituelle'.[38]

* * * * *

It would be tempting to associate Jaccottet's open-work with grace and Ponge's fastidious stopping up of gaps with gravity, but in fact, as we have seen, it is on the balance of gravity and grace that a poem depends, and gravity is a prerequisite for grace more generally. As is most clear when thinking of dance, gravity is needed to make grace graceful: even if it may be true that it is the momentary apparent freedom from gravity that gives a gesture its grace, the moment is in fact still subject to gravity's force, and the grace comes not from overcoming gravity but coinciding or corresponding with it. As writers from Schiller onwards have always emphasized (most succinctly, Disraeli: 'Grace, indeed, is beauty in action', quoted in the *OED*), grace is mobile, it is a passage, or what Jaccottet calls an 'inflexion'. It cannot be arrived at deliberately, but depends on chance, that is, on what falls ('chance' shares its etymology with 'cadence'). It involves a certain acquiescence in or concord with the way things fall, and by that token it soon ends, it is not a state. The poetry that combines gravity and grace, 'une parole rythmée' (*La Semaison*, p. 356), lends just enough weight to what is fleeting, to the volatility of the world; and aerates the solidity and density of matter, opening it out into a tissue of meanings and correspondences and making it what Jaccottet, borrowing from Rilke, often calls 'intérieur'. He sometimes associates poetry with snowfall — 'la poésie illuminant par instants la vie comme une chute de neige' — and points to 'ce caractère d'*exception* qui lui est naturel' (*La Semaison*, p. 407). Elsewhere, in one of his many attempts to anchor poetry in the everyday, he speculates that 'le monde infini' might be reflected:

> non plus dans le miroir de l'ostensoir quand on le tire de son coffret d'or, non plus sur la page d'un grand livre poétique, mais, un instant, un instant seulement et qui suffirait, sur un peu de neige entrevue par la fenêtre embuée au moment de se lever, en décembre, ou sur la poignée d'une porte qu'on était occupé à fourbir. Peut-être...[39]

Another world in this, 'l'illimité' in 'la limite', that is a possible definition of grace, and falling snow, the beauty of the snowflake forming as it descends and fading on the ground, might be thought the epitome of grace understood as an operation that espouses gravity.

★ ★ ★ ★ ★

The poems of *Airs*, brief, fragile, and apparently weighing little, are full of images of suspension and hesitation, but the thought is offered that these things are the conditions that make the poem possible, as in the opening verses:

> Peu de chose, rien qui chasse
> l'effroi de perdre l'espace
> est laissé à l'âme errante
>
> Mais peut-être, plus légère,
> incertaine qu'elle dure,
> est-elle celle qui chante
> avec la voix la plus pure
> les distances de la terre (p. 421)

To be 'peu de chose' gives no protection against 'l'effroi' and doesn't banish it, but neither does it result in melancholy — rather in a hope tempered by uncertainty, which is the proper complexion of hope. The poem embraces lightness, but without forgetting its conditionality; it balances grace and gravity in its themes (beginning with 'peu de chose', ending on 'terre'), as the possibility that lends the poem to itself. The voice is not pure, but it is as pure as possible. It also combines gravity and grace in another way, in that it seems to be a version of the Emperor Hadrian's famous address to his soul, 'Animula vagula blandula':

> Animula vagula blandula,
> Hospes comesque corporis,
> Quae nunc abibis in loca,
> Pallidula rigida nudula,
> Nec ut soles dabis iocos?[40]

The first verse of 'Peu de chose...' can be read as a loose translation or rearrangement of Hadrian's first two lines, but the second then works by lifting off from the Latin, invoking not the vagueness of 'loca', but 'les distances de la terre', and omitting any equivalent for the negative adjectives 'pallidula rigida nudula': 'l'âme errante' is not naked, the 'peu de chose' it still has left is enough for its airiness to drift into song. Once we are aware of the source, it becomes part of the poem, whose lightness depends on the ballast of the Latin lying beneath it, which it lets appear through the words but leavens and alters into the tenor of *Airs*.

The collection is full of this lightness which does not forget. It sees the world in a way which can be said to be scientifically accurate and visionary at once — 'Ce monde n'est que la crête | d'un invisible incendie' (p. 425) — and it traces an exposed and tentative living on a surface which knows of its depths. The poems pick out a trajectory 'entre pierre et songerie' (p. 424), in a world which is made up of the texture of material things and our reflections upon them, a space we can never be quite sure we inhabit. The lightness of being means that it is always eluding us, and the poems, guided in part by Jaccottet's discovery of the haiku, attempt, in their stripped down state, to articulate precisely that elusiveness.[41] Unlike in the previous collection, *L'Ignorant*, or in the next one, *Leçons*, they use minimal punctuation and in particular never end on a full-stop, being as interested in letting things slip through them as in catching hold of anything (filters are also a kind of net). They are attentive to what happens at edges, to the meeting of one thing with another: 'La parfaite douceur est figurée au loin | à la limite entre les montagnes et l'air' (p. 433). One poem in particular ponders the relationship between incommensurables which cannot not be brought together, such is our strange habitation of the world:

> Poids des pierres, des pensées
>
> Songes et montagnes
> n'ont pas même balance
>
> Nous habitons encore un autre monde
> Peut-être l'intervalle (p. 438)

Jaccottet later quotes this poem in 'Éclaircies', the final part of *Paysages avec figures absentes* (as it happens (?) just after a long quotation from Simone Weil). There he presents it as an attempt to:

> saisir en poème [...] ce sentiment qu'il doit y avoir *deux mesures, deux ordres de mesure*; parce que ce que nous vivons, douleur ou joie, dans une vie, ou même en un bref instant, nous comprenons bien que c'est sans rapport avec les millions, les milliards d'années ou de kilomètres de la science.

The feeling that something in us escapes number might be, Jaccottet says, 'l'ébauche d'une espérance' (p. 531).

But these comments seem to me almost to falsify the poem in their strict separation between 'ce que nous vivons' and 'la science' ('sans rapport'). The poem relates at least as much as it distinguishes, so that the first phrase invites us to consider how the weight of stones and of thoughts might belong in one line, one breath. 'Songes et montagnes', by inverting the order, only increases the sense that the collocation is not that of a clean distinction, and the sounds of the words, too, suggest a seepage between them. The line 'n'ont pas même balance' implies that 'songes' and 'montagnes' do not weigh down on the scales in the same way — though 'avoir balance' is hardly a ready-made phrase — and yet the poem creates a kind of balance between them nevertheless, an imagined equilibrium which might in fact be a prerequisite for the 'intervalle' between them. Whereas the comments in *Paysages avec figures absentes* seem to say that our true life occurs outside the ambit of what is describable by science, the poem suggests rather that it occurs, or 'perhaps' occurs, at the point where the mental order and the physical order intersect, or perhaps, if we take 'intervalle' more literally, in a gap between them. The precise sense of 'intervalle' and its syntactical value are left unclear, or open. It is natural to read it in apposition to 'un autre monde', but we don't quite have enough information to do so confidently, and in an unpunctuated poem the capital letter on 'Peut-être' makes a separation. Slightly dislocated and suspended as it thus is, 'l'intervalle' ends the poem with a kind of verbal flicker which opens it out and perhaps creates (or 'insinuates'?) the kind of 'interval' it speaks of, giving us something and taking it away at once. It is a gesture full of grace, and depends as such on the grave tempering of 'peut-être'.

Notes to Chapter 14

1. Philippe Jaccottet and Gustave Roud, *Correspondance 1942–1976* (Paris: Gallimard, 2002), p. 239.
2. Paul Valéry, 'Le Cimitière marin', in *Œuvres*, ed. by Jean Hytier, 2 vols, Bibliothèque de la Pléiade (Paris: Gallimard, 1957), I, 147–51 (p. 148).
3. Philippe Jaccottet, *Taches de soleil, ou d'ombre: notes sauvegardées 1952–2005* ([Paris]: Le Bruit du temps, 2013), p. 55. Cf. Simone Weil, *La Pesanteur et la grâce* [1947] (Paris: Union générale d'éditions, 1962).
4. Jaccottet, *Taches de soleil*, p. 58.
5. For 'souffle', see especially the crucial early pages of *La Semaison*, in Philippe Jaccottet, *Œuvres*, ed. by José-Flore Tappy and others, Bibliothèque de la Pléiade (Paris: Gallimard, 2014), pp. 354–56. Where possible, references to Jaccottet's works will be to this edition, given as page-numbers in the text.

6. Philippe Jaccottet, *Ponge, pâturages, prairies* ([Paris]: Le Bruit du temps, 2015), p. 69. For the Rilke translation, see Jaccottet's anthology, *D'autres astres, plus loin, épars: poètes européens du XXe siècle* (Geneva: La Dogana, 2005), p. 48.
7. Philippe Jaccottet, 'Joubert, Senancour, Amiel', in *Une transaction secrète* (Paris: Gallimard, 1987), pp. 34–41 (p. 36); originally in *Gazette de Lausanne*, 9/10 April 1966.
8. See Jaccottet, *Taches de soleil*, p. 177.
9. See Jacques Borel, 'Philippe Jaccottet: poète de l'insaisissable', in *Poésie et nostalgie* (Paris: Berger-Levrault, 1979), pp. 125–64. Many others have used the word *insaisissable* when talking of Jaccottet, including Jean Starobinski in 'Philippe Jaccottet: parler avec la voix du jour' and 'Philippe Jaccottet traducteur', both collected in *La Beauté du monde: la littérature et les arts* (Paris: Gallimard, 2016), pp. 784–92 and 793–99. They take it from Jaccottet himself in *La Semaison*, see *Œuvres*, p. 354.
10. Jaccottet, *Taches de soleil*, p. 58.
11. As in 'Grâce rendue à la grâce (Georges Schehadé)', *Nouvelle Revue Française*, 456 (January 1991), 75–81.
12. The poem is 'To What Serves Mortal Beauty?' and the translation Jaccottet cites is by Pierre Leyris: '*de Dieu la beauté suprême, la grâce*' (*Taches de soleil*, p. 168).
13. Published respectively on 14 April 1950 and 21 November 1951. The 'Chronologie' in the Pléiade *Œuvres* notes that Jaccottet 'reread' Weil in 1950 (p. L). See also Judith Chavanne, 'Présence de Simone Weil dans l'œuvre de Philippe Jaccottet', in *Simone Weil et le poétique*, ed. by Jérôme Thélot, Jean-Michel le Lannou and Enikö Sepsi (Paris: Éditions Kimé, 2007), pp. 255–69.
14. In his notebooks and other writings Jaccottet usually puts quotations from other writers in italics. Where this is the case italics are also used here.
15. Philippe Jaccottet, 'Notes', in *L'Entretien des muses: chroniques de poésie* (Paris: Gallimard, 1968), pp. 26–30 (p. 29).
16. Seamus Heaney, in Dennis O'Driscoll, *Stepping Stones: Interviews with Seamus Heaney* (London: Faber & Faber, 2008), p. 468.
17. Philippe Jaccottet, 'Ver le "vrai lieu"', in *L'Entretien des muses*, pp. 251–57 (p. 251).
18. See also Jaccottet, *L'Entretien des muses*, p. 255. The Bonnefoy poem can also be found in Yves Bonnefoy, *Poèmes: Du mouvement et de l'immobilité de Douve, Hier régnant désert, Pierre écrite, Dans le leurre du seuil* (Paris: Gallimard, 1994), p. 106.
19. Philippe Jaccottet, 'Approche de Ponge', in Jean Pierre Vidal, *Philippe Jaccottet: pages retrouvées, inédits, entretiens, dossier critique, bibliographie* (Lausanne: Payot, 1989), pp. 11–12 (p. 12); originally published in *Pour l'Art*, 2 (September/October 1948).
20. Jaccottet, *Ponge, pâturages, prairies*, pp. 15–16.
21. See in particular Michèle Monte and André Bellatore, *Le Printemps du temps: poétique croisée de Francis Ponge et Philippe Jaccottet* (Aix-en-Provence: Publications de l'université de Provence, 2008). Several of Jaccottet's articles on Ponge are gathered in *L'Entretien des muses* and *Une transaction secrète*. Many more are uncollected.
22. Philippe Jaccottet, 'Comme un salut, de loin', in *Une transaction secrète*, pp. 240–44 (p. 243).
23. Philippe Jaccottet, 'A propos du *Grand Recueil*', in *L'Entretien des muses*, pp. 115–20 (p. 116).
24. Francis Ponge, *Le Parti pris des choses* (Paris: Gallimard, 1986), p. 38. This poem is included in Jaccottet's anthology *Une constellation, tout près: poètes d'expression française du XXe siècle* (Geneva: La Dogana, 2002).
25. Quoted in 'Approche de Ponge', in Vidal, *Philippe Jaccottet*, pp. 11–12.
26. The conjunction of Ponge and Hölderlin is also present in Jaccottet's *Paysages avec figures absentes* (in *Œuvres*, pp. 1447–49). For another instance of the Hölderlin phrase, here translated in one piece, see p. 1053.
27. The translation he quotes is by Nobuko Imamura and Alain Gouvret.
28. Jaccottet quotes only these two opening lines, in German, and gives in a note his own prose translation of the whole poem together with one in verse by Jean Tardieu.
29. See for example *À travers un verger*: '*des histoires de voyageurs franchissant un col dans un tourbillon de neige*' (p. 556).

30. Philippe Jaccottet, 'Contribution à l'année Shakespeare (*Le Conte d'hiver*)', in *Une transaction secrète*, pp. 28–33 (p. 33).
31. See William Shakespeare, *The Winter's Tale*, ed. by Stephen Orgel, Oxford World's Classics (Oxford: Oxford University Press, 1996), p. 176.
32. See Roger Pearson, *Unfolding Mallarmé: The Development of a Poetic Art* (Oxford: Clarendon Press, 1996), pp. 285–92 (on Mallarmé's 'art of insinuation').
33. In a note, Jaccottet supplies the translation by Pierre de Labriolle: 'Tout corps tend, en vertu de sa pesanteur, vers la place qui lui est propre: mais un poids ne tend pas nécessairement vers le bas: il tend vers la place qui lui est propre. Le feu monte, la pierre tombe' (*Ponge*, p. 64).
34. See Weil, *La Pesanteur et la grâce* (Paris: 10/18, 1962), p. 13: 'La pesanteur morale nous fait tomber vers le haut'.
35. Stéphane Mallarmé, *Poésies* (Paris: Gallimard, 1992), p. 62.
36. Philippe Jaccottet, 'Remarques', in *L'Entretien des muses*, pp. 299–310 (pp. 303–04).
37. Jaccottet makes the same distinction, without pursuing it or quite applying it to that between Ponge and himself, when he sets 'l'ébauche' against 'le tableau achevé', 'le premier jet' against the 'ensemble' (*Ponge*, p. 44).
38. Stéphane Mallarmé, letter to Léo d'Orfer, 27 June 1884, quoted in Pearson, *Unfolding Mallarmé*, p. 294. Jaccottet quotes this, up to the colon, in an early article, noting that Mallarmé called the request that provoked it 'un coup de poing' ('La Poésie est aussi un plaisir', in Vidal, *Philippe Jaccottet*, pp. 16–18 (p. 17), originally published in *Suisse contemporaine* in May 1949).
39. Philippe Jaccottet, 'Remerciement pour le prix Ramuz', in *Une transaction secrète*, pp. 297–303 (p. 303).
40. *The Penguin Book of Latin Verse*, ed. by Frederick Brittain (Harmondsworth: Penguin, 1962), p. 61.
41. On the haiku's significance for Jaccottet, see above all: 'L'Orient limpide (*Haïku* de R. H. Blyth)', in *Une transaction secrète*, pp. 123–31; the notes for August 1960 in *La Semaison* (pp. 363–64); and the volume *Haïku présentés et transcrits par Philippe Jaccottet* ([Montpellier]: Fata Morgana, 1996).

— 14 —

Feathers, Scales, and Hollow Eggs: Lightness and Weight in Mercè Rodoreda's *La plaça del Diamant*

Laura Lonsdale

> What then shall we choose? Weight or lightness? [...] The only certainty is: the lightness/weight opposition is the most mysterious, most ambiguous of all.
> MILAN KUNDERA, *The Unbearable Lightness of Being*[1]

In *Quanta, quanta guerra* (1980) [War, So Much War], a work almost symbolist in the quality of its images, the Catalan novelist Mercè Rodoreda wrote that 'El que tenien de més bonic [les bombolles de sabó] era que després de tanta paciència per veure-les sortir de la canya i de tant tornassol, mentre volaven es fonien com si les punxessin' [The most beautiful thing about [soap bubbles] was that after all that patience, waiting for them to emerge from the cane, and all that iridescence, they would disintegrate in flight as if they had been punctured].[2] As a possible allegory of a writer's craft this image of lightness, beauty, patience, iridescence, and transience stands out among the images of war and necessity that mark out in Rodoreda what Calvino, in response to Kundera's 'unbearable lightness of being', has called the 'ineluctable weight of living'.[3] The opposition between lightness and weight, an opposition as existential as it is artistic, is prominent in Rodoreda's best-known novel *La plaça del Diamant* (1962), set in Barcelona before, during, and after the Spanish Civil War and narrated by a woman, Natàlia, dubbed 'Colometa' by her overbearing husband, Quimet. Translated by Eda O'Shiel as *The Pigeon Girl* (1967) and by David Rosenthal as *The Time of the Doves* (1981), the novel is a verbal modelling of the 'colom' or pigeon — semantically indistinguishable from the dove in Catalan — translating the hollow fragility of the bird's skeleton and eggs, its fevered domesticity and its torpid flight into the structure, imagery, and tone of Natàlia's narration.[4] Suffering first the weight of an unhappy marriage and later of a terrible war, Natàlia's account lacks all levity but abounds in lightness, a lightness at once artistically positive and existentially negative.

The image of the soap bubble refers to lightness and impermanence, though also to patience and time, to craft, as qualities of beauty. And sure enough Rodoreda's prose is highly crafted while lacking any heaviness in its verbal texture; instead it combines a naive and untutored lexical simplicity, proper to Natàlia's voice, with a complex of images that anchor the text in its own poetic reality. This is important to observe because, without a sense of the anchoring nature of the novel's images, Natàlia's account threatens to float free of all but the powerful but ultimately inessential statement of personal experience. Critics have often noted the novel's refusal to engage more directly and overtly with its historical and political context,[5] and Nance's idea that it should be read in light of the slogan 'the personal *is* political' is arguably a defining critical starting point in readings of the novel, whether the politics in question are feminist or Catalan.[6] But though Natàlia 'seems to live and speak outside history',[7] Rodoreda's novel remains one of the most powerful, as well as one of the most beautiful, literary testaments to the Spanish Civil War.[8] For Calvino, to look too directly at reality is to let 'the weight, the inertia, the opacity of the world' stick to and petrify writing, while it is the 'indirect vision' that allows Perseus to cut off Medusa's head:

> To cut off Medusa's head without being turned to stone, Perseus supports himself on the very lightest of things, the winds and the clouds, and fixes his gaze upon what can be revealed only by indirect vision, an image caught in a mirror.[9]

Calvino sees this as 'an allegory on the poet's relationship to the world, a lesson in the method to follow when writing', though he simultaneously recognizes that myth relies primarily on a 'language of images' in which meaning is enclosed in the 'literal narrative, not in what we add to it from outside'.[10] In the same way, the language of the novel's images refers the reader to historical and political reality in the manner of Perseus looking at Medusa's reflection: the text may be realist in its evocation of a physically concrete environment and the subjective specificity of the narrator's voice, but it is the novel's images that encode its reality and its relationship to the outside world, and give novelistic ballast to its autobiographical form.

Though imagery may give the novel formal ballast, the images themselves are principally of hollowness, along with its associated qualities of brittleness, emptiness, and fragility, and its opposite attributes softness, sponginess, and fullness. The choice of hollowness as a core image is an interesting one precisely because it evokes a space capable of and even receptive to being filled, and to that extent evokes emptiness and fullness, lightness and heaviness simultaneously. The core image of this core image is pregnancy, or, more accurately speaking, pregnancy is the most concrete manifestation of this relationship between hollow space and the penetration or invasion of that space, also manifested in Quimet's expulsion of a tapeworm from his gut. The very physical reality of Quimet's tapeworm is preceded by a psychosomatic illness causing him pain in one leg, the two illnesses combining in the reader's mind to evoke a phantom pregnancy, and associating pregnancy therefore with internal consumption. Quimet's later claim that he has tuberculosis brings this imagery together with his corrupted lungs and Natàlia's mental picture, after his death in the civil war, of his unburied ribcage in the sand. These images of hollowness, internal consumption, and corruption centred on Quimet both derive and depart from the initial association of him with wood, the weighty substance of his occupation as a carpenter. During a late afternoon visit to Barcelona's Park Güell in the early days of their relationship, Natàlia begins to feel, as Quimet talks incessantly about wood, that she is fading with the light, becoming more insubstantial as he gains in density; the association is reinforced in the following chapter (Chapter 5), when Quimet talks of nothing but wood over a meal with Natàlia's father. This chapter also introduces woodworm and worm-eaten wood as another recurring image of hollowing out and internal consumption, and ends with a statement of Natàlia's existential lightness: 'però és que a mi em passava que no sabia ben bé per què era al món' [my problem was that I didn't really know why I was in the world].[11]

If Quimet ends, in Natàlia's picture-making, as an unburied ribcage in the sand it is no doubt in some sense poetic justice for his outrageous hypochondria, itself an extension of his laziness, profligacy, childishness, apishness, and unkindness. All his fullness and presence, his wish that after the war he might burrow into his home as a woodworm into wood, is lost to this image of bleached bones exposed to the sun and the wind, as even the weight of the grave is denied to him. If Quimet is ultimately denied weight, Natàlia herself is consistently denied lightness, weighed down by work, childcare, and, most particularly, the deprivation caused by the war. Yet Natàlia's fears gravitate not so much around weight as the loss of physical integrity in the form of invasion, emptying, splitting, and internal consumption, all of which evoke hollowness and fragility. She is horrified by the physical changes she experiences in pregnancy, by the swelling that threatens to lift her into the air like a balloon, an ambivalent image of both heaviness and lightness that puts her pregnant body in the amorphous company of rainclouds, cloudy seas, and spongy, impermeable substances like cork and feathers. As the war approaches and Natàlia becomes more exhausted by work, and as the pigeons she and Quimet bred from a pair increasingly invade their living space — circulating like blood through a body with the dovecote as its heart, jokes Quimet — Natàlia begins in a spirit of 'revolution' to shake the eggs with their half-formed chick inside, an action that leads to a long period of sleepless nights and bad dreams:

> I em despertava a mitjanit, com si m'estiressin els dintres amb un cordill, com si encara tingués el melic del néixer i m'estiressin tota jo pel melic i amb aquella estirada fugís tot: els ulls i les mans i les ungles i els peus i el cor amb el canal al mig amb una gleva negra de sang presa, i els dits del peus que vivien com si fossin morts: era igual. Tot era xuclat cap al no-res altra vegada, pel canonet del melic que havien fet assecar lligant-lo. I al voltant d'aquesta estirada que se me'n duia, hi havia un núvol de plomes de colom, flonjo, perquè ningú no s'adonés de res. (*PD*, p. 131)

> [And I'd wake up in the middle of the night feeling like someone had tied a rope around my guts and was tugging on them, like I still had that cord on my belly button from when I was born and they were tugging all of me out through my belly button and as they tugged everything went out: my eyes and hands and nails and feet and my heart with that tube down the middle with a drop of black blood caught there and my toes still alive but feeling like they were dead... it was that same feeling. Everything sucked out into nothingness again through that little tube that had dried out after they knotted it. And all around that tugging which was taking me away there was a soft cloud of dove feathers so no one would see what was happening.][12]

The 'softness' of the feathers is in Catalan 'flonjo', spongy not downy, with both the lightness of the insubstantial and the heaviness of the inert, impermeable enough to conceal but not to protect. The umbilical cord and heart valve are reminiscent of the hollowing, consumptive worm, while harking back to Natàlia's fear of splitting in childbirth and her impression of butchered animals in the market before war broke out. Existentially light, yieldingly passive, heavy with both duty and necessity, Natàlia dreams of her days as a shop assistant selling chocolates, a peaceful, reconciled time before war and marriage when, as she observes later, she sold 'xocolatins plens i xocolatins buits amb licor a dintre' ('solid chocolates and hollow chocolates with liqueur inside') and walked 'com una persona al costat de les altres persones' (*PD*, p. 166) ('like a person among other people').[13]

The hollowness that pervades Rodoreda's imagery is also present in the novel's structure, in the form of gaps and non-sequiturs. In Chapter 14, as mentioned above, Natàlia describes shopping at the market: after a powerfully poetic description of its smell of sea and death, of glassy-eyed lambs' heads and offal-sellers with waxen faces, of the gold-capped smile of a fishmonger with her basket of fish and the multiple reflection of a lightbulb in each fish scale,[14] Natàlia drifts into an anecdote about her greengrocer and then, after an ellipsis, begins again: 'I tot anava així, amb maldecaps petits, fins que va venir la república' (*PD*, p. 94) ('And life went on like this, give or take a few small headaches, until the Republic came').[15] While this apparent clumsiness might be evidence of Natàlia's lack of purchase on the world around her, it is also much more than just that. As a structural device, if we can call it that, the elision of the anecdotal and the transcendental creates a hole in the text that lightens it, stripping out the weight of all that seems most important. But at the same time the mention of the Republic at this moment and without further preamble gives symbolic weight to the images of death, and also to the images of life, that precede it: the lamb and the fish not only link with the dove in the public symbolism of Christian iconography, but the heart, the shell, the fish, and the fish egg reappear and are freighted with additional private meaning throughout the course of the novel. Though initially her elision might suggest the narrator's clumsiness and torpor, and make her impressions feel light and lacking gravity, all of which is important to our understanding of Natàlia as both character and narrator, by substituting absence for presence Rodoreda evokes powerfully both the everydayness that accompanies major events and the symbolic transcendence of both the everydayness and the events: she does not look Medusa in the face and her account of the coming of the Republic is not turned to stone.

Another example of the use of gaps and non-sequiturs to generate symbolic value can be found in Chapter 12. In a similar way, Rodoreda allows her narrator to indulge in a long descriptive passage, this time of dolls in a shop window, before introducing a surprising contrast; but on this occasion the contrast is yet more marked because the description is both more naive and the non-sequitur more abstracted:

> Sempre allí, bufones a dintre de l'aparador, esperant que les compressin i se les enduguessin. Les nines sempre allí, amb la cara de porcellana i la carn de

pasta, al costat dels espolsadors, dels picamatalassos, de les camusses de pell i de les camusses imitació de pell: tot a la casa dels hules.

Em recordo del colom i de l'embut, perquè en Quimet va comprar l'embut el dia abans d'haver vingut el colom. (*PD*, p. 89)

> [They were always there, so sweet in the shop window, waiting for someone to buy them and take them away. They were always there, the dolls, with their porcelain faces and paste flesh, beside the feather dusters and carpet beaters, the leather dustcloths and imitation leather dustcloths; all in the shop selling oilcloth.
>
> I remember the dove and the funnel, because Quimet bought the funnel the day before the arrival of the dove.]

At this point we have heard nothing about either the dove or the funnel, but the suddenness and incongruousness of their chiastic appearance gives them all the round presence of an allegory, however enigmatic. The nickname 'Colometa' is enough to tell us that the dove will have significance of some sort, but at this stage the association between it and the funnel is unclear: relying on sight and on sense, which their raw status as images demands, there seems to be a physical association between them based on fragility and hollowness. This is made plain at the end of the chapter, when Natàlia tells us that:

> I el colom ferit i l'embut van ser dues coses que van entrar gairebé juntes a casa, perquè el dia abans del colom, en Quimet va comprar l'embut per abocar el vi de la garrafa a l'ampolla, tot blanc, amb un voraviu blau marí, i va dir que anés amb compte perquè, si tenia la desgràcia de caure'm a terra, s'escrostonaria. (*PD*, p. 90)
>
> [And the injured pigeon and the funnel were two things that entered the house around the same time, because the day before the pigeon appeared [Quimet] had bought a white funnel with a dark blue rim for pouring wine from the demijohn into the bottle, and he said to take care because, if I had the bad luck to drop it on the floor, it would crack.][16]

Their fragility, hollowness and whiteness take us back to Natàlia's first appearance in the plaça del Diamant, when Quimet named her 'Colometa', in her white dress with the gold seashell clasp on her handbag, with all the colouring and vulnerability of an egg; but it also points forward to what Natàlia does not yet know: that the children will become in her mind like the pigeons, fragile, febrile, and pestilential; and that, after long years of war and on the point of starvation, she will look out the enamel funnel for the purposes of poisoning both herself and her children. Lying hungry with them in bed she has nightmares:

> I van venir unas mans. El sostre de l'habitación es va fer tou com si fos de núvol. Eren unas mans de cotó fluix, sense ossos. I mentre baixaven es feien transparents, com les meves mans, quan, de petita, les mirava contral sol. I aquestes mans qui sorten del sostre juntes, mentre baixaven es separaven, i els nens, mentre les mans baixaven, ja no eren nens. Eren ous. I les mans agafaven els nens tots fets de closca i amb rovell a dintre i els aixecaven amb molt de compte i els començaven a sacsejar: de primer sense pressa i aviat amb ràbia, com si total la ràbia dels coloms i de la guerra i d'haver perdut s'hagués ficat en aquelles mans que sacsejaven els meus fills. (*PD*, p. 160)

[And then I saw those hands. The ceiling became soft like a cloud. The hands were cotton, boneless. And as they came down the light shone through them like my hands when I was a little girl and I held them up against the sun. And as they were coming down from the ceiling the hands which had been together pulled apart, and as they were coming down the children stopped being children and turned into eggs. And those hands picked up the children who were shells with yolks inside them and lifted them up very carefully and started shaking them. First slowly and then furiously, as if all the fury of the doves and the war and losing was inside those hands that were shaking my children.][17]

Just as before, her anxieties are centred on an image not of weight but of spongy softness and fragility, as she imagines a reverse birth, a reversion to the egg, equivalent to the umbilical cord nightmare that preceded her own shaking of the pigeon's eggs. If the umbilical cord-worm voided her, the fragile eggshells of her children threaten to crack and spill their precious yolk. Through the visual association of the dove and the funnel, Rodoreda brings together all the strands of her novel's imagery — ribbons and cords are among the novel's most recurring images, connecting visually with both the worm and the umbilical cord — pointing backwards and forwards in novelistic time, inwards to a network of images around the loss of physical substance and integrity, and outwards to the reality of war and the pain of having lost. But, most importantly for our purposes, the introduction of these images in abstraction lends them an immediate and striking symbolic weight that does not contradict, though it anchors, their everydayness.

The attributing of symbolic weight to images is important not only in compensating for the perforations in Natàlia's narrative, but in indicating different ways in which lightness and weight can attach themselves to words. Symbols and allegories can, after all, be their own form of petrifaction, a 'frío juego de abstracciones' or cold game of abstractions, as Borges put it.[18] What releases symbols and, especially, allegories from this weight is the mobility of their signs, their ability to incorporate a range of possible meanings rather than a single, fixed meaning. But if petrifaction, total presence, is at one end of the scale of possibilities where symbolic value is concerned, empty reference is at the opposite end of that scale. Quimet, associated as we know with weight, but condemned ultimately to hollowness and evisceration, is the master of the empty referent. His mysterious habit of expressing disappointment and disapproval with the words 'pobra Maria' [poor Mary] leaves Natàlia perennially confused; and though undoubtedly she is literal-minded in asking Quimet's friend, Mateu, if he ever knew a girl called Maria, she can hardly be blamed for failing to understand his meaning. Natàlia's own name, evoking both birth and Christmas (*Nadal* in Catalan), along with the novel's parody of other elements of the Christmas story, are sufficient to put this name in its religious context, while Quimet's particular formulation of it — 'pobra Maria' — evokes the leverage among Catholics of sentimental guilt. This is reinforced by the sermon given by the priest, Mossen Joan, at Natàlia and Quimet's wedding, a re-telling of the story of Genesis in which Adam scolds Eve for hurting a flower: a particularly risible distillation of the moral content of the Creation story, especially in the novel's brutal context of war and its impact on a woman.

Internally to the novel, Adam's admonition succeeds in pointing forward once again to Natàlia's traumatic experience with her children, who are 'com flors mal cuidades' (*PD*, p. 121) [like neglected flowers], and brings the weight of the serpent to the visual imagery of umbilical cord, worm, and ribbons; but it also lightens the content of the biblical story to the point of absurdity, while leaving intact its kernel of feminine sin and guilt. Quimet's 'pobra Maria' points to nothing in particular, to no woman, idea, or event in particular, but nevertheless slots with robotic precision into the cultural construct from which it automatically and unthinkingly derives. The combination of inexplicable motivation and automatic authority is a feature of Quimet's behaviour more broadly, revealing the weight of his own position in the gender hierarchy and the lightness of his understanding of the nature and source of his authority, which has therefore to be constantly and arbitrarily re-affirmed. For example, having provoked an argument with his mother about the lack of salt in his food, and having brought to bear Lot's wife on the weighty matter of seasoning, he then mentions the devil in terms that are head-spinningly vacuous: 'I en Quimet aleshores va dir que el dimoni, i quan va dir, el dimoni, va callar' (*PD*, p. 62) [And then Quimet said 'the devil,' and when he'd said, 'the devil,' he shut up]. Though he is unable to follow up his references, they nevertheless stand in public symbolism for the moral source from which he believes his authority to derive, and in that sense are both vertiginously light and crushingly heavy. Though Natàlia never broaches the subject of morality or religion directly, her mental image of the church after the war as the belly of an enormous fish full of eggs that, in her mind, are also bullets, and her later sense when she is at peace that a seashell with the sound of the sea is a church with Mossen Joan as a pearl inside — a pearl she inserts from her own necklace to keep the lonely sea company — indicates a diminishing of the Church's power, if not perhaps its beauty, in her imagination over time.

The arbitrariness of the decontextualized is also a feature of Natàlia's depiction of the physical environment, which has itself been read as allegorical.[19] The genteel but faded house in which she is given work as a cleaner — before she is sacked for Quimet's republican sympathies — is a 'trencaclosques' (*PD*, p. 109), a puzzle made of balconies, archways, skylights, and glass doors, connections and divisions both insubstantial and disorientating. Access to the house is both difficult and confusing, full of disembodied voices 'que, quan em cridaven, no sabia mai d'on venien' (p. 109) [which called me, though I could never work out where they came from] and misleading doorbells:

> Li vaig preguntar d'on venia el timbre; i la senyora em va dir que el timbre que havia sentit era el timbre del jardí, que trucava la galeria, mentre que el timbre de la porta principal trucava al capdamunt de l'escala del rebedor. (*PD*, p. 114)

> [I asked her which bell it was because I couldn't figure out where the ringing was coming from; and the lady told me the bell I'd heard was the garden bell that rang on the porch, while the main doorbell rang in the front hall at the top of the staircase.][20]

The very accumulation and precision of detail in Natàlia's description of the house contributes to this feeling of confusion, the idiosyncrasy of the physical space overlaid with trivial, headachy anecdote:

> Vam sortir a la galeria descoberta del baixos que eren pis i, per l'escala que hi havia damunt del pou i del safareig, vam baixar al pati de pòrtland, sempre ple de bitlles perquè al nen li agradava molt jugar-hi. La senyora em va explicar que la seva filla necessitava repòs perquè tenía un mal, i em va explicar el mal que tenia la seva filla, que li venia per culpa d'haver volgut canviar les bótes de les camèlies de lloc. [...] El metge els havia dit que no se sabria el mal que patia la seva filla mentre no tingués un dels ronyons de la seva filla a la mà. I això, el metge, que no era el seu, perquè el seu feia vacances, els ho havia dit quan estaven drets damunt dels graons de marbre de l'entrada principal, al costat de la trapa que donava damunt mateix de la banyera de rajola de València. (PD, p. 109)

> [We came out into the veranda on the ground floor that was the flat and went down the stairs over the washhouse and well and into the cement yard that was always full of skittles because the kid liked playing skittles there. Madam told me her daughter needed to rest because she was ill and she said her daughter was ill because she'd moved their pots of camellias. [...] The doctor had said he couldn't say what was wrong without opening her up and looking at one of her kidneys. And it wasn't her doctor, because hers was on holiday, and he'd said that when they were standing on the marble steps in the main entrance, by the trapdoor with the view of the bath with the Valencia tiles.][21]

The disorientating nature of the house and the sickness and decay Natàlia observes in its garden is linked to the family's obfuscation, their tendency to lie, cheat, and be evasive, to a lack of solidity in what appears a solidly built house. In a sense the house functions as the physical equivalent of Quimet's 'pobra Maria,' as an empty symbol of social rather than moral power, as the family draws on the social capital represented by the house to avoid working and to cheat those who do, as they cheat Natàlia herself out of a proper wage by confusing her. The connection between social and religious power, particularly in the context of the civil war, goes without saying. Like Quimet, Natàlia's employers are guilty of drawing on received ideas and stored power, a dead weight of reference that is empty and incapable of generating new meaning, as the accumulation of pointless and exhausting detail indicates; and so the house embodies both what is most disabling in the symbolic and most disheartening in the real.

Natàlia's intention to kill herself and her children marks a turning point in the novel, as she is saved by an offer of work at the shop where she used to buy birdseed, and where she now goes to buy the cleaning substance that will kill them. From this point on her fear of disintegration begins to recede, as the possibility of regaining her physical and mental integrity is offered first by her paid employment, and then by her marriage to the shopkeeper Antoni. A war veteran, Antoni is both sexually impotent and facially pockmarked, attributes that in the novel's universe of images come to mean not damage but wholeness and innocence, the visible impressions of his scars contrasting with the invisible corruption of woodworm, consumption, rottenness, and infestation: 'A la llum ennuvolada els foradets de la verola semblaven més enfonsats a dintre de la pell. Cada foradet rodó amb una pell més nova, una mica més clara que la pell que es té del néixer' (PD, p. 174) ('In that cloudy light the pockmarks on his skin seemed deeper. Each pock was round and the skin on them was newer and a little lighter than the skin you're born with').²² The association of Antoni with innocence and integrity is key to Natàlia's recovery though problematic within the wider context of the novel, given that his relatively comfortable postwar existence suggests that, unlike Quimet, he fought not for the Republic but for Franco's Nationalists, an unmentioned possibility that leaves a yawning hole in the narrative while highlighting the passive or pragmatic nature of Natàlia's choices. While there is an inevitable, if elusive, political comparison to be drawn between the rotten but virile Quimet and the integral but castrated Antoni, Natàlia herself is symbolically implicated in the atrocities of the war while remaining marginal to its politics in her struggle to survive. Both her genocidal destruction of the eggs and her intention to kill herself and her children with cleaning fluid evoke the rhetoric of cleansing on both sides of the political divide, charging her domestic work with the symbolism of the war and associating cleaning with carnage, as Norah Lynn Gardner has pointed out; and in this context it is perhaps Antoni's irreparable but healed damage that acts as his guarantee, irrespective of his political allegiance.²³

Antoni's innocence and integrity are further emphasized in the final chapter, as Natàlia presses her ear to Antoni's back and listens to his heart beat, feeling his interiority and placing her finger in his navel to keep him whole. This act not only corresponds to her dream of being emptied through the stub of the umbilical cord but has an evident phallic connotation too, as her twin anxieties of being emptied and filled, of lightness and weight, are relieved. Of even greater relief, perhaps, is the scream that is 'tan ample qui li havia costat de passar-me pel coll' [so huge it was hard to get out of my throat] and which brings up 'una mica de cosa de no res, com un escarabat de saliva' (*PD*, p. 206) [a little bit of something and nothing, like a beetle made of spit]. The act of bringing something up, tiny and beetle-like, refers us back to the woodworm and relieves her of a hollowing parasite, though it is also in her mind representative of lost youth. In addition to the finger in the navel and the scream, the novel's final chapter offers a third form of symbolic resolution: returning to her old apartment building, Natàlia inscribes, deeply and with a knife, the name 'Colometa' in the door. She would have liked to go inside and touch the pair of scales engraved on the wall of the stairwell — an unequally balanced set of scales carved into the plaster with a punch, which she would touch with her fingers and by which she would sometimes pause for breath during the hardest days of her life — but she cannot get access to the building. The carving of her name on the door throws off the weight of the name 'Colometa' and yet gives the experience associated with it gravity and depth through inscription: she finally makes a mark. The inscription, the shout, and the finger in the navel are forms of both (self-) protection and assertion in response to existential lightness, though the brevity and transience of life, the loss of youth, remains. Standing in the shadow of a doorway watching her slim and healthy adult daughter in the sunshine, she becomes aware that Rita's shadow stretches all the way to her feet, imagining it as a lever that will lift her up into the air. Rita, who is like Quimet in looks and temperament, has in Natàlia's mind a weight and exteriority in contrast to which she fades or is in shadow, but the imagery here is not of a loss of integrity, which in association with her husband articulated anxieties about sex and pregnancy, but of the passage of time that signifies the substitution of one generation by the next:

> Em va semblar que l'ombra de la Rita, a terra, era una palanca, i que a qualsevol moment jo podria anar enlaire perquè feien més pes el sol i la Rita a for a que l'ombra i jo a dintre. I vaig sentir d'una manera forta el pas del temps. [...] El que roda i roda a dintre del cor i el fa rodar amb ell i ens va canviant per dins i per fora i amb paciència ens va fent tal com serem l'últim dia. (*PD*, pp. 193–94)
>
> [I kept imagining that Rita's shadow, on the ground, was a lever, and that at any moment I might be lifted into the air because the sun and Rita were heavier outside than the shadow and I were inside. And I felt very strongly the passage of time. [...] The time that goes round and round our heart and makes it go round with it and which changes us inside and outside and patiently makes us what we'll be on our final day.]

Though the thought is a melancholy one, and does not compensate for or resolve the unequal balance of forces in Natàlia's life, it lacks the anxiety of earlier perspectives on death and disintegration, the combination of Rita's slim body, round legs, and crown of fine hairs in the sunlight conveying an abiding sense of lightness and weight in harmony. In the same way, the novel's closing image of puddles full of sky, with a bird 'que [...] sense saber-ho esbarriava el cel de l'aigua amb el bec' [that [...] unknowingly broke up the sky in the water with its beak], is an image in which two things combine not parasitically or amorphously, but with contentment.

To return to Calvino: for him, lightness can be manifested in literature in 'at least three different senses':

> First there is a lightening of language whereby meaning is conveyed through a verbal texture that seems weightless, until the meaning itself takes on the same rarefied consistency [...]. Second, there is the narration of a train of thought of psychological process in which subtle and imperceptible elements are at work, or any kind of description that involves a high degree of abstraction. [...] And third there is a visual image of lightness that acquires emblematic value.[24]

Rodoreda's writing manifests all three of these senses and qualities of lightness, while keeping in tension the oscillating values of weight and lightness in artistic and existential terms. Natàlia's unconscious fears of hollowness and softness are deeply inscribed in the novel's imagery, which itself gains both gravity and grace through the careful manipulation of its symbolic power. Rodoreda's light touch conveys Calvino's sense that 'writing is a metaphor of the powder-fine substance of the world', avoiding both the hollowed out empty referent and the petrifaction of abstracted symbolism, and parodying the excesses of realism while generating a work alive with poetic reality.[25]

Notes to Chapter 15

1. Milan Kundera, *The Unbearable Lightness of Being*, trans. by Michael Henry Heim (London: Faber & Faber, 1995), p. 5.
2. Mercè Rodoreda, *Quanta, quanta guerra* (Barcelona: Club Editor, 1981), p. 55. All translations are mine unless otherwise indicated.

3. Italo Calvino, 'Lightness', in *Six Memos for the Next Millennium* [1985], trans. by Patrick Creagh (London: Vintage, 1996), p. 7.
4. The lack of distinction between pigeons and doves in Catalan is reflected in the three English translations of the novel to date, especially in the title of the first two, Eda O'Shiel's *The Pigeon Girl* (1967) and David Rosenthal's *The Time of the Doves* (1981). Neither doves nor pigeons appear in the literally translated title of the most recent version by Peter Bush, *In Diamond Square* (2013), though he renders the nickname Colometa as 'Pidgie' to communicate the unromantic nature of the birds in question. Rosenthal's doves acknowledge the novel's lyrical tone and the metaphorical value of the birds, while pigeons convey the toughness and lack of sentimentality of Natàlia's existence. My preference is for Rosenthal's doves, largely because the name 'Pidgie,' though in keeping with Quimet's voice, conveys only what is dull and stupid about the birds; it lacks the lightness of the name 'Colometa' while giving it a comic levity absent from the original novel.
5. See for example Enric Bou, 'Exile in the City: Mercè Rodoreda's *La plaça del Diamant*', in *The Garden Across the Border: Mercè Rodoreda's Fiction*, ed. by Kathleen McNerney and Nancy Vosburg (Selinsgrove, PA: Susquehanna University Press, 1994), pp. 31–41 (p. 33); and Josep-Anton Fernández, 'The Angel of History and the Truth of Love: Mercè Rodoreda's *La plaça del Diamant*', *MLR*, 94.1 (1999), 103–09 (p. 104).
6. Kimberley A. Nance, 'Things Fall Apart: Images of Disintegration in Mercè Rodoreda's *La plaça del Diamant*,' *Hispanófila*, 34.2 (1991), 67–76 (p. 67).
7. Fernández, 'The Angel of History and the Truth of Love', p. 104.
8. García Márquez wrote a moving testament to the then little-known author on her death in 1983: 'Al parecer, pocas personas saben fuera de Cataluña quién era esa mujer invisible que escribía en un catalán espléndido unas novelas hermosas y duras como no se encuentran muchas en las letras actuales. Una de ellas — *La plaza del Diamante* — es, a mi juicio, la más bella que se ha publicado en España después de la guerra civil' [Hardly anyone outside Catalonia seems to know who she was, that invisible woman who wrote beautiful, hard novels in magnificent Catalan such as are rarely to be found in contemporary literature. One of her novels, *In Diamond Square*, is in my opinion the most beautiful to have been published in Spain since the civil war' (Gabriel García Márquez, '¿Sabe usted quién era Mercè Rodoreda?', *El País*, 18 May 1983, <http://elpais.com/diario/1983/05/18/opinion/422056813_850215.html> [accessed 9 April 2016].
9. Calvino, 'Lightness', p. 4.
10. Ibid.
11. Mercè Rodoreda, *La plaça del Diamant* (Barcelona: Hermes, 2005), p. 36; hereafter referred to in the main text as *PD*.
12. Mercè Rodoreda, *The Time of the Doves*, trans. and intro. by David Rosenthal (Saint Paul, MN: Graywolf Press, 1986), pp. 112–13.
13. Ibid., p. 167.
14. See Mercè Rodoreda, *In Diamond Square*, trans. by Peter Bush (London: Virago, 2013), p. 63.
15. Ibid.
16. Rodoreda, *In Diamond Square*, trans. by Bush, p. 58.
17. Rodoreda, *The Time of the Doves*, trans. by Rosenthal, p. 145.
18. Jorge Luis Borges, 'Nathaniel Hawthorne', in *Otras inquisiciones* (Madrid: Alianza, 1997), pp. 80–113 (p. 86). Borges goes on to say that some writers think in images (e.g. Shakespeare, Donne, and Victor Hugo) while others think in abstractions (e.g. Julien Benda and Bertrand Russell). One is not a priori better than the other, he argues, but 'cuando un abstracto, un razonador, quiere ser también imaginativo, o pasa por tal' (p. 86) [when an abstract thinker, a reasoner, tries to be imaginative, or appears to be so], then allegory becomes 'un género bárbaro o infantil, una distracción de la estética' (p. 85) [a barbarous or infantile genre, a distraction from the aesthetic].
19. See Bou, 'Exile in the City'.
20. Rodoreda, *The Time of the Doves*, trans. by Rosenthal, p. 93.
21. Rodoreda, *In Diamond Square*, trans. by Bush, p. 80.
22. Rodoreda, *The Time of the Doves*, trans. by Rosenthal, p. 161.

23. Norah Lynn Gardner, 'Dirty Doves: Domestic Cleansing and the Spanish Civil War in Mercè Rodoreda's *La plaça del Diamant*', paper given at The Spanish Civil War and World Literatures conference, Institute of Modern Languages Research, University of London, 11–12 July 2016.
24. Calvino, 'Lightness', p. 17.
25. Ibid.

— 15 —

The Permissions of Translation

Patrick McGuinness

The poet and translator C. H. Sisson called his translations, of which he did many, 'fishing in other men's waters'.[1] It's an arresting remark, and because our metaphors for translation usually cast it in a more positive light, there's something enjoyably bracing about his imputation of both sterility and trespass. Sisson goes against the things we like to tell ourselves: that translation bridges cultures, crosses borders, explores the world and brings back riches; that it finds the universal in the particular and shows us that we're all different enough to be interesting to each other, but not so different that we've got nothing to say.

What I want to begin with is not Sisson's negative imputations, but the metaphoricity of the language we use to describe translation. Unlike writing poems, painting pictures, composing music, making engines, or discovering vaccines, translation is always 'like' something else: a process that apparently can only be explained by other processes. As when we explain complicated things to a child, we often end up saying what translation is like, not what it is. This is because we are surer of what translation resembles than of where its identity lies. Translation is already, in that respect, a metaphor.

None of this is news, but it is relevant to what I want to explore here: fake translations that are real poems, translations with no originals, and poets who go through the performance of translating in order to produce a fictional heteronymic 'original' poet, as well as new poems with fictional cultural, linguistic, national, and political hinterlands. We call these 'pseudo-translations', doubtless because 'pseudo-' is a less loaded qualifier than 'fake', but also to differentiate them from hoaxes. The distinction is important. The 'permissions' of translation in this context are the permissions not of translation itself (there are no originals, remember), but the permissions given to the poets by exploiting metaphors of translation in order to create new poems — poems that are original and yet that toy, fictionally, with the possibility of having existed elsewhere, in a different time, place, and language, and thus of not being original at all. This sounds like a Borgesian enterprise, perhaps, but one that manages, I hope, to balance the playful and the serious, the creative and the academic.

If we are bothered by the negativity implicit in Sisson's fishing metaphor, it is not because his unflattering images are fanciful, but because we recognize them all too well. The fishing metaphor sounds good, we think, and the foreign waters give translation a swashbuckling, fearless, exploratory aura. There's nothing more poetic, as Mallarmé knew, than a figure on the prow of ship facing choppy seas and unpredictable weather, hearing the sirens sing and navigating unknown realms. We just don't like the imputation that we're stealing someone else's fish.

In terms of metaphoricity, we can use I. A. Richards's vehicle/tenor division: we may agree on the vehicle (fishing), but the tenor is ambiguous; are we poaching from the territories of others, or are we casting our nets wide in the endlessly-replenished ocean of an international maritime free-for-all? If we disagree with the note of reproof in the tenor of Sisson's metaphor, the vehicle is one we are familiar with.

There are reasons Sisson can say what he says. The first is that he was a prolific translator, and the second is that he was a prolific poet. In these respects, he had paid his dues to both activities. Sisson knew whereof he spoke, and the 'fishing in other men's waters' comment should be understood quite specifically to be about the poet-translator, and the relationship between the poet as poet and the poet as translator.

Behind the fishing metaphor lies a sense of the poet having somehow used up his own resources, whether personal (the 'other men' being other writers) or cultural (the waters being national). Fishing disputes, as we know, arise out of all sorts of rights, counter-rights, claims and counter-claims, that are set in and argued about according to international maritime law. The fishing metaphor maps uncannily well onto debates about translation because they are about where national boundaries start and finish, and where territorial frontiers extend into the briny oceans where one wave and one fish look much like another but apparently are not. Many arguments about translation look a lot like fishing disputes (and are about as interesting), but the analogy captures very nicely the more numinous literary anxieties we have about ownership, territory, borders, language, cultural ecology, geo-political power, national identity, and national culture. And also with the notion of 'rights': who can and can't fish here? In at least one other respect too, the analogy fits: just as, when you take your boat into unauthorized waters, the border police come speeding up alongside you to check your papers and see what you've got in your hold, so when you translate something there'll always be someone ready to complain, accuse you of ignorance or bad faith, or tell you you've caught the wrong fish, strayed into the wrong waters, or used the wrong kind of net.

I want to avoid going over the usual debates about translation, about fidelity to the original, about the translator's cultural or linguistic 'qualification', and about the aesthetic pay-off (a good version, translation, adaptation) versus its ethical cost (appropriation, a silencing of the original, unbalanced power-relations between languages). They are instructive debates precisely because translation is always about more than translation, and there exist plenty of very good books about them. However, to the standard metaphors of distance and closeness (topographical) and fidelity and betrayal (moral) with which we discuss translation, I'd like to add the gravitational metaphor: the suggestion that the original must still exert a 'pull' on the version, and that the relationship between a translation's 'grace' and an original's 'gravity' is what determines the success of translation as an art. We might think of the original poem as having a heft, a mass, a *pesanteur* of its own, and that the laws of translational gravity are what keep the translation, the version or the adaptation, 'grounded'. The purpose of this essay is to explore what happens when a translation has no original — where the poet frees themselves from the laws of translational gravity while at the same time opening those laws up for examination and scrutiny, as well as for creative engagement. To ward off any imputation of postmodernism, I want to signal my interest in this category of writing for what it tells us about poetic creation, and about poetry and translation conceived not as different activities but as different points on the same continuum.

Before leaving Sisson behind I would like to suggest that his fishing metaphor is a bathetic echo, conscious or not, of Keats's poem 'On First Looking into Chapman's Homer'. The poem is famous for the way it celebrates the translator's skill in making the original speak, or seem to speak, in ways that are both true to it and new to it:

> Oft of one wide expanse had I been told
> That deep-brow'd Homer ruled as his demesne;
> Yet did I never breathe its pure serene
> Till I heard Chapman speak out loud and bold:[2]

Though Keats knew plenty about Greece, he could not read the language — unlike Byron or Shelley — and his Greeklessness was mocked by several contemporaries. It is thus honest as well as fitting for him to admit that the voice he hears is that of Chapman and not Homer. A proper classicist and less discriminating intellect (or quite simply a better bluffer) would surely have opined on whether or not *Homer*'s 'voice' was coming through. But then again, Keats implies, a proper classicist might have missed the point, by focusing only on what can be *heard* and *told* of Homer rather than what can be *breathed*. To breathe something in is to internalize it, to live *in* it and because of it, to make it part of you. Something subtle and qualified, but also rather radical, is being said about translation, and it can be traced across Keats's lines in the movement from the passive and removed 'had been told' to the active 'I heard Chapman', rendered even more dynamic and arresting by 'speak out loud and bold', until we reach the point where the original is *breathed*. Homer, in this poem, is experienced in terms of the function where life and language meet: breath. He isn't *read*, he isn't *heard* and he is no longer merely *told of* — these are merely relative degrees of mediation, increments of closeness or distance. Homer is *breathed*. Keats was trained in medicine, and breath and breathing have particular resonance in his poetry not just because they join life to language, but because, in their lack or in their negative, they join death to silence. Breath is life, and because breath is measure and rhythm in poetry, it is also the life of the poem. What it might be to breathe something in terms of a powerful poetic presence is caught in Mallarmé's disquieting description of Baudelaire, or his shadow, as an invigoratingly deadly gas: 'un poison tutélaire | Toujours à respirer si nous en périssons'. What Keats is breathing is tutelary and life-affirming, and while it might be Chapman's words he *hears*, it is Homer's air that he *breathes*.

That passage in Keats from 'told of', to 'heard', to 'breathed', is like a backwards articulation, a taking of language back to source: from the heard, to the spoken, to the mouth that utters and makes its words from the breath of life. Read like this, the poem is hugely ambitious in what it implies — much more ambitious than the lines that follow, which, however splendid, are much more straightforward to parse:

> Then felt I like some watcher of the skies
> When a new planet swims into his ken;
> Or like stout Cortez when with eagle eyes
> He star'd at the Pacific — and all his men
> Look'd at each other with a wild surmise —
> Silent, upon a peak in Darien.

The freedom usually attributed to the translator is here once more transferred to the reader. It isn't Chapman looking through the telescope or captaining his ship, it is the reader. Translation — or rather, reading translations — is both horizontal exploration (across land and sea) and vertical exploration (skies, stars, and planets). It has both vectors covered. When Keats wrote these lines, the two activities he described, astronomy and conquistadorianism, were generally positively viewed. Now these once-glorious metaphors are as likely to have the opposite effect; and, depending on who is reading them, more likely to. Cortés began the process that destroyed Aztec civilization, and his expeditions opened the way for colonial exploitation and genocide. As for 'new planets swimming into our ken', today's Keats might reflect on the irony that the first thing human beings do when they reach a new planet is stick a national flag in it. Behind every Newton is a Homais, and Homais has gone galactic. In other words: in knowing the world, do we merely reduce the world to what we know? It's a Flaubertian proposition, and it seems valid to ask it of translation too. Whether you're on Cortés's flotilla or Sisson's fishing boat, the same metaphor that sponsors the image of translator as world-widening explorer sponsors the image of translator as world-shrinking, homogenizing asset-stripper.

Because the arena in which these tensions are most obviously found is poetry in translation, translating without an original suddenly begins to seem like a sensible precaution...

The authors I will consider here — David Solway, Christopher Reid, and Derek Mahon — create poetry that depends, in order to work, on the idea that what we are reading exists in another, 'original' language, form, and context, and where the idea of translation as a process of gain and loss enables them to achieve certain fictional and poetic effects that would not otherwise be available. Though the parallel text has gone, the (reader's) mentality of the parallel text remains in fictional play with its spatial and temporal arrangements: the 'side by side' facing-text, or the original that is somehow, in time and place, 'behind', 'before', or underneath the translation that is 'from' or 'after' it. The recto-verso dialectic, which is, in pagination terms, a concretization of the before/after dialectic of source text and target text, remains as a ghost in the machine: a necessary fiction, like a creation myth of translation itself, that underpins the pseudo-translation.

Poetry has a long and colourful tradition of invented poets, and it's important to distinguish the fictional poet, the heteronym, or the alias from, say, the hoax or the parody, such as the French Adoré Floupette, author of the *Déliquescences* (1885) and the great Australian surrealist Ern Malley, author of *The Darkening Ecliptic*.

Both 'poets' were parodies, and Ern Malley was an outright hoax as well. Floupette and Malley each had a pseudo-biography whose purpose was to situate them as absurd and tragi-comic versions of the *poète maudit*. Not only were their verses send-ups of the avant-garde poetry of the period, but their imagined lifestyles were caricatures of the bohemian poetic life. If parody and hoax succeed, it is because they are distillations of the poetic culture as well as affronts to it: Calibanesque mirrors in which it sees itself unflatteringly delineated. The parody and the hoax, and inventions like Ossian, have different tales to tell and I am not concerned with those here. Nor am I going to discuss Pound, Eliot, Yeats, and the modernist 'mask', Valery Larbaud's Barnabooth or Gide's André Walter, or other instances of ironic self-distancing in modernist writing, where post-romantic *malaise* is disowned through the kind of displaced confession that allows the poet to revel in its tropes while claiming to see through them. In these contexts, irony becomes the last stand of sincerity, not its negation. And as for the list of invented poets, it would make a United Nations in itself, from the multiple heteronyms of Machado (who called them 'apócrifos') and Pessoa to Max Jacob's Morven le Gaélique, from John Peck's Hi-Lo, via Peter Russell's Quintilius, to Geoffrey Hill's Sebastian Arruruz, via Nabokov's John Shade and Pasternak's Zhivago poems.

My interest here is in real poems that are fake or pseudo-translations, which come with imagined authors and evince translation processes, and cultural, personal, and linguistic relations between translator and translated, that are part of their fictional coming into being. Above all, I am interested in how the pseudo-translation creates a sense of the absent original's 'gravitational pull': in Mallarméan terms, we might think of it as the creation, through the *ombre exprès* of pseudo-translation, of the *objet tu* of its non-existent poetic source.

I

My first poet is 'Andreas Karavis', a creation of the Canadian writer David Solway. Karavis is a good place to begin because he is a Greek fisherman poet, and thus helps us expand on Sisson's remark about fishing in other men's waters. *Karavi*, or καράβι, means a boat or a ship, and Solway's Greek heteronym, we are told, often writes on his boat and gives his poems away 'with the evening's catch'. Karavis is a 'unilingual' Greek with only a smattering of English, but he is cultured, ironic, and self-taught, having read widely in the Greek classics, notably Homer and Hesiod.

Karavis is fully enough conceived to give rise to a whole volume of selected poems, *Saracen Island* (2000) and, in 2001, *An Andreas Karavis Companion*. In both books, Solway casts himself as translator and friend of Karavis, but also as his guest. In the preface to *Saracen Island*, he thanks Karavis for 'open[ing] his home' to him, and for showing himself to be 'a gracious and impeccable host'.[3] The idea of the translator being a guest in the home of the original is a delicate and satisfying one: what sort of guest will the translator prove to be?

The book comes with a photograph at the front, which Solway tells us is a rare picture of Karavis, a substantial critical-biographical introduction, a note on

Greek orthography and pronunciation, and a twenty-five-page commentary on seventy pages of poems from across Karavis's enigmatic career. Karavis's life and work are situated in relation to Greek history, politics, and literature, and while the poet himself may not have existed, the contexts into which he is placed are unmistakeably recognizable ones. Similarly, real people are thanked by Solway for perhaps imaginary help, as is the Arts Council of Canada for what may have been a real bursary. *Saracen Island* is arranged to resemble a critical edition, with the kind of apparatus befitting a major international discovery. Solway had been sporadically publishing Karavis poems in journals before the book came out, and in October 1999 *Books in Canada* ran a selection of Solway's 'translations', an interview with Karavis, and a brief note by the journal's editor entitled 'Great Authors of our Time: Andreas Karavis'.[4] Solway had thus prepared the ground, and though some journal editors and critics were aware of Karavis's fictionality, the initial effect was of a hoax. The hoax element itself is amusing but not especially interesting, except insofar as it opened up the question of where the poem's identity is located. But perhaps the question of where a poem's identity is located should be the first and only question we ask of it?

This is how Solway explained his experiment in an interview with the *Danforth Review*:

> I also realized that the primary intent of my project could not be regarded as deflationary in the hoax tradition of Stewart's and McAuley's Ern Malley or Kent Johnson's Hiroshima poet, Araki Yasusada. Quite the contrary. [...] Neither was he conceived as a 'forgery' in the antiquarian tradition of Rowley and Ossian, prototypes of the ambition to inject a pseudo-past or native strain into a problematic national present or, as the case may be, of the wish to put one over on a credulous public. [...] He was, rather, an extended trope or metaphor of the desire for transformation and his poems a metonym for the reconstructed self. This meant that Karavis had to be self-substantiating and I could not, at least initially, readily expose his origins as an imaginative projection, a disembodied wraith or something only made-up. A fiction cannot at first be recognized as fictitious if it is to do the practical work for which it was designed. For this reason, and for my own sake, I needed to make him as authentic and believable as possible since I was not interested in perpetuating a deception but in creating a style, and ultimately in recreating a self.[5]

Solway is being a little disingenuous here — he organized a launch for his book in Montreal, invited the literati, and even arranged for a man in a fisherman's cap to move through the crowd looking Greek and poetic (it was the Solway family dentist) — but what is valuable in his exercise, Solway tells us, is 'creating a style'. Solway further explains how the 'practical work' of poetic renewal is dependent on maintaining a 'self-substantiating' fiction. This is not so different from the modernist mask, or the Pessoan heteronym, or the Machadian 'apócrifo', but in Solway's case the 'job' of translating, the fictional friendship with Karavis, the immersion in Greek language and politics, are part of a ramifying backstory that the 'translations' evoke. In this respect, it is more like Nabokov's *Pale Fire* than Pound's *Hugh Selwyn Mauberley*.

Since Karavis, Solway has invented several more poets to whom he has attributed entire collections, also with biographical introductions and notes: Rhys Savarin (Dominican), Nismene Rifet (Turkish), Alim Maghrebi (Arabic), and most recently the thirteenth-century Franciscan friar 'Bartholomaeus Anglicus' ('Bartholomew the Englishman'). It has become his mode, to the extent that we could speculate that Solway's *propria persona* has been squeezed out by his personae. There is a law of diminishing returns to this, not least because Solway's deep knowledge of Greek and Greece made Karavis, the first-born of his fictional progeny, a more persuasive and dimensional figure than his siblings. Perhaps this is because, while it's possible to translate from a language one doesn't know, one can only do genuine pseudo-translations from a language one genuinely knows.

There is a further question: are there different degrees of inexistence for the invented poet? Solway calls his invented poets 'ostensibles', which he defines as follows in the publisher's catalogue: 'poetic voices and artefacts which he regards as constituting an extended trope or metaphor of the desire for transformation'.[6] The poet claims that the 'ostensible', a good word for the otherwise clumsy 'translated heteronym' or 'translated mask', provides the poet with an opportunity for 'transformation'. That's fine, replies the reader, but why not just write new poems? Because (offers the critic) the ghost-process of translation, with its linguistic challenges, its cultural specificity, the imagined original's own relationship with its real literary tradition, even the personality of the original poet — in other words, the fiction of translation's gravitational pull — is part of the literary product and not simply part of its process. By the time Solway writes the *Karavis Companion*, he discusses his friendship with Karavis, filling him out much as a novelist might deepen and sketch a character: we are told Karavis thinks Seferis is a fraud, Rilke 'effeminate', and Pound and Eliot 'pretentious'; he likes some of Neruda but reckons him a 'narcissistic political infatuate'; he has tried to escape the influence of Cavafy, whom he admires, and considers Sikelianos to be his master. Solway is Boswell to Karavis's Johnson, but a Boswell who has invented Johnson.

Solway/Karavis's *Saracen Island* is thus an achieved work of poetic-translational method-acting, and the 'Ostensible' known as 'Karavis' is a fictional-poetic creation born from the trope of translation. Here is one of Karavis's poems:

> I am the one who speaks,
> a voice become your voice
> as you read, aloud or silently,
> tracing a course with your finger.
> Yet I am spoken by another
> whose voice I cannot hear,
> whose recitation escapes me,
> whose language is adrift
> in dark uncharted waters
> even the shark and dogfish avoid.
> I am the channel
> between one I cannot hear
> and one I cannot see.
> I am the exile

>   in the desolate margins,
>   the sentinel on the coast.
>   I stand by the broken jetty.
>   The sun turns me to salt.[7]

Using this poem in an attempt to invigorate a translation class, I tried an experiment whereby I furnished one set of students with Karavis's biography, another set with Solway's, and a third with no information other than the poem. The results were interesting because they all engaged with the question of where the poem's 'identity' was located. The Karavites thought of it as a classic Greek elemental-metaphysical poem, a cousin of poets such as Odysseus Elytis or George Seferis, with a bit of Zorba the Greek thrown in. They also (thanks to information about Karavis's self-taught knowledge of Homer and ancient Greek literature) read the poem as a meditation on the relationship of past and present, of the poet 'adrift', or in 'exile', in a language that is both his and not his. One student also read it as an anxiety about 'measuring up' to his literary forbears, and several saw shades of Homer's *Odyssey* in the precarious seafaring situation.

The students who were told it was a poem by a contemporary Canadian poet, who spoke several languages and taught literature in a university in the bilingual metropolis of Montreal, thought it was the opposite: a sophisticated poem about the stimulations and the disorientations of linguistic in-between-ness and intertextuality. Two students supplied the context of Quebec's contested language politics, and saw in trigger-words like 'exile', 'margins', and 'adrift' a meditation on the tensions of a bilingual poet in a bilingual culture, and who could only 'express himself', or write poetry, in one language — despite being able to write with equal ease in both.

Those who knew nothing about the author of the poem saw it as an allegory of the poem itself, and of the poem's uncertainty of being heard, and perhaps even of having been spoken. They further suggested that it was the poem itself speaking, describing the perilous journey it makes across the sea of language, unsure — as one student put it — 'whether once it's set out on the sea it belongs to the hearer or the speaker, the writer or the reader'.

It is a tribute to Solway's skill that all of these interpretations, in an Empsonian three-for-one offer, can be enjoyably entertained without ever cancelling each other out. The same key terms (sea, voice, seen/heard, unseen/unheard, exile, margins, coasts, self and other, channels, navigation and drift) conjure up readings that, however different, meet at certain critical junctures of the poem's interpretations. Moreover, each group responded to the poem's possessive pronouns — who is speaking? who or what is being spoken? whose voice 'is become' whose? Is the poem the boat and translation the channel? — in ways that were, for all their local difference (grizzled fisherman, sophisticated professor, or Anon) very similar.

The poem may also be about translation, about its own heteronymity as a pseudo-translation, and about the heteronymity that perhaps all translation foists upon both translator and translated. Solway is clearly fishing in other men's waters, but the fish don't exist until he has caught them, the other man is himself, and the 'uncharted' waters are waters he has invented. Karavis provided Solway with the opportunity of being a different kind of poet, to inhabit another version of himself, and it is worth insisting on the creative element of what might sometimes appear to be a postmodern game. The poets I am discussing here understand that the fiction of translation enables creativity by the seemingly paradoxical process of abolishing the original as translation's point of 'origin', only to conjure it back, more powerfully, as the translation's terminus or destination. The pseudo-translation doesn't 'come from' an original, it 'goes towards' it; it is not born of it, but gives birth to it, creating the poem-shaped *ombre exprès* from which an *objet tu* of the original poem can be deduced.

At the creative level, imagining a voice that 'speaks through' you, and positing yourself as a translator, enables a different kind of relationship with your writing identity, and by creating translations that seem to defer to something that came before them, to an ur-state, you also take poetry back to its first question: is poetry made or is it found?

Lost in translation? You cannot lose what you never had. Gained in pseudo-translation, then?

II

Christopher Reid's *Katerina Brac* is an altogether different volume, though it plays some of the same games in a more restricted manner: there is no introduction, and there are no references to the original language from which the poems are 'translated'. From the name Katerina Brac we might be led to imagine Czech, Slovak, Polish, or any of the nations of the former Yugoslavia. The book has no apparatus or notes of any kind — just poems — and yet the cover and blurb are significant.

The cover first: in large letters, we have the name Christopher Reid, then below it as a title and in italics, *Katerina Brac*. The traditional Faber & Faber poetry book livery of its time is there: the **ff** logo in the background with a portrait-formatted inset of a woman in dark glasses, smoking. The picture is designed to look like a battered photograph: private, pocket-worn, furtive, and folded. Folding has a special Mallarméan sensuousness and secrecy, but Brac's is the foldedness of samizdat and political risk. It exudes the Cold War, and rarely can the cover of a book have triggered such a complex yet specifically-delineated set of expectations. These expectations are endorsed on the book's back cover:

> The testimony of Katerina Brac may strike readers as typical of the artist under pressure, but the way in which this still too little-known poet addresses her situation remains startlingly individual. In presenting a selection of her work, Christopher Reid demonstrates his awareness both of the translator's responsibilities, and of the paradox whereby a poet must become the creation of his or her translator.[8]

The word 'testimony' is loaded for maximum topical-political traction, while the coy statement (which Reid wrote himself, a clear sign that the book's external and material aspects are part of the fiction) about the poet becoming the creation of their translator seems like an invitation to guess the trick.

Katerina Brac appeared in 1985, the year Gorbachov was elected General Secretary of the Soviet Communist Party. *Glasnost* was not quite in the air, and the fall of communism seemed far away. East European poetry, however, was thriving and translation was one of the major channels through which readers engaged with culture behind the Iron Curtain. My own experience of reading, in the British Council library in Bucharest, poets such as Holub and Herbert and Szymborska, and closer to home Ana Blandiana and Marin Sorescu, in British poetry magazines such as *Modern Poetry in Translation, Poetry Review, PN Review*, was one of the great discoveries of my two pre-university years in Romania in 1986–87. The most notable of these magazines, and the most curious and questing and brave, was Ted Hughes and Daniel Weissbort's *Modern Poetry in Translation,* which sustained and maybe even created a climate in which East European poets were read and discussed in Britain. Many of them went on to be published by UK and US publishers, and 'translated' by poets such as Ted Hughes, Seamus Heaney, Michael Longley, Elaine Feinstein, and others.

These translations were often done through the 'prose crib', something which used to be quite commonplace but is now less favourably viewed. The 'famous' British poet would take the 'raw material' (a term I'll come back to) of a native speaker's prose version of the original poem and 'turn it into' an English poem. It was always an ambiguous exercise, appropriative and hierarchical despite the generosity of its motivation in the context of the Cold War. Translation in this respect was also an act of solidarity, and the doubts I have about this method, along with the cultural assumptions and habits exemplified by this method, are all retrospective — at the time I was grateful and inspired and enlightened. It therefore seems churlish to list the three distortions for which that translation culture was responsible. But here they are: firstly, there was the implication that the original poems and poets needed to be mediated by British poetic celebrity in order to reach an audience, and that the translations were 'not yet' poems until they had been touched by a poet on 'our side' of the translational process. Original text, raw, translated text, cooked, was the implication. Secondly, it was understood that the famous Anglo-poet didn't need to know any languages before translating 'from' them because there would always be, somewhere along the line, a 'crib' provided by a native. Little has changed there. And thirdly, there was the way in which not very good poets were promoted simply because they were political, thus boxing East European poetry into a space where their subjects had to be extreme, or political, or so ironically apolitical that they became even more political; or the poets themselves had to be dissidents or exiles. Several Romanian poets I knew back in those days lamented how, as they saw it, the UK/US poetry markets had created a sort of export version of East European poetry, and how certain subjects were expected of these poets if they were going to 'make it' abroad: repression, suffering, persecution, ironic attitudes, and, yes, 'testimony'. In other words, it seemed that the East European poet was already, to some extent a 'persona', a creation of the translation process and of the translation culture, further 'translated' into literary marketing and publishing economics. The word 'testimony' was everywhere, and though I never read *Katerina Brac* when I was on the other side of the Iron Curtain, I can vouch for the reception context in which the book appeared. Her audience was primed.

I came to *Katerina Brac* long after my brief period in Cold War Europe, and soon after I had written my own pseudo-translations of the Romanian poet Liviu Campanu, a disconsolate dreamer with neither the gravity for politics nor the grace to float free of them. But Reid's book is an altogether different work. *Katerina Brac* is an experiment in creating not just fictional translation, but fictional translationese: a graceful attempt to replicate the laws of translational gravity by implying that the poems are, as translations, still weighed down and pulled back by their originals. By this I mean that Reid creates 'versions' which, in their mattness, their opacity, and their awkward lyricism, confront the reader with an illusion of what has been lost in translation. They do this at the same time as expressing the sense of language and speech being compromised in an unfree society, making their ethical modesty about their non-existent originals match, at the linguistic level, the thematic and ethical concern with compromised language under totalitarian duress: Reid's versions are themselves, in that respect, a kind of 'testimony'. In contrast to the translations being produced at the time by other poets, which tended to strive for immediacy of expression, high style, grandeur of pitch, and a general (unspoken) sense of 'improving' the originals — in short, striving to be 'cooked' poems and not 'raw' translations — Reid uses *Brac* to do the opposite. Pseudo-translation here becomes an exercise in poetic self-abnegation, showing us the toll that translation takes on its original.

Katerina Brac is not an exercise in the virtuosity of poetic Englishing, but an exploration of the approximation of translation, its maladroitness, heaviness, estrangement, dullness, and blur, its feeling of always being 'at-one-remove'. This is what, I think, Reid means by the 'responsibility' of the translator: a modesty whereby one serves the original and defers to it, with a translation that makes sure that the reader knows or infers that the original is better. *Katerina Brac* is about the distancing and muffling of what is 'lost' in translation, except that it is all gain, because there was nothing to start with. The gain *is* loss, or rather such a detailed, textured, dimensional illusion of loss that it becomes a kind of gain. For a poet, this is a cute poker game to play, a series of highly skilled bluffs: nothing less than successful original poems masquerading as failed or failing translations.

Just as 'Karavis' has a ready-made tradition of Greek poets into which he can be inserted, 'Brac' has a clear family resemblance to East European poets such as Szymborska, Holub, Zagajewski, and Sorescu, whose works were 'found' in translation by English-language readers during the 1970s and 80s. Their poetry is skittering, indirect, coded, spare, ludic and sad, painful and absurd, existing in and because of the 'double état de la parole': a public language hollowed out by officialese and censorship, and a private language cracklingly alive with ambiguity and irony. From the little that we can piece together of her biography, Brac is educated, comes from a village, and has a long- or recently- lost lover whom she thinks of and sometimes addresses with a mix of regret and prudent wisftulness: the way you would talk to someone familiar if you thought you might be overheard by strangers.

Reid's *Katerina Brac* as a book is authentic because it puts language at stake, makes language the issue, and gives the illusion of containing transliterated idioms, clumsily-Englished collocations, a deliberately-crafted awkwardness that creates the pretence of coming from elsewhere through disrupted linguistic, cultural, and political channels. The poems contain clues to this, and to their status as 'lost in translation' homages to originals that never were. They also appear to belong to a world — Eastern Europe, 1985 — where language is already all translation, everything always means something else, shot through with doublespeak, and where personal relations and granitic officialese share the same compromised channels.

The book opens with the poem 'Pale-Blue Butterflies', and here are its first two stanzas:

> Once again, magically
> and without official notification,
> it was the time of the year
> for the pale-blue butterflies to arrive.
>
> They came in their millions —
> an army composed entirely of stragglers
> filling the sky,
> the gust-driven trash of migration.[9]

This certainly has the laconic off-key-ness of something that might have sounded better in another language: 'it was the time of the year for', 'to arrive', 'composed entirely of'. It feels recognizably East-European too, with the deadpan juxtaposition of 'magically' and 'without official notification' which is also a yoking-together, where magic and official notifications are as unreal as each other. But 'gust-driven trash of migration' is of a different order, more intense and vibrant, though as a compound participle it can also sound 'translated': it is alive and pulls the poem upwards not just into the sky but into capital H History — refugees, defectors, post-war resettlements, persecutions, and other elements we might expect from a book 'by' a certain Katerina Brac appearing in 1985. The butterflies might also make the reader think of the military fly-bys and parades beloved of East European leaders, alluded to metaphorically in a world where you cannot say what you mean, and where human interaction is contaminated by metaphor because to speak directly would be to incur sanctions. A scene is set, culturally and politically and geographically, but also linguistically: the sense of the translation's 'other', its first self as a poem, somewhere behind these numbed snippits of translationese with their occasional, felicitous, pangs of *mot juste*. The poem sustains this mix to the end:

> There followed an unscheduled
> season of summer thunders:
> colossal rearrangements
> somewhere at the back of the mind.[10]

The way each word seems weighed to be as ambiguous but also as cleanly inoffensive as possible — a mode which censorship creates in writers in unfree societies — is typical of Brac's writing. Yet at the same time it clearly bears some relation to Reid's *propria persona* poetry at this time: the martianism of which he and Craig Raine were the exemplars, and which we cannot blame him for trying to escape.[11]

In 'A Tune' Brac suggests the inner world, the world of thoughts, through the image of the radio 'thinking aloud': 'I have heard the same song | in numerous clever disguises', she writes, and the radio is never just a radio in this tripwired language: the radio which gushes official speeches, news about Five Year Plans and patriotic music is also the radio which enables you to tune into news from the West, and whose frequencies the authorities try to jam.[12] Translation, then, as jammed frequency? While Brac is referring to the way the subterfuge-language of poetry works its way around the clunking mechanisms of censorship and officialese, Reid himself might be reflecting on translation's 'numerous clever disguises', and on his own, as in the poem 'Like a Mirror':

> To have possessed you
> like a mirror
> in which you glanced once,
> pulled a face and passed on.
>
> But wait: can mirrors
> be said to have memories?
> yes, there is always behind the surface
> an inordinate heaviness.[13]

In a 2012 interview, Reid makes the same point as Solway does about how translation, and the fiction of translating, enables poetic re-creation:

> I had the bright idea that the best way not to sound like myself was to write somebody else's poems for them. So I took an imaginative holiday to a distant part of the world and found Katerina Brac.[14]

This is how it happens:

> One of the things that is problematic about reading foreign poetry, from a language you don't have, is that you're taking a great deal on trust, and the person you're trusting is the translator. So I had a sense that I knew what a translator's voice was more clearly than I knew the voices of certain Eastern European poets. What I was trying to catch in Katerina's poems was the hint that behind my inadequate English there was something rather rich and wonderful to which the reader lacked direct access but which was nonetheless present as a kind of ghost or intuition.[15]

For all his voice-throwing, shape-shifting skill, Reid has produced a work of 'testimony' to the honesty of the fake translation, and to the loyalty it displays, as a true poem, to an original that never existed. Reid dramatizes the lack of direct access to an original, makes translation confess to the channels by which it imperfectly does its — nonetheless necessary — work. In so doing it also conveys muffled human relations in an unfree world, and the fidelity and unfaithfulness of translation become metaphors for the slipperiness and coercions of language. Reid's

Katerina Brac is one of the few examples in modern poetry of the virtuosic refusal of virtuosity: poetic grace deferring to translation's gravity.

That *Katerina Brac* has been translated into Polish is a fitting epilogue to her story: a translation waiting for an original. And yet, since Brac may also be Serbian, Slovenian, Croatian, Czech, Russian, Bulgarian, etc., there may well be a time when this particular 'translation' is outnumbered by 'originals'.

III

'Tous les mégots de siècles se ressemblent,' wrote Huysmans: 'every century's butt-ends look the same'. Derek Mahon has made much of the resemblance between his own late twentieth century and the 'mégot' of the nineteenth: the Franco-Anglo-Irish *fin de siècle* of Mallarmé and Laforgue, Symons and Beardsley, Yeats, Synge, and Wilde. The most francophile of poets, Mahon would have enjoyed the neatness of publishing *The Yellow Book* in 1997, followed by his *Collected* in 1999, on the centennial — on the millennial — cusp. Dates have their own poetry, and for a poet as attuned as Mahon to their symbolic power, the calendar too can be made to rhyme.

While there are plenty of false starts in poetry, there are also plenty of false endings, and if there's one thing the *fin de siècle* is rarely about, it's the *fin*. To coin a Beckettian pun, the *fin de siècle* was 'terminatal', not just because the old and the new, the dying and nascent co-existed, but because they often turned out to be the same. Mahon is a terminatal poet — the 1890s are his demesne, as befits a writer obsessed with endings. The last two decades have been terminatally productive for Mahon, a *finale* rather than a *fin*, with *Harbour Lights* in 2005, *Life on Earth* in 2008, and *An Autumn Wind* in 2010, as well as a number of adaptations, translations, and pamphlets. A *Collected Translations* appeared in 2016, as well as translations of *Cyrano de Bergerac* (2004) and *Oedipus* (2005). The 'autumn wind' is clearly also a second wind. As for *Collected Poems*, seasoned finisecularists would have realized that if Mahon knew *fin de siècle*, he'd be back soon enough with a new one. Sure enough, a *New Collected Poems* came out in 2011. It is almost a hundred pages longer than the first, proving, as Thom Gunn wrote, that 'you add to, you don't cancel, what you do'.[16] With Mahon, however, the 'adding' comes with a regrettable tendency to revise, as well as occasionally re-title, his poems, generally to their detriment. Critics have puzzled as to why Mahon does this — perhaps it is a way of suggesting that poems are never *set*, that they are still wet, malleable, open, and thus resist the finality that their appearance in a book forces upon them. A *New Selected Poems* followed in 2016.

Mahon's earliest work already has a theatricalized irony, a *rire jaune*, that marks him out from the Northern Irish poets, notably Heaney and Longley, with whom he came to prominence in the late 1960s. In an early version of a poem from the early 1970s, 'Beyond Howth Head', Mahon is already:

> rehearsing for the *fin de siècle*
> gruff jeremiads to redirect

> lost youth into the knacker's yard
> of humanistic self-regard.[17]

There is also an early scepticism about the 'role' of the poet, a question given particular sharpness by Northern Irish politics, a context against which the following lines might seem deliberately provocative and arch:

> A chiliastic prick, I prowl
> Among the dog-lovers and growl,
> Among the kite-fliers and fly
> the private kite of poetry — a sort of winged sandwich board
> El-Grecoed to receive the word;
> An airborne, tremulous brochure
> proclaiming that the end is near.[18]

If the young Mahon was jaded, he was at least freshly jaded, and the analogy of the poet as a kite-flying, sandwich-board prophet is clever, surprising, and stays just this side of the laboured. It's more Laforgue than Huysmans.

Mahon was just waiting for the calendar to catch up and give him some poetic dates to rhyme with his poetic states. His late-nineties *Yellow Book* pose — part-languid observer of a rising tide of Celtic Tiger tat, part ironic Luddite (preferring, in one poem, the fur on the edge of the typewritten letter to the computer screen) — was never really about endings and exhaustion, but about what could be made, lyrically, from what he called in 'Hangover Square' 'the forest of intertexuality'.[19] Mahon has always been in search of the clearing in the intertextual forest, and managed to make poems even when there were no clearings to be found. From the beginning, he has negotiated cultural and literary saturation, and in this respect he is the most *fin/ale de siècle* of our poets. Where other poets might simply have walked away, rebelled, or tried to start afresh (the three most obvious recourses), he always turns that choking surfeit of models and examples to his advantage. There are no clean slates, and Mahon has kept faith from the beginning with this sense of the crowdedness of the terrain.

Mahon has always translated, either directly from French or from cribs from other languages. In the foreword to *Adaptations*, he makes the traditional distinction between 'translation' and what he calls 'recreative (and recreational) adaptation'.[20] Of the latter, he says, 'poets use it to keep the engine ticking over'. This is different from Solway's and Reid's idea of self-reinvention through pseudo-translation, but it shares with them the idea of translation being an activity that feeds the production of original verse. The notion of translation as a creative interzone is something Mahon elaborates in the foreword to *Echo's Grove: Collected Translations* (2016), where he writes at greater length about negotiating between languages he knows and those for which he requires a prose crib; 'approximate with zest' is his advice: 'refuse pedantry and intimidation'. It is an uncontroversial idea, however thrustingly expressed, but the most extraordinary statement in Mahon's foreword comes in brackets, and as if in passing, in a discussion of translation ethics: '(As for Hindi, my "Raw Material" sequence owes so much to real Indian poems that it must be considered unoriginal and so qualify for inclusion.)'.[21]

The parentheses confer a modesty on that statement that is quite belied by the audacity of the proposition: that his pseudo-translations of an imagined Hindi poet are so indebted to real Hindi poetry that their 'unoriginality' qualifies them to be included in a book representing Mahon's life's work in translation. This takes us back to the question I posed about varying degrees of inexistence among invented poets. Mahon's trick is to imply that 'unoriginality' is the token of the reality of the fake originals. The Hindi translations in question are of the poet Gopal Singh, who first appeared in *An Autumn Wind* (2010), and then a year later in *Raw Material* (2011), a book of Mahon's translations. Singh has therefore had three incarnations-cum-recyclings in the Mahonian *œuvre*: in a book of original poems, masquerading as a translated poet; in a book of translations, masquerading as an original poet; and in a book of collected translations included appendictically as an unreal poet whose existence owes so much to the real that he 'qualifies' as an extension of it. Gopal Singh's interzonal status is further compounded by his absence from Mahon's 2011 *Collected* poems, even though his inexistent existence predates the publication of that book, as well as from the 2016 *New Selected Poems*. Mahon seems to be indicating that pseudo-translation 'belongs' between poetry and translation, and exists as an 'appendix' to both.

I am more concerned with what function 'Gopal Singh' fulfils in Mahon's work than in the Borgesian *faufilements* of his publishing history. The first thing to say about Gopal Singh's poems is that they are of a piece with Mahon's lifelong interest in recycling in its broadest sense, in exactly those things the early, middle, and late Mahons are so consumed by: the possibility and impossibility of the new, the illusoriness of both endings and beginnings, the anxieties of repetition and reiteration, and a culture where everything has been said, read, done, made, spoken, and heard many times before. This poetry of lateness implies, too, a sense of lateness being a fit subject, and perhaps the only subject left in a world of eternal returns. This is why there are so many landmarks in Mahon's poems, 'harbour lights' we could call them, what Baudelaire named 'Phares', by whom the artist navigates, but against whom he also risks creative shipwreck: other writers, painters, poets, the ancients and the moderns, and all the accumulation of great works and monuments that make up a canon or a tradition. But in Mahon there's also a lot of, well... rubbish: trash, junk, detritus, scraps, cast-offs, the used-up, and the thrown-away, and the stratum of second- and third-rate literature that furnishes a culture but does not outlast it, except as intellectual landfill in the form of footnotes. We think of 'A Disused Shed' or 'A Garage in County Cork': Mahon knows that a culture's dustbin is the double of its library, its disused shed the lost twin of its museum.

Literature is recycling, tradition is recycling, translation is recycling. In Gopal Singh Mahon invents the poet of recycling, as if to render, explicitly and yet obliquely through pseudo-translation, the themes that have haunted his poetry from the start. While I was writing this piece, Mahon published an essay entitled 'Rubbish Theory' in a limited edition pamphlet of prose called *Olympia and the Internet* (2017). Here, he endorses critics, notably Hugh Haughton, who read his own poetic concern with rejectamenta through Michael Thompson's seminal 1979 book

Rubbish Theory. Late Mahon, 'autumnal Mahon', has become more ecologically-aware, and where his earlier work explored rubbish and clutter and crowdedness for their metaphorical value, his recent writing is more urgently concerned with the realities of environmental destruction. 'Rubbish Theory' begins:

> We hear of a sea of rubbish, hundreds of miles wide, in the Pacific. Inquire further and you find this is only one of several in the oceans, albeit the largest, and is actually composed of two, the interacting East and West Pacific Gyres that combine to make up the Great Pacific Garbage Patch north of Hawaii.[22]

It is surely through the kind of higher randomness we call poetic justice that these hideous 'interacting' gyres of toxic detritus should share their name with the 'gyres' of Yeats's *A Vision,* or the 'widening gyre' in his poem 'The Second Coming':

> Turning and turning in the widening gyre
> The falcon cannot hear the falconer;
> Things fall apart; the centre cannot hold;
> Mere anarchy is loosed upon the world,
> The blood-dimmed tide is loosed, and everywhere
> The ceremony of innocence is drowned;
> The best lack all conviction, while the worst
> Are full of passionate intensity.[23]

Yeats's gyres are interlocking cones of energy that represent the drawn-out, fertile period of overlap between eras: a vibrant fusion of endings and beginnings. These gyres are the 'interacting' currents of a 'sea of plastic' that represent the overlap between the era of consumerism and the era of ecological disaster.

Mahon's poetry begins by negotiating a choking surfeit of literary models, and finishes with a choking surfeit of refuse, scrap, litter, and waste. From metaphorical recycling as a way of figuring the anxieties of literary influence in early Mahon, we arrive, in late Mahon, at poems which imagine recycling as a sort of Yeatsian *spiritus mundi*. This is where Gopal Singh, whom we can think of as Mahon self-recycling, comes in, because Gopal Singh's central conceit is between recycling and the Hindu notion of reincarnation: the ultimate form of recycling, as in his poem 'Raw Material':

> Only material forms die
> says the *Gita*,
> the dusty soul within
> alone survives
> even as we discard
> one body for another.[24]

Like Solway and Reid, Mahon gives Gopal Singh a story: born in Kashmir in 1959, we are told he has published ten books of verse, most recently *Kacha-Maal*, or कच्चा माल. Mahon renders this as *Raw Material*, though it more exactly means 'waste goods', or 'rubbish'. As for the poems, we are told: 'Singh's is a densely intertextual poetry which frequently references the work of others — Bengalis, Tamils — with the result that it almost reads like a telescopic anthology of the contemporary Indian canon; but his distinctive voice is unmistakable'.[25] This could function as a useful description of Mahon himself, or at any rate a Hindi version of Mahon. As for how the translation was arrived at, this too has its own story: 'he provided literal drafts for these rather free versions and approved the results,' Mahon tells us, before thanking the Arts Council of Ireland for a (real) visit to India. Like Solway and Reid, it seems important to Mahon to fictionalize the translation process, not just to offer fictional translations or invent a poet. Why? One answer, I think, is that Mahon, like Solway and Reid, wants to make translation into a story or a narrative of transformation, and not just an end-product of a transformative process. The story is about a kind of recycling, the passage of material from one form (one language, one culture, one religion, one belief-system, one economic situation) into another.

Unlike Reid, Mahon does not forbear to write in his own voice — on the contrary, he throws his voice rather than silences it. Translation is, here, the extension of the poetic ego rather than its self-abnegation. Gopal Singh's poems read like relocations of Mahon, and Solway's term 'Ostensible' seems apt: someone you could, in a different time and place, be. Take this, Gopal Singh's 'The Great Wave':

> If 'waste is the new raw material' as they say
> our resources are infinite: on black beaches
> carrion, groceries, sewage, wide-open fridges
> fought over by frenetic gull and crow.
> Tractors haul the wreckage, dead car and cow,
> balconies, splintered bits of bungalow.
> On the last rock some soapstone Madurai
> devotional figures... A post-tsunami sky.[26]

This has all the trademarks of Mahon's themes and idioms;[27] only the Madurai figures mark this beach out as Indian, and the religion as Hindu. But Gopal Singh's religion is crucial to Mahon: it is the religion that promises reincarnation. In 'Recycling Song', Mahon allows himself to allow Gopal Singh to be even more explicit:

> 'What goes around'... The *Gita*
> warns us that we never die,
> something escapes the blaze.
> Our smoke and methane rise
> above the world of matter
> in viral columns to a busy sky.
>
> Throw nothing out; recycle
> the vilest rubbish, even
> your own discarded page.
> Everything comes full circle:
> see you again in heaven
> some sunny evening in a future age.[28]

Gopal Singh, and the fictional act of translating Gopal Singh, enable Mahon both to recycle and reincarnate himself. Singh's poetry of recycling and reincarnation is a logical extension of the themes that have haunted Mahon's poems from his earliest work. Singh even asks, in a poem called 'A Child of the Forest', if he will 'ever outgrow | the babble of words?' The forest in question is Mahon's 'forest of intertextuality', in which Mahon and Singh are each other's 'intertexts': intertextuality *is* recycling, intertextuality *is* reincarnation.

We have had gyres, which evoke Yeats, and now we have Singh, who evokes (recycles? reincarnates?) J. M. Synge, another of Mahon's tutelary presences. With Mahon, the further we go from Ireland, the closer we come to it. As Rimbaud tells us: 'on ne part pas'.

★ ★ ★ ★ ★

I have explored the different ways in which these poets — Mahon, Reid, and Solway — have used pseudo-translation to explore the laws of translational gravity. With Solway, the translator is a guest in the house; with Reid, the translator bears 'testimony' to the original; and with Mahon, the translator recycles and reincarnates, and is recycled and reincarnated in his turn.

Notes to Chapter 16

1. *The C. H. Sisson Reader*, ed. by Charlie Louth and Patrick McGuinness (Manchester: Carcanet, 2015), p. 485.
2. John Keats, 'On First Looking into Chapman's Homer', in *Complete Poems*, ed. by Jack Stillinger (Cambridge, MA: Harvard University Press, 1982), p. 34.
3. David Solway, *Saracen Island: The Poems of Andreas Karavis* (Montreal: Vehicule Press, 2000), p. 9.
4. <http://www.booksincanada.com/article_view.asp?id=1258> [accessed 25 September 2018].
5. David Solway, interview in the *Danforth Review*, <https://canpoetry.library.utoronto.ca/solway/tdrint.htm> [accessed 25 September 2018].
6. <https://www.guernicaeditions.com/title/9781550716153> [accessed 25 September 2018].
7. Solway, *Saracen Island*, p. 97.
8. Christopher Reid, *Katerina Brac* (London: Faber & Faber, 1985). The cover is integral to the way we read the poems inside it, and it seems visually as well as historically illiterate for Faber & Faber to have got rid of it in their recent re-issue (lemon yellow cover, no picture,). The new blurb, meanwhile, states that the collection is 'presented as' translation.
9. Reid, *Katerina Brac*, p. 9.
10. Ibid., p. 10
11. In a fascinating article on the return journey of the pseudo-translation, that is to say, the return journey to a place it never began from, Kasia Szymanska explores the Polish translation of *Katerina Brac* by Jerzy Jarniewicz and Leszek Engelking. Szymanska argues that 'The Polish back translation of the original pseudo-translation creates the next link in a potentially infinite chain of translations in which the original ceases to play a role' ('Can Mirrors Be Said to Have Memories? A Polish Katerina Brac Looks Back at Her English Reflection', *MLN*, 132.2 (2017), 432. Szymanska interviews Jarniewicz, for whom Reid's book was symptomatic of cold war cultural relations: 'Katerina translated into Polish is a mirror in which we can see how the others see us..., to what extent these poems are 'ours' and whether we really find ourselves in them' ('Can Mirrors Be Said to Have Memories?', p. 428. I am grateful to Kasia Szymanska for stimulating discussion in the preparation of my own essay.
12. Reid, *Katerina Brac*, p. 11.
13. Ibid., p. 46.
14. Kathryn Maris, 'Truth and Dare: An Interview with Christopher Reid', *Poetry London* (Spring 2012), <http://poems.com/special_features/prose/essay_reid.php> [accessed 25 September 2018].

15. Ibid. See also 'Katerina and Her Kind', *Metre*, 12 (2002), 90–93, and Elizabeth Frost, 'Found in Translation: An Interview with Christopher Reid', *Electronic Poetry Review*, <https://www.epoetry.org/issues/issue6/text/prose/reid.htm> [accessed 25 September 2018].
16. Thom Gunn, *Selected Poems* (London: Faber & Faber, 2017), p. 181.
17. Derek Mahon, 'Beyond Howth Head', in *Collected Poems* (Oldcastle: Gallery Press, 1999), p. 54. These lines do not survive in the most recent edition of *Collected Poems*.
18. Derek Mahon, 'Sunday Morning', in *New Collected Poems* (Oldcastle: Gallery Press, 2011), p. 117.
19. Derek Mahon, 'Hangover Square', in *New Collected Poems*, p. 211.
20. Derek Mahon, *Adaptations* (Oldcastle: Gallery Press, 2006), p. 11.
21. Derek Mahon, *Echo's Grove: Translations* (Oldcastle: Gallery Press, 2013), p. 15.
22. Derek Mahon, 'Rubbish Theory', in *Olympia and the Internet* (Oldcastle: Gallery Press, 2017), p. 22
23. W. B. Yeats, 'The Second Coming', in *Poems*, ed. by A. Norman Jeffares (Basingstoke: Macmillan, 1989), p. 294.
24. Derek Mahon, 'Raw Material', in *Echo's Grove*, p. 191.
25. Derek Mahon, *An Autumn Wind* (Oldcastle: Gallery Press, 2010), p. 66.
26. Derek Mahon, 'The Great Wave', in *Echo's Grove*, p. 201.
27. See 'Beyond Howth Head' for instance: 'Spring lights the country; from a thousand | dusty corners, house by house, | from under beds and vacuum cleaners, | empty Calor gas containers, | bread bins, car seats, crates of stout, | the first flies cry to be let out, | to cruise the kitchens, find a door, | and die clean in the open air' (in Mahon, *New Collected Poems*, p. 54).
28. Derek Mahon, 'Recycling Song', in *Raw Material*, p. 199.

Dancer

David Constantine

This five-year-old dancing to the music of a man
Who died a long long time ago, when I tell her
She is very graceful she nods as though to say
You don't need to tell me that, and goes on dancing

Not knowing and nor would it interest her to learn
What kind of grace I'm telling her she has. For it isn't
That of the music nor a matter of whether
She keeps time or not. The man who made the music

And died too young was a child to the bitter end
And I think he'd have loved almost as much as I do
The way her right sock will keep coming down and how
Pulling it up again, she jigs on her left foot

Without a smile. Her grace is a serious matter
But as if through the eyes of the old mask, through aeons of tears
Broke such jolly tunes the celestial bodies
Skipped and skated. Her time's not exactly his but nor

Does she use his music merely for her back-cloth
It's more a place and her way of being in that place
Free to keep what time she likes. So I think Lilith
Danced in Eden and the flames and waters of the earth

The trees, the stones and all kinds of other living things
In a solemn gaiety danced their own dances
With her. And it's true, child, you don't need me telling you
You're graceful. The words, words, words: you're lighter without them.

INDEX

Acquisto, Joseph 70, 83
Adam, Antoine 137
Adorno, Theodor W. 146, 149
Anam, Tahmima 8
Atwood, Margaret 8
Augustine 188

Bach, Johann Sebastian 188
Balzac, Honoré de 31–32, 153
Barbey d'Aurevilly, Jules 33–34
Baudelaire, Charles 40–41, 42–43, 44, 45, 46, 47–50, 51, 55, 70–84, 96, 97, 100, 103, 107, 131, 135, 139, 140, 209, 222
Beardsley, Aubrey 220
Beaujour, Michel 42, 49
Beckett, Samuel 146–60, 220
   'Le Calmant' 146, 147, 148, 151–52, 154–55
   'L'Expulsé' 146, 147, 150–51, 152, 156–57
   'La Fin' 146, 147, 148, 149, 152–53, 155, 156, 157
Beckford, William 112–27
Beethoven, Ludwig van 6
Benjamin, Walter 55, 59
Bennett, Claire-Louise 20
Benoit, Eric 125
Bergson, Henri 161, 163–64, 169, 171, 173–74, 175
   Essai sur les données immédiates de la conscience 164, 169, 173
   Matière et mémoire 164, 169, 171, 174, 175, 176
Berlin, Isaiah 25
Bertall 30
Bertrand, Aloysius 48
Beyoncé 6
Blanc, Charles 30–31, 35
Blanchot, Maurice 125
Blandiana, Ana 217
Bonnefoy, Yves 161–77, 182–83, 187
   L'Été de nuit (Pierre écrite) 163–75
   'La Présence et l'image' 162–63
Borges, Jorge Luis 115, 124, 200, 207, 222
Boswell, James 213
Bourdieu, Pierre 51
Bousquet, Joë 182
Boy George 6
Bradford, John 12
Broome, Peter 71
Burke, Edmund 120

Buson, Yosa 186
Butler, Judith 17
Byron, Lord 125, 140, 209

Calas, Jean 24
Calvino, Italo 195, 196, 204
Campanu, Liviu 217
Casanova, Pascale 157–58
Catani, Damian 70
Cavafy, C. P. 213
Caws, Mary-Ann 165
Celnart, Madame [Elisabeth-Félicia Bayle-Mouillard] 31
Cézanne, Paul 6
Chapman, George 209–10
Chardin, Auguste 122
Chateaubriand, François-René de 98, 124
Coetzee, J. M. 8
Cohn, Robert Greer 48
Colet, Louise 33
Connor, Steven 148
Cortés, Hernán 210
Courtenay, William 118
Cozens, Alexander 115
Crébillon, Prosper Jolyot de 25
Creed, Martin 19
Crépet, Jacques 137
Culler, Jonathan 70

Dante 80, 147, 155, 157, 187, 188
Davies, Paul 146
Dawkins, Richard 12
De l'Isle Adam, Auguste 35–36
De la Barre, François Poullain 25
Delacroix, Eugène 64
Deleuze, Gilles 131, 164
Delille, Jacques 96
Derrida, Jacques 9, 13, 15, 16
Devéria, Eugène 55, 60
Disraeli, Benjamin 1, 190
Douglas, Mary 29, 34
du Bouchet, André 186

Eaves, Will 20
Eliot, George 13
Eliot, T. S. 211, 213
Elytis, Odysseus 214

Emin, Tracey 6, 18
Empson, William 2, 214
Euclid 26

Feinstein, Elaine 216
Felski, Rita 19
Fields, Gracie 10
Flaubert, Gustave 29, 40–54, 91, 96, 103, 104, 114, 147, 210
    'Hérodias' 40, 43–51, 103
    Madame Bovary 30, 32, 33, 34, 36, 40, 43, 50, 51, 151, 152
    La Tentation de Saint Antoine 114
Floupette, Adoré 210–11
Franco, Francisco 203

Galland, Antoine 115, 116, 117
Gardner, Norah Lynn 203
Garrett, John 117
Gautier, Théophile 93, 96–99, 101, 107, 114
    Emaux et camées 93, 96–99, 100, 101, 107
George, Stefan 123
Gide, André 211
Giorgione 6
Girard, Didier 118
Girardin, Madame de 29–30, 31
Goethe, Johann Wolfgang 26, 96–97, 98, 99, 186
Goncourt, Edmond de 32–33, 35
Goncourt, Jules de 32–33
Gorbachov, Mikhail 216
Guattari, Félix 131
Guenot-Lecointe, Georges 29, 30, 31, 34
Guerlac, Suzanne 173
Gunn, Thom 220

Hadrian 191
Hamilton, Emma 122
Hamon, Philippe 59
Haughton, Hugh 222–23
Head, Dominic 15
Heaney, Seamus 191, 216, 220
Henley, Samuel 123–24
Herbert, Zbigniew 217
Herter Norton, M. D. 149–50
Hesiod 211
Hiddleston, James 73, 74
Hill, Geoffrey 1–2, 211
Hirst, Damien 18
Hockney, David 6
Hölderlin, Friedrich 182, 185
Holub, Miroslav 216, 217
Homer 168, 209, 211, 214
Hopkins, Gerard Manley 1, 181
Houssaye, Arsène 48
Hughes, Ted 216
Hugo, Victor 94, 95, 97, 98, 100, 151

Huysmans, J.-K. 34, 40, 220, 221

Isherwood, Baron 29, 34

Jaccottet, Philippe 178–94
    Airs 178, 179, 186, 190–92
    Paysages avec figures absentes 182, 192
    Ponge, pâturages, prairies 183–90
    La Semaison 179, 180, 181, 182, 190
    Taches de soleil, ou d'ombre 178, 181, 182–83
Jacob, Max 211
James, Clive 155
Janvier, Ludovic 146
Johncock, Ben 8
Johnson, Samuel 213
Joubert, Jean 178–79
Jouvin, Xavier 28
Joyce, James 16, 157, 168
Juvenal 17

Kant, Immanuel 10, 13, 166
Kay, Jackie 6
Keats, John 209–10
Kerr, David 65
Keymer, Thomas 115
Kraus, Chris 8
Krueger, Cheryl 43, 44, 49–50
Kundera, Milan 195

Labiche, Eugène 32
Labitte, Adolphe 113, 126, 127
Laclos, Pierre Choderlos de 25
Laforgue, Jules 220, 221
Lamartine, Alphonse de 96
Larbaud, Valery 211
Leconte de l'Isle, Charles Marie René 93–96, 98–111
    Poèmes antiques 93–94, 95, 96, 98, 99–102, 107
    Poèmes barbares 95, 100–06
Leibniz, G. W. 26, 156
Logan, Kirsty 8
Longley, Michael 216, 220
Lonsdale, Roger 124
Loti, Pierre 34
Louis-Philippe 35, 56, 60, 61, 64
Loutherbourg, Philippe de 121

Machado, Antonio 211, 212
Mackintosh, Sophie 7
Maclean, Mary 45
Mahon, Derek 210, 220–25
Mallarmé, Stéphane 2, 3, 6, 40, 42, 85–92, 93–96, 98–104, 107, 112–29, 130, 147, 166, 170, 187, 188, 189, 207, 209, 211, 215, 220
Malley, Ern 210–11, 212
Marchal, Bertrand 119
Marder, Elissa 43

Marlowe, Christopher 116
Marmontel, Jean-François 25
Marx, Karl 17
Maupassant, Guy de 3, 33, 130
McAuley, James 212
Mérimée, Prosper 125
Merleau-Ponty, Maurice 134, 144
Meyer, Grace 10
Michelangelo 8
Mikriammos, Philippe 134–35
Miller, D. A. 17
Miller, Henry 154
Mills, Kathryn Oliver 42–43, 44–45
Milton, John 121
Mohammed 116
Monnier, Henri 60
Montagu, Edward Wortley 115
Montesquieu 26, 114
Moore, Marianne 2

Nabokov, Vladimir 151, 211, 212
Nance, Kimberley A. 186
Nancy, Jean-Luc 164
Nelson, Admiral 121, 122
Nelson, Maggie 20
Neruda, Pablo 213
Nerval, Gérard de 29, 42, 105–06
  'El Desdichado' 139–43
Ngai, Sianne 10
Nietzsche, Friedrich 17
Numa [Pierre Numa Bassaget] 55–69

Offill, Jenny 20
Olds, Marshall C. 123
O'Shaugnessy, Arthur 124, 126
O'Shiel, Eda 195
Ovid 6
Owen, Wilfred 134–35

Parker, Cornelia 19
Parreaux, Alfred 113, 117
Pascal, Blaise 26, 72
Pasternak, Boris 211
Pearson, Roger 2, 3, 4, 6, 7, 20, 51, 93, 97, 103, 107, 130, 147, 187, 188
Peck, John 211
Pessoa, Fernando 211
Philipon, Charles 56, 60–61, 64, 65, 66
Pichois, Claude 137
Piranesi, Giovanni Battista 120
Plato 164, 166
Ponge, Francis 183–89, 190
Porter, Max 20
Pound, Ezra 211, 212
Proust, Adrien 153

Proust, Marcel 44, 147, 152–55

Raine, Craig 219
Rancière, Jacques 119, 130, 144
Reid, Christopher 210
  Katerina Brac 215–21, 223, 224, 225
Richards, I. A. 208
Ricoeur, Paul 17
Rilke, Rainer Maria 147, 152, 190, 213
  Duino Elegies 179
  The Notebooks of Malte Laurids Brigge 149–50
Rimbaud, Arthur 93, 113, 118, 119–20, 225
Rodoreda, Mercè 195–206
Rosenthal, David 195
Roud, Gustave 178
Russell, Peter 211

Said, Edward 114
Scherer, Jacques 85, 86, 87, 88, 89, 90, 91, 125
Schiller, Friedrich 8–9, 25–26, 112, 190
Scott, Walter 28, 100
Sedgwick, Eve 17–18
Seferis, George 213, 214
Shakespeare, William:
  Measure for Measure 1
  A Midsummer Night's Dream 161, 163, 166, 169, 174
  The Winter's Tale 11, 16, 20, 162, 187–88
Shelley, P. B. 209
Sikelianos, Angelos 213
Sirven, Pierre-Paul 25
Sisson, C. H 207–08, 209, 210, 211
Smith, Ali 6–23, 152
  Artful 19, 149
Smith, Zadie 8
Solway, David 210, 211–15, 219, 223, 224, 225
Sontag, Susan:
  The Volcano Lover 121
Sorescu, Marin 216, 217
Staël, Madame de 125
Staffe, Blanche 31
Stendhal 2, 3, 6, 20
Stewart, Harold 212
Symons, Arthur 123, 220
Synge, J. M. 220, 225
Szymborska, Wisława 216, 217

Tadié, Jean-Yves 153
Tait, Theo 16–17
Thompson, Michael:
  Rubbish Theory 222–23
Todorov, Tzvetan 48
Turner, William 120

Valéry, Paul 25, 40, 41–42, 44, 46, 51, 150, 178
Vasari, Giorgio 8

Verlaine, Paul 85, 86, 93, 100, 113, 118, 188
Vinken, Barbara 46, 48–49, 50
Voltaire 3, 6, 24–27, 114, 124, 125, 147, 155–57
    Candide 24–25, 26, 155–57

Wagner, Richard 95, 96, 121
Walsh, Joanna 20
Warhol, Andy 18
Weil, Simone:
    Attente de Dieu 181–82, 184
    La Pesanteur et la grâce 1, 71, 93, 94, 106, 107, 178, 179, 181–82, 188, 192

Weissbort, Daniel 216
Whistler, James 123
Wieland, Christoph Martin 25
Wilde, Oscar 123, 220
Woolf, Virginia 24

Yasusada, Araki 212
Yeats, W. B. 165, 211, 220, 223, 225

Zagajewski, Adam 217
Zola, Emile 3, 32, 34, 35, 130

www.ingramcontent.com/pod-product-compliance
Lightning Source LLC
LaVergne TN
LVHW061250060426
835507LV00017B/1994